MORAL EMOTIONS

Northwestern University
Studies in Phenomenology
and
Existential Philosophy

Founding Editor †James M. Edie

General Editor Anthony J. Steinbock

Associate Editor John McCumber

MORAL EMOTIONS

Reclaiming the Evidence of
the Heart

Anthony J. Steinbock

Northwestern University Press
Evanston, Illinois

Northwestern University Press
www.nupress.northwestern.edu

Copyright © 2014 by Northwestern University Press. Published 2014.
All rights reserved.

Printed in the United States of America

10 9 8 7 6 5 4 3 2 1

Library of Congress Cataloging-in-Publication Data

Steinbock, Anthony J., author.
  Moral emotions : reclaiming the evidence of the heart / Anthony J. Steinbock.
    pages cm. — (Northwestern university studies in phenomenology and existential philosophy)
    ISBN 978-0-8101-2955-9 (cloth : alk. paper) — ISBN 978-0-8101-2956-6 (pbk. : alk. paper)
    1. Emotions (Philosophy) 2. Emotions—Moral and ethical aspects.
3. Ethics. I. Title. II. Series: Northwestern university studies in phenomenology & existential philosophy.
B815.S74 2014
128'.37—dc23

2013039156

∞ The paper used in this publication meets the minimum requirements of the American National Standard for Information Sciences—Permanence of Paper for Printed Library Materials, ANSI Z39.48-1992.

For my parents,
Marie and Samuel Steinbock

Contents

	Acknowledgments	xi
	Introduction: The Distinctiveness of Moral Emotions	3

Part 1. Moral Emotions of Self-Givenness

1	Pride	31
2	Shame	67
3	Guilt	100

Part 2. Moral Emotions of Possibility

4	Repentance	137
5	Hope and Despair	160

Part 3. Moral Emotions of Otherness

6	Trust	197
7	Loving and Humility	223
	Conclusion: Moral Emotions, the Person, and the Social Imaginary	261
	Notes	279
	Bibliography	319
	Index	333

Acknowledgments

The reflections and clarifications of method that follow are in some way as much a result of these analyses as they are the direct motivation for them. In part, they came as an attempt to carry out a phenomenology of the emotions in the tradition begun by Edmund Husserl, and developed by Max Scheler, Martin Heidegger, and Maurice Merleau-Ponty. But they also evolved as an attempt to do phenomenology with others. Sparked by a question concerning how to do phenomenology, I continued this project of a phenomenology of the emotions in group meetings that started in a café, holding weekly and biweekly gatherings with circulating interdisciplinary students and colleagues over several years. Those meetings gradually developed into what is now the "Phenomenology Research Group" (PRG), which is an integral part of the Phenomenology Research Center (PRC).

My initial orientation was and has remained phenomenological. But because of the questions raised in what Herbert Spiegelberg and Ed Casey might call a "sym-phenomenologizing" effort, the descriptions that were planned according to certain preconceived ideas spontaneously developed, and led to ongoing elucidations concerning phenomenology as a method. This entailed a clarification and interpretation of phenomenology's relation to psychology, anthropology, ordinary language philosophy, analytic philosophy, eidetic analysis, the role of examples, and phenomenological first-person and second-person descriptions.

I am grateful for and to the many members and associates of this research group, local, national, and international, who have contributed invaluable insights in our discussions in several different venues. They are too numerous to be mentioned here. However, I do want to recognize some of the long-standing participants and interlocutors who have helped to shape my thinking on these matters in important ways: Leslie Brown (who has provided me with intellectual as well as moral support), John Brittingham, Christina Gould, John Hartmann, Iris Hennigfeld, Yinghua Lu, Jodie McNeilly, Frédéric Moinat, Christopher Paone, Fabrício Pontin, Thomas Price, Rebecca Rozelle, Mohammad Sayeh, Jessica Soester, Lucian Stone, and Shai Yeshayahu. I am grateful to Thomas Ruble, a newer member to this group, for his diligent reading of this book and for his conscientious work in developing its index. I am appreciative of former dean Alan Vaux and dean David DiLalla (Southern Illinois University, College of Liberal Arts) for their initial support to conduct this research group in the Phenomenology Research Center. My appreciation also goes to provost John Nicklow and dean Kimberly Kempf-Leonard for their kind support of this Center and of this book.

I have especially benefitted from the demanding and incisive readings of the manuscript at nearly all stages by my long-time teacher and friend Art Luther, and from lengthy conversations with him. My gratitude extends, too, to Jana Trajtelová, who invited me to present this work in a series of lectures and seminars as a visiting professor at Trnava University, Slovakia; she also generously commented on an earlier version of this manuscript. I wish to thank Dan Zahavi for our discussions, and for the collegial and engaging atmosphere of the Center for Subjectivity Research in Copenhagen, Denmark; this provided me with two main occasions as visiting professor for developing earlier aspects of this work on the moral emotions. I am also indebted to Sara Heinämaa, who offered me thoroughgoing comments on an earlier version of the book. My thanks also go to my children, Joseph and Samara, for providing me with insights in ways they could hardly imagine. Finally, I would like to thank Jane Bunker, director of Northwestern University Press, for inviting me to submit this work to the Press; I am grateful for her and managing editor Anne Gendler's attentiveness and expertise in seeing it through its various stages to publication.

MORAL EMOTIONS

Introduction

The Distinctiveness of Moral Emotions

My intention in this work is twofold. First, it is to give a fuller and richer account of the human person than is customarily available in interpretations that restrict evidence in human experience to the perceptual and judicative dimensions, broadly defined. I do this by describing certain key moral emotions. To bring these moral emotions into consideration in this way, I describe them in original phenomenological analyses, paying attention both to how they give themselves in experience, as well as to their structural characteristics and interrelations. Such a critical perspective requires a careful, detailed analysis of the emotions' modes of givenness (e.g., in relation to others, their temporal meanings, their possibility structures) and attention to how they can yield a broader sphere of evidence where persons are concerned.

My second aim, also accomplished through these analyses, is to show how the moral emotions can play a distinctive role in addressing the problems associated with "modernity" and those encountered at the impasse of postmodernity. The description of the moral emotions, as emotions of self-givenness, emotions of possibility, and emotions of otherness, enables me to suggest the ways in which they reveal unique dimensions of freedom, how they can take a leading role in shaping civic life and relations of power, and why the moral emotions should not be relegated in such discussions. I conclude this work with reflections on what the moral emotions can tell us about who we are as persons, and what they tell us about our experience and concepts of freedom, normativity, power, and critique. In this way, the moral *emotions* point to the possibility of contributing to the social imaginary of the modern and its postmodern variants, in a field where such interventions have been predominately guided by communicative ethics, rational theories of justice, the discourse of psychoanalysis, and the intercession of bio-politics. In addition to pointing to different conceptions, for example, of freedom, normativity, and critique from the perspective of the moral emotions, one of my other conclusions in this regard concerns the way in which we understand the role of the emotions in the crisis of reason, modernity, and postmodernity. That is, if the moral emotions give us new insights into our social imaginaries, it is not because they constitute a new beginning (in relation to the old beginning of wonder, theory, or reason). Rather, it is because the emotions have been there all along, yet as subordinated in terms of what they are able to contribute; and it becomes a matter of recovering their distinctive contributions to who we are as persons, interpersonally. If there is a crisis, it is not in reason; nor is it a matter of coming back to the true sense of reason; rather, it concerns the way in which the emotions had lost their distinctive evidential footing, and had been consigned to either reason or to sensibility.

In the "Introduction," I describe (1) what is at stake in the moral emotions having a distinctive structure of experience and evidence that is irreducible to other kinds of experience, (2) the scope of the moral emotions as interpersonal, and what distinguishes them both as "moral" and as "emotions," and (3) the method by which I investigate the emotions, namely a phenomenological method. In doing so, I describe briefly the place of ordinary language philosophy in a phenomenology of the moral emotions.

The Emotions: Do They Have a Distinctive Structure?

Modernity can be credited with many things, among them the recognition of individual subjectivity, the value of freedom, the practice of critique, and the prominent role that rationality plays in them. Modernity also marks the emergence of an innovative social imaginary, the consequences of which we are still living. Addressing these issues in the concluding section of this work, I call attention here to what has been dismissed both in the enthusiasm for these modern features, and in the contemporary criticism of modernity, for example, from criticism levied by German idealism, psychoanalysis, phenomenology, and critical theory. What have been sidelined are the emotions, especially, the moral emotions.

It is well known that having identified cognition with rationality, and rationality with the meaning of (predominately male) human beings, the emotions became the province of what is non-human, instinctual, and characteristic of women, children, animals, and the mentally impaired. Far from having any evidential import, far from being able to disclose the meaning of persons, emotions were customarily regarded as irrational ruptures of objectivity, violations of human potential, and ultimately devoid of any spiritual or philosophical significance. They became merely subjective matters devoid of an objective or rational grounding, and thus had no legitimate bearing on the purpose or meaning of human existence. How many times do we still hear the words of caution: "Don't let your emotions get the better of you!" As Max Scheler observed, modernity no longer understood the emotional sphere as a meaningful symbolic language; it was no longer allowed to govern the sense and meaning of our lives. Instead, emotions were regarded as blind processes running their course in nature; as such, they required a rational technology for restraining them so that we would not come to harm, and so that human activity could be truly spiritual, cognitive, and meaningful.[1] The entire realm of the emotions, and everything alogical, was surrendered, becoming either an object of the psychology of inner perception, a matter of individual interior ethics, or the subject of intellection belonging to the province of judgment as inferential acts of thought.[2]

Rather than hearkening, say, to a feeling of calm or agitation at an event, the love of a person before us, the shame of communal inaction, the guilt of a deed, the trust of a stranger, or even the self-centered pride at our own doings—in order to examine how and what they can reveal to us about ourselves and our being with others in the world—we instead become very practiced in ignoring them, and as a result, we dull our sensibilities to them as providing a social and political compass. Yet, with Scheler, if logic wants to investigate the structure of interconnections and relations, or the acts through which we grasp these logical interconnections, it is a sign of unsurpassed arbitrariness to carry out these kinds of investigations into modes of givenness and essential connections only in the case of perception and thinking, but to abandon to psychology the remaining part of spirit.[3] It is arbitrary because our experience shows that there are different kinds of cognition and evidence which have their own integrity and which are not reducible to, say, rational, volitional, or even instrumental knowledge—even if the latter have become for us the predominant ways "to know," or rather, to experience something given in an evidential manner.

It would be one thing simply to declare that the emotions do have a distinctive structure, that they have their own kinds of evidence, and that they are revelatory of the person. But my intention is to illustrate through the description of the moral emotions treated here how they have their own structure, their own kinds of evidence, their unique "cognitive" styles, and how they are revelatory of the person as interpersonal—without them either somehow being tied to rationality in order to be meaningful, or on the contrary, being ostracized from the sphere of evidence because they are not rational. Thus, in distinction to some contemporary thinkers on the emotions, these analyses show that some emotions are directly moral, and further that moral emotions have an evidential dimension and are not merely supports for judgments.[4] Showing this, however, requires overcoming the prejudice that the human person is exhausted in the dualism of reason and sensibility.

Such a wearied dichotomy between reason and the sensibility where the emotions are concerned had already come under fire in transitional existentialist figures like Nietzsche and Kierkegaard;[5] it was challenged systematically by classical phenomenologists like Scheler, to whom I have already alluded, and to some extent, by Heidegger, Sartre, Marcel, and Strasser;[6] more recently, it has been tackled by more contemporary thinkers like Jankélévitch, Waldenfels, Depraz and Varela, Johnston and Malabou, Sheets-Johnstone, Solomon, Thompson, and Zahavi, working in an interdisciplinary capacity with philosophers, psychologists, cognitive scientists, and evolutionary biologists.[7]

Of course, one could argue that the dualism between reason and sensibility had been undone when it was recognized that there is not only an intending and a fulfillment of meaning, and thus evidence (adequate or inadequate) on the level of judgments. Judgment, it has been maintained, is not the sole province of truth and evidence because there is also an intending and fulfilling process of sense (and thus a kind of evidence) that takes place on the level of bodily kinestheses, in "passive" syntheses, and not only in "active" syntheses. Is this not a discovery already announced by Husserl, some of his followers, and their conceptions of phenomenology? Is this not the herald of a decisive break?

For my part, even this openness to sense and meaning-givenness can be misleading where the emotions are concerned. That is, we can admit that there is an advancement made in epistemology when we have discovered that there are ways in which sense is formed in and through bodily kinestheses, or that evidence can arise in sensible experience (from the placement of a foot on a step while talking to a friend, to detecting a familiar tune while reading) without the explicit intervention of egoic acts or consciousness actively passing judgments on that experience. But the presupposition in all of this can still be that there is one basic order of givenness—what I have called elsewhere presentation[8]—parsed out in terms of active and passive variants.

Accordingly, it does not address our concerns if now we displace the emotions from the realm of judgments to sensibility, citing the fact that the sensible is also susceptible to sense and evidence. Rather, at stake is an entirely different or unique order of givenness and evidence peculiar to the emotional sphere, such that it is relegated neither to the order of judgments nor to the order of sensibility (i.e., the whole realm of presentation: judicative or perceptual). The question is not whether, for example, judgments or propositional meanings are founded in sensibility or perceptual sense (and as a whole constituting the order of presentational givenness); rather it bears on whether the emotional sphere as such is founded in perceptual sense and/or judicative meaning in order for it (the emotional sphere) to be evidential in personal existence, or instead, whether the emotional sphere is another irreducible order, with its own kinds of evidence, modalizations, and so on, and whether the sphere of the emotions themselves, as having their own kind of cognition and evidence, might be founding for other kinds of knowledge (see chapter 7 and "Conclusion"). At least this is what is at stake in such questions.

Let me therefore formulate the problem concerning the evidentiary structure of the emotions in a still more subtle way, but in a way that might also remain problematic for a typical phenomenological approach. We can ask: are the emotions *founded in* certain epistemic acts that have relations to objects in order to exist for us, or do they have a *unique structure* that is independent of such acts? In traditional phenomenological terms: do acts peculiar to the emotional sphere simply follow the coordinates of the noesis: noema structure of intentionality? This is not to ask if they have no intentional structure, but only if the noesis: noema structure is the only form of "intentionality" that could define the emotions. Do they rely on this structure to gain their integrity and evidence? Or does the emotional sphere, which concerns the person (and not simply the subject as perceiver or knower), have an essentially different structure?[9]

We find an initial and extremely clear discussion of such a problematic in Husserlian phenomenology, first in Edmund Husserl's *Logical Investigations,* and, with certain modifications, later in his *Ideas.* Allow me first to explain what Husserl means by these kinds of acts and their relation of foundation. In this way, we can have a clearer understanding of the issues involved, and after the concrete analyses of these selected moral emotions, we can adduce the extent to which acts of the emotional sphere have a unique structure such that they are not merely modifications of other epistemic acts or to be governed by epistemic acts in order to be significant.

While Edmund Husserl is often credited with realizing that consciousness is always consciousness of something, this insight was already well prepared by Descartes, Kant, and Hegel, among others. Husserl's groundbreaking insights did not simply involve the discovery of the intentional structure of consciousness, but concerned his unique phenomenological approach that allowed him to describe the "how" of giving (sense, meaning) of "what" something is (the being of the object) in relation to the power and limits of subjectivity. In the *Logical Investigations,* Husserl described this relationship under the heading of "objectivating acts." An objectivating act is that intentional act which "refers" to an object in and through a certain sense. Thus, an objectivating act is that kind of act which allows there to be an intending and intended object. This is known generally as the intentional structure, and is what Husserl also calls a process of *Gegenständlichung,* that is, the process by which something acquires the status of a *constituted* "object"; in this way the process is a kind of object-giving or "objectivating."

An objectivating act is not only that intentional act in which an object is given as sense, but it is also such that it needs no additional, adjuncting act in order for an object to be given. A non-objectivating act is said to be an act that is "founded" on an objectivating act, requiring the latter's structure.[10] The objectivating act is what allows the non-objectivating act to have this intentional structure, to have an act:sense correlation through which something is given beyond the one who executes acts. Examples of non-objectivating acts are acts of valuing, willing, and emotional acts.

Husserl's initial portrayal of the structure of objectivating acts is carried over into his discussion of the intentional relational in the *Ideas.* In brief, the intentional structure was in part characterized by means of the "quality" and the "material" of the act in the *Logical Investigations,* and with certain important qualifications, was later articulated in the *Ideas* such that the intentional relation could be described under the rubric of the "noesis" or intending side of the relation and the "noema" or the intended side.[11] Accordingly, the characterization of the relationship between objectivating acts and non-objectivating acts is also carried over into Husserl's discussion of intentionality.[12] After describing the "higher spheres" of consciousness in the noesis and noema of judgment, Husserl writes: "Analogous statements hold, then, as one can easily see, for the emotional and volitional spheres, for mental processes of liking or disliking, of valuing in any sense, of wishing, deciding, acting. All these are mental processes which contain many and often heterogeneous intentive strata, the noetic and, correspondingly, also the noematic ones." Thus, emotional acts are founded in more basic essential intentional epistemic acts, giving the latter a peculiar privilege: "a perceiving, phantasying, judging, or the like, founds a stratum of valuing which overlays it completely."[13]

To say that emotional acts are founded in more basic intentional acts means for Husserl that the emotions are dependent upon "objectivating" ones because they require those characteristics of the latter in order for the "non-objectivating" act to mean something beyond itself as presented under a certain sense. Thus, either acts have an epistemic structure (basically a "rational" structure) or they are—in this case—the province of mere instinct and have no cognitive value. The founded acts are called "higher" because the noeses and noemata (acts and senses) are "built" upon the founding levels, though they, too, form a distinctive, new unity of epistemic processes such that the new object-structure will have its own modes of givenness, its "characters," its manifold modes of being intended.[14]

Even though the founding and founded dimensions constitute a new "object," the founding relation is such that these "upper" levels and strata of the total phenomenon can be "abolished" without the remainder ceasing to be a concretely complete intentional experience.[15] As noted, when describing the founding-founded structure of acts and senses in the *Ideas,* Husserl initially considered examples of lived-experiences such as liking or disliking, valuing, wishing, deciding, or doing. Deciding, for example, belongs to the province of volition, but in order to will something and to decide as a willing, I still have to intend or "mean" the object in some way, where the meaning given is the meaning of the object. The "analogous" point Husserl wishes to draw here is that such experiences contain manifold intentional noetic and noematic strata.[16] As intimated above, a new sense is constituted when it is founded upon, yet encompassing, the founding structure. "The new sense brings a totally new dimension of sense," for example, when we see not just the painting, but experience it as a beautiful painting, the machine as a useful machine, and so on.[17]

A valuing that is founded upon a "perceiving, imagining, judging, and the like," by virtue of its adjunct status, qualifies the founding-founded whole as, for example, a "wishing" (for the hot coffee over there) even though the valuing dimension can be removed, leaving intact, mutatis mutandis, the perceiving founding stratum; or again it could be removed and leave a judicative dimension, for example, "that the coffee is certainly hot." Here, the founding-whole can also be teased apart from the founded without damaging the underlying basic structure.

Where valuing is concerned, then, Husserl suggests that the perceptual sense of the object, the perceived as such, belongs to the perception, but in higher-order valuing, it is also integrated into the "valued" as such, as a correlate to the concrete valuing, *whose* sense it (the perceptual sense) founds.[18] Accordingly, we must distinguish the objects, things, characteristics, affair-complexes that are given as valued in the valuing, and the presentings, judgings, imaginings, and so on, which found the valuing, even though the whole new intending may give the object in a unique belief modality, say, as "certainly ugly work of art," or "probably valuable machine."

The relations of founding are multifarious, and can describe the relation of parts to wholes,[19] or the way in which the judgment (as the noematic correlate) is founded upon the perceptual sense, as the judging act is founded upon the perceiving as a being-positing process: doubting-being, possible-being, deeming-being-likely, rejecting- or negating-being are all modifications of a basic "simple" givenness and positing of being that is given in a straightforward attitude. This is also the sense in which Husserl conceived of passive syntheses (in a "transcendental aesthetic") to be founding for meaning constituted in active synthesis (peculiar to a "transcendental logic").[20]

Now, Husserl's notion of foundation [*Fundierung*] is not the problematic issue here. In fact, it is one of those concepts that Eugen Fink termed "operative" in the sense that it can be taken up in a variety of contexts, and depending upon the context, shift in nuance.[21] Husserl wants to stress by such a founding structure that the relation is not a causal one between, say, perceptual and emotional acts; nor even is it a "reciprocal" relation, which would presuppose an exchange of causes. Rather, the founded has to be understood as an "elaboration of" the founding beyond what could have been anticipated in advance, but to which the founding dimension gives a radically new meaning, and which it "needs" in order to be in this unique way.[22] At issue for us is not the founding relation, then, but the fact that the emotional sphere is said to be founded in a more basic "epistemic" intentionality, meaning that the emotions are to be understood as having the same kind of intentional structure, the same kind of rational import, the same kind of givenness, evidence, and so on, as the purely judicative or perceptual sort.

We can ask: Is Husserl correct when he contends that there are analogous distinctions in the emotional and volitional spheres of experience where this founding is concerned? Are the volitional and the emotional spheres of the same mettle so that we can make such a comparison in the first place? Is the emotional sphere really analogous to the judicative, and in this way only to be actualized by being "founded" on the perceptual, objectivating, positing act, or even itself on a judging or an imagining act? If this is the case, then—to give just one example—trust would itself have to be either a kind of judgment, something founded in a decision to trust, or a blind belief.

But is trust a kind of judgment, as a rational decision, or as an epistemic assessment of risk? Is hope a kind of expectation, an optimism of what might come to be, or a belief in the future? In what follows, I show that the structures of moral emotions, for example, through the temporal modes of givenness, through other kinds of self-givenness, modalizations of possibility, and relations to otherness, suggest the order of a unique emotional sphere that is "non-founded" in the sense described above.

To be sure, Husserl realized that it would be ridiculous to place the "valued" or the "likeable" in the same series as the "possible," the "presumable," or the "indeed."[23] But we must pursue this line of inquiry and ask whether emotional experiences are dependent upon such epistemic founding experiences so that only in this way do they have a cognitive dimension, and only in this way do they constitute a meaningful experience.

We will see throughout these analyses that the moral emotions are *not* such that the so-called strata could be stripped off, leaving us with an integral, self-subsistent founding objectivating layer. Rather, they show themselves to be self-subsistent, as another kind of experience that has its own style of givenness, cognition, and evidence, and that is irreducible both to epistemic acts, on the one hand, and to instinct or "private feelings," on the other. In this way, they become another clue to who we are as human persons in the moral universe, and enable us to redress our contemporary place in the world.

Moral Emotions

Emotions are revelatory of human persons. My descriptions of the emotions attend not only to the meaning and structures of the particular experience in question (say, shame, hope, or trust), disambiguating them from related phenomena, and identifying possible cross-cultural invariants. I aim more deeply at a fuller and richer picture of the human person (fuller than a rationalistic or a generally epistemic account would give us), guided by an examination of certain key emotions. I consider the emotions I treat as "key," as we will see through these analyses, because they reveal in optimal ways central meanings of what it means to be a person.

As a starting point, and merely by way of introduction here, I understand by person that dynamic movement and orientation that lives through acts, that en-actment which unfolds on the level of spirit, or more exactly, is discernible as the spiritualization of the concrete lived-whole of the human being. I acknowledge such an understanding as a point of departure because for the purposes of this work, it is important not to identify "person" with the formal constitution of the self, with the sense of self as the "minimal self," which is the first-person character of experiential life,[24] or with the so-called narrative self, which can be understood as the culturally or linguistically constituted "self."[25] Even though I use the expression "self" throughout this work, I use it in a much more general and non-specific way, and not, for example, in Zahavi's more technically rich sense.

Further, I understand the person as absolute in terms of his or her uniqueness and irreplacability, given and creatively en-acted. As absolute, the person is not absolved from relation, but rather absolved from the relativity of being a thing or object in relation to things or objects. One of the insights garnered here is that the person is inherently interpersonal. One way I speak of the person as absolute and interpersonal is as the "Myself"—the person as receiving him- or herself in terms of "who I am," in the accusative (and as a consequence as reflexive), as directly interpersonal, intrinsically relational, and not self-grounding. As I suggest throughout this work, first-person experiences like "I cannot do otherwise," "what is my way," "is this really 'me,'" and so on, suggest some of the deepest experiences that qualify me, Myself, as who I am or who I am to become. While the descriptions of the moral emotions in this respect requires the explication of vocational experience, I treat the latter in another work.[26] Again, this Myself, which is expressive of the dimension of person as interpersonal, is more robust than a minimal or alternately narrative sense of self—although this says nothing against the necessity of a minimal sense of self-awareness as Zahavi has characterized it. But again, all this is merely by way of introduction because part of the task of this work is disclosing the meaning of person through the moral emotions.

By emotions, I understand those experiences that pertain to the domain of feelings (or what some would call the order of the "heart"), but which take place or are enacted on the level of spirit.[27] Emotional en-actments uniquely open up the sphere of persons, that is, that specific sphere of givenness through which the human being is revealed not merely as subject, but as person, having its distinctive sphere of evidence. (It is distinctive, for example, from that kind of perception or apperception through which the lived-body is given in its own way.)[28]

By moral emotions, I mean those emotions that are essentially interpersonal or that arise essentially in an interpersonal nexus. Rather than understanding the moral sphere as pertaining to an individualistic concept of the human being relevant only to the interior makeup of the subject, I understand the moral sphere as expressing human exis-

THE DISTINCTIVENESS OF MORAL EMOTIONS

tence as interpersonal coexistence and in this way informing the sphere of "praxis." Rather than moral conduct referring to a set of norms that "ought" to govern human action, moral praxis is revealed through the moral emotions, which as we will see, evince norm-constitution and norm regulation within experience itself, and are in this sense "normative." The legitimacy of norms that emerge (e.g., through shame, guilt, trust, loving, etc.) originate from the experience in which they are given and the interpersonal register in which they are lived. Thus, my usage of moral and normative from a phenomenological perspective does not correspond to the attempt to infer how the world ought to be or to prescribe conduct.[29] Further, my attempt is distinct from the first-order moral questions about what is good and bad, and the meta or second-order questions concerning the epistemology of moral thought that we might find in thinkers who have helped shape these discussions like Mark Timmons and Terry Horgan.[30]

The use of "moral" in "moral emotions" is meant to evoke the irreducible interpersonal dimension of experience. I prefer the expression "moral" here to "ethical," despite certain contemporary conventions, because it is my way of stressing the interpersonal character of the experience, as a manner of experiencing, a mode of givenness, rather than presupposing an "ethical subject" who is somehow given prior to that experience, or who can be considered merely in the nominative case, isolated from others.[31] With the expression "moral" I also would like to eschew the assumption that we are dealing with a process of mere deliberations and dilemmas, whose goal in "ethical conduct" is something oriented toward individual propriety or salvation of one's own soul, or simply doing the right thing according to either fixed or arbitrary norms.

Equally important for this work is the sense of moral as "vertical" in a twofold sense.[32] The moral is vertical in the sense that persons are "absolute," unique, as finite, and not merely relative or interchangeable. I therefore tend to speak of an absolute moral (interpersonal) experience, but not a universal ethical one. The moral is vertical in another sense: moral experience is irreducibly moral, but it is also the experience implicitly of not being self-grounding. While the inter-Personal dimension of experience (or what I have called elsewhere religious experience) may not be explicit in the moral, it is implicitly connected to it, and alternately, the moral implicitly opens up to, or "de-limits," the inter-Personal.[33] For something like computer ethics, business ethics, engineering ethics, this need not be the case, whereas, by contrast, for what has been developed in terms of a "care ethics," such an interpersonal dimension is evident.[34] It is certainly appropriate to use the expression "ethics" or "moral" in any way one will—but I present this clarification as notice of the way in which "moral" is employed in this work, and for these reasons.

Under the heading of emotions, I include experiences like remorse, regret, optimism, pessimism, panic, disgust, or sincerity—just to scratch the surface. But these are not essentially *moral* emotions because they do not in all instances exhibit an interpersonal relation. So, whereas disgust or wonder could relate to a person, it may exclusively relate to an object without an interpersonal dimension ever coming into play. However, this characteristic is not alone sufficient to distinguish an emotion as a moral emotion. An emotion could be expressed in a subject-object relation in one respect, but be subtended by a deeper relation, for example, if in and of itself the experience would give me to myself as not self-grounding—in this respect being in relation to another and be constituted as a moral emotion (as in the case of hope, as we will see below). So while there are emotions that exhibit a subject-object relation like dread or courage (vis-à-vis an event), and while they might also be shared by human persons or within a relation to the world or objects in the world, they are not given with any deeper relation. Finally, belonging here are those emotions that not only are not interpersonal, but may not even exhibit a subject-object relation. Emotions I have in mind here, emotions that are not moral emotions (or what Heidegger would call "moods") include anxiety and boredom.

The moral tenor of the emotion is not gauged according to whether it is judged to be "good" or "bad," or whether the emotion fits accepted standards or conforms to norms. Rather, the moral tenor of the emotion can be weighed according to how it opens up or closes down the interpersonal nexus. This understanding is more in concert with the way that Henri Bergson characterized "open" and "closed" morality, where the moral sphere is founded in dynamic (not static) religious experience.[35] Each in their own way, the moral emotions are expressive of person-to-person relations; they illuminate a creative dimension of person and an *interpersonal* dimension of freedom. This is perhaps more clearly seen in emotions like hope and repentance, but it also holds for emotions of self-givenness like shame and guilt. When pushed to their core, what all the moral emotions reveal is the "person" *as* interpersonal (as from and with finite persons) and *as* inter-Personal (as from and with infinite Person).

I examine the moral emotions according to three central rubrics: emotions of self-givenness, emotions of possibility, and emotions of otherness. Under these rubrics, I investigate what I consider to be key moral emotions. Why they are key will become clearer below, but in

THE DISTINCTIVENESS OF MORAL EMOTIONS

general, it concerns how they express these central features just mentioned, how they are exemplary of the moral emotions, and how they are essential to who we are as persons. For emotions of self-givenness, I treat chiefly pride, shame, and guilt; for emotions of possibility, I investigate principally repentance, hope, and despair; for emotions of otherness, I focus on trust, loving, and humility.

While these central features (self-givenness, possibility, and otherness) are evident in all of these moral emotions, they are patent in different ways. The ones that more directly characterize a specific modality recommend themselves to be treated under that specific heading. For example, even though trusting is directly a relation to otherness, an emotion like shame also essentially exhibits such a relation, while shame's primary experiential weight or main "contribution" is as an emotion of self-givenness. I explain in more detail the meaning of these categories below.

While almost all works on the emotions do not take up the unique temporal orientations and meanings of the emotions, this work does feature the temporal dimensions of the experiences. Here is why: if the moral emotions have their own modes of givenness peculiar to the kind of experiences they are as personal and interpersonal, they may not necessarily map onto the familiar temporal life that we see in the presentational structure of time-consciousness, that is, in the sense of the presentation, retention, and the motivated protention of objects. Of course, there is always a retention and protention of any given psychophysical experience, so in this sense, the process of self-temporalization does relate to these experiences as experiences that are mine. Yet, the temporality of some of these emotional experiences is not simply founded in these presentational structures of time-consciousness, nor does it carry on or elaborate these structures. For presentation, retention, protention, and more actively, remembering and expectation, are *modes of temporal givenness;* and if there are experiences that exhibit different kinds of givenness and different kinds of evidence (e.g., epiphany, revelation, disclosure, etc.),[36] then we can at least suspect that this will hold for their temporal modes of givenness as well.[37]

The moral dimension of the emotions pertains not only to the dimension of spirit, but to the interpersonal nexus in which they arise. There are of course many other emotions that could be classified as moral emotions and warrant being treated here, though they may only get a cursory nod in their direction: embarrassment, atonement, sympathy, empathy, envy, jealousy—just to name a few. Indeed, some of these emotions are examined by way of comparison or distinction, articulated around the main moral emotions studied here, those that take the point for elucidating the meaning of person in this work. In the case of loving, which is a fundamental moral emotion, I reserve its systematic treatment for another work connected to this one, although loving is explored throughout this work and introduced in a more concerted manner under its own heading in relation to humility. Because of my specific interest in disclosing the distinctive structure of the emotions, thereby disclosing the meaning of person, and connected to this, showing how the moral emotions can and should intervene where the problems of our social imaginaries are concerned—because of this, my goal is not to be exhaustive in the treatment of the moral emotions, and indeed, I do not consider the moral emotions described here to be exhaustive, though for various reasons they can be considered exemplary or key. While they will have implications for psychological discourse on the emotions and the way they are treated in analytic, empirical, and phenomenological literature alike, an intervention in this respect is not my primary objective.

Finally, for the purposes of this work, I distinguish affects from the emotions and specifically the moral emotions. Affects or the affective life pertain to who we are as psychophysical beings: liking or disliking, pleasure or pain, being ill at ease, arousal, sadness, excitement, nervousness, anger, aggressiveness, distress, and so on, as they may pertain to goals and motives. While significant in their own ways, they will not be considered as a part of this work.[38] By alluding to this distinction between affects and emotions, I want to emphasize that I do not start from the notion of person and then deduce something as an emotion (e.g., assert that this is a person, observe that this person has an experience and conclude that it is an "emotion" or "moral emotion," or inversely, this is an "animal" and it has affects). Wittgenstein reflects: "One can imagine an animal angry, fearful, sad, joyful, startled. But hopeful? And why not? . . . Can only those hope who can talk?"[39]

For my part, I leave open the possibility that, for example, a wolf, dolphin, elephant, or chimpanzee, while not human, could through emotional acts become "person" in our sense. If we encounter a grieving elephant, an ashamed dolphin, a loving chimpanzee, a trusting wolf—and not simply "higher intelligence"—then we might just be confronting "person" here. I don't think we can know that it is, for instance, an ashamed dolphin in any decisive way by testing for objective similarities between ashamed humans and dolphins, because this still presupposes that we can identify the experience of shame originally. Instead, if this happens, if we become cognizant of shame, love, pride, trust, humility, it is because they will have opened up interpersonally in and through the very emotional experience itself, with its own kinds of evidence, modalization, and so on, peculiar to that sphere of experience (the sphere of the emotions), and not adjudicated outside of that sphere.[40]

In any case, for me, it is not that an animal cannot hope because he or she is an animal or has not mastered language. Rather, it is that through hoping (or trusting, shame, guilt, etc.) the dimension of person as interpersonal is creatively opened up in its richness and fundamental mystery, and that "person" is revealed and originated in these and other emotions, and most profoundly, in what we have called the moral emotions. In this way, they become interwoven with and co-revelatory of the universe of interpersonal acts.

Phenomenology of the Emotions

The emotions analyzed here are described in fresh phenomenological descriptions. They utilize contemporary empirical psychological studies to the extent that they contribute to the elucidation of the experience in question, though far from the phenomenological analyses being superseded by them, the very methods and foundations of these other studies are also in question where the moral emotions are concerned.[41] Further, to say that these are fresh or original phenomenological analyses means that it is not a matter of simply citing past phenomenologists either, but of utilizing the latter only to the extent that they help elucidate the emotion under discussion.

While this is a phenomenological approach, I take many departure points into the emotions: sociological, political, linguistic, anthropological, historical, and so on. In particular, I bring ordinary language philosophy into this discussion of phenomenological method, not because I want to raise the time-worn specter of the relation between "continental philosophy" and "analytical philosophy," but because of the important and unique interrelations in method where an undertaking of a phenomenology of the emotions is concerned. Since we often deal with the emotions linguistically in order to identify an experience, say, as shame, repentance, humility, or pride, we encounter both similarities and differences between phenomenology and ordinary language philosophy. In the following pages, I suggest how ordinary language philosophy can work with and be enlisted to provide leading clues within the general phenomenological enterprise of describing experience: elucidating the emergence of meaning, the hermeneutic task of interpreting that experience, and the conceptual clarifications of experience and its structures.[42]

Phenomenological method. Phenomenological method is undertaken as a way to liberate the "matters" that we experience so that what they are and their very appearing are not taken for granted in the experience of them. Phenomenology is thus attuned not only to *what* appears to us, but to *how* this "what" is given. The what of appearing counts as the thing itself, the being, as well as the structure, the essence, or the a priori of the matter; the how of appearing is the way in which the matter gives itself, the manner in which it is encountered or experienced—in short, its mode of givenness. It is characteristic of phenomenology to approach the matter in question in any number of ways, but all of them will have these two methodological components concerning the "what" and the "how" of the experience.

One of the best known ways in which this method is carried out begins by holding in abeyance or "bracketing" our everyday assumptions that characterize our being in the world. It puts out of play those prejudices and inherited validities about being, so that we do not take the meaning of their being for granted. This process is typically known as the *epoché* (from the Greek expression), meaning "suspension." Rather than denying or doubting being, it is a process of withholding assertions about what we unquestioningly accept. Such a process is undertaken in order to see how the meanings are constituted, that is, how something is given and how it is accepted as such, so as to understand the structures of those meaningful experiences.

Bracketing is complimented by another move. It is not simply a matter of freeing the constituted sense, but retrieving the dimension of "constituting" sense. Because it is a process of going back to the origination of sense-giving, this aspect of phenomenology is commonly known as the "reduction." When we go back to the origination of sense, one immediate source for description is first-person experience.

The risk in such a procedure that appeals to "my" experience as a source of description is that phenomenology might become a new exercise in autobiography. This is one reason why phenomenology does not stop at the phenomenological "fact" of my experience, but investigates the structural, essential, or shared components of that experience. Such a process is at all possible because the eidetic structures of experience are given in the concrete fact of experience. So, while many experiences can serve as examples or instances to get at the essential structure, in principle only one is sufficient; but at least one is necessary, since the essence is only given in and through the particular, which constitutes the latter precisely as an instance of it.[43] This is why Scheler can assert that Siddhartha Gautama, the Buddha, was able to understand the whole of world suffering, its intrinsic unity or core of sense, by a chance encounter outside the palace walls, concretized in the instance of, for example, a beggar (also without himself having suffered in this way).[44]

In pursuing a phenomenology of the moral emotions, we are concerned with how the emotional experiences emerge, what they are like as experienced, how they are lived through in various modes of givenness, and the essential structures of those emotions. These sorts of issues can enlist a variety of approaches. For example, we might start by examining an experience, statically in the "now-phase" of the experience; we might inquire into its givenness over time in remembering or anticipating. We could imaginatively vary the example of an experience to get at its essential structure. We could begin *by presupposing* active accomplishments of meaning, utilizing them as leading clues to critical investigations of sense-giving. By "leading clues," I mean guides to a phenomenological analysis that serve, but are themselves not necessarily or strictly speaking phenomenological analyses.[45] We could go along with already accepted descriptions gleaned from the sciences; we might use the analyses and results, say, of cognitive psychologists; we might utilize the fieldwork of cultural or physical anthropologists; we could use the political-historical reflections of other thinkers; we could even press into service the work of other phenomenologists. But if we undertake such approaches, then we take them as points of departures for (or again, as "leading clues" to) a constitutive analysis into the very genesis of sense. The point of all of this is to elucidate, as broadly and fully as possible, experience—its genesis and structures—in its dynamic origination.

The seemingly simple question "What is pride?" therefore solicits phenomenologically a host of interrelated questions: How does pride emerge at all when it was not present beforehand or predestined to be that act which restricts and refuses contributions of meaning? How is it that shame emerges as a creative response to pride, and not something else or some other diremptive experience, like guilt? How is it that there is something like repentance—of all possibilities—that arises originally as a reply to guilt or to shame and as a recovery of ourselves, when nothing had prefigured this? In short, if the actualization of meaning is radically original and creative; if the person may not even know he or she has this "capacity" for the emotion until it is actually realized; if the emotion is not pre-given in the makeup of the person; "how" does it emerge at all? In what ways does the emergence of these moral emotions constitute the person? To what extent are they shared experiences; to what extent are these experiences cross-cultural?[46] Methodologically, how are we to undertake these kinds of investigations?

Through the *epoché* and reduction, or critical phenomenological reflection, the "natural attitude" as such comes to the fore *as* that attitude that takes meaning for granted and posits being as simply there. The natural attitude is not only that attitude that pre-reflectively experiences the world in a commonsense way; the natural attitude also encompasses the "naturalistic attitude," that is, a reflective posture that may try to make the natural pre-reflective attitude more precise, more exact, like we find in the natural, physical, or technical sciences. For example, to render the color red more exact in terms of the physicist's wavelengths may seem to clarify experience, but actually it does not make the reflection on the meaning of red any more "critical"; similarly, to speak now of "moral cognition" on the model of rational cognition in the name of conceptual rigor would do little to clarify that field of experience and its own kind of evidence. In fact, not only does such a "scientific" reflection presuppose a certain order of experimentation and validation as true, it can become forgetful of the way we see red or experience moral emotions, and even demean the everyday experience in the process, taking itself for the "true," and superimposing itself as that upon which the everyday is founded. This forgetfulness and reversal, which become like "second nature" to us, constitute their "naiveté." Thus, certain kinds of reflective attitudes can also be mundane, insidiously so, and still remain outside of philosophical-phenomenological critical reflection.

Phenomenology is a special kind of reflection that acknowledges the basis of reflection, but distances itself from this basis. It does this in order to bring the everyday into relief, to see the process of the everyday's origination, to witness the initial strangeness of meaning in what has become for us so obvious, and thus to describe the process of meaning formation in its opening unfamiliarity which has long since been taken for granted within everyday practicality. In reflecting on the sense-giving process itself, we grasp it in its living process so that we can glimpse how and what it "means," "intends," or "accepts." This is in part how phenomenology becomes "critical."

Such a movement is expressed in the qualitative shift in perspective from what something is to how it is given. Because phenomenology is a special kind of reflective, mindful attentiveness that is attuned to givenness which occurs *within* experiencing itself, phenomenological description can occur within the very process of experiencing the matter, while simultaneously being at a distance through an attentive reflection. To do so, it can draw on current experiences, on rememberings of past experiences, on first-personal plural accounts, on real or fictional experiences, or figures that are exemplary for these purposes; it can appeal to second-person exemplary instances, or instances that make themselves available in dialogue. These avenues are especially important in describing the moral emotions because of the peculiar style and nature of the experiences. In any case, they don't seem to be accessible in the same way as desks, cups, or tables.

I approach the emotions under consideration from several different angles, for instance, from situational contexts, by means of historical examples, by beginning with other thinkers' insights, by tracing some connections in the history of ideas. These provide what I described above as "leading clues." I also rely on many examples in this work to describe and to hone in on the particular emotion under discussion. When dealing with the moral emotions, deeply personal examples that go directly to the core of who we are obviously come to the fore, and they can be illuminating for this very reason. But sometimes extremely mundane examples may also be just as illuminating. They can be elucidating for two reasons. First, in the phenomenological method, the very simplicity and commonness of the example is no longer taken for granted in using it as an example, and to this extent, its immediacy is transcended in the direction of that which enables the situation to arise as such, toward the originating of the very banality. By bringing such common examples into focus, we go beyond the commonness in the example, and this opens a new world of meaning, as it were, that was taken for granted in the ordinary. The point is to see the fundamental strangeness or mystery in the ordinary, but now *as* it is taken for granted.

Second, because we are examining not just the mode of givenness of the experience, but the essential structures of the experience, we should be able to find the same structure, say, of guilt, hope, or trust in the most simple to the most complex, in the most banal to the most profound of experiences. It should disclose the generative structures present in the everyday and their dimensions of meaning-constitution.[47] This is how a phenomenological approach can not only describe the moral emotions, but in getting to the core of such interpersonal experiences (where the roles of freedom, creativity, normativity, and critique emerge in unique fields of interpersonal experience), a phenomenological approach can enable us to see how the transformative dimensions of the moral emotions have been effaced in modernity and postmodernity, and suggest why they should be reintegrated into such a project.

Ordinary language philosophy. These considerations bring me now to the possible role of ordinary language philosophy in this phenomenological undertaking of describing the moral emotions. I would like to take an all too brief look at ordinary language philosophy because of the way in which we sometimes take our leading clues for a phenomenological analysis when dealing with the emotions. When we describe emotional experiences are we simply describing a familiar meaning, some term that we use in common or a sense upon which we agree? One of the main contributors to what we understand as ordinary language philosophy is J. L. Austin.[48] In his "A Plea for Excuses," Austin attempts in part to clarify the philosophical study of conduct, in particular freedom and responsibility, by investigating excuses (and the usage of various terms that are related to excuse, such as extenuation, mitigation, justification), and in this way shed light on ethics. This is significant for our purposes because he also uses this foray as a study in method.

Since words are tools, he contends, we have to be clear about our usage of words. In fact, how a word is used, or what we mean by it, is identifiable with what is there, with the *being* of the thing.[49] This is why ordinary language philosophy, according to Austin, examines not simply what we say when we use this term, but what we should say when . . . , and thus why and what we should mean by it.[50] For example, to understand what trust is, we examine what words we should use in relevant situations. When we do this, we look not merely at words, but at the realities we use the words to address.[51] Thus, *what* trust is, its essence, amounts to the usage of the term "trust" in that context or what we mean by trust linguistically in that statement. The functional insights here, gleaned from Wittgenstein, are that the life of the sign is its use,[52] that the meaning of a word is its use in the language,[53] and that our concepts are tied to essential human situations and that they are part of the form of life.[54]

For Austin, the familiar usage of the term "hallowed by ordinary language" can work well for practical purposes, and in this way be illuminating. Accordingly, the more attentive we become to words and how we use them, the more we can sharpen our perception. To do so, he not only suggests working with the dictionary, but imagining a variety of situations in which the word/meaning under consideration arises.[55] As words are tools, not facts, we need to tease them apart from the world so that we can realize both their inadequacies and their familiarities, and so that we can "re-look at the world without blinkers."[56] The effort here is to call our attention to befuddled thinking where it appears to be the most transparent, disclosing misleading thought when it is taken to be the most irreproachable. Thus, if there is a problem in our use of words, the way to address the problem is in language and by taking a clue from the ordinary, familiar, commonsense way in which they have become meaningful for us. As TeHennepe writes, the extent to which the existential dimension of philosophy lies in its return to the philosophical significance of the ambiguous world of lived-experience is the extent to which ordinary language philosophy has such an existential purchase by appealing to the everyday way in which we use language.[57]

While we would agree with Russell that we do not want to reduce philosophy to lexicography, we cannot agree with his further charge that the problem with the results of ordinary language philosophy are that they are too "inexact," too "everyday" to be a part of philosophy.[58] In my view, one of the virtues of ordinary language philosophy is that it precisely maintains its contact with everyday experience. The advantage of this approach is that it directly expresses the natural form of consciousness from the natural concept of the world; it wants to reach understand-

THE DISTINCTIVENESS OF MORAL EMOTIONS

ing by examining the term in the contexts of its actual use. To the extent that it is descriptive, it returns to a vital, living engaged standpoint.[59]

Indeed, contrary to Russell, it does not help us philosophically to replace the natural attitude of questioning, "what we should say when," with a positivism of the exact sciences akin to the technical vocabulary of the physicist or chemist in the name of clarity and truth (naturalistic attitude). This just leads to a new form of dogmatism that was already criticized by Wittgenstein and Husserl alike. If there is ambiguity in ordinary language philosophy or in the concept of the natural world, it does not thereby mean that we should negate the natural expression of life or replace it by a positivistic worldview, in order to conform to a rational model of knowledge governed by the exact sciences giving us supposed clarity about our world.

Even if the ordinary is not critical—and by this I mean here that it does not examine directly meaning-constitution or how sense is generated individually and interpersonally—it can still function as a source for philosophical and critical reflection, and it can become the context in which theories about the world are tested. For us, the difference between ordinary language and ordinary language *philosophy* is the distance that reflection takes from ordinary language by bringing the ordinary into focus as such. It is no longer possible, in one sense, for ordinary language philosophy to remain ordinary language. But while Austin characterized the task as prying words from the world so as not to remain myopic in view, he never thought of ordinary language philosophy as "the final arbiter . . . of phenomena." It does not have the "final word" for him, but instead is "the first word."[60] Were it not for the clumsiness of expression, he conjectures, he would even suggest calling what he is doing "linguistic phenomenology."[61]

Ordinary language philosophy can function as a "leading clue" to the critical elucidation of the phenomena, as do other leading clues.[62] It belongs as much to what we call a lifeworld ontology as do psychology and anthropology.[63] But it has a special resonance here because of its access to emotional experiences, an access that does not presuppose more complex theories and their substructions, and therefore it serves as a possible way into a more critical investigation.

Ordinary language philosophy can be helpful to a phenomenology of emotions insofar as it may orient the discussion or hone in on phenomena. (And phenomenology, especially generative phenomenology, does not ignore historical or linguistic presuppositions, but creatively works from them in an effort to elucidate those very experiences.) But this does not mean that ordinary language, like any lifeworld ontology, can substitute for a critical investigation, since it is the experience and its clarification which is the point of the description and appeal. This is something that Austin himself does, though he does not acknowledge it as such![64] The point is not to presuppose the accumulated meanings; still less is it a matter of constructing theories without reference to experience, but to investigate their how of givenness—for example, the modes of temporal and spatial givenness, their constitution of possibility, how we are self-given in them, how the emotions are lived in relation to otherness, how they open or close our being with others, their peculiar positive or negative valences—and through this attention to their sense, the clarification of their essential structures. By taking advantage of pre-constituted familiar meanings and assertions about being as leading clues to a constitutive analysis, as a whole, ordinary language can be taken as part of an overarching phenomenological analysis, and the results of ordinary language susceptible to phenomenological clarification.

Let me give an example. Let's say that we start to investigate the meaning of trust by examining the way we use it, and further, that we begin with the expression, "I trust my footing" (while I am ascending a mountain cliff). Having examined the temporal modes of givenness of something being "reliable," the role of the past, familiarity, and so on, in this experience, and having compared it to the experience of trust (to take advantage of the later analyses presented here), we notice that the usage of "trusting my footing" does not clarify the meaning of trust at all. In fact, it is misleading. As I take my posture on the rock face on this climb, I live the rock and my feet not in an attitude of trust, but of reliability, taking advantage of a past confidence and expecting a certain outcome.

Again, presupposing the phenomenological analyses below, this point of departure does not get to the core of the trust as realizing my freedom as being bound to another, not depending upon a past, and temporally as proffering myself in vulnerability as the basis for an expectation. In no way do I impute a free agency to my feet or to the rock face in such a way that they might freely betray me—and if I did, it would be an entirely different situation. The differences can be seen *in the way in which we live through the experiences*. This will differentiate the experiences that we may call "trust" from "reliability"—but it is not the predetermined sets of meanings that are adjudicating. Though indeed, the ordinary usage of trust can help us as a leading clue in discerning what it is, or in this instance what it is not, to take this usage of trust here to be its meaning or being would be very deceptive. We can find similar examples with emotions used below: hope, shame, desperation, humiliation, and many others. In this case, not only is the usage of trust not the final word, it may not even pass for the first word.

Certainly, in some cases, the usage of the term can give us important insights. For example, if I want to determine the temporal orientation of hope, I can begin with the statement: "I hope that did not happen," to see if it makes sense to speak of hope in relation to a past. Instead, such a beginning gives us a clue to the futural significance of hope. Here the temporal mode of givenness of hope coincides with its encompassing linguistic sense. The final appeal, however, is what takes place in terms of the lived-experience of hope. Or we can take a different experience, say, repentance. While I might say that "I will regret that tomorrow"—knowing myself and what I am about to do, and how I will feel about it later—I do not say that "I will repent that tomorrow" *because* I experience repentance spontaneously as responsive to guilt or shame, and I do not *live* it as something I already anticipate. When I examine what happens when I experience this emotion as a response to shame or guilt, I discover it as a sincere revolution of the heart to change my ways (namely, repentance).

We can get a hold of different insights into the emotions and to who we are as persons depending upon our starting points. For example, analyzing the statement "I hope I do not get a flat tire"—mundane as it may sound—will probably yield different results from analyzing the statement "the cat is on the mat." But what is decisive is the underlying experience and what it reveals about our being with others and possibilities for transformation and meaning constitution. The statement "I will love you for five years" makes perfect linguistic, grammatical, and semantic sense, but it does not make phenomenological sense because the very movement of loving is to go to infinity, without foreseen limits, even if in fact that love does end in five years. This statement has an interpersonal or moral meaning that is different from its merely linguistic one, and to presuppose the linguistic sense as a true or final adjudication of its meaning and structure would be misleading according to its experiential, phenomenological sense. This is because—as an investigation into its temporal modes of givenness, its relation to the mode of possibility, and its orientation to otherness show—loving is initiated without predefined or expected temporal, modal, or interpersonal limits.

With its emphasis on experience, which includes linguistic experience, phenomenological reflection is trained on the way in which something is *given* to us and on its essential structures. Yet, there are experiences that are lived through which may or may not be readily available in language or expressed by a concept. The common experience of sensing that an expression is not quite right, or realizing that we do not have a concept for that particular experience point us in this direction. Very often it is the experience that gives rise to the formulation of not just a new term, but a new concept. There are experiences for which we have no vocabulary; the more fundamental is the experience, the more evident this becomes. Being attentive to the experience, however, can enable us to formulate and to reformulate new concepts and new vocabulary. What we call mystical experiences and the struggle with ineffability—which however is not confined to mystical experiences but is especially clear here—brings this point home. Sometimes there are no ready-made terms or concepts available, and neither usage (let alone common or everyday usage) nor predetermined concepts coincide with the experience, the "meaning," or the "being" of what is given. There is at most a fumbling for a language that the mystic never knew even existed because he or she brings it into being to try to be "worthy" of the experience.[65] Here, the experiences usher forth language and concepts never at their or anyone's disposal prior to this, and then such language only functions meaningfully by evoking, not provoking, that experience.

If, as Marcuse reluctantly concedes, ordinary language is indeed of vital concern to critical philosophical thought, then it is also the case that in the medium of critical thought, the "humble use" of words, like we find in ordinary language philosophy as in a lifeworld ontology, loses its plain meekness and reveals that "hidden" something.[66] This means that there is both a more transparent and a more opaque critical dimension in the descriptions by phenomenology and even by ordinary language philosophy when the natural becomes unnatural, the ordinary unordinary. In its own appeal to experience, in its own employment of the everyday, critical reflection brings into relief the meaning of the everyday such that the meanings cannot remain in the universe of ordinary language. We can side with Wittgenstein: "Unfamiliarity is much more of an experience than familiarity,"[67] since the fundamental strangeness, the mystery of appearing, originating emergence of meaning through which the concepts first take form is brought into relief *as* both hidden in and available in the everyday.

The reflective transcendence of phenomenology in relation to the ordinary or the average everyday is essential to understanding the ordinary and the average everyday. To bring forth the unfamiliar in the familiar expressively is to clarify experience. If ordinary language has a critical function, it is to take advantage of what is already revealed in ordinary discourse, "to make the established language itself speak what it conceals or excludes."[68] If this is the case, then the ultimate aim of ordinary language is to clarify experience, not to clarify terms or the way we use terms. If, however, the ordinary wants to remain ordinary, then it is to be taken within a more encompassing critical thinking without resorting, on the other hand, to the exactitude of the technical or natural sciences. For my purposes, this critical approach, at least as it is employed here where the moral emotions are concerned, is phenomenological.

Part 1

Moral Emotions of Self-Givenness

This first part of *Moral Emotions* concerns the emotions of self-givenness. The main emotions of self-givenness that I focus on in this work are pride, shame, and guilt. I briefly touch on related and antithetical emotions in this part, such as embarrassment, self-love, being proud of, self-confidence, modesty, remorse, and so on, primarily as a way of drawing distinctions. My focus, however, is on these three privileged experiences of self-givenness. I prefer the expression *self-givenness* to characterize these moral emotions rather than calling them, say, emotions of self-awareness, self-consciousness, self-appraisal, and the like for the following reasons.

First, other figures—from Kant to Sartre—have shown that I am self-given in any experience in order to have an experience. Self-givenness, for example, does not have to be occupied by higher-order acts of self-reflection or self-judgment in order for this self-givenness to take place. These experiences of pride, shame, and guilt are unique, first because I am given to myself explicitly in distinctive ways in the very experience, but second, also because they are emotional experiences in which self-givenness explicitly occurs.

Second, the sense of self-givenness in these emotions has been approached by others dealing with the emotions under different rubrics. For example, Gabriele Taylor has referred to them as emotions of "self-assessment." She does this because they concern certain beliefs in oneself in relation to social norms, where what is believed amounts to the assessment of the self.[1] Teroni and Deonna,[2] like Fischer and Tangney, among others, place these emotions (along with other emotions like envy, jealousy, embarrassment) in the context of the psychology of self-conscious emotions.[3] Fischer and Tangney especially recognize the fundamental, inherent role of others in these emotions, maintaining that they are established through socially reciprocal evaluation and judgment. They argue in fact that these emotions have their own integrity, are not individualistic, though they are self-conscious, and that they testify to the fact that human behavior is fundamentally social.

Rather than characterize pride, shame, and guilt within a *psychology* of "self-conscious" emotions, however, I describe them *phenomenologically* within a philosophical perspective. Further, they are treated not with respect to just any kind of individual or social behavior, or the means by which it is externally or internally sanctioned, but with regard to their *moral* significance.[4] That is, they are treated not simply as human, but as *personal* or more precisely, *interpersonal* emotions, having fundamentally therefore a spiritual significance. They reveal the moral sense of the person in the dynamic process of becoming; they do not just disclose a psychological state.

So, while these emotions do exhibit a cognitive dimension—a dimension widely recognized in contemporary literature, and a far, positive step from considering them as irrational[5]—they themselves are not reducible to their epistemic functions. My experience of guilt, for example, is not reducible to my knowledge of guilt and what it can do in relation to the fear of punishment or to accommodating myself to others.[6] In this case, it is not simply a matter of being self-aware through the emotions, though they do have this function. The awareness, however, is rooted in emotional tonalities and valences that bear on the becoming of the person.

While self-consciousness can apply to any epistemic acquisition, even those that are specifically singularizing (like the examination of my conscience, theoretical speculation, etc.), pride, shame, and guilt also bear on ways in which I am not self-grounding, and hence as given to myself; they presuppose *how* I am given to Myself in the accusative, and thus self-given as in relation to another or others.

There is indeed a possible critical dimension peculiar to shame and guilt. But this is prior to assessing myself, because the critical dimension that calls me into question (and is available for a subsequent assessment or adjudication) is spontaneous and in this sense pre-judicative. In pride, I am given to myself explicitly, but *not* in any critical manner that calls me into question, and certainly not in a manner of assessing myself. It presupposes my position in the world as the arbiter of meaning over the contributions of others and the world, and results as we will see in a self-dissimulation. Shame and guilt are modes of critical self-giving in the sense of being thrown back on myself, but not in any reflective epistemic manner, though being called into question in this way is available for self-assessment and judgment.

Self-givenness is the most general feature of these emotions, of course, and does not specify the unique contribution of each experience, but it does give them their unity of sense. Pride, for example, is not evaluative or potentially critical like shame or guilt; shame and guilt are not self-dissimulating in the way that pride is, though pride is a kind of self-givenness.

I begin with an exposition of pride among these moral emotions of self-givenness. I do this because pride is not just one emotional experience among others, not even just one among those emotions of self-givenness. Rather, it is peculiar in its moral significance because in pride, I place myself before others, and in a practical way, I resist the contribution others make, all the while presupposing their contributions in my actions through a peculiar self-salience. This movement makes it a fundamental turning point in moral life, and serves as an implicit and explicit experiential nodal point for shame and guilt, not to mention repentance and humility. Shame and guilt each and in their own ways have a genetic relation to pride, as personal reactions to pride, even if they are not reducible to this tie. They also set up a dynamic that points to the regeneration of a future, eliciting repentance (and forgiveness), and humility as responses to pride, and toward the reconciliation with others through the reshaping and reorientation of the person.

1

Pride

As with all the emotions treated here, pride, like shame, guilt, hope, trust, and so on, can be approached within more limited strictures. For example, it can be treated either sociologically, psychoanalytically, neurologically, or anthropologically. This is justified because trust, for example, does arise as a sociological phenomenon, guilt as a psychoanalytic one, and so forth. But we would miss the import of these experiences if we limited them to these levels and did not consider them within the full context of the human person. This means that it would be misleading to detach the sociological or the psychological meanings, for instance, from the encompassing framework of the person in which they emerge. This framework of the person is comprehensive of what we call "spirit," and this is why the broader context of these emotions needs not only to take into account the sphere of the moral and the divine, but also to be attentive to how the former are situated in relation to the latter. Because the emotions appear in these spheres, they are susceptible to description, and it would be incumbent upon a more restrictive reading (say, that wants to treat the emotions *only* in a psychological perspective) to prove otherwise.

I begin with the experience of pride as a moral emotion for several reasons. First, pride gives us an important starting point because it can be qualified as a moral subjective attitude: I am given to myself, but in a way that is not self-revelatory, precisely in a dissembled manner. Second, although it seems counterintuitive, pride as a subjective self-oriented act is essentially an interpersonal experience; pride concerns how we are given to ourselves in relation to others. Third, there are genuine basic experiences that are elaborated in pride; while they are peculiar kinds of self-givenness, they are not sufficient "to cause" pride, and this points to the creative, initiatory, "personal" dimension of pride. The emergence of pride raises the question concerning how pride not only is a moral experience (as the resistance to others through the insistence of self), but how it emerges as a moral experience, and further, what creative responses can call pride into question. Finally, pride is not just one emotional experience among others, but a real creative turning point in the meaning of human person such that other emotional experiences of self-givenness such as shame and guilt can function in their style of self-critique as original challenges to pride. These considerations also point this investigation to privileged experiential modes of self-givenness treated in the following two chapters, namely, on shame and guilt.

In this chapter, I begin by investigating pride as an interpersonal experience (1) and then examine the basic experiences that are creatively elaborated in pride (2). After characterizing pride as a moral subjective attitude by describing the peculiar self-givenness involved here (3), I describe pride as non-self-revelatory and entertain the possibility of a "moral reduction" (4). The issues of pride being called into question, and pride as non-self-revelatory, provoke a discussion of how pride is self-dissembling and actually self-limiting (5). As this negative or restrictive movement, pride is founded in the positive movement of genuine self-love (6). These determinations allow pride to be distinguished from phenomena often conflated with pride, like being proud of, boasting, and self-confidence (7). This serves as the transition to the experience of shame as a moral self-revelatory emotion.

Pride as an Interpersonal Experience and as a Moral Emotion

Insofar as pride entails an exclusion of otherness (in ways I will explore below), pride can be understood as a closing down or narrowing movement in and through a peculiar assertion of the self. The contention that pride is essentially an *interpersonal* experience, namely, that it has an interpersonal basis, and that it unfolds only in an interpersonal nexus, might sound contradictory at first because pride is usually thought to devolve upon the self. Pride, therefore, is a peculiar starting point because pride, in which the self is self-given, always already occurs within the context of others. Thus, the self as given in pride is not really a self-sufficient point of departure. Pride is interpersonal because it presupposes an implicit movement toward others, and includes others only by resisting them in the constitution of who I am through the vaulting self-valuation. Thus pride is a twofold movement. It is both (1) a subjective self-movement, as (2) a resistance to others. This twofold movement is what gives to pride both what we might call its "truth-character" (see the "basic experiences" below) as well its "dissembling-character."

Due to this dissembling character, pride is not self-revelatory, even though it may strike us as such due to the peculiar focus that we have on ourselves in pride. For example, I can be conceited about my accomplishments without—hypothetically—the intervention of others in any way. Yet in order for such an experience to be pride, this conceit would have to be constituted in and through the positing of and resistance *to others* in the same movement. I do not have to resist others actively in order to live in the movement of pride. It is sufficient to fixate on the basic experiences (that I detail below) to such a qualitative extent that it winds up being a resistance to others in my very presupposition of these others and their contributions. So, rather than pride being the putative happy confluence of excitement or joy and personal efficacy in a reciprocal relation with shame,[1] pride is simultaneously the insistence on the self as the denial of shared meaning, and hence the resistance to the interpersonal nexus. In this way, pride "blinds" me to others in the sense that I do not see them, and in the sense that I presuppose them, while nevertheless refusing their contributions. In pride, I take myself as sovereign.

Placing myself as *the* constitutive source or as the *highest* constitutive source, I admit no significant contribution of sense from the outside; but in pride I do so as excluding the others which I presuppose in this exclusion. This is why if pride is to have sense, it must occur within an interpersonal nexus. A complete reduction to myself as the point-zero of meaning-constitution actually begs the question, since it begins with an abstraction from others from the very start. I would have already withdrawn from the interpersonal context from the very beginning in order to see how others get their meaning from me. If I were to take this abstraction as an isolated meaning-giver as my starting point, I could never have access to the experience of pride.[2]

For example, it is possible to identify as prideful the individual who takes all or the major credit in a group project; pride is evident in someone who wants to be called out as special in front of others, to be recognized, say, as the better or best painter deserving special recognition among his peers;[3] we can see the movement of pride, for example, in patriarchy when men capitalize on women's contributions, taking credit for the accomplishments in their name, thereby including them through their exclusion, materially-reproductively and spiritually-emotionally.[4] One can discern pride in cultural accomplishments that we take to be our own through the labor of others; I would go so far as to say that even though there are other meanings surrounding this as well, the attribution of the invention of the cotton gin to Eli Whitney in the place of the real designer, Katherine Littlefield Greene, is expressive of pride. One can also detect the movement of pride in what Agamben has characterized as bio-political sovereignty (as we will see below in chapter 2), where others are included precisely through their exclusion; we can see pride operative in making others in our own image (which is another way of expressing self-assertion as resistance to others); and the movement of pride is expressed in the myth of the "self-made man," as the person who is self-grounding; and precisely because he made it (ostensibly all himself)—which is expressive of this self-grounding character—he takes himself as *deserving* the gain, in whatever form. Even narcissism can be seen as an expression of pride, and not the reverse.[5] While not exclusive, all of these can be interpreted as examples of pride because they share this basic movement of self-insistence and presupposition of others through their exclusion.

Whereas smugness might be an artful expression of pride, I could be conceited without any interpersonal nexus, but I could not be prideful.[6] A Nietzschean overman, for instance, could never be accused of pride. Statements like: "Well, that's all because of me; it's just the truth," could register a mere statement of fact; it might be a mistaken assumption; it could be an overestimation; it might be an expression of my conscience; it could be an entirely different phenomenon, like sheer meaning-giving, but it would not be pride.[7] The fact that Mr. Darcy in Jane Austen's *Pride and Prejudice* expects to be regarded in certain ways, to keep a certain company, and holds himself to a high standard that he may not hold others to is not necessarily pride in our sense because it can exist within the sphere of solitude—though this sense has fallen for us colloquially under the rubric of "pride."[8] It is more accurately self-esteem, moral superiority at best, or arrogance, as we will see below.[9] For example, I can be selfish in my acquisition of toys (I want them all for myself, I don't want to share), or I can be self-centered in a conversation at a party (I want all the attention); but in order for this to be lived as pride, this experience has to be accompanied by an "I deserve it" in the face of others.

Accordingly, pride is not simply the epistemic non-recognition of others, not simply self-esteem or vanity. For in vanity, I implicitly give myself over to the opinions of others, adopting the judgments from those very others I seek to surpass by being showy or showing off how good I am.[10] But pride is the refusal of or resistance to the contributions of meaning by others to my very self and to the world—contributions among which I implicitly or explicitly live. This is why pride can also take the form of refusing help or receiving instruction from others ("I can do it on my own," "I don't need anyone to teach me how to swim"), as well as assuming the contributions of others as my own, and in this sense, refusing the contribution of others.[11]

Descartes understands such a resistance to the contribution of others as one of the defining characteristics of pride (*l'orgueil*). For example, Descartes describes pride in distinction to true generosity:

whereas generosity proceeds from the will to make good use of our free will, holding nothing more important than doing good for others and disdaining individual interests, pride arises when "glory [*gloire*] is regarded as nothing but usurpation," when gifts are used to depreciate all others such that the more glory/gifts I ascribe to myself, the more prideful I become.[12] This would be the justification for calling pride "vainglory" as does Hobbes,[13] and of Rousseau placing pride (*l'orgueil*) among the spirit of domination.[14]

Pride therefore is never innocent. In epistemic terms, we might be tempted to say that it is a second-order denial of what I know on the first order. Still, we want to be careful about how we portray pride merely in terms of knowledge, because pride is not situated on an epistemic continuum (as more or less belief, recognition, or awareness, say). Pride is a *moral* emotion, belonging to a moral dimension of experience, because it is a resistance to others and to their contributions to shared meaning in and through asserting myself as *the* only or the highest source of meaning. I am given to myself in pride as self-grounding. It is no coincidence that the bodily posture attributed to pride, even as a synonym for pride, is not just being puffed-up, but being "stiff-necked"—unable to turn to or recognize others; and it is also telling that someone like Dante could speak of pride in terms of the "proud neck," and that the metaphors associated with entering the first level of purgatory to overcome pride are portrayed as a suppleness of bowing one's head.[15]

Having suggested that pride is morally problematic, it would be simplistic to rebuke the experience of pride as if it arose from nowhere, as if it were simply some wild or random design that the ego invents, something that had no impetus or spur. Even though pride is understood to be an ultimately negative moral emotion because of its resistance to otherness—by claiming the contributions of others as my own or refusing the contribution of others—we do find that there are fundamental experiences that function as "lures" for pride given within experience itself. Specifically, there are at least five such basic experiences, two that arise on the level of the person as such, three that can be found pertaining to the aesthetic dimension of our lives.

Basic Experiences as Lures for Pride

This fundamental context within which pride emerges is a positive orientation toward others, ultimately a creative openness toward another as loving (and trusting, sympathy, etc.).[16] The orientation of pride can be seen as a negative one, not because it is deemed good or bad, but because it narrows in a qualitative sense rather than opens to the interpersonal sphere that it presupposes. It is itself a creative turning that fixes on what we can call "basic experiences," and, retrospectively, "lures." Pride emerges within a basic interpersonal nexus, and this interpersonal nexus is evinced by the very experience of pride itself.

Pride emerges in the interpersonal nexus by means of "basic experiences" constituted in the movement of pride as lures for pride. By "basic experiences" I mean those fundamental features of being a person or an embodied being, ways of being that we find "given" and that can be taken for granted. I discuss these basic experiences below, each in their turn. In and of themselves there is nothing wrong with them; in and of themselves, they are fundamental experiences of ourselves.

These basic experiences can take on meaning retroactively as "lures for pride" when they are viewed after the fact and within the very movement of pride. By "lure," then, I do not mean a motivation or cause that preexists pride and then provokes pride, but rather that "condition" that is fixed upon (such that the basic experience in question becomes a nonrelational relation). Viewed within the circuit of pride, within a pride already accomplished, the basic experiences become constituted as contributing to this experience. But the fact that we can identify such conditions or lures does not mitigate the fact that pride emerges as another creative, personal way of being with others. Indeed, it is a spontaneous, expressive mode of experiencing that differentiates itself from other experiences, having a phenomenologically identifiable unique structure. We must accordingly identify the structure of pride guided by these basic experiences that serve as conditions or lures.

On the one hand, pride is not arbitrary, because it draws on elements that arise *within experience* and that become precisely lures in the direction of pride from the standpoint of pride. These are what I characterize as personal and aesthetic basic experiences. In a general sense, pride works from the inherent value of ourselves, as we are given to ourselves in specific ways. As such, they harbor something "true" or "affirmative" in the movement. These basic experiences are not nothing or insignificant. Yet, this affirmative moment of them (that can be taken up in humility—see chapter 7) should be conflated neither with the positive valence that accompanies any act of pride, nor with pride's negative moral tenor. Whereas shame has a negative valence, as we will see, but can be positive (as self-critique when it is not a matter of debilitating shame), pride is always given with a positive valence, but is morally negative. This is not because it is "bad" according to prescribed norms, but due to its contraction of the field of interpersonal experience in favor of self-salience. Further, even though these experiences can be described and articulated conceptually as basic experiences, they are not first thought and then applied.

On the other hand, to say that pride is non-arbitrary because there are basic experiences does not mean that they are causes, justifications, or rational necessities that have to lead to pride; they are not "potentialities" for pride prior to the pride-experience. Given the basic positive orientation of the person as *immediately and directly* interpersonal; given that these basic experiences do not *cause* pride or are not reducible to pride; given that pride as a moral emotion is not an affect, not merely a psychological disorder, not an impulse or a product of practical intelligence, *how* is it possible for pride to arise as an ultimately negative moral emotion? For there is nothing in these genuine human experiences that says we must fixate on them such that "I" take myself so seriously (as self-important, as grandiose, etc.) that I include others only excluding their sense, worth, or in general, their contributions. Pride is not a compulsory experience, but a creative, free emergence that works from these basic experiences, and that are taken up into the current of pride. Let me now turn to explicating these basic experiences.

Basic Experiences as Lures for Pride on the Level of Person

As intimated above, by person, I understand that core of the dynamic orientation of acts, whereby who the person is becomes precisely "in" the intrinsic coherence of its creatively oriented movement, the most central sphere of which is the emotional one, and the most profound revelation of which is loving.[17] When I write of pride pertaining to the dimension of person, I mean those experiences that impact most deeply on this aspect of the human being.

Individuation as uniqueness: person as absolute. As persons, we are not merely particular beings who exist under a universal concept (say, the concept of humanity, children, parents, etc.); the latter is how we would understand the relation of a particular thing to its essence. As persons we are not simply singular, which is how we might understand ourselves in terms of our psychophysical individuality. This is something we as human beings share with all psychophysical life. For example, Pasha, my pet cat, or a quasi-familiar wild animal (the woodchuck living in our backyard) can be distinguished singularly by her peculiar practical intelligence, her respective quirks of habit, her style of behavior. This is because there is a more developed process of internal individuation expressed through, for example, practical intelligence, vital drive, and habit.

From particularity and singularity, I distinguish "uniqueness," which is a feature of the spiritual individuation peculiar to persons (where human beings are also persons, but where "person" is not a priori limited to the species human being). As persons we are *individuated* as unique, which is to say, absolute. As absolute or unique, persons as such can be predicated neither of singularity nor of plurality, and are neither relative, particular, nor universal. While I have treated this notion of uniqueness in another work,[18] I can summarize here by noting that persons are irreplaceable, unrepresentable by virtue of this givenness and creative enactment. No one can take my place as person. For this reason, I can experience myself as "like no other." This absoluteness or uniqueness, which is not only "given" but generated historically in fundamentally creative ways, ultimately concerns the problematic of "vocations."[19] My point here is simply that the implicit or explicit experience of "myself" as absolute and relative to no thing, the experience of myself as unique among persons, and in this sense as irreplaceable, can constitute a lure for pride.[20] Taken in and of itself, this is a positive affirmative moment, a "truth character" within pride—though this remains, as we will see, a limited (indeed self-limiting) perspective.

Ability-to-be. Related to the absolute uniqueness of the person, we find another basic experience as lure for pride, namely, as we take ourselves up as an ability-to-be. By the ability-to-be, I mean the power we have (in our freedom) to control a (personal) situation—or the extent to which we can control a situation to master a (personal) task, like learning a musical instrument, executing a proof in mathematics, performing magic tricks, competing in a race, mastering a language, engaging in civil disobedience, and so on. Here, building up my personal identity through such activities is unproblematic and should not be equated with pride, since trying to make sense of myself, for example, is not necessarily the exclusion of others. Occurring in the sphere of historical purposiveness, the ability-to-be ranges from simply making a decision and seeing it through, to determining my own way in life, being able to choose a path and to follow it. Not only the ability to execute acts in the rational or emotional sphere (thinking, denying, loving), initiating actions in work or play, the ability-to-be also entails being able to take responsibility for those actions that are "freely" or creatively executed.

Further, we find ourselves as the ability-to-be in the sense that we can take ourselves as the source of our own being. That is, not being confined to a situation, we can take up a de facto situation and give it and ourselves a figurative significance; "we can escape our lot in life," we make something of ourselves that was not given in our horizon of possibilities—born into a Midwest town, I can become a champion alpine skier; I can make plans and realize them even when objectively everything goes against them; I can project a future for myself and out of sheer expressive means give my life-situation new meaning.

Of course, we do not have to be explicitly aware of ourselves in our ability-to-be in order for it to be functional; since this ability is given in and through our everyday experiences, we can remain "buried" in our very living it. One way in which we can become aware of ourselves in this capacity is by no longer taking the meaning of things for granted. That is, by holding in abeyance our presuppositions about the world, we can discover explicitly that the things have the sense they do because we give them their meaning in the first place. For example, we can see the ways in which the world takes on sense through our meaning-giving in language, artistic accomplishments, technological advances and creations, through our remembering and expectations. We can discover ourselves, therefore, as the *constitutive sources of meaning*. Reflectively, we may no longer take ourselves for granted as constitutive sources, but in our freedom realize ourselves as the source of these accomplishments.

Basic Experiences as Lures for Pride on the Aesthetic Level

By the aesthetic level of the human person, I understand that level of experience that pertains to the constitution of space and time through our psychophysical modes of comportment. Thus, "aesthetic" means perceptual or bodily comportment in the original sense of "aesthesis," and not immediately, at least, the matter of art or beauty.[21] In the following, I treat three aesthetic basic experiences, the first dealing with the experience of myself as an absolute bodily presence, the second with the experience of myself as an ability-to-do or an "I can," and the third with self-temporalization.

Aesthetic absolute presence. Not only does pride have lures on a spiritual or personal level, it also has lures on an aesthetic or psychophysical level. For example, while we might presuppose our body to be a mere thing among things, we have experiences that go in a different direction, namely, we experience our body as lived (what we call the "lived-body"), and that it is not given in a way that things are given. It therefore cannot be a mere thing among things, but a "ground-body" for the relative givenness of objects. For example, objects in my visual or tactile field are given as left and right in relation to my body; I can move around or away from them in a way that I cannot move around myself; things are oriented by me in relation to my body as here and there, as present and absent in ways that are radically distinct from my body's self-presence.[22] I am given to myself as absolutely "Here" in relation to the here and there of things, and in this respect, I experience myself bodily as the "zero-point of orientation" for objects.[23] Indeed, while we can take a perspective on things, we cannot take a perspective on our body *insofar* as it is in the process of, say, seeing, touching, tasting, smelling, and so on. In short, insofar as we experience ourselves as lived-body in the functioning as a zero-point of orientation and as absolute presence, we have a genuine aesthetic psychophysical basic experience that can be appropriated and lived as pride.[24]

Ability-to-do. The givenness of the lived-body as absolute presence and as zero-point of orientation has a related aesthetic experience which also proves to be a lure for pride. This experiential lure is rooted in the body as an "I can," as my ability or power to do. The "I can" as the ability-to-do is the experience of our relative freedom in relation to functioning in a milieu. It is most obviously manifest in our kinestheses, that is, in our micro and macro bodily movements that negotiate our passage through a milieu and dealings with objects. In this respect, the "I can" is expressed in our power to move as our power to do something, though it can be understood more generally than that.

Certainly, our lived-body as "I can" is tempered by an "I cannot."[25] We not only experience the triumph of our ability-to-do as we become stronger or as we move from childhood to adulthood, say, in mastering tasks. There are also objects that become "obstacles" because I cannot overcome them; there are impediments that challenge my ability-to-do—synchronically in a current slice of time, and diachronically, say, as we age. But that something can be constituted as an "obstacle" at all presupposes the evidence of an "I can." So, even though there is evidence of an "I cannot," it is always grounded in and relative to the basic experience of myself as lived-bodily as "I can." And it is this experience of the "I can," as the basic ability-to-do, that genuinely motivates an experience of pride which has aesthetic roots or what we can call an "aesthetic" pride.

Self-givenness and self-temporalization as an experiential lure for pride. Because self-temporalization is intimately related to self-givenness, I treat both here where the aesthetic basic experiences are concerned. In a subsequent section in the context of self-confidence, I elaborate upon the specific temporal orientation and temporal meaning of pride. Let me begin with the issue of self-givenness.

In any experience, not just the "object" is given, but as Immanuel Kant, Edmund Husserl, Martin Heidegger, Michel Henry, and others have recognized, the subject is also given "to itself" in the givenness of the object. This is what it means "to have" an experience. But this does not mean that the subject is itself given as another intentional object, for in that case we would have an infinite regress, and it would beg the very question of givenness. Rather, in the experience of, for example, the bicycle, I am aware not only of the bicycle, but of my experience of the bicycle "transparently" in the experience of the bicycle. The difference here is not a difference of "objects" (internal and external objects), but a difference of givenness: object-givenness and self-givenness, or as others have called it, manifestation and self-manifestation, disclosure and revelation as self-temporalization, passive auto-affection, or self-awareness.[26]

Self-givenness can be understood as an immediate or direct givenness. While figures like Michel Henry might insist that self-givenness is absolutely distinct in the sense that it is fully self-sufficient vis-à-vis an orientation toward the "outside" or a "hetero-manifestation," others in the phenomenological tradition do not: such self-givenness has temporal gaps (it is chiasmatic in Merleau-Ponty, ecstatic in Heidegger, mediated in Hegel).[27]

In either case, self-givenness is so intimate and distinctive that it easily remains "invisible" to a transcending perception. Self-givenness cannot be given like an object, and hence must always remain on the limit of givenness as long as we define givenness by object-givenness.[28] But if we are open to different kinds of givenness, then "I" need not be merely presupposed as a condition for the possibility of the appearance of any object, but more precisely, given. Here we can account for a genuine self-givenness of a different kind in and through which there is an experience of anything as intentional sense.

Whether I am self-given in such a way that no otherness or transcendence plays a part of this self-givenness (Henry), or whether this self-givenness is mediated by otherness, ultimately, integrating this otherness into a self-presence, self-awareness, or self-givenness is that without which there would be no givenness of objects of any sort. This self-givenness is implicated in the process of self-temporalization. Let me explain.

In external perception an object is given in evidence. In terms of the form of time, the present is necessarily fulfilled. Whatever was intended, however it was intended, even if my protentions or expectations were disappointed or in doubt, something arises in the present. But even if something else does appear otherwise than expected, even if I am disappointed by the new appearance, something emerges in the present, in evidence, even if without apodictic certainty. This is another way of saying that even if the presently enduring object or occurrence (like a tone) ceases, the process of the enduring itself cannot cease; the enduring, as Husserl has called it, is "immortal."[29] Something can usurp something else as the new enduring thing, even if for a moment, because the cessation itself, as the cessation of the object, presupposes a non-cessation, which is to say, it presupposes consciousness to which the cessation is given.[30]

Thus, we could conclude that consciousness of the present is immortal. But this is too narrow a scope, because such a putative immortality would only last in that moment of conscious intending. There are, however, deeper temporal considerations that bear on the subject and not just a momentary conscious intending. For example, when I remember something (e.g., when something present recalls something past), "I" am awakened to it more actively, and a deeper, broader temporal life emerges co-relative to the emergence of an object as such. Remembering is an identifying activity that can repeatedly come back to the same presentation beyond the present, also conferring a density on the object as such over time. Through iterative remembering, we arrive at an identical unending time in the mode of unending past such that the whole of subjectivity, in terms of my genesis of time, cannot have a starting point "in" the past, thus cannot be born, and in this respect "is" "eternal."[31]

Similarly, every Now also has a future horizon constituted through protentions and expectations that sketch out a new Now. I not only expect a Now to arrive, but I expect a whole flux and its streaming-off into retended pasts that can be remembered. This directedness of the future is oriented toward the mobile zero-point of the Now in relation to which I stand as subject. The anticipations that give something "identical" as an object can only be fulfilled through the occurrence of presents and through the identifying processes of remembering after the perceptions have elapsed, even if what now occurs disappoints what I had expected. What never gets disappointed, however, is the form of an expected present; I experience not only possibilities, but the necessity of fulfillment. While what is expected can never be apodictic, with respect to its form, expectation is apodictic. The structure of the constitution of new presents and of progressing time-consciousness is an experienced necessity. The subject lives on and therefore it is inconceivable that the subject as time-constituting would cease.[32]

This is simply to say that I am given to myself in the process of constituting time, and insofar as I am self-temporalizing, I constitute the very sense of past, present, and future, and therefore cannot be "before" or "after" myself. Accordingly, gaps in consciousness like sleep, fainting spells, or any disruption of sense are integrated into an overarching concordance of temporal continuity such that there are no decisive gaps in such self-temporalization. In this respect, I am given to myself as not arising, not ending, but in the eternal process of self-genesis.[33] Within the scope of self-temporalization, I am the ultimate source of meaning. Let us consider further how I am given to myself as self-temporalizing.

As self-temporalizing, I am not given to myself as filling time.[34] I am not temporalized from the outside, locatable in objective time, since I am the source of that time. To attempt to locate the self-temporalizing process in time would be to presuppose object-time as the already constituted standard, and then to apply it to myself as the measure of temporality, becoming forgetful of myself as self-temporalizing in this very process. Certainly, there are beginnings and endings within the temporal genesis. But within the genesis of self-temporalization, I am not before my own birth and I am not after my death, since the very senses of before and after are constituted within temporal genesis. I do not constitute my birth or my death; therefore, in terms of self-temporalization, I experience myself as always was and as always will be.

Following out these observations, it is possible to say that as absolute, I am the source of meaning and I am the meaning source of myself. To that extent, I can be considered as constitutively self-grounding. To the extent that I am self-temporalizing and self-grounding, I cannot simultaneously be constitutively before or after, that is, outside of myself—again, where the process of self-temporalizing is concerned. I am the origin of time. Thus, we have the givenness of an *eternal* being in the process of becoming that is constitutively independent where the genesis of meaning is concerned.[35]

Thus, self-givenness in self-temporalization can be understood as a basic experience and lure for pride insofar as I am given to myself as self-grounding, as the absolute source of time, as "eternal," and therefore "prior to" being before and after myself.

My primary purpose in mentioning these basic experiences in the general movement of pride is to show, first, that pride does not just arise out of nowhere, and that there are several fundamental experiential senses emergent in our lives that can be elaborated as pride. To locate these specific basic experiences is not the same as justifying pride; for pride is a creative emergence within the fullness of the human person such that in its enactment, it becomes a feature of human persons, but not a necessity. Discerning these basic experiences in this way is an effort to point to a "positive" moment that occurs in the broader movement of pride, and as such has something of a truth-character to it, precisely at those nodal points mentioned above: personally, absolute uniqueness, and the ability-to-be; and aesthetically, the absolute lived-bodily presence, the ability-to-do, and self-temporalization. But the fact that these basic experiences are not themselves pride also suggests that pride is a novel emergence, a creative actualization of the person in an interpersonal nexus. Once it emerges as a historical and personal event, there will be different "responses" by the person that also arise on this level of experience—responses that I treat below. Before I turn in this direction, let me continue to explicate pride by characterizing it as a moral subjective attitude. Here we will see that pride takes these basic experiences too seriously, as it were, such that I fixate on them in asserting myself as the primary source of meaning, and further by taking myself to be self-grounding, putatively removing myself from (interpersonal and inter-Personal) relations.

Pride as the Subjective Attitude

I noted that pride is an experience that takes shape within an interpersonal context such that pride can be understood as a twofold movement, namely, as a positive self-insistence and a resistance to otherness. As unfolding within interpersonal relations in this way, pride is situated within the moral sphere of experience. In order to develop these insights into pride, I characterize pride as a moral "subjective attitude." Let me do this by relating it to what phenomenology calls an epistemic "natural attitude."

Phenomenology terms the posture toward being (the world, objects in the world, the real, etc.), which lives directly with the being of things such that it takes their meaning for granted, the natural attitude. It is called *natural* or mundane because we invest ourselves fully in the "world," in the being of things, *in terms of an overwhelming forgetfulness* of the subjective contribution to the meaning of those matters: the ferns outside the window, the rock cliff, the bicycle, even myself. It is also called natural, because it occurs as a matter of course. We are simply there with the matter of concern, and the latter is accepted as ready-made. Even if a question or an assertion were to arise concerning what the thing is, say, as doubtful, probable, likely, indeed, or not it at all, we still live and act by being transported "there" directly in an unproblematic way by presupposing the thing's meaning. This is quite "natural." If I kick a stone on the street, I don't have to think about how the stone appears to me, how I contribute to its kinetic sense, or kicking's own kinesthetic sense in order to kick the stone; my relation to its meaning is directly already there in such a movement. The same holds for thinking a thought, making a judgment, or exploring an idea.

It is through a peculiar kind of reflection, which phenomenology practices, that allows me no longer to focus on *what* something is in a straightforward manner, and that enables the very direct acceptance and presupposition of the being of things to be disclosed as naive. Holding in abeyance the assertion concerning the object's being, I turn my attention instead to *how* "it" is given, *how* this what "appears" such that it is no longer taken for granted, and instead, is examined in terms of its *sense-givenness*. This is not a further objectifying reflection that turns inward on the self where now an introspection takes the subject for granted as what he or she is. Rather, this is a reflection that examines the perspectives, the contexts, the how of appearing through which something is accepted as such in the first place. The general change in attitude, then, is attentive to how something gets accomplished, how sense emerges *as* given, or in phenomenological parlance, how its sense is "constituted" (and not how its being is created). Where previously we directly accepted the world in an unproblematic way, now the world is given as a "problem" in the positive sense of the term because now we are concerned with the very origins of the world's meaning. The mundaneity of the world is lost in terms of our naive acceptance of it, and it is "gained" in the sense that the worldliness of the world comes to the fore. Accordingly, Husserl described one aspect of the transcendental concept of the lifeworld as the "world-horizon"—that which is radically unique as constitutive source, neither singular, nor plural, nor object, but that from which an object gains its sense as object.[36] Here the world as horizon contributes generatively to sense-emergence.

The emergence of this dimension of *constituted sense* or sense-givenness points us immediately to the correlative dimension of *sense-constituting* or sense-giving. Even though the sense-giving process is what is closest to us, as Martin Heidegger might say, it is the most forgotten, hidden, or elusive, in part, because through it we are launched directly at the thing constituted, and naturally "away" from the giving-process itself in favor of what is given. Nevertheless, when we do ask after how something takes on sense or its modes of givenness, we can inquire, for example, into spatial perspectives, how it is given from the front or back, up or down; we can examine the horizon within which an object emerges as such; we can explore kinestheses or bodily orientations and movements through which the object appears; we can investigate how something is given as thought, how it is doubted, imagined, asserted, denied; we can examine temporal perspectives as well, such as how something is present, how it is retained, anticipated, recollected, and so on. In short, the insight gained through such a change in perspective is that there is a *constitutive dimension of sense,* correlative to the constituted dimension, and further, that the constituting dimension as sense-giving is the enigmatic origin or source of meaning.

Why is it instructive to call pride a moral subjective *attitude*? The natural attitude pertains to the variety of ways in which meaning is given as presentational givenness.[37] Because the moral sphere has its own kinds of givenness, evidence, and is susceptible to its own kinds of modalizations, the presuppositions peculiar to it have their own kind of attitude. While the expression "attitude" might seem too much of a merely mental operation, and misleading in evoking the moral dimension of pride, I find the term "attitude" to be appropriate, and not simply because it already resonates with the well-known phenomenological expression. Rather, I understand "attitude" here in the sense that it is used in dance, that is, as a dynamic posture held within encompassing movement.[38]

But why, then, understand pride as a *subjective* attitude? Just as the natural attitude obfuscates the source of sense-givenness by taking meaning for granted as already there, pride obfuscates, or more accurately *resists* other sources of sense-constitution in and through the *insistence* on my own powers (or marveling on who I can be, what I can do). There is nothing wrong with the "subjective," for example, as the dative of experiencing.[39] But in pride, I resist others as contributing sources of meaning to who I am or to whatever the context or matter might be—in favor of assuming those contributions as my own and asserting myself as *the* source and thus over others. Pride is a subjective attitude in this sense. It thus has a moral and not merely epistemic significance. Asserting myself over others can range from resisting the implications of others in what I do and in who I love, by taking myself to be all deserving, to not admitting that I am wrong, to attempting to fashion others in my own image, for example, by imposing my ideals on another person. In short, the *natural attitude* takes for granted the world as the horizon of meaning and the subject as meaning-giving. The phenomenological attitude regains the world as meaningful in relation to the subject and intersubjectivity as constitutive sources. Pride as a *moral subjective attitude* refuses not just the constitutive role of world as horizon, losing it in its constitutive function as horizon of meaning, but other "subjects" who contribute to its meaning and even to my own being-sense.

Ultimately, pride resists any other source of myself in positing myself as self-sufficient and self-grounding. Thus, in resisting the contribution of others, I posit or presuppose myself as sufficient for sense, and as self-sufficient for my own origins. Further, because the interpersonal context is actually a constitutive basis for pride to be pride, pride must resist the interpersonal nexus (the contribution of others) in presupposing it *in and through* positing the self as the sole meaningful source of sense and as its own origin as self-grounding. When we push this analysis to its core, we see that in pride I have to assert myself in a secular context while presupposing a religious one. I am first among others, and this salience of self is taken as self-grounding. This is not a matter of arbitrarily importing a religious dimension into pride; rather, this dimension of experience is disclosed from within the experience of pride itself. In these ways, I find pride fittingly characterized in the moral register as a "subjective attitude" corresponding, mutatis mutandis, to a natural attitude.

Now, if we were to remain solely within the epistemic attitude, we might conclude that such a perspective is fully adequate because in my freedom, I finally see myself as a constitutive source of meaning, and no longer take this for granted. Or if we were to examine the prospect of a self-givenness that would be sufficient unto itself more critically, we might conclude that such a perspective is only problematic because it is short-sighted or does not account for a fuller range or complexity of givenness.[40]

However, I find it necessary to distinguish a mere reflective omission of other constitutive sources from what is going on in the experience of pride. For the former might merely be a matter of conceiving self-awareness abstractly, showing up a perspective as naive or undiscerning. In distinction, the experience of pride arises when I live myself as the major, predominate, or sole constitutive source in the presence of others as excluded, and limit myself to myself as self-grounding. Phenomenology, which lives inside of the experience it describes, can disclose these experiences or point the way to them or to their fallacy. And phenomenological analysis, as radical reflection, can serve as a critique, and help to disclose pride as such. But pride would only be an issue to the extent that the phenomenologist himself or herself as human person asserts him- or herself as the source at the same time as he or she resists other sources. Thus, the epistemic natural attitude cannot be equated with the moral subjective attitude, but can (only) function meaningfully as a leading clue to the experience of pride. Pride is a subjective attitude in the moral sphere by positing the self over others as the primary constitutive source, including them only in their exclusion through my self-salience.

This does not mean that the phenomenological attitude cannot disclose the inherent meanings of pride, since it, phenomenology, is open in principle to all kinds of givenness. Even if it begins as a purely academic task, in giving itself over to the matters themselves, it can discern the moral and religious dimensions of the experiences in question, and function critically in this way. Would that practice then not have at least implicitly moral and religious meanings, then? My point is that to treat the moral subjective attitude of pride as akin to an epistemic natural attitude suggests that pride is a kind of *nachträglicher* starting point that did not have to be, but as emergent, as a kind of historical a priori, as Marx might call it, it is the most difficult to overcome.

Placed therefore in the broader context of human experience, it is telling, for example, that Augustine opens his *City of God* with the problems of the proud, and by implication the necessity to begin by overcoming pride; Dante considers the first cornice in passing through purgatory to be that of the proud.[41] This is the most arduous beginning and after this, everything else on the ascent is said to go more easily.[42] Likewise, Rousseau considers pride—the assumption I merit the gift that I did not give myself—to be the most dangerous and the most feared of human emotions, because it is the most difficult to destroy.[43]

Pride as Non-Self-Revelatory: The Possibility of a Moral Reduction

Within the natural attitude we are hidden from ourselves in terms of our constitutive powers. It is a phenomenological reflection that runs counter to such an attitude by revealing us to ourselves in terms of our powers and limits of meaning-giving. For example, Husserl claims at one point in his work that it is "wonder," in particular, the wonder of the problem of the world, that spurs our calling into question the natural attitude; and it is the "unnatural" phenomenological reduction (the *epoché* and movement going back to the origins of the constituting dimension) that discloses us to ourselves.

Despite the fact that there are "basic experiences" elaborated upon as pride in experience, pride is nevertheless not self-revelatory. It is not self-revelatory because pride dissimulates the interpersonal dimension of Myself. How is it the case that I can be so attentive to myself in pride, yet *not* be revealed to myself in this experience? Is there such a thing as a "moral reduction"—to play on phenomenological terms—that could call pride into question and reveal me to myself as I "am," Myself, as relational and not self-grounding? Thus, there are two interrelated moments here with respect to pride: that which calls pride into question, and that which reveals me to myself.

Let's begin with what *cannot* call pride into question. Here there are two issues: whether I myself am sufficient to call pride into question, and whether it is merely a matter of bringing the matter to explicit awareness.

What cannot call pride into question is the source of pride itself, namely, my own subjective activity. To try not to be prideful is not only to exercise my will, but it is to be oriented to the selfsame self. As Rousseau cautions in a different context, let us not go and reproduce pride in our own efforts to combat it; even to pride myself on conquering prejudices, he continues, is to be subjected to them.[44] When someone *tries* not to be prideful or *tries* to be humble (which is distinct still from merely putting on a show of humility), we often notice an ingenuousness when we see such a display. There is something phony that comes across precisely because "I" am what is at stake in this attempt.

Taylor points out that "Mr. Darcy" does not simply think his status, taste, or learning is superior to others, but that he is superior in the only areas that matter, and further that being able to fall short of such high standards is in this sense itself a point of pride.[45] Similarly, Rabbi Dov Baer, the Chassidic Jewish mystic, writes that there is a great danger for someone who realizes that he is very close to God, but that any remaining fault or any distance from God is the "only" thing he has left to conquer.[46] As Saint Teresa of Avila observes, this can also take the shape of a distress over the sins and failings of others, thereby taking pride to be humility.[47]

Let's assume, however, that the matter lies in not being completely self-cognizant, that I am not exactly aware of being prideful: once I call it to my attention, or once someone else calls it to my attention and I re-present it to myself as such—can I overcome pride in this way? Can such a becoming aware or representation (through psychoanalysis, confession, or meditation) modify my orientation of pride? We know all too well of examples—from ourselves and others—when we do realize that we are being prideful, when it is called to mind or pointed out, and we simply respond: "So what, it is not pride, it is just true," or more defiantly, "So what, there is nothing wrong with it."

First, we should recognize that pride is an original "shift" in orientation in the meaning of what it means to be a human person. Merely becoming cognizant of this fact through any sort of representation cannot address this shift. Second, if I am not revealed to myself in pride, the exercise of my intellectual self-will seems to do just more of the same. Rather, since pride occurs as a moral experience, what calls pride into question is some emotional response or act that issues from the same dimension of our existence or coexistence. And this happens, third, as an overcoming of that pride, such that it catches me unawares and even against my will—as we can see in the next chapter. This overcoming does not emerge because now I feel or think that pride is "bad" or that another asserts or opines that my pride is "bad"; rather, I am struck from another, from a source that is ultimately not my own, and in a way that calls that pride into question, and further that might initiate calling pride into question in a more active manner. The point here, however, is that while I may gain clarity that I am prideful, this is not (yet) the overcoming of pride.

Accordingly, I may have the best intentions in trying not to be prideful, but the fact is that trying not to be prideful is still to be concerned with myself by way of my calling myself into question—which is still a devotion to my-self. This is why self-doubt or self-denigration, being disappointed in myself or beating myself up about things, for instance, is not an answer to pride, but again another expression of it. Perhaps there can even be a "sweetness" in self-loathing as when one wallows in self-doubt; it is why Bernanos writes in the voice of the Country Priest: "To doubt oneself is not to be humble, I even think that sometimes it is the most hysterical form of pride, a pride almost delirious, a kind of jealous ferocity which makes an unhappy man turn and rend himself. That must be the real truth of hell."[48] The fact that there can be such a sweetness even in self-doubt as well as more positive forms of pride show that pride is always accompanied by a positive valence. This goes in the direction of exercising my effort, my will, and the positive estimation of myself. (This can be contrasted with the experience of shame or guilt, which are always colored by a negative valence.) This is no doubt why Hume associates pride with a kind of pleasure.[49]

To combat pride, then, one cannot strike at the basic experiences, as if personal uniqueness, the ability-to-be, absolute lived-bodily presence, the ability-to-do, and self-temporalization were now of negative value or the moral culprits. They are not. They are positive experiences that can be creatively appropriated and lived in the direction of a radical self-salience and self-grounding. Self-destruction, like self-hatred, only presupposes the *disvalue* of myself. Not only are they still preoccupied with myself, hence unable to overcome pride, they may lead to what Nietzsche recognized as a false altruism grounded in ressentiment. In this case, one merely turns toward others as a way of avoiding or negating oneself, where however the self would still insidiously be the motivating factor.[50]

We might even ponder whether all the contemporary talk of the "absolute Other" and "ethics as first philosophy"—Levinas notwithstanding—is really a concern with ethical comportment, or instead an attempt to seek refuge in the "other" as a fleeing from the responsibility toward the self, a reaction of self-hatred—not to mention the eclipse of serious work to be done in epistemology and on the meaning-structure of subjectivity.

In any case, when the mystics write of the "annihilation of the self" (say, in the case of the Islamic mystics like Rūzbihān Baqlī), they are very clear that this does not originate from myself or my own efforts, but that Allah ("the God") takes over the work, that it comes from Transcendence or Truth. Even *after* the annihilation of self [*fanā*] which follows upon union, there can be a sustaining of personal self, a "*subsistence*" or an "*abiding*" [*baqā*] whereby "I" am "given back," as it were, in my uniqueness, and sustained only by God.[51]

So, unlike the epistemic reduction, calling pride into question is not a result of the exercise of my freedom by honing in on myself. For the critique of pride as a moral experience shows the "core-self" as relational Myself and as given to myself inter-Personally and interpersonally. This is not to say that there are not practices that might help to inculcate a disposition toward another as a dis-position of the self, like obedience, in the sense of *obedare* or listening deeply, like silence, poverty, fasting, doing mitzvahs or acts of *tzedakah* (justice and charity). But here the orientation is in the service of another, not that I want to overcome *my* pride (e.g., for my self-improvement). It is no coincidence, for example, that Michel Henry writes in the context of Eckhart that living the mystery through a kind of "bracketing" is ethical in nature, and that it requires a practice of renunciation, for example through becoming "poor in spirit" as a condition of the transformation of existence.[52] But the point is the transformation of existence, not the self.

If, then, we are to consider—only in passing for now—emotional acts and experiences that challenge pride, we can see that there are many of them. All of them are "other-oriented," for example, trusting, loving, humility, even self-giving emotions like shame and guilt. But not all interpersonal experiences call pride into question, for even pride is also at root an interpersonal experience. And if we want to speak of a moral reduction of pride, where pride is understood as a moral subjective attitude, then the "reduction" of which we speak cannot be something that I initiate, but rather, something that comes from another. If I attempt to overcome pride, I just hold more tenaciously to myself, and all I get is more restless effort. Hence, the moral reduction in the case of pride is something I cannot perform like I can a philosophical reduction, because instead, it brackets me; "I am reduced"—to Myself (as not-self-grounding, as relational)—I am humbled.

The experiences mentioned above bracket a moral subjective attitude through a kind of moral reduction by having shifted the orientation to the other person by the other person or persons, and in this way, away from myself. I am reduced in the presence of the other person. But such experiences, while they may call pride into question, do not reveal me to myself in "being reduced." There are, however, privileged experiences in which I am "reduced" where pride is called into question, and that reveal me to Myself, and one of them is shame. In shame, I am revealed to myself through a diremptive experience as exposed before another. This perspective on shame and pride significantly underscores the difference between this view of pride and that of Jean-Paul Sartre's.

As we will see in the next chapter, for Sartre, shame is the experience that I "am" or that I have a nature outside of my lived freedom, being over there for the Other. Sartre interprets shame as "original" (the fact that I am as an object-being for the Other-as-subject) and that *upon which* pride is grounded—pride in both senses of *fierté* and *l'orgueil*.[53] Pride in the sense of *fierté* is only a resignation (resigning myself to being that external nature) and a primary *reaction to* shame that is in "bad faith." It is in bad faith because I take up what the Other confers on me as an object in order to affect the Other in his or her freedom to sanction me in my objectness. Pride in the sense of *l'orgueil* is an "authentic attitude" because it is an affirmation of my freedom; yet it is still founded on shame because I affirm myself as that *free* object by which I confront the Other as object.[54] For us, however, it is shame as self-revelation in a diremptive experience that calls my freedom into question, and more specifically, the subjective attitude that is characteristic of pride (even though shame has other functions than this).[55] I will take up shame in the next chapter. Suffice it for now to have pointed to this experience that can only appear as privileged and fundamental in relation to the issues we have encountered with the experience of pride.

The fact that pride is non-self-revelatory, and the fact that "I" cannot overcome pride through my activity or will, is only part of the issue of pride as a moral subjective attitude, and what makes pride complex and elusive as an emotional act. Pride is not only non-self-revelatory, it is also self-dissembling. It is self-dissembling because it resists the interpersonal nexus that is constitutive of myself in positing itself as self-grounding. Pride dissembles the relational Myself. This dissembling aspect of pride shows how pride, while not completely arbitrary (because of the basic experiences that are elaborated upon as pride) is nonetheless *self-limiting*, and to this extent if not fully arbitrary, then precisely *"subjective."*

Pride as Self-Dissembling and Self-Limiting

I mentioned above that despite the personal and aesthetic basic experiences that are elaborated as pride, and despite the fact that pride concerns myself, pride is not self-revelatory. I suggested, further, that pride is not self-revelatory because it is actually self-dissembling. We often say, for example, that there is something "false" about pride; we also speak of times when someone is not justified in pride, or we call it a "false pride." It is often said that there are illusions of pride or that pride deceives us. What is the nature of this deception? These are important everyday clues to a deeper understanding of pride as an emotional movement. On our understanding, we do not mean by these statements that I have merely overvalued myself, as if I could simply ratchet down the self-appraisal and leave pride behind. Rather, we understand that it is the very assertion of myself in the presence of and over others that is not justified (in a manner to be determined below). So, while we can identify so-called truth moments as basic experiences as lures for pride, we need to investigate the sense of these contravening "falsifying," quasi-arbitrary, subjective dissembling moments of pride because they show pride's self-centering as inherently self-limiting.

The very experience of pride points in this self-dissembling direction because it presupposes the very interpersonal context that it resists; thus in positing my own self-sufficiency, I presuppose others who would challenge this self-sufficiency in the very resistance to the contribution that they do make. Put in grammatical terms, the assertion of myself in the nominative as "self" dissembles the deeper interpersonal, relational core of "Myself" as accusative, as given to myself at the heart of this "self."[56] This twofold movement of pride explicated above dissembles the integral, co-contributing sources to who I am and what I do, and as not receiving myself from another as Myself; in this way, pride is self-dissembling.

If we examine the basic experiences of self as lures for pride that we treated above, we can see in each instance how pride is self-dissembling as self-limiting. Pride is not dissembling by accentuating these positive basic experiences; taken by themselves, they are not arbitrary, for they emerge from an experiential basis for them. But taken as a whole movement, pride is self-dissembling because it occludes dimensions of experience that are also co-given in this experience, namely, Myself as relational, Myself as given to myself, others as co-constitutive of who I am and what I do, and the contribution by others to the meaning of the world. The extent to which pride is subjectively arbitrary is the extent to which it *limits* the very constitution of the self, the world, and thus is self-limiting.

In the case of personal basic experiences, pride takes the absolute uniqueness of myself as self-given, and in the assertion of the latter, not as given to myself. Thus, it is self-dissembling insofar as I take my actions as emergent from my self-grounding character. Gripping human experiences like "what am I do?" "who am I to become?" "what is my path in life?" "I cannot do otherwise than this," "this is who I am," and so on, could have no meaning if I were completely self-determining or self-grounding because if I were, I would be the very cause of my self-determination and these questions would be so transparent that they would be answered in the very instant they were posed. Such questions might arise as merely academic questions, but then they could take no existential purchase. It would not help to say that I am just not aware of myself, and hence I raise these questions, make those assertions; for this just redoubles the question and perhaps puts it on a different plane, say, in terms of the narrative "other" in the self, or the other as portrayed in psychoanalytic theory.

We could raise the issue on the other extreme, say, with the radically thrown character of the individual like we find in Heidegger's rendition of the relation between Dasein and Being. But we would not find the experience of pride here either. It is true that Heidegger understands Dasein as not self-grounding, since Dasein is a thrown-projection.[57] Nevertheless, if Being (or *Ereignis* or the "It gives") withdraws in favor of the giving, abandoning Dasein to itself in a thrown forgetfulness of Being, then we would be hard put to account experientially for (or be accountable for) something like pride. Why? Because there is no experienced interpersonal nexus that is resisted since my thrown transcendence is already the forgetfulness of the "Source."[58] If, however, this "Source" is given as "Person" as loving, like in the Abrahamic traditions, evidenced in the experience of the mystics, or as clarified phenomenologically in tradition following Max Scheler, then asserting myself as self-grounding is not due to a forgetfulness, no matter how primordial, but is the emergent resistance to the interpersonal nexus.[59] Pride can then be experienced as placing myself as first among others, acknowledging others as I appropriate their contributions, at the same time as removing them from contributing or refusing their contribution to my own sense and the world we share. I am sovereign.

Through pride I exercise my freedom by unilaterally assuming others into the field of my overall experience, rather than binding myself to them, co-foundationally as in experiences like trust (see below, chapter 6), and I implicitly make others, for example, useful to me, rather than placing myself in service to others. These interpersonal dimensions are resisted in the experience of pride, but *present as resisted,* and in this way pride is self-dissembling.

Aesthetically speaking, the lived-body is not given like an object among objects, and so it is not present to itself like an object, though I can take an objectifying view on myself. We have seen that the lived-body is given as an absolute presence in relation to the relative presence and absence of things, and further, that the lived-body functions as a zero-point of orientation. Insofar as this is the case, it is not constituted by objects, but is grounding for the spatial (and temporal) orientation of objects. This can become a lure for aesthetic pride, but need not be. For example, I can legitimately assert the integrity of myself if this means resisting being reduced to an object. This is not to say that the lived-body is immalleable as a zero-point of orientation; sometimes I have to tilt my head according to a painting in order for it to be meaningful to me; sometimes I have to orient myself by a building or mountain to find myself spatially.

Rather, aesthetic pride and the self-dissembling peculiar to this pride consist not only in defying the intercorporeal constitution of sense by asserting an "I can" over others' co-participation,[60] but takes the absolute presence of the lived-body as exclusively self-grounding. To take the lived-body as self-grounding means that the lived-body is not grounded in or upon anything but itself, and that it is solely "responsible" for its own spatial and kinesthetic sense in its self-moving. In relation to objects it is a stable ground that is not grounded by the objects it orients. In this way, it is a self-grounding as ground-body and absolute presence.

Here we find Edmund Husserl's fundamental investigations into spatiality and kinestheses instructive. His analyses show that not only do physical-bodies have sense in relation to my lived-body, but my own lived-body as the ground-body for the spatial and kinesthetic sense of objects gains its kinesthetic and spatial sense *in relation to the Earth-ground* (*Erdboden*).[61] In this way, the lived-body as ground-body and absolute presence is itself dependent upon and relative to the Earth-ground as an absolute constitutive source. Thus even the lived-ground-body is grounded—without the lived-body becoming reduced to the status of a relative object.

Even when we do recover the lived-body from its object status (the reversal accomplished by the medical and physical sciences), the assertion of the lived-body as self-grounding still accomplishes the reversal or the resistance that we call aesthetic pride. It does this, that is, so long as we limit the reversal of the reversal to the self-grounding lived-body. One way this takes place is by projecting the Earth as just another object (e.g., a planet among others) which is subject to the control of my body, as merely relative to my constitutive powers. The fact, then, that the lived-body has constitutive powers is not the issue; this is a genuine givenness, and can become obfuscated when we regard the lived-body merely as an object-body. When we live the body as self-grounding in a *self-limiting way*, however, we can lose the Earth in its sense as Earth-ground such that it can become transformed into the mere resource of object-bodies that are subject to manipulation, subject to my I can, at my free disposition.[62] Such an "earth-alienation" in this view would be a product of aesthetic pride.

Because the Earth never withdraws, its reduction to an object for the lived-body (rather than as the ground of the lived-body) is due not to a neutral Earth-forgetfulness, but to an *Earth-resistance,* an imposition of the lived-body as self-grounding over the Earth. The very source for spatial sense (without which there would be no verticality or horizontality) is now uprooted and projected by and from us as an object in space "up" or "down" or "splayed out" as a planet among planets orbiting the sun, viewed now as the big blue marble from "outer space." Applying the Earth's grounding sense to ourselves, where the earth is potentially under our control, we can interpret such a resistance as influential for ecological exploitation and environmental disasters. Husserl locates this resistance, what we call aesthetic pride, in modernity, not with the subjectivism of Descartes, but with Copernicus and the Copernican revolution. Thus, Husserl sees his task as reversing the Copernican revolution.

For us, the point is that aesthetic pride is self-dissembling because in its recovering or insistence of the *genuine* grounding character of the lived-body for objects (from its putative status as an object), it *limits* the recovery to this point, and dissimulates itself as given to itself from the Earth as ground, and thus as an absolute presence relative to and grounded in the Earth as absolute aesthetic ground. While I would not call the overcoming of aesthetic pride the recovery of the "interpersonal," I would call it the recovery of the *intercorporeal.*

We can find similar ways in which aesthetic pride is self-dissembling, namely, by the way in which it conceals contributions others make in my very self-temporalization. For example, while sleep is a rupture that is given within the overarching concordance of self-temporalization, birth and death are not, and as such cannot become constitutive features of that self-temporalizing process. But this basic experience as a lure for pride, when taken as expressive of pride, occludes the historicity of my experience. For example, not only am I constituted with and through others as a family member, as a compatriot, or in general as a member of a community—synchronically—I assume and appropriate myself from my progenitors and give myself over to those who follow. Not only do my parents assume a new constitutive sense now as "father" or "mother," and myself as "son" or "daughter" through my birth or adoption; I become constituted as "father" or "mother" through the birth of child or adoption. None of this could have meaning within mere self-temporalization, and pride generated from this experience occludes these very dimensions. Instead, we share a "generatively communal time" that transcends the iterative quality of remembering, where the latter is itself encompassed by historical memory through generations that can be reiterated through birth and through narrative.[63] What is subjectively arbitrary here is the limitation of temporality to self-temporalization.

Whereas, within self-temporalization, I am given to myself by myself such that I am self-grounding, within generative temporality, I am given to myself "from" a homeworld, my progenitors, home-companions, from something outside of myself, yet which encompasses me. Thus, if I experience myself as absolute as self-temporalizing, this absoluteness is itself given to itself in relation to a deeper absolute. Further, if I am given to myself in such a way that birth and death are constitutive features, then I cannot be the ultimate source of meaning and I cannot be self-grounding. The ultimate source of meaning in the aesthetic register of temporality is generative temporality, in which I am given to myself as self-temporalizing. In order to highlight the self-dissembling dimension of pride taken in its aesthetic temporal dimension, we could say that "I *am* eternally given to myself as *self-giving*" or "*I give* myself to myself, eternally." What is dissembled is the following: "(I am) *given to myself* as self-giving by generative historicity."

In each instance in pride, I key off of certain basic experiences, through which I limit myself to myself; by insisting on myself as the primary or sole giver of meaning, through which others are eclipsed in that process, by positing myself as my own source, I am actually self-limiting. What pride dissembles is that I am not self-grounding, that I am given to myself as Myself, in the accusative, and that I am a co-constitutor of meaning, a constitution that ebbs and flows according to the context. Further, it dissembles a co-functioning and intercorporeal nexus in which the lived-body is not only ground-body, but even as ground-body for sense, is itself grounded in a deeper ground, and further as self-temporalizing, is given to itself within generative historicity. If pride is dissembling and self-limiting, it is because it is a creative movement that negates or restricts a positive movement. This positive movement is loving, in which pride is founded. A mode of loving is genuine self-love. Although a discussion of self-love anticipates the later treatment of loving and humility in chapter 7, I address self-love here briefly both because, phenomenologically speaking, self-love founds pride, and because it is systematically important to disambiguate self-love from pride.

Self-Love and Pride

In an everyday way of speaking, we tend to conflate pride with self-love. But on the basis of these phenomenological analyses, we can distinguish genuine self-love from pride.

In every case, loving is oriented personally toward the beloved as an opening to the depth or richness of its intrinsic value; this entails, as we will see below, an opening to the beloved's own possibilities that cannot be anticipated in advance and can only be revealed in the movement of loving. It is an opening to infinity, as it were, which is ultimately in the direction of holiness. This movement should not be mistaken for an attempt to improve another, for this would amount to fashioning him or her in my own image, which is a more insidious form of pride.

With such a provisional understanding, it is legitimate to speak of a genuine self-love. What we mean by this is that loving is directed toward the absolute uniqueness of who the person is, Myself—as who I am *to be* in the dynamic sense, as from another.[64] Superficially, pride seems to have this valuing of self in common with self-love, or even with maintaining one's own integrity. But the internal sense of these acts is quite different.

First, a genuine self-love is an openness to who I "am." It is more precisely an openness *according to* who I am and to who I am to become, and certainly not in the direction of destruction or limitation. Self-love, however, presupposes the experience of *vocation*, or very generally speaking, of being given to myself in some way or ways—ways that are to be developed or generated creatively. This relates to what the ancients called "self-knowledge." Since I develop the theme of vocational experience in another work, I will not treat it here in detail. Suffice it to say that vocational experience is an experience of being given to myself as Myself, through nonviolent insistence and creatively appropriating or dynamically originating that givenness *as* from another;[65] it can be revealed in experiences like "I cannot do otherwise," "that's just not me," (as Marx might put it) "I don't feel at home when I am at work," and "I am becoming Myself."

Fundamentally, the Myself is always given as before another, and thus most radically, inter-Personally. This is why vocational experience will ultimately have a religious tenor (in the sense of being placed in the moral universe by and before, e.g., the Holy, the Godhead, Ultimate Reality). To insist that I "must" love Myself suggests a responsibility to who I am becoming as given for others and for myself, which is in the process of generation. While this might be a peculiar way of articulating the experience, I want to emphasize the creative "normative" dimension that we find in the experience of loving (see chapter 7). But here the "must" has the sense of Al Lingis's "imperative," which entails a being bound in freedom, where I am not the source, and where it is not a determining necessity.[66] Loving Myself (which is different from being fascinated with myself) is only determined, therefore, in and through the "response." While I "must" love Myself in self-love, in pride there is no such imperative, for pride is arbitrarily subjective in this respect, dependent solely on my self-valuation. Whereas self-love is delimiting and opening relationally, pride does not simultaneously open beyond itself.

Or it does, but it does so as self-limiting, and therefore can develop into an infatuation with or fixation on myself.

Now, if we were tempted to treat Myself, which is already relational and interpersonal, on the same level as the "Self," the attentiveness of self-love and pride might look similar. After all, they both ostensibly recognize the value and uniqueness of the person. But there is a decisive difference. In self-love, I can be attentive to the value and uniqueness of Myself without at the same time positing myself as the source of that value and uniqueness, or positing myself over others. Strictly speaking, I cannot overvalue Myself in this sense. As we will see below under the next point, I can be proud of Myself, without this being pride because the weight of significance in being proud of is the "other"—here myself as self-given or relational—and not my own self. Rather, the problem where pride is concerned is letting my "self-worth" blind me to others, becoming enthralled with myself, and in this way occluding their value while presupposing it for the occlusion and self-insistence. Using things or instruments in a way that allows me to flourish is not the same as everything being there to serve me no matter what. I "must" love another as Her or Himself, as another "must" love me as Myself, as I must love Myself. But this imperative flashes forth from or according to "Myself," and not from me.

In fact, in self-love, I cannot ultimately take myself as the source of Myself; if I love Myself, I am open to who I am as given to myself, but as unfolding. In pride, however, I cannot recognize the value and uniqueness of Myself without me also positing myself as the source or cause of this. In pride, I take myself as self-grounding, asserting or presupposing myself as the origin of who I am, and not independently of that positing. Further, self-love can never be static in the sense of arresting development because loving is oriented to the fullest possible becoming of the beloved, toward boundless fullness or depth. A care of self is rooted here in self-love. On the contrary, pride is precisely not self-love, since what is really at issue is myself as the subjective source of who I am. While self-love is open as the person changes, pride is either a resistance to such dynamism or is a subjectively arbitrary alteration. Pride can even be a resistance to *how* I am given to Myself and to refuse service as Myself to others. Self-love, however, can modify as the person modifies, since it is "in" dynamic becoming as an openness to how I am given to Myself as from another.

Even if I were to concede that I am given to myself in pride in some way, then it is I who have given myself to myself—and this serves as the basis of the myth—so pervasive, for example, in capitalism—of the "self-made man." So, while I can experience self-love in being oriented positively toward who I am and can be dynamically and creatively, in pride I must also be the constitutive source of that subjectively arbitrary becoming. This presupposition of being my own constitutive source, of being self-grounding, also dissembles the very interpersonal dimension of being given to Myself. This holds as well for what some may call the "habit of pride." The fact that it is a habit does not ameliorate the creative dimension of pride, since such a repetition in habit would have to be a creative re-institution of that pride-moment in each case. In the Abrahamic religious traditions, this is understood as "idolatry."

All of this holds mutatis mutandis for the collective person as it does for the individual person.[67] This is not only how we can experience a national pride, but also how there can be a genuine self-love of a homeworld. But in the latter case, such a self-love occurs *in its co-foundational* relation with alienworlds, as expressive of the movement of Generativity.[68]

In this way, too, pride is distinctive from standing on the integrity of who I am. Insisting on my integrity is consistent with the givenness of Myself. In many cases, it might arise by resisting a patronizing or controlling attitude, defending Myself against being used as a tool or objectified as a thing. Further, to oppose becoming who I am not, or to defy being forced to become who I am not (in humiliation, in violence), is also positive. In neither instance are these matters of pride, but of what we can call standing on my personal integrity, which is grounded in at least the first sense of the personal basic experience cited above. Affirming my integrity, as rooted in self-love, is not reducible to pride because the personal value in question is not reducible to "me" who would cause it, but can be recognized by anyone, and not just because I subjectively assert it. Now, if integrity were reducible to pride, then the corrective could be to denigrate oneself, to attempt to diminish the value of oneself, or to go down the road of self-defeat, and so on. Standing on one's integrity (which is grounded in self-love), however, cannot admit the denigration or depreciation of Myself. On the level of aesthetic pride, it could go in the direction of devaluing the body, or valuing illness over health.[69] This is why care on the level of the body can be a positive affirmation of the ontological value of health.[70] Exercise and training, for example, can be a way of caring for the body, a practice of mastering the body, shaping it, literally "body-building."[71]

Being Proud, Boasting, and Self-Confidence

The distinction between self-love and pride gives us a clue to the distinction between being proud of (or taking pride in), and pride, as well as boasting, and self-confidence.

PRIDE

Being proud of, taking pride in. Being proud of something presupposes the inherent value of the person, thing, or event of which I am proud. Further, when I am proud of something I express a relation to the matter about which I am proud and myself. But I am not the main issue here; rather, it is the affirmation of the other and my relation to it.

Let me attempt to make this clearer with an example and a further distinction. We can distinguish an "I am happy for you" from an "I am proud of you." Let's say a friend has received her first job, and I express an "I am happy for you." This is a direct relation to the event of the person getting a job, and I simply express my pleasure at her having received the job. Aside from the fact that I am happy about this, there is no relation to myself involved in this congratulatory gesture. But let's change the situation to highlight the difference between this and being proud of. Let's suppose I am the one who received a job, and a colleague with whom I have had little or no contact does not say, "I am happy for you," but "I am proud of you." Let's suppose, further, I never really liked this person in the first place, and I even did everything I could to avoid this particular person. At least two things could be experienced. I could experience this as an insult, as arrogance, say, and at the very minimum I might feel uncomfortable—precisely because he is linking himself to my new success, and perhaps to me in some way (intentionally or not). To say, "I am proud of you" in such a situation implicitly or explicitly ties me to that person or to that event. "To be tied to" here is the more general sense of the connection; it could also go in the direction of "taking responsibility for."

There are ways in which such a situation may not be insulting to me. For example, the colleague may understand himself as part of a larger community, and I take the "I am proud of you" as really reflecting a "we" are proud of you, for example, as if the individual sees himself as representative of the larger community. But it is hard to imagine a situation in which I would embrace the imputed tie of the person when—in this extreme example—I wanted no ties. In a more neutral situation, I may be pleased that this person wanted to be tied to me, and thus, I could be happy that he is proud. The main point of these examples, however, is to show that being proud of implies or imputes a connection of myself to the other person or event, or the other person to me and/or what I have done.[72] Not only their recognition of our mastery as we grow and develop, but also this personal connection is in part why we as children want our parents to be proud of us. But by the same token, we do not want our parents to claim responsibility for what we have done and in this way be the source of our accomplishments. In this case, the interpersonal dynamic tension would disappear.

Thus, in pride I experience myself as the source of myself, the thing made or of what happens; and this allows me to draw attention to myself, to assert myself in pride and turn a blind eye to others. In being proud of, however, I value the thing itself, and not just because it is identified with me in some way. Yet, being proud of can turn to pride when I experience myself as the source of the value of the other thing, or when I (as source) take precedence over the other. But in being proud of, the *what* it is or *what* we have done—in general, the world has the horizon of meaning—has the point of emphasis; in pride, I myself as the only or highest source take priority. Moreover, in pride something only has value *because* it is I who has it or values it.[73] It is for this reason that what Michael Lewis characterizes as "pride" is really the experience of being proud of or taking pride in something.[74] Similarly, what Mascolo and Fischer identify as that appraisal pattern that mediates pride (in which, for example, an accomplishment has a socially valued outcome) would amount to being proud of or having pride in, but not pride as we understand it.[75]

Accordingly, I not only can take "pride in" my garden that I have tended, but I can meaningfully engage in a pride that builds personal or communal identity, like "gay pride." In this case, one can reappropriate a feature or qualification that was denigrated previously (being gay, being "black"), and reaffirm it with a positive orientation because what is being emphasized is the positive value—in these cases—of the person in being gay ("gay pride"), in being black ("black pride"), and so on. But these qualities have an integrity independently of the fact that I assert them, even though it is "I" or "we" who are now asserting them. In other words, it is not *because* I assert them that they have value, but I assert them because of their inherent (previously unrecognized or demeaned) value, and therefore, I am related to them in this way. This is why being proud of can tolerate others as contributors in a manner that pride cannot.[76] Self-esteem is not the problem here, but it is the esteem of myself over another that could become the matter of pride. Accordingly, what I mean by "excessive pride" is not a disproportion to an arbitrary standard held by myself or another;[77] rather, I mean that pride is itself excessive because it eclipses others by virtue of myself.

We can imagine a woman like the mother and concert pianist, "Charlotte," in Bergman's *Autumn Sonata*. Incessantly speaking of herself and being self-occupied in her daughter's (Eva's) presence, even though they have not seen each other for seven years, she hardly allows her daughter to have her own experiences or to share in them.[78] On one level, Charlotte was simply being beneficent. After "generously" giving up her touring possibilities at that time in order to devote herself to her family, Charlotte lavished attention on her daughter. But Eva disambiguates it. Charlotte did nothing but impose her own image on her (Eva) with a vengeance, a sort of "perfect repetition" of meaning, without any dialogue or consideration of Eva: new hair style, correct posture, braces on teeth, and so on. Again, Charlotte's "outward" interest toward Eva all came back to herself; in asserting her presence, she arrested the meaning of Eva so that there was nothing left for Eva to do of herself or that could disrupt this dominating presence.

To the extent that Charlotte had an inkling of pride, she was no longer merely being benevolent, even for herself, for pride presupposes the others one resists or triumphs over. Indeed, it would be difficult to say that Charlotte was even proud of Eva. In being proud of, the person or event at least has value outside of myself, even if I relate myself to this person or to the event. But for Charlotte, Eva can only make a contribution if she, Eva, does it Charlotte's way, from her style of playing the piano (Chopin's Prelude No. 2 in A minor) to the general style of being. She only tends to recognize others when she is the source of those others. Indeed, her putative generosity tragically fails to be interpersonal. "Don't my critics say that I am generous with my music?" she asks her manager on the train as she leaves Eva and her disabled daughter. The tragedy of pride lies not in the valuing of self, but in the occlusion of others on behalf of the self.

Boasting. Boasting is a peculiar kind of exposure before others that is irreducible to pride. We can begin with some obvious differences between boasting and pride. Whereas pride, like self-admiration or vanity, can take place without it being linguistically expressed, boasting is always communicated linguistically. In a related manner, boasting always takes place directly before others as the "to whom" I am boasting, whereas pride need not have an interpersonal audience. Finally, boasting can be rooted in pride, but it can still remain boasting without being tied to pride.

Let me push to the core of this latter insight by observing boasting in a most unlikely place, namely, as it occurs in the tradition of the Sufis or Islamic mystics. At first glance, one might find it curious, if not paradoxical, that there is a tradition of boasting in a mystical tradition when more commonly the mystical practices are renowned for avoiding anything that smacks of self-indulgence or drawing attention to oneself.

What we know today as Sufism, however, grew out of an Arabic culture, and Islamic mystics creatively adapted this culture in their own spiritual practices. In particular, they took up the rhetorical pre-Islamic Arabic boasting contest [*mufākhara*]. In a specific spiritual lineage, which encompasses Sufis like al-Husayn ibn Mansur al-Hallāj, Abu Yazid al-Bisṭāmī, and Rūzbihān Baqlī, their "boasts" gave evidence to their mystical experiences in what are known as "ecstatic sayings."[79] But these hermeneutic dialogical pronouncements, Carl Ernst observes, served as evidence of mystical experiences for others, because they originated from the authority of experiences of the divine, not from oneself. Thus, although "I" give them voice, they are not ultimately about "me."

From the outside or for the neophyte, the boasts can appear (and in fact did appear) to be heretical and were punishable by death. But for the mystic, these ecstatic sayings were literally expressive to others of experience in the form of witnessing, and not pride. For this reason, writes Ernst, unabashed boasting was not only permitted, but encouraged.[80]

Granted, this might appear to be an extreme example for such a seemingly simple act like boasting. My point in citing this case is to show that and how boasting is essentially distinctive from pride. Though boasting is before and to others, it is not a resistance to an interpersonal context. While boasting does exhibit a relation to oneself (as does being proud), and even might most often be found to be *about* oneself in everyday occurrences, it need not be "from" myself before others, and "about" myself as an exclusion of others. In this extreme example it can be a form of witnessing (something not possible for pride), and thus is essentially distinct.

Self-confidence. As we saw above, since the temporality of pride is so intimately related to the matter of self-givenness, allow me to explicate the temporal orientation and temporal meaning of pride in order to determine the difference between pride and self-confidence. In pride, I am given to myself as if first among others, either "before" others could intervene, or as if their givenness or contribution to meaning were nonintegral to my experience, and in this sense I am structurally before others. It is not just the fact of self-temporalization in which the self is given as constituting and constituted, but the way in which the self is self-given in pride that constitutes its orientation and its meaning.

We saw how the dimension of temporal self-givenness is a fundamental self-givenness for the experience of pride, and this gives us a clue to the temporal orientation and to the temporal meaning of this experience. First, the temporal orientation of pride is the "present" in a twofold sense as it is governed by self-givenness. (1) The self-givenness in pride is the present in an *immediate* sense, that is, insofar as I who inhabit this present in self-givenness am not able to be crossed out in that selfsame experience.[81] (2) The orientation is the present in the broader sense of what we can call the living-present which *encompasses* the retended past and the futural protentions. In this case, the orientation is the present, but as I transcend the present and integrate what is beyond the immediate present into an overarching living-present.

Second, the temporal meaning of pride is intimately related to its temporal orientation. Pride springs from myself toward myself such that the very temporal meaning of pride is the present in both the immediate sense mentioned above, and in the sense of the encompassing living-present. Even though I am constituted as subject in the repetition of remembering, the ultimate point of this process as a feature of pride is myself through the reintegration of the past (and "subjectification" of what is other). Rather than the generation or transcendence of new meaning, this is the reproduction (without decisive difference) of the same structures which have already come to light. Its meaning is to remain within the present self as self-giving and self-given. For example, pride does not have an ultimate futural orientation (like we will find with the experience of hope or repentance). Neither does its meaning rest in the past (like we find to be the case with guilt). Even though we could speak of an expansiveness in pride (suggestive of its spatial significance), it is an expansiveness of the self (over others and their contribution), which is not to be conflated with transcendence of self. In this respect, the temporal meaning of pride is "present."

Accordingly, we do not require evidence of the past in order to have the experience of pride. This is the case even though one can look for "evidence" of pride after the fact. If we compare this to the experience of self-confidence, we find an important difference on this score. In self-confidence, the experience of the past is essential. Self-confidence is based on the concordance of the past and the concordant unfolding of experience. By concordance we mean that the experience in question has been confirmed and reconfirmed in a harmonious manner and in such a way that is sufficient for an expectation of activity to be generated in order for this activity to be continued. This can support "confidence," or at higher levels, self-confidence, and in a differently qualified way, "success." Further, on an interpersonal level, self-confidence is in no way a resistance to the contribution of others. I can be confident in my ability as a carpenter to build a house without positing myself as the source of that activity. My self-confidence might even assist others, for example, in building a proper house for them. Further, while pride is interpersonally exclusive in its inclusion, self-confidence is not a resistance to the contribution of others.

In this way, I find the temporal orientation and the temporal meaning of pride to be the present such that pride could only exist in the present; self-confidence, on the other hand, essentially requires the past for a future project.

Conclusion

The chapter on pride has done two things. On one level of analysis, it has provided a description of the experience of pride in terms of its distinctive meanings and structures. To this end, I interpreted pride as a moral, interpersonal emotion which is expressed through a dual movement of self-insistence and through this self-salience, the resistance to and refusal of contributions from others. Pride obfuscates Myself, limiting Myself as relation to myself as self-grounding. I examined personal and aesthetic basic experiences of self that are taken up creatively as pride, and then characterized pride as a moral "subjective attitude." As such an attitude, the self-givenness in pride is not only non-self-revelatory, but is self-dissembling. Nevertheless, pride is susceptible to a moral reduction that calls pride into question, but this was seen as not being able to originate from the very movement of the self as a prideful self. To help hone in on the distinctiveness of pride, I attempted to disambiguate it from self-love, standing on my integrity, being proud of something, even boasting and self-confidence.

In and through these descriptions, however, I have been aiming at something more, namely, a fuller and richer picture of the human person. Pride gives us a clue to the meaning of the human person by the fact that pride is freely enacted and by being expressive of that very freedom. It does not preexist as a "potentiality" in human nature. Rather, pride is a creative emergence within the sphere of persons, enacted as it were, and now continues to co-originate with the meaning of persons. But even as original, pride's originating freedom cannot combat itself precisely because of its refusal of and resistance to others in the execution of its self-freedom. Its very self-givenness is self-dissembling and self-limiting. While we saw how a person can be directed toward him- or herself in ways that are not necessarily interpersonally destructive, such a refusal of or resistance to the contributions of others in pride discloses the person as essentially interpersonal; the latter shows up even at the core of a subjective attitude. Moreover, pride ultimately aims at a sphere of the absolute, where the self fills this void by positing itself as self-grounding. But the very interpersonal nexus that is presupposed in positing myself as self-grounding points to deeper dimensions of the person, with implications that are moral in the large sense (social and political), and religious. In the next chapter, I will look to shame as a privileged moral emotion that is self-revelatory, and in this way is able to call pride into question.

2

Shame

> One does not make a revolution out of shame.... Shame is itself a revolution.
> —Karl Marx

Pride emerges freely, creatively, qualifying dynamically who we are as persons. Yet it is self-limiting and self-dissimulating regarding who we are as persons. Pride is not of such a mettle that "I" could call it into question; a moral reduction of pride is not something that "I" can perform. Shame arises within the emotional sphere of the person in a way that reveals me to myself. Shame is lived as a diremptive experience, occurring even against my will, but it also emerges as a creative response, most deeply to the movement of pride. In this way, I am reduced in shame—to Myself—I am humbled, such that I am unable to justify myself in my self-salience as resistance to others. Being thrown back on myself in the presence of another, halting me in my tracks, shame provokes a self-revelatory and possibly self-critical experience that is not evident in pride.

Shame is a complex moral emotion, and it is impossible in the scope of a chapter to treat every dimension of it. For the purpose of describing shame as a moral emotion in the context of disclosing the meanings of the human person, I limit myself to the following aspects of shame. By way of introduction to the dynamic of shame, I treat the relation between life and spirit as a locus of shame (1). I then consider shame along with embarrassment as diremptive experiences (2), focusing on the self-revelatory quality of shame in its positive self-givenness (3), its negative valence, and the possibility of a debilitating shame (4). It is in relation to such a positive self-givenness that shame can be interpreted as a "moral reduction." After examining the interpersonal character of shame (5), I address the problem of shamelessness (6), and then the peculiar temporal structure of shame (7).

Life, Spirit, and Shame

The issue of shame has made frequent appearances in philosophical, spiritual, religious, psychoanalytic, and literary traditions, but it has also gained wide currency in contemporary thought and discourse, especially in relation to the concept of life. As such, it has been explored as having ontological, existential, personal, psychological, and even bio-political significance. I would like to introduce the experience of shame as a matter of spirit in relation to life by briefly examining its emergence in three relatively contemporary thinkers who have examined it in this respect: G. W. F. Hegel, Max Scheler, and most recently, Giorgio Agamben. I do this because these thinkers, in their own ways, identify a "tension" or "conflict" peculiar to shame, thus providing us with a leading clue to that experience. I will then turn to a more detailed phenomenological analysis of shame.

In his *Phenomenology of Spirit*, Hegel addresses the experience of life in the dialectic of lordship and bondage. Here, inchoate self-consciousness risks its specific existence by projecting death as a possibility in order to show that it is not merely a form in the flux of life in general. If its death were simply vital, putting an end to its natural setting would mean putting an end to itself and rejoining the unending flux of life. Anxiety, however, intervenes and becomes a surrogate biological death; it grants to determinate existence the loss of itself. In anxiety, the specific existent does not experience itself as a determinate existent, but rather, experiences the radical indeterminacy of its being as a whole. It experiences the negation of its particular form without having to sacrifice its particular form. Anxiety, here, is the meeting point between individual self-consciousness as implicit spirit, and life.[1]

In Hegel's *Encyclopedia*, however, we have a different account of the relation between life and the emergence of spirit as individual consciousness. The awakening of consciousness to life is described as shame (not anxiety, fear, or even guilt for that matter). Shame is evidence of the distance between the human being and sensuous life, something that is only accomplished from the perspective of spirit. It is for this reason, writes Hegel, that animals do not experience shame. Furthermore, he reflects, the human feeling of shame is the spiritual and moral origin of clothing; by contrast, the physical need of dress is only a secondary matter. This distance of life and spirit, and of spirit becoming conscious of itself as life, which is marked by shame, is essential to spirit, even if it is not the final goal of what it means to be human.[2]

This intimation of the relation between shame and life is studied in a more phenomenologically acute manner in the work of Max

Scheler. Placing shame at the interstices of life and spirit, Scheler studies shame within the encompassing perspective of a philosophical anthropology, disclosing its ontological significance. He depicts shame as rooted in the tension between the unending movement of life and the finite individuality of the person or spirit. In fact, shame can only arise by virtue of the emergence of spirit. According to Scheler, shame arises spontaneously when, for example, we are living in and through an act (spirit) and are suddenly turned back on ourselves in a way that highlights the personal (unique, individual) quality of the finite being against the background of life in general.[3] Belonging to the fundamental conditions and origin of shame therefore is the presence of spirit, of life, and something like a disequilibrium, unbalance, and a *disharmony of the human being* between the sense and the claim peculiar to a spiritual person and the necessities of life.[4] Or put differently, it is a tension experienced between higher or deeper value orientations in relation to lower drive-related strivings.[5]

Certainly, not every kind of turning back on oneself is an experience of shame. But shame is an experience of a conflict, namely, of the essential claim and genuine sense of those acts and their *personal* point of departure with their concrete and actual *modes of existence*. This is why Scheler suggests that one of the primary functions of shame is self-protection. What he means by this, however, is not a protection from others, as Gabriele Taylor seems to imply when she employs this expression,[6] but a protection of the individuality of a process of becoming through the unique *personal* orientation in relation to the entire sphere of what is general or common in the vital sphere. Though I will take this up in more detail below, it is important to note here that because the positive value of the self is given in shame as the basis of any valuation, the negative value of action is founded in the positive value of self. Being ashamed about something is then a retroactive reaction of shame that goes back to the maintenance and protection of the positive value of the self in which the loss of this value is suddenly glimpsed. Accordingly, all feeling of shame goes to the positive felt value, never toward a negative value.[7] We can summarize the experience of shame in Scheler, then, as an ontological tension between spiritual and life orientations, and as the personal tension between the uniqueness of the individual and life as common to all.

The relation between shame and life also arises as a fundamental concern for Giorgio Agamben. Allow me to devote a little more space to Agamben in this introduction to shame because the structure of sovereignty that he describes (in relation to which shame emerges) shares the same structure as pride, articulated in the context of bio-politics.

Relying on the implicit distinction in the Greeks between *zoē* and *bios,* Agamben describes life, respectively, in the mode of "bare life," that is, life peculiar to all living beings as living, life in general, and life as it pertains to the individual or collective person, the manner of living peculiar to them as politically qualified life. The interpenetration of bare life and qualified living as political eventually constitutes the zone of indistinction, a zone that arises through the "state of exception."[8]

By state of exception, Agamben means the way in which bare life is included in politics through an exclusion of bare life from power, receiving its determination (its inclusion) by virtue of its very exclusion. A premier example of this is the phenomenon of the "camps."[9] The camps, Agamben writes, were born out of the state of exception and martial law. The state of exception (and the decision of life—and death) is the right of the "sovereign." Legally placed outside the law and having the legal power to suspend the validity of the law, the sovereign can institute the state of exception by beginning a temporary suspension of state law. This temporal dimension of the state of exception becomes a permanent spatial arrangement of bare life and equated with juridical rule itself.

Further, the meeting point of bare life and the political in the human being constitutes the human being as *homo sacer.* *Homo sacer,* the "sacred man," is the seemingly contradictory figure in Roman law who at once cannot be the object of ritual sacrifice, but who can be killed by anyone with impunity, without it being considered an act of homicide.[10]

In sum, the humanity of the living human being is constituted in the "politicization" of bare life.[11] Thus, the state of exception as the structure of sovereignty is the originary structure in which law refers to life and includes it by suspending it. Killing human life which is banned (which is not ritual sacrifice) is both outside the law (abandoned by the law) and yet legal, not punishable as homicide.[12] What is produced is a zone of indeterminacy or zone of interpenetration of bare life and politics, life as such and a way of life. What Agamben calls the structure of sovereignty, the process of including in and through the very exclusion, is the structure of pride. Is it any wonder that pride and sovereignty (personal or political) have so much in common?

In his notes for and preceding the trilogy of *Homo Sacer,* Agamben had considered the experience of shame. Primo Levi, he writes, has shown that there is not merely a national shame with respect to other peoples, a shame like we might find in Marx,[13] but a shame of being human.[14] What Agamben is on the verge of discovering in this early text is that shame cannot be limited to an incidental experience (like "Italian shame"), but must be understood as a *fundamental (political) experience of being human* today, and hence "the most emotive tonality of subjectivity."

In the third volume of his treatise on *homo sacer*, *Remnants of Auschwitz: The Witness and the Archive*, Agamben devotes an entire chapter to the problem of shame.[15] Weaving a suggestive analysis through figures ranging from Levi to Heidegger to Kafka, Keats, de Saussure, and Binswanger, Agamben characterizes shame as the very structure of subjectivity.[16]

Shame emerges as fundamental to human subjectivity because it is the revelation of the conflict that emerges at the very interpenetration of life in general and individual life, the ever-present tension between anonymous life, corpus, and the qualified life of the political citizen. Functioning in the service of politics, bare life no longer has its own special region and can no longer be separate from politics; still, human beings distinguish themselves from their own bare life and simultaneously maintain a relation to that bare life in an inclusive exclusion. For Agamben this interpenetration of life in general and individual life is today already the implication of bare life in *politically qualified life*. The sphere of implication or indistinction is the condition of shame such that all life is always already political and such that all political life would have to be constituted as shame.[17] Self-loss and self-possession, servitude and sovereignty are experienced as shame: "In shame," writes Agamben, "the subject thus has no other content than its own desubjectification; it becomes witness to its own disorder, its own oblivion as a subject. This double movement, which is both subjectification and desubjectification, is shame."[18]

Because shame is the experience of bearing witness to the desubjectification or inhumanity of the human subject *as* a human subject, Agamben can link the experience of shame to bearing witness and testimony, and to the discursive or linguistic reality of the individual who says "I" vis-à-vis anonymous vital functions.[19] As the hidden structure of all subjectivity and consciousness, shame is the event of enunciation through self-revelation in relation to living being. Thus, it is shame that is expressive of bearing witness to a tension, that is, both to our inhumanity and to our humanity, but—and this is decisive—from the perspective of our humanity as attested to by the unique individual.[20] Shame is thus possible because the identity between the human and the inhuman is never complete, and even though there is a zone of indistinction with regard to bare life and the political citizen, there is still a non-coincidence allowing a self-givenness in the style of shame.[21] At the same time, the disclosure of ourselves through shame reveals to us a new task, or at least, as Agamben suggests, the beginning of repentance and revolution in the direction of an unforeseen and unforeseeable future for humanity.

With these accounts of shame from Hegel, Scheler, and Agamben, we have a set of leading clues to the experience of shame as a fundamental and constitutive feature of human personal experience. Let me sum them up here. For Hegel, shame is the awakening of consciousness to life as evidence of the interval between spirit and life; for Scheler, shame is an originary experience of the tension within the human being of person and life in which the individual is turned back on itself revealing its positive orientations against which the negative is measured; for Agamben, shame is a bearing witness and testimony of individual subjectivity to our inhumanity, yet *as* human in the interpenetration of bare life and politics. While none of these thinkers takes shame as a phenomenon of life merely, they do evaluate shame as an experience that arises in relation to life. Yet, in order for shame to function in the fundamental ways that they suggest, it has to be understood more explicitly as a personal mode of self-revelation.

I develop these insights further in this direction in order to discern the meaning and structure of the shame experience. Although shame is often the topic of psychoanalytic, psychological, and therapeutic works,[22] I explore the meaning of shame and its essential structures from a philosophical, and specifically, phenomenological perspective.[23]

In what follows, I examine shame as a diremptive experience in which I am revealed to myself as exposed before another. The self-critical dimension of shame that arises in self-revelation and allows us to reorient ourselves also emerges in the context of the interpersonal dimension of shame such that we are able to account for the phenomenon of shamelessness. It is in this respect that shame calls into question pride as the structure of sovereignty. This analysis will enable us to consider the temporal structure of shame and to evaluate whether shame can be prospective, thwarting shameful action.

Diremptive Experiences: Embarrassment and Shame

A diremptive experience is an experience of a unity in difference of orientations, where one orientation is more basic than another and, as it were, "measured" against another. This diremptive experience can be taken up in different ways where this appropriation on the level of the person is understood as a *creative,* "spontaneous" elaboration of the diremptive experience. To say that a diremptive experience can be lived creatively is to say, on the one hand, that such an experience did not have to be appropriated in this way, that it is a response on the level of the person to an existential situation, and lived out improvisationally in this manner and not in another, prior to the level of a rational choice of what to do. Once realized as such, these various realizations become historical a prioris for the meaning of persons. Some of the creative, personal elaborations of a diremptive experience that I will treat below are embarrassment, shame, and guilt.

The diremptive dimension peculiar to shame is what others have identified in shame, generally speaking, as a "conflict," "tension," "disharmony," or "non-coincidence." This is not to say that all "tensions" give rise to shame.[24] Rather, shame is a unique way (one way among other creative responses) of living this tension such that it can evoke a reorientation. My point is that without this unity in difference of orientations, shame would not be self-revelatory. In order to give shame as a diremptive experience sharper contours, let me contrast it with that of embarrassment. (I will take up guilt as a diremptive experience in the next chapter.)

Both embarrassment and shame are kinds of diremptive experience. A diremptive experience can occur as a mere infraction or rupture (an anomaly), or as a more substantial rivalry or challenge.[25] Embarrassment emerges as a diremptive experience of the first kind, namely, as a mere discordance of a concordant dynamic orientation of who I am. For example, if I show up at someone's house and discover that I have holes in my socks, or if I misstep and trip while trying to impress a group of friends, I might be embarrassed insofar as these events are experienced by me as mere ruptures. Notice that in embarrassment there is a kind of rupture in the experience, namely, the event disrupts my expectation, and is given as an incidental infraction of my general character: I am usually well dressed, but now I have holes in my socks; I am usually graceful, but I tripped foolishly in front of my friends.

Whatever I experience as a diremption in embarrassment is constituted merely as an infraction of an otherwise concordant flow of experience. The event or action—the diremption—will function as an index to who I am, and *via negativa*, reveal me to myself in a certain way. Taylor is on the right path when she observes that shame is "weightier and more shattering" than embarrassment,[26] as long as we do not mean, as Lewis maintains, that embarrassment is a mild version of shame.[27] What I object to here is placing embarrassment and shame as if on the same quantitative continuum, when in fact they are qualitatively distinctive, even if they are both modes of diremptive experiences. Thus, we need to examine what can be meant by shame being "weightier."

Shame emerges as an experience when the lived-diremption is

given as more than a mere infraction, that is, when the event or action qualifies me in some way and threatens a "re-configuration" of my character. Accordingly, against the background of my character, the event or action will be given not merely as an anomaly, but as the emergence of a new discordant concordance that diverges from the former concordance. There are now two (or at least two) competing ways of being. However, even though there are two potentially competing orders or ways of being, they are not given on the same level; one is experienced as more "basic" than another. Without (1) this co-givenness and (2) without one being more basic, there would be no shame, but merely alternative ways of being.

A discordant concordance begins the institution of a new sense that calls into question the previous internal coherence, say, the "lived teleology" of the person; it institutes a possible new orientation such that the latter clashes with the former. On the one hand, a countervailing incident is given with *enough severity* to call another into question; on the other, it is given such that it threatens a *more basic orientation* with which I feel myself more aligned.[28] This divergence of "teleoi" constitutes the normative contrast and can give rise to shame.

Now, any of the particular situations I gave above as examples of embarrassment *could* also solicit the experience of shame, depending upon the context; for example, if showing up with holes in my socks is an (unwelcome) part of who I am, or if it reveals me as an insensitive person. So, if it is a reflection on my character (or if it reflects "poverty" and poverty is something to be shunned because of accepted values), then it might provoke shame. Perhaps it reflects poor taste or being sloppy. For example, if the house is dirty, I might be ashamed to have someone over; as an external sign of my character, I might experience shame, and not merely be embarrassed (perhaps it is dirty just this one time). The point is, if it bears on me, then we will experience shame. Even if my house is dirty only once, but if I experience it as somehow expressive of myself, I will experience shame and not merely embarrassment.

This means that the difference between embarrassment and shame is not a quantitative one; what constitutes the embarrassment is not that it only occurs once or once in a while. A single event can also elicit shame if that event or action reflects who I understand myself to be and threatens it. Rather, shame is a qualitatively unique emotional experience that bears on the becoming of the person. Having characterized shame as a kind of diremptive experience that is taken up creatively and lived as shame, I would like to investigate it more deeply as a mode of self-revelation.

SHAME

Shame as Self-Revelation

Shame is an experience in which we are turned back on ourselves, lived as a distinctive kind of diremptive experience through which we are thereby revealed to ourselves. It is in this respect that shame can be understood as a "moral reduction" and as able to call pride into question.

Let us examine a paradigmatic example of shame from the Western Abrahamic tradition. This tradition places shame at the origin of "the beginning" and casts it as one of the primordial emotional experiences, defining what it means to be a human person in relation to our deeper possibilities. Let us recall that shame emerges in the account of Adam and Eve (the first persons) in the story of creation, "In the beginning," or Bereshit/Genesis—the first book of the Tanach or Bible. My contention is that shame is not the mere fact of bodily exposure, when Adam and Eve supposedly discover themselves as naked, but rather, the dynamic of self-revelation before the Holy.

After Adam and Eve have eaten of the Tree of the Knowledge of Good and Evil at the center of the Garden of Paradise—something they were forbidden to do—God is said to ask, "Where are you?" This question does not really concern spatial location (presumably, God would know where the inhabitants of Garden were located). Rather, God is calling for a response. The question "where are you?" calls for an acknowledgment of how one is disposed to or oriented toward God. Notice that when God is said to ask this of Moses or Abraham, they are said to respond immediately with *"hineni,"* or "Here I am." In other words, they are directly disposed to God, without question and without hesitation. Adam and Eve, on the other hand, hide from God, which is to say, they have removed themselves from the movement of holiness, and accordingly (in some way) are not oriented toward God.

Shame is the self-revelation to Adam and to Eve that they have somehow turned away from God—whether it is by not taking responsibility for their actions, disobedience, or more fundamentally, pride. Thus, shame is most radically an interpersonal phenomenon as an inter-Personal self-revelation. In this example, *shame tells Adam and Eve "where they are,"* now, and how they are disposed (and not disposed) to God. Adam and Eve are *exposed* before God as dis-oriented from God. Accordingly, the "Fall" is the "moment" of dis-orientation from the Holy, as disclosed in the experience of shame.[29] Without this fundamental dimension of shame as self-revelation, other modes of shame are relatively insignificant.

Shame is an interpersonal self-revelation, and in this respect I am not only given as exposed before another, but as *receiving myself from another.* In this interpersonal framework, Adam and Eve are *given* to themselves as shameful *from* holiness. Even though we can say that they are given to themselves as shameful from the direction of holiness (the Holy), there is nonetheless a dimension of *personal creativity* in this shame that redounds upon the first persons. For in order for Adam and Eve to experience shame at all, it goes to their "credit," as it were, to be still basically oriented toward God and as the basis upon which any disorientation is gauged. It is from this underlying orientation toward God that their disorientation is revealed as shameful. Otherwise, Adam and Eve would have been simply "shameless." I return to this point below.[30]

The self-revelation peculiar to shame is "spontaneous" in the sense that it arises of its own accord, although it is not something I egoically initiate (as is in the case of self-reflection or self-examination of conscience). Shame calls me into question; it is not something that I will, and is in fact an experience I want to avoid. It holds me in check precisely in my sovereignty over others as self-salience and resistance to others. But just because this aspect of my freedom is called into question as insistence/resistance, it does not mean that shame is not "creative" or that it does not occur within the sphere of the person. It is a creative, original emotional experience (and not an affect); I must be so oriented or disposed in such a way that I could be stricken by shame. Otherwise, I would not experience shame at all. Shame is not caused; the same set of circumstances may not provoke shame in every case. They might just give rise to embarrassment, for example, or to self-disappointment or self-doubt as modifications of pride. Likewise, this cannot be attributed to differences in cultural norms or mores, for we can have the same variation of experiences within the same cultural setting or small groups, and different experiences may or may not arise. Indeed, there are occurrences in which I am exposed to others, in which I am engaged in a questionable activity, or a disposition of pride, and so on, and I do not experience shame at all.

The creative personal dimension of shame as self-revelatory enables shame to have a critical dimension; it can modify how I understand myself and how I am to be. Contrary to concluding, as does Bernard Williams, that shame is expressive of a "loss of power," shame is expressive of a self-revelation, even though I am not in control of the way in which I am revealed to myself (which again does not mean that there is not a core of personal creativity in shame).[31] This is why a self-revelation, especially of the type shame, always *matters to me;* it is, we could say, impassioned. While auto-affection and self-awareness as kinds of self-givenness always take place in the constitution of the self, shame as a mode of self-awareness only occurs in certain circumstances and under certain conditions.[32]

Having highlighted the personal, creative dimension of shame in self-revelation, I now explicate the self-revelatory dimension of shame in terms of the positive self-givenness presupposed in shame, and distinguish the negative valence of shame from debilitating shame.

Contrary to many theories of shame, shame is not possible without a genuine self-love and positive self-valuing. We encountered the phenomenon of genuine self-love when it was distinguished from pride. To recap: by genuine self-love, I mean the self-givenness of *personal* uniqueness, and being oriented toward the depth of who I can become as person, relationally, as Myself. Shame concerns who we are as persons. If we understand by "religious" not the adherence to a religion or dogma, but a dynamic orientation that coincides with loving in the direction of holiness, then shame is fundamentally religious since I experience myself as being given to "Myself" (as inherently relational), and the "loving" as being open to that good-in-itself-for-me, as an experience of being not self-grounding. This orientation is exemplary for other modes of shame that we might experience, be they political, moral, social, economic, or ecological, and they in their turn express this dimension of self-revelation.[33] Hence, Scheler can write that shame is a feeling of self-love because shame is a reaction of a consciousness directed toward higher values and at the same time and on the basis of which a lower-level act is oriented.[34] It is by virtue of the experience of the positive value of Myself that an act or event giving rise to shame can be weighted as negative.

Moreover, according to Scheler, "being ashamed about" is a retroactive reaction of shame, which—like all feeling of shame—goes back to the maintenance and protection *of the personal uniqueness* in which the loss of this positive value is suddenly glimpsed.[35] As we saw above, shame is an emotion of self-protection, not in the sense of protecting myself from others, but in the sense of protecting the positive value of Myself that is challenged by an action or set of circumstances. This is why we can be ashamed of a lack of shame, and why, in distinction to repentance or remorse, being ashamed is always a moment of self-love that is disappointed.[36] But this also means that shame can have a transformative dimension as a reorientation of the person (individual or collective). For this reason, not only Marx, but Agamben alludes to the fact that the experience of shame is the beginning of a revolution (and repentance, as we will see, its realization).[37]

As an experience of genuine self-love and the positive value of self, shame, as "a trailblazer to 'ourselves,'"[38] is the basis of implicit and possible explicit self-critique. Accordingly, shame is not originally a form of self-deception as some claim, but is a way of overcoming self-deception. The sense of clarity of mind in shame (more precisely, trying to avoid it) is captured by Pheadra in Euripides's *Hippolytus* when she says "I am ashamed of what I have said. / Cover me. Tears come from my eyes, / and my look is turned to shame. / To have one's thinking made straight is painful / but madness is an evil. To die / without awareness is best."[39] In short, it is the positive self-givenness in shame that allows us to be self-critical as reorienting ourselves. In this sense, shame can give us our bearings such that without it, we might remain lost.[40] This is no doubt why at the end of Bergman's film *Shame*, the characters (who lack shame) are stranded for days on end in a small fishing boat in an open, horizonless sea.

The Negative Valence of Shame and Debilitating Shame

Although shame has the positive value of the self in view, shame carries with it an implicit self-critique such that shame is given with a negative valence. This is one reason why shame is often confused with a depreciation of self, and why it is mistakenly cast in a predominately negative manner.

The negative valence of shame is *inherent in any experience of shame,* even those are seemingly trite. Let's suppose I am at a friend's house and I see a set of new racing wheels for his bike. With respect to an experience of shame, several things could occur. (1) He tells me how hard he has worked to buy these wheels, and I feel ashamed because all of my racing equipment was given to me at little or no cost. (2) I steal his wheels from his basement and put them on my bike. My friend sees his new wheels on my bike at a race; I know he notices them, but he says nothing. I feel ashamed that I am not living up to who I could be as a friend, and in this respect, that I took these wheels. (3) My friend sees the wheels, demands them back, and I am ashamed, not because I stole them, but because I got caught: I think: "And you call yourself a thief; you should be ashamed of yourself" (namely, for not being a better thief).

What these examples have in common, like others that impact us more significantly, is an experience of un-comfortableness, dis-grace, dis-honor, un-worthiness, being ill-at-ease that issues forth in and through these countervailing tendencies. This "dis," "un," or "ill" shows up shame as a self-givenness that is colored by a *negative* valence. Aristotle probably has this aspect in view when he defines shame as pain or disturbance in regard to bad things.[41]

By negative valence, I do not mean that the purpose or the result of shame is negative; indeed, it can yield positive results, for example, when it reorients the one experiencing shame to a more integral life in accordance with his or her, or even a society's, deeper orientation. Phil Hutchinson is correct in not considering shame to be simply "regressive," as is generally thought to be the case. As he remarks, an affluent society that allows its cohabitants to suffer from a poverty that could be easily avoided is shameful, and to experience shame here is not something regressive.[42] In fact, such a shame might bring clarity to move us in a more morally profound orientation. In short, there are positive effects of shame just as there are debilitating and destructive ones; but these should not be reduced to the negative valence inherent in shame.

The negativity here is peculiar to how I experience shame in the duration of shame. No matter what the circumstances, I experience a discomfort. Indeed, shame is so "un"-comfortable, so "dis"-agreeable, and so on, that I do not *want* to experience shame. Even if it can be instructive, even if it can provoke self-critique in a positive direction, I do not welcome shame. Hence, we want to avoid shame *even if it is not necessarily to be avoided*. This is what I mean by its negative valence. The negative valence of shame is so essential to the feeling of shame that it cannot be experienced without this implicit, integral negative tenor. We never like to experience shame, and even if one argues that we do, it would be the peculiar discomfort or negativity that we would seek.

The negative valence that occurs in and through the shame-experience, moreover, does not arise primordially from a reflective self-assessment or self-judgment. Such a negative valence, contra Leon Wurmser, occurs *prior* to a negative self-judgment.[43] Blushing, downcast eyes, lowered head, staying quiet, covering one's face before another, feeling exposed, shirking of body posture, feeling small—all of these are bodily expressions of shame that take place prior to active self-assessment.[44]

Certainly, disappointment in myself or self-criticism may arise reflectively and after the fact of shame. But the experienced "dis" or negative valuation that does arise in shame arises *as I am revealed to myself in a particular way*. Only later might I criticize myself, be disappointed in myself, doubt myself, or take steps to address shame, and so on.[45] This negative valence is in part what connects the experience of shame to guilt, and also distinguishes it, in large part, from related experiences like pride. For example, we saw that in pride (like the related phenomena of being proud of something, self-esteem, boasting, self-confidence), my experience is colored with a positive valence. Even when actions go against shared social norms or expectations, like illegal wiretapping, union-busting, embezzlement, if I experience pride or am proud about what I have done, the experience will be given with a positive valence.

Debilitating shame is a particular kind of shame that neither exhausts the meaning of shame, nor is to be reduced to shame's self-revelatory, self-critical characteristics, nor especially to the negative valence of shame. It may be objected that if shame can be debilitating, we might need to account for shame with a more neutral term of "self-awareness" rather than the more positive sense of "self-revelation." My point, however, is that whether the self is "given" in a way that is there for a positive self-critique or is given in a debilitating way, whether it originate in a well-ordered or disordered heart, what is taking place in shame is a revelation of the self *that is not neutral*.[46] I am revealed to myself in this way or that, and I take it so seriously (as true, whether or not it is, objectively speaking, valid), that I am thrown back on myself before others in an experience of shame. In fact, shame could not be debilitating if I were not *revealed* to myself in a positive manner, and if I did not experience myself as *revealed* to myself, with an import and veracity. Therefore, shame is not a neutral self-awareness or "low-level" self-awareness as in auto-affection;[47] rather, it is a kind of self-revelation. This is why shame can be debilitating in the first place.

Debilitating shame arises from what we might call, according to Scheler, a "disordered heart."[48] In debilitating shame, I am given to myself through distortions of value, either on the part of others or myself. In examples of emotional or physical abuse, cultural hegemonies that prescribe value ideals (economic, social, political, and bodily), what is given is a "disordered" norm of self and others. Children of abusive parents, foreigners who speak, look, or dress differently, the poor, and others, may live with a projected and internalized low self-esteem resulting from a disordering of value, having originated from a hatred by others.[49] The problem with debilitating shame, however, is not shame, but the disordered heart at its root.[50] (I treat the experience of humiliation, which actually belongs here as a mode of debilitating shame, below in the chapter on humility because of the common and unfounded confusion between humility and humiliation.)

Where the disordered heart is concerned, I can (a) live through the disorder in such a way that I recognize it as such, or (b) I can live it *as* disordered where the disordering is invisible, as it were, and where the disordering becomes the norm. Marx's critique of the alienation of species-being (*Gattungswesen*) gives an excellent example of such a disordering. In this instance, spiritual values (creativity, freedom) are subordinated to life values (subsistence), use values, or even commodities to such an extent that one "willingly" sacrifices the former for the latter. Such a distortion closes off what can appear as value, limits the becoming of another, and thus moves in the general direction of hating rather than loving. Such a disordered heart can provoke a debilitating shame. In short, for debilitating shame, I am not able to live with others in an open coexistence because it shuts down the interpersonal nexus.

Debilitating shame can have many sources. For example, other people I trust or love might impose a false or destructive "self-image" against which any action is measured. Relying on evidence gathered as a psychiatrist, James Gilligan—and following him, James Hart—maintains that the most violent crimes (especially those associated with psychopathology) have arisen in those who have been deeply shamed by being violated in their childhood.[51] Another can make me feel unworthy when there is no "cause" for this unworthiness, or never release me from "unworthiness," whether actual or fictitious, such that I can no longer justify myself (or become justified) before another or before myself.[52] This is why we think of debilitating shame as "unwarranted" and even tragic.

In debilitating shame, the potentially self-critical dimension of shame is reduced to self-destruction and can lead to self-hatred. For example, in an essay on race pride, "On Being Ashamed of Oneself," W. E. B. Du Bois writes that through an internalization of racism, and eventually matters of education and social status, "colored Americans" had become directly and indirectly ashamed of themselves. In particular, he pointed to the dynamic of an upper colored group not wanting to be represented before white people by "untrained and uncultured colored folk," or being mistaken for them. This discloses, he writes, the "secret shame" of being identified with such people over whom one has no real control, and ultimately revealing a kind of love of what is not oneself and a consequent shame of being oneself.[53]

I mentioned that this arises from a disordered heart because the presupposition of shame that moves in the direction of a positive self-critical response—at least in a religious, ethical, or "ontological" register—is another who is loving or good. In debilitating shame, I have to value the value ideal that the other has of me and, in some way, take it over as mine such that it becomes that against which I measure myself. When *debilitating* shame arises from another, it is through a reversal of loving, namely, hating that shame becomes destructive or self-destructive. Shame, which presupposes a genuine self-love, is debilitating when it results in self-hate.

What qualifies shame as debilitating, however, can be different for different cultures and different religious and spiritual contexts. For example, while we might call a shame that results in suicide in the West a debilitating shame (say, because it is a closure of life of the individual person), for the samurai (where the greater honor of the community is in play and within the broader context of reincarnation and transitory nature of life), shame that leads to ritual suicide or seppuku is not debilitating. On the contrary, it is a testimony to the individual's honor and courage beyond the dishonor.

My main point in noting this, however, is not to reduce one form of shame, what is called debilitating shame, to all aspects of shame. Phenomenologically speaking, we must distinguish the negative valence experienced in shame and as inherent in all shame from a debilitating shame that can issue from a disordered heart.

Although the topics of the absence of shame and shamelessness belong by implication to the discussion of shame as a mode of self-revelation, I defer the discussion of these topics until the section that follows the role of others in shame. This is because a proper understanding of experiencing shamelessness requires situating it in a first-person plural interpersonal context.

Summary: Shame as a moral reduction. Allow me to summarize the role that shame plays thus far. Shame, at its core, is a positive self-givenness grounded in self-love, and essentially cannot be equated with a debilitating modification of shame. I am called into question in shame (from another), and this being called into question is self-revelatory. While being called into question is felt as the negative valence of shame, I am given to myself in a way that is both critique and affirmation. It is critique insofar as one orientation or way of being is experientially contested, and it is affirmation insofar as the latter occurs on the basis of a "root" orientation as who I am. Such a tension or diremption in the unity of experience, as instigated from the outside, constitutes a *self-givenness; I am turned back on myself before another* where this self-givenness reveals to me who I am (even against my will or my liking). As such shame is precisely self-revelatory, self-opening, and not self-dissembling or self-limiting. In shame, I am "reduced," in the phenomenological sense, to Myself, as who I am before another.

In this way, shame can call pride into question and serve as positive self-critique (and as we will see, can possibly lead to repentance), even though as a creative emergence, it does not have to be appropriated as a positive self-critique. The "can" here is not an abstract possibility, but it is meant to evoke the sense in which shame as a personal moral emotion arises as an immediate kind of experiencing as an expressive/transformative mode of being with others. Finally, even though shame is nothing "I" do in an active sense, this shame that I feel and that befalls me is still a creative, original and originating response, issuing from the essential core of the human person. Otherwise, I would experience no tension; there would not be something about Myself that could persist to experience a diremption of this sort; otherwise, there would be a mere absence of shame or what we can identify as shamelessness.

Shame and Otherness

Thus far, I have characterized shame as an experience of a diremptive movement whereby I am revealed to myself in a way that has religious, spiritual, moral, and epistemic implications. Many figures in the history of philosophy have also recognized the fundamental social dimension of shame. As a brief sampling: for Aristotle, shame occurs before others who we admire and whose opinion matters to us;[54] Descartes understood shame as arising before the opinions of others, even though it is a kind of sadness grounded in self-love;[55] for Spinoza shame was understood as a lessening of a feeling of self-worth coming from the outside;[56] Kant took shame as an anxiety originating in the regard of a person contemporary to me.[57]

Although these and other figures implicitly point to the social dimension of shame, let me (a) explore its social character by examining two contemporary examples of the social dimension of shame, the first from Jean-Paul Sartre, the second from Emmanuel Levinas. I highlight these two figures because they both give what have become regarded as classic examples of shame, and because they both situate shame within the dimension of social existence—with differing implications. Then I (b) address various modes of otherness, and finally (c) examine the phenomenon of interpersonal shame.[58]

The social character of shame. Whereas in the Abrahamic tradition the "Fall" is this reversal of directedness from the Holy as before the Holy (where the [self]-revelation of this diremption is shame), for Sartre the primordial "Fall" is the existence of the Other itself. This is due to the fact that for him the Other is the hidden limitation of my free possibilities, making the Other the very being of my shame.[59]

The experience of shame for Sartre is irreducible to the exposure of my body as object or to something like appearing naked before the Other. Rather, shame arises as the matter of my freedom being objectified. I am reduced to being, where my bodily being is just another instance of being in general. According to Sartre, although I live transparently in the intentional directedness of the "consciousness of . . ." through the other, "my" free intentionality becomes reified, and it is shame that reveals to me that I *am* this being, *in-itself*.[60] I am ashamed *of* myself *before* the Other because I live through a radical diremption, namely, I am conscious of myself (my freedom) as escaping myself and being given as an object—a diremption brought on by the Other.[61] The Other, contends Sartre, is not the objective condition of my shame, but the very being of it.[62] I am not ashamed of what I am, but *that* I am.

This dynamic of shame is perhaps nowhere so evident as in Sartre's paradigmatic "keyhole" example. Being completely caught up in peering through a keyhole and listening at the door, I suddenly hear footsteps in the hall, with the accompanying sensation that someone is observing me (it is immaterial whether there is really someone there, or I just imagine it). Shame is self-revelatory for Sartre because it "reveals to me the Other's look and myself at the end of that look."[63] "Shame . . . is the *recognition* of the fact that I *am* indeed that object which the Other is looking at and judging. I can be ashamed only as my freedom escapes me in order to become a *given* object."[64]

The problematic aspect of Sartre's account is neither the fact that he captures the diremption of my experience between two versions of myself, nor of a distinction between how I am for myself and my exposure to others. Problematic, rather, is his rigid ontological dualism that allows him to miss the phenomenon of shame in its full integrity. Granted that I experience shame before another, we might inquire into different experiences with others that provoke shame, but that do not unfold in his "subject-object" ontology. If this is the case, then shame cannot be reduced to the being of the other. I want to inquire into how shame may be given as an interpersonal (not subject-object) phenomenon.

Let us consider the following example. Suppose I am a young, gifted mathematician, who after a short time has reached the top of his class, but who now no longer feels it is necessary to make any effort to cultivate that ability. It is altogether possible that another person—a parent, a teacher, a mentor, a loved one—approaches me in the integrity of who I am (and not in a patronizing manner, like, "I am going to change you or make you better"). This person, by example, instruction, compassion, or unconditional love, may show me who I am such that I see for myself that I have not been living up to who I am or who I can be. In his loving, insightful, or compassionate attitude, he may know me more deeply than I do myself, so that through his eyes, I measure what I have done according to who I am in this dynamic sense, and I am invited to become who I am. Given my past or present actions, I might experience shame, not because I am placed as a thing among things in the world, becoming an object for myself, experiencing my freedom as escaping me. Rather, for the first time, say, I experience through the Other my freedom as who I can become, and I am ashamed I have not done what only I am capable of doing.[65]

In this way, I can be revealed to myself by another as more than I am being now, and in this way provoke an experience of shame from a perspective which is in some sense who I am, and in another, which is beyond who I am, which I am and which I am not yet. It is a lived diremption, productive of shame, but in an interpersonal and not subject-object nexus.[66]

The interpersonal and moral dimension of shame comes to the fore distinctively in the work of Emmanuel Levinas. Levinas's main determination of shame in one of his main works, *Totality and Infinity*, originates from the givenness of the Other in relation to my arbitrary freedom.[67]

On the one hand, the subject is the ongoing practice of freedom, the power of mastering its world (through enjoyment, use, comprehension, etc.). The subject simply does what it does where it is able. This freedom is both non-justified in the sense that it needs no justification to be exercised, and it is unjustified because as a freedom originating in myself, whose only recourse is the self, it needs no "outside" justification. By itself, the subject is neither just nor unjust.[68] The presupposition here is that the exercise of freedom and mastery is a relation with things (in the mode of disclosure), such that the subject needs neither to be justified, unjustified, or just. In this respect, I as "ontological solitude" am, my spontaneous freedom is "naive," "innocent."

On the other hand, the determinations of freedom as independent of any Other are abstract, for I am always already a moral person. For Levinas, concretely in the face of the Other, my freedom appears as *morally unworthy*. Through the givenness of the Other, I am thrown back on myself *as* freedom, as a freedom that is *unjustified* and *unjust* before the Other: I cannot justify myself, my occupation with myself, in the face of the Other. This experience of *unjusti*fied unworthiness—which before the Other Levinas calls "moral unworthiness"—is the experience of *shame:* "Thus this way of measuring oneself against the perfection of infinity is not a theoretical consideration; it is accomplished as shame."[69]

Shame, accordingly, is the beginning of moral consciousness because it is the welcoming of the Other, which calls my freedom into question.[70] Structurally, not temporally, as my freedom runs along naively mastering things in the world (disclosure), it is abruptly confronted by that which resists such appropriation, only because the Other *gives him- or herself differently* (revelation).[71]

Shame is engendered *in* a freedom that feels itself arbitrary *by* welcoming the Other who has imposed him- or herself on me. "My arbitrary freedom," writes Levinas, "reads its shame in the eyes that look at me."[72] This shame amounts to a critique of the self, instigated by the Other—indeed, it could not originate in me—by showing up myself, my freedom as "not-innocent," as not justified. "Morality begins when freedom, instead of being justified by itself, feels itself to be arbitrary and violent."[73] Shame, engendered by the Other, is an invitation to *tzedekah*: justice, righteousness, charity.

In distinction to Michael Lewis, we would have to say that I am revealed to myself *in and through* being exposed to another, where this other can be, but is not necessarily, a concrete other.[74] Accordingly, and contrary to what Guenter Seidler would contend, shame does not emerge when *my boundary has been violated* (say, by being exposed to another), for shame is an interpersonal phenomenon, and not simply a subject-object one.[75] In short, by exposure before another in shame, we do not mean the bare fact *that* I am exposed before another; rather, it concerns *how* I am given to myself as exposed to another, since, as we saw above, I also receive myself from another in the self-revelation of shame.[76]

Modes of otherness. There are many dimensions of otherness that are evident in shame, and this otherness need not be a concrete other. Being exposed before another in shame can take shape in the personal presence of the Holy, another human being, such as a mentor, a parent, a partner, or an oppressor; or otherness can be given in the experience of a collective person, as we will see below, such as a family, a social group, or an organization. On the other hand, shame can take place in the presence of social norms and even in terms of an anonymous other, for instance, as before a camera lens.[77] I experience shame that is motivated by the expectation of others or in the context of accepted social norms.[78] The same kind of shame would hold, for example, for the experience of a personal or social defect. It is in this context that shame for being poor could arise as a possible experience—where not being poor is a social value that might be tied to an ethos of "hard work," accumulation of wealth, pride in social standing, and so on.

But shame can also occur before myself as another. The principal way in which I am exposed to myself as another is when I am before myself as the vocational self or "Myself."[79] The Myself as vocational is "another" in the sense that it is myself, but as *given to me,* hence, as I receive Myself. I stand before Myself as given over to myself.

This "Myself" is open to religious as well as sociological and psychological meanings, namely, as receiving myself from outside myself. Derivatively, therefore, this Myself can occur as an occupational or professional self in which "I" am given to myself by others who have given me this role or function, to whom I have a duty, or who have given me their trust and have appropriate expectations of me to fulfill my role (say, as a public official, a police officer, a teacher, or more generally as a compassionate human being). When I do not measure up to these expectations or do not fulfill these appropriate duties, I may experience shame.[80] Further, myself as another can also be analyzed more generally in terms of personal norms, an "optimal" self, and still differently in terms of a profession, as long as it concerns who I understand myself to be: a father, a mother, an artist, an athlete, or even a pickpocket.[81] Thus, I could experience shame, and not merely embarrassment, if I do not or am unable to provide for my family, or generally if I do not or am unable to perform well.

As suggested, the otherness before which I am exposed might also be non-personal. For example, it is possible to experience shame before social norms and mores, or even before the "thing itself" such as an artistic medium like dance, music, sculpture, whereby shame would arise by not doing, for example, dance justice. In this way, I might experience shame about falling short of what I was trying to accomplish even if no one else actually sees what I have produced or failed to produce.[82]

Interpersonal shame. Shame does not concern just the individual, nor is shame only an interpersonal phenomenon in the sense that it takes place before another. Having social and political significance, shame is interpersonal in the sense that it can be shared and co-experienced, synchronically and generatively. For example, as a United States citizen, I can experience shame at having begun a so-called "preemptive" war in Iraq, even if I, as an individual, was against the aggression. As a person, I can experience shame at the bombing of Hiroshima and Nagasaki, even if I was not yet born when this happened. As a human being, I can experience shame at the use of petroleum products in the face of disastrous damage to ecosystems off the Gulf Coast and the coasts of Africa due to oil spills. The reason I can experience shame in these instances has to do with the constitution of homeworlds in relation to alienworlds.[83]

For shame to arise, I have to have appropriated—implicitly or explicitly—the sense that stems from that particular community or tradition, and experience this "homeworld" not just as a "we world," but as "*our*" world in which I play a constitutive role. It is not the mere fact that I was born into this group, that culture, this family, and so on, but the process of having made its values, its meaning my concordant, optimal, typical, and familiar world "home" through processes of appropriation and disappropriation. In shame, the conflict or diremption that I experience has to presuppose the home as the basis of that experience, and cannot be so severe that I would no longer experience that world as home—in which case, something else would be constituted as home. My concern is not to say when and where this could actually happen, but only to point out that the extent to which I experience or still experience shame, no matter how removed I may feel from my homeworld, and no matter how severe I feel the diremption, this is the extent to which I am or am still a co-constitutor of that very homeworld as a "home-companion." In this way, I can experience shame for my homeworld, for my present home-comrades or my home-progenitors.[84]

It is also within this context that I can experience not only something like "I am ashamed for what we did," and not only a "you should be ashamed of yourself," but an "I am ashamed of you." In order to have an experience of *myself* being ashamed of *someone else,* we have to be integrated in the same homeworld as co-constitutors. Thus, we might hear a parent say to a child "I am ashamed of you" when he or she acts up in a public place. This is because the child is expressive of the home, and also because the parent and home are exposed in a particular light, co-revealing the collective person of the home and the parent to themselves in a specific manner, namely, that goes against the home's and parent's orientation. This dynamic of unity and difference is the same as we saw above, but now expressed in terms of co-relation of individual and collective persons.[85]

Accordingly, where the experience of shame is concerned, there can be no experience of something like a "complete stranger." Whereas in trust, the complete stranger has to be able to be given, because one trusts the other in a non-anticipatable open future,[86] in shame, another cannot be given as a complete stranger. That is, although I may not know this other person (of whom I am ashamed), in order to experience shame, this stranger must be integrated into the home in some way: he or she is perceived as being of the same religion, from the same town or country, having a shared style of dress—that is, in some way implicitly or explicitly constituted as a home-companion. Thus, being ashamed of another is a modality of being ashamed of "ourselves."

Finally, I can have an "other-orientation" in shame. That is, I can act in such a way that I do not cause another shame. What is distinctive about this mode of shame is that it is not concerned with shame of the self, but is sensitive to the shame that another might experience. This not only presupposes a sympathy toward the other person in order to experience how and that another might experience shame (and then possibly to prevent it, perhaps by pretending not to notice a dishonorable act), but it brings up the experiential issue of shame's relation to the future. This is something I take up in the section on the temporality of shame.

Absence of Shame and Shamelessness

Rainer Krause, in his "Psychodynamik der Emotionsstörungen," introduces a helpful distinction between the absence of shame and shamelessness.[87] Before discussing this distinction, it is worthwhile to ask if such a distinction can be meaningful phenomenologically. That is, do we have first-person access to such experiences in order to make these distinctions? I think we do, but it is important to note that I cannot experience either the absence of shame or shamelessness as an isolated individual. Instead, I experience the absence of shame or shamelessness of another. It is in this sense, but only in this sense, that the absence of shame and shamelessness make sense in a phenomenological description.

Whereas I do experience shame in the present (as we will see below), I experience neither my own absence of shame nor my own so-called shamelessness in the present. Either I experience shame, or I do not. But it is possible to experience another as lacking shame or as shameless.

When I experience another as lacking shame, I experience him or her as not having a shame experience or even as being incapable of shame. When Primo Levi was liberated from Auschwitz by the Red Army, he could recognize in the young soldiers a shame: "It was that shame we knew so well, the shame that downed us after the selections, and every time we had to watch, or submit to, some outrage: the shame the Germans did not know, that the just man experiences at another man's crime."[88] It is on the basis of a perceived lack of shame on the part of another that I might assert that he or she should experience shame. Even the more pedestrian expression "you should be ashamed of yourself" discloses this. The other person is perceived as not experiencing the shame that should be felt, but it is given as a shame that does occur as a self-revelation within the collective person.[89]

My experience of the absence of shame in another—who perhaps, I think, should experience shame—is different from the experience of another as shameless. While there might be a kind of innocent malevolence when I experience the absence of shame in another, on the contrary, I experience a kind of insolence or assertiveness of self against others or social norms when I experience another as shameless; for me who experiences the other as shameless, it is she who is doing wrong, but she persists in the wrongdoing against all decency. Allow me to examine this more closely.

From the outside, or retrospectively, we attribute the following to the shameless person: he somehow has an inkling of a normative "diremption," but he does not let himself be moved by it; he feels himself going against something we share, but he simply does not care if and how he is exposed to another; she knows that her actions go against social conventions, accepted norms, and that it might be "wrong" from this perspective, but she continues anyway. She is ostentatious and has an intimation that her actions are "showy."

I still maintain that I cannot experience myself *as* shameless (even though I might look back on my past and reflect that I was shameless). Shamelessness indicates an experience of someone else, but it is accessible phenomenologically because it presupposes that this other is given within our first-person interpersonal world, our homeworld. Thus, while we do not experience shamelessness from a first-person singular perspective, shamelessness can be experienced from a first-person plural perspective, and only in this sense, as we will see below, ourselves as shameless as belonging to a homeworld. For example, we can experience the British Petroleum CEO as "shameless" because he is implicitly a home-comrade of our homeworld who shares (or should share) the values, norms, and types of "our" world. Here, for us, the other person should feel shame, but for some reason does not. For us, he goes against the shared moral compass in which shame would arise or this action would not take place. Since to experience shame is to experience a bifurcation in unity of orientations such that one orientation is more basic than the other, then for another to be shameless (from our perspective) is for the other to be so removed from a putatively *shared basic orientation* that he cannot feel the shame he should feel. Again, we would have to have appropriated the other as a home-comrade, as co-constitutive of a homeworld, in order for such an experience to arise. This is why Andrei Tarkovsky can have *Nostalghia*'s Dominico say vis-à-vis a society that has lost its way at its very core: "What kind of a world is this if a madman tells you that you must be ashamed of yourselves!"

If we go back to the example of Adam and Eve, we can say that even though Adam and Eve are disoriented from God, the fact that they experience shame at all through the disorientation also means that they are still fundamentally oriented toward God in order to experience shame. Otherwise, they would have been described by the faithful of the Abrahamic tradition as "shameless." Thus, for Spinoza, although shame is not desirable, it is nevertheless good because it shows the desire to live honorably.[90] If Adam or Eve had turned away completely from God, that is, not experienced shame as expressive of a turning away grounded in a more profound orientation, they would have experienced themselves in a fully new direction as "self-grounding"; they would have experienced pride par excellence (not shame). Adam or Eve could have become, for the faithful, "Lucifer." The fact that they are still said to experience shame shows that there is an originating orientation on their part, and in this way that they creatively align themselves more fundamentally in the direction of holiness (and in this sense that later is more basic than the turning away from).

Accordingly, we can distinguish between a sense of shamelessness that accompanies a refused sense of shame within the individual, and another sense of shamelessness that is given without the sense of shame on the individual's part, but is given from within the homeworld. Thus, only in the sense of belonging to a homeworld would it be possible to say "we" are shameless.

In the first case, shamelessness would imply a willful, knowledgeable violation of accepted norms, accompanied by a kind of self-insistence like we would see in pride. For this reason, we would hardly say of the politician who does something wrong and then apologizes that he is shameless. But if the individual persists in the same ill conduct, like BP trying to drill off the coast of Alaska at the same moment it cannot control one of the worst "spills" off the Gulf Coast, or if the CEO attempts to cover it up, or worse, does not bother covering it up, we would experience him as shameless. This implies that he knows better and that he can do better. It is not a matter of a "moral weakness" that falls short of a norm, but a violation or problem that is brought to light or has already come to light but is ignored. For us, he should experience shame such that he should stop and restore relations with others, but he continues despite the givenness and expectations. To the extent that we participate in this movement as belonging to the same homeworld, it would be possible for us to experience shamelessness in this co-responsible sense.

To conclude this discussion of shamelessness, we can make a distinction between two types of this phenomenon. In the first case, one experiences shame, but keeps involved in the activity that gives rise to shame, and in this sense is "shameless," going against the self-revelation in shame. In the second case, one persists in an activity beyond all decorum, say, and should experience shame—but does not—even while persisting in this activity. There is a conflict or diremption in "our world," that is, where the homeworld is concerned, and thus a shame opened to home-comrades. Thus "we" experience the activity as brazen, as untenable, and ultimately as shameless.

The Temporality of Shame as Presencing

In this section I consider the temporal determination of shame as presencing, and examine the possibility of a "prospective" shame. I do this, first, to show the temporal unity of shame as presence, even if the "self" in question is the past, present, or futural self; and second, I want to determine whether and the extent to which shame has an impact on future actions—as it is often claimed—and to qualify the specific futural quality instead as shyness.

The temporal unity in shame as presencing. Shame presupposes a lived-through unity that endures through the diremptions in experience. While there is a self-diremption in shame, there is just as much a unity, or as we would also say, an "internal coherence" as it centers on self-revelation as self-presence. To make this point, let me examine this from three different temporal perspectives.

I am always the one, now, experiencing anything. But more specifically in the following example, it is the past action in relation to me now that shows up as shameful—but all the while presupposing a unity in difference of orientations. Let's imagine that as a chess player, I get overconfident and quit practicing, and I do poorly in my matches. Years later, I become ashamed not only of how I performed in the past, but how I had squandered my talents, my training, and how I had dishonored my teachers—veering away from my "true" self that I have recently discovered or rediscovered. Here, if I feel shame for something done in the past, it is (a) my present self who experiences the shame (b) where the past is in reference to myself now in an internal coherence of the "same."

It is, however, possible to experience shame from a different temporal perspective. For example, I can experience shame for who I am now in relation to who I was before. Here we might experience the following: "I used to be this or that kind of person, but now look at me." Given the internal coherence of the person, this presents an interesting dynamic because evidently, the reference for the shame is not the present self, but the past self. I do not measure up now in significant ways to how I was before. I am ashamed for what I have become. Again, if I were simply *identified* with my past, for better or worse, I would not experience shame. Here, however, there is an experienced diremption which goes in a different direction.

In this case, the "norm" of the self against which I measure myself for the experience of shame arises from the past, and I turn away from Myself in this way. Again, it cannot be a completely past self because then I would have no commerce with it at all. I must still experience myself as "that" person in the past who has commerce with who I am now; I am still that "past" self: that concordant/optimal self in relation to this concordant/non-optimal self, in the larger internal coherence of who I am and becoming. Still, the movement is a movement away from an optimal myself as actualized in the past; it is not myself as who I can become, but as who I already was. This recognition of shame aligns me with my past self; it is not myself in the past who experiences shame, but the past Myself, *who I am still.* Shame reveals me both as disjoined from and connected to myself, again through a unity in difference, and this is one of the reasons we can describe the temporal meaning of shame as presencing.

Let's say I experience no discrepancy in my past and my present actions such that there is only an experienced "identity" that remains, at the very least, implicit. But after speaking with a friend, or after gaining some insight into myself, I experience shame about something I did in the past or am doing now. In order for me to experience shame about my past/present, I have to experience myself as already ahead of myself. This "being ahead of myself" is most profoundly what I have called above the "Myself" as the vocational self whereby personal norms and expectations, or an "optimal" self, can be understood as elaborations of the Myself; here, the Myself is not some abstract futural self objectively posited by me or for me.

But where the future in shame is concerned, I am this Myself such that who I am now conflicts with who only I, Myself, am and can be. Modally put, it is I, as able-to-be myself, who experiences shame—the self from that perspective—and not the present self (though it is no other than the present self). Shame arises here by not living up to who I can be, even if I have never yet become that person. Again, if I do not experience this Myself as who I am/can be, what I do now will not be given with as a diremptive experience. It will just be something else I do.

Temporal meaning of shame. Shame is a mode of self-revelation that occurs through a diremptive experience as exposed before another. When considering the temporality of emotional experiences, we distinguish between two senses of its temporality: (1) the object-orientation and (2) the temporal significance of the experience.

Where shame is concerned, we notice that the shame experience (in the sense of "1") can be directed toward something past (I am ashamed of what I did) or the present (I experience shame when "caught" in a present behavior, e.g., burglary, making bad coffee, not knowing how to read, etc.). But shame itself does not seem to possess a futural directedness. Even if I do experience something like: "If I do this, I will feel shame," this is not yet the experience of shame.

Rather, if something is going to count in shame, then it is going to have to be given *as* accomplished. I will take this up again in the chapter on guilt, but let me be specific here that by accomplished, I do not mean that I necessarily achieve something consciously or that an action has been completed. An accomplishment, instead, is a constituted sense that, in order to become what it is for me, it is "accepted" in such a way that it elucidates not just the moment, but predispositions and orientations. Accordingly, for sense to be constituted it does not have to be a "product" of an ego; simply acquiescing, appropriating implicitly, taking for granted, and so forth counts in this sense as an accomplishment. In short, the object-orientation of shame is the past and the present.

When we inquire into the temporal *meaning* of shame, we are not inquiring into something like its "purpose," but rather, we are asking after its inherent temporal significance. Shame has a predominately temporal meaning of presence which entails the future insofar as shame's meaning encompasses the *recovery* of the self through self-revelation. I may be ashamed for what I did before, but my shame for the past originates and resides in me in the present with an implicit openness to the recovery of "who I am" through self-revelation. This "am" points to the temporal significance of shame as presence. Thus, although I may want to rectify what I did or find out what went awry in shame, the experience of shame does not imply this rectification or apology—this experience is more allied with guilt in terms of its dimension of responsivity. Further, whereas in repentance there is a transformation of the meaning of the past and a liberation for the future (as we will see in chapter 4), shame is temporally self-presencing as a self-revelation implicitly open toward recovery.

This presencing feature of shame can be further elucidated by comparing it to the experience of guilt. Let's say I have made derogatory remarks about an acquaintance. Reflecting on the situation now, I can't believe that I was the kind of person who would publicly impugn his integrity, especially now that I know he holds me in high regard. I am ashamed of myself. Suppose in the same event, I damaged the other person's character. In response to the transgression that produced guilt, the offended person can forgive my transgression; but in shame there is nothing to forgive, and likewise, there is nothing that another can do to alleviate my shame. I may apologize and she may accept my apology, but strictly speaking, there is still shame. This is because the alleviation of shame does not come from another; there is nothing the other can do like he or she can do in forgiveness. Rather, shame is alleviated when the circumstances or context of the shame change or when I change. Michael Lewis writes, for example, that by acknowledging shame, one can make attempts to eliminate it, for example, through forgetting or denying shame, confession, laughter, and so on, which are all attempts to move away from the shamed self.[91] But whereas guilt concerns *what* I have *done* or *omitted,* shame bears on *how* I *am.* Thus, I *am* ashamed before you (shame) for what I *did* to you (guilt).[92] As we will see below, this bears directly on the problem of repentance as a transformation of who I am.

SHAME

Prospective shame. If shame is a presencing, temporally speaking, is there any sense to something like anticipatory shame—not just the fact that I might anticipate a shame, but that shame has a future anticipatory quality, what we can call a "prospective shame"? When Plato suggests in the *Laws* (647a-b) that the type of fear called shame (*aischynê*) is what will prevent me from doing what is dishonorable;[93] when Nietzsche writes in *Beyond Good and Evil* that *"die Scham ist erfinderish"* ("shame is inventive")—whereby I am prompted to invent a mask in order to avoid shame provoked by others and the self;[94] or when Taira Shigesuke writes in the *Bushido* (*The Code of the Samurai*) that cultivating the practice of doing right begins with the fear of being disrespected such that I do right out of a "sense of shame"[95]—what does all this mean for the experience of shame in terms of the future?[96]

Let us recall that in the experience of shame, an experienced diremption occurs in terms of what I experience now or what has taken place in relation to a more basic orientation. The point here is that this diremption is already taking place. If the shame is taking place as presencing, then shame might be able to stop us from *continuing to do* what is dishonorable. In this way, shame can provide a clarity of mind (as figures from Scheler to Dōgen suggest), and through a self-revelation that occurs in shame, it can show us how we are oriented so that we do not continue in the same way. Thus, the experience of shame cannot be a prophylactic in the sense that it cannot prevent what has not occurred, though it can serve as a guide of "no longer" doing something dishonorable.

But, we might ask: Is there not a different futural sense to shame as these representative observations from Plato, Nietzsche, and Shigesuke seem to imply? In what sense is there an anticipating shame, and is this the same as prospective shame?

We can discern the following senses of the future in relation to shame. (1) Shame in relation to the expectation (of me) on the part of another. This has to do with the possibility of social norms being integrated into our own personal orientations, as well as how another (like a mentor or parent) might be oriented toward us. (2) Shame in relation to the expectation of myself. Here we would speak of the vocational self, Myself as another, or personal norms. (3) Anticipating shame (for example: I know that if I will do this, I will be ashamed of myself). We need to examine this more closely.

Anticipating shame is an epistemic act in the sense that it takes place in the straightforward attitude of belief. Allow me to summarize briefly these basic temporal modes of futural givenness. A protention is the most passive form of this futural orientation and can be investigated in a phenomenology of association. A protention arises on the basis of something given in the present and is "immediately" retained. Through the presentation and retention, a futural orientation is sketched out such that the givenness will be concordant with what has already been given. Basic kinestheses have this structure, from eye movements to walking. It is for this reason that when the protention is disrupted, we experience that something has gone awry (and opens the possibility for surprise). An expectation and anticipation retain the basic structure of a protention, but because they are "active," their motivation is less tied to the immediate givenness of a present/retention, and can be more correlated with my "free" initiation.

In all of these cases, my futural orientation occurs in a straightforward attitude of belief and is modalized, for example, in terms of probability or likelihood. Thus, anticipation as an epistemic relation is an intention that "portends" a fulfillment. Accordingly, I can anticipate (or intend) an event that will provoke shame: if the event takes place (if I do this or that), I will experience shame. But shame itself is not the intention toward shame. Shame as self-revelatory does not have the same structure of intention and fulfillment. To anticipate an experience of shame is not the experience of shame.

Accordingly, Plato's, Nietzsche's and Shigesuke's allusion to a prospective shame can mean one of two things: either I anticipate shame (say, on the basis of past experience) and it prevents me from doing something dishonorable—in which case I have not yet experienced shame. Or, I have already experienced shame—in which case I am already doing something dishonorable, and the self-revelatory character of shame "invites" me *no longer* to do something dishonorable, and to recover who I am.

The only other feature we might want to consider here is whether or not anticipating shame somehow already implies a kind of living in the anticipation and thus already qualifying my character as somehow shameful: "I am such a person who would think of doing something like this?" But here again, anticipating that I would do something dishonorable is not the same as anticipating shame. It is the anticipation of doing something dishonorable (in the future) that would provoke an actual experience of shame *now*.

Finally, we can describe an anticipatory quality often ascribed to shame in the experience of *shyness*. Let's take the example of someone who will not speak up around others, especially in larger gatherings, like a student in a classroom. We may want this person to speak up and say her view, speak her mind, give her analysis. Some languages may want to express this by saying that we hope this person will not be ashamed, and therefore will speak up in class. Yet, this person has nothing about which he or she would be ashamed. Instead, because of this futural dimension, I suggest we mean by this that we hope this person will not be *shy*.

SHAME

I therefore interpret shyness as the anticipation of the exposure before others in a diremptive experience, an experience that carries a negative valence, or the anticipated exposure or diremption lived as a shame-to-come, and in this sense only as an anticipated shame.

Conclusion

I opened this chapter on shame by suggesting that shame is a creative response to pride as something that "reduces" me—to Myself—and I developed this matter of shame in relation to pride, beginning with the interrelation of life and shame, and by relating the self-insistence/resistance of others that we find in pride to that sovereignty and the state of exception. Let me now revisit that complex of issues that arose in the introductory exposition.

Generally speaking, we saw how shame was interpreted as an experience that emerged spontaneously on the part of the individual in relation to unending life as such. This dynamic tension that arises in shame does not occur within life alone, but from the perspective of "spirit" in relation to life. Shame is not limited to a relation of the person within the vital sphere simply, but concerns the becoming of persons, individually and collectively.

It is true that Agamben understands life, bio-politically, in a broader sense than a mere vital élan. The phenomenon of the sovereign, the co-emergence of the state of exception, the camps, and the constitution of the human being as *homo sacer* all point to this fact. The relation of shame and life has broader implications, therefore, than mere textual exegesis of Agamben, and thus it also points to a deeper problem in relation to which shame is highly relevant to interpersonal experience and the dynamic I explicated under the heading of pride.

For example—to stay with Agamben—if the very meaning of the nation state, its relation of power to the social sphere, and the discourse of rights is tied to the constitution of the human being as *homo sacer;* if bio-politics comes to the fore as the constitution of the zone of indistinction in which the human being cannot be sacrificed, but can be killed with impunity, what would the political and social spheres, what would "life" look like outside of this structure? Does Agamben, then, not have to assert the overcoming of the nation-state, and so on, in order for the human being to become emancipated, that is, no longer given as *homo sacer*? Might we accuse Agamben of advocating anarchy, of not leaving us with any "positive" solution, or leaving us with a kind of bio-political hopelessness, defeatism, or apathy?

This might be the case were it not for the intervention of shame, and it is no coincidence that it is the *emotional* experience of shame that gets highlighted in his work. Shame is relevant as more than a mere psychological feeling.[97] In fact, Agamben himself maintains that it is the harbinger of repentance and revolution; as such, the role of shame plays a significant role, and indeed, it is through shame that we are not left with a static, abstract negation of the current order. This can be surmised not only by the prominent role accruing to shame by Agamben, but by the structure of shame ascertained by these phenomenological analyses.

As we saw, shame is an experienced diremption in which a particular situation is given in tension with a more basic orientation; although the situation in question is sufficient to call the more basic orientation into question, something is still given as more fundamental such that it is the latter to which we are "truly" aligned. The phenomenological analyses presented here showed shame more precisely as self-revelatory, indicating *both* a departure *and* path of return to who one "is"—"is" understood here in the dynamic sense of a becoming according to a deepening of possibilities. The fact that we can experience shame at all, even from the perspective of sovereign pride, even as *homo sacer* and in the state of exception, even in a zone of putative indistinction, has to mean that we are in some sense already ahead of ourselves in a different direction—even if we cannot put our finger explicitly on the meaning of that direction.

Further, shame in its positive sense—not in the debilitating sense—is founded in a genuine self-loving. Loving does not presuppose a static "self," but is oriented toward the deepening of who we are in such a way that the "self" of self-loving cannot be determined in advance. Given this kind of experience, Agamben—for example—cannot be blamed for not saying what comes after the nation-state; nor is it at all inconsistent not to be able to specify in a concrete way what a post-nation-state order of power and civil life will look like. This is not only because it has not yet happened, but because it is peculiar to the nature of loving (and hence, persons) that persons are not able to be objectified, predictable, and fixed in a historical epoch or reducible to history, but in a qualified way, are at the source of history.

That shame emerges with a negative valence not only allows us to take stock, or gives us pause about a current or past course, but simultaneously provides us with a leading clue (or leading clues) to an orientation to who we are most deeply in an interpersonal nexus. Provided that this is not a debilitating shame, which can only occur through a distortion of loving and a disordered heart, shame can therefore orient us along these lines which may have not yet been historically relevant. As dynamically present, the self-revelatory character peculiar to shame cannot be reduced to the anticipation of shame, and in this sense cannot be prospective, even though it can and does function as self-critique for transformative activity. The very possibility of the experience of shame makes us susceptible, communally, to shamelessness. But this ultimately goes back to a diremptive experience in which we are thrown back on ourselves such that we cannot *not* respond from a positive distance to the shamefully qualified situation.

For the purposes of this analysis, I want to highlight some of the salient features concerning the meaning of person that we have discovered so far regarding shame—features that will also become relevant later. Shame as a diremptive experience points to the possibility of the person becoming alienated from him- or herself and others, and it shows how tenuous is this alienation because shame can so easily slip into a debilitating shame. But this diremptive experience also points to the fact that the person is fundamentally integral in and through such a dynamic tension in a twofold sense. This notion of being integral means both that the person is a unity of experience in the tension or disequilibrium of shame, and that a person can be brought back to him- or herself in a posture of integrity, as in line more deeply with who I am.

Further, shame shows how an attitude of active mastery cannot define the person; not only does that mastery falter in its very pursuit in the case of combating pride, but it can be called into question through an experience like shame. Moreover, self-givenness as self-revelation occurs in the presence of another, and this suggests not only that I am dependent upon another for my own self-givenness, but that who I am is intimately connected to others: I receive myself from others not only in social connections, but in a religious context. Shame points to the experience of receiving Myself in the sense of being given to myself, and in this way not self-grounding. Shame suggests that peculiar to the person is the fundamental experience of vocations. Yet, even in shame, which is an experience that befalls me and is an experience that I do not initiate, I am nevertheless, as person, creative—shame is not caused, not necessary, not instinctual, or pragmatic.

Finally, shame offers us a distinctive model of normativity that emerges interpersonally—through a love of other and genuine self-love—and a model of critique. This sense of critique is not a rationally motivated process, or one instigated simply by myself alone, but originates an interpersonal process in relation to who I am. In this case, a redirection is already implicit in the very experience of shame. From this perspective, even shamelessness might become a relevant sociopolitical category.

3

Guilt

Like pride and shame, guilt as an emotional experience is a kind of self-givenness that has interpersonal significance. Guilt, like shame, is able to call pride into question in the mode of a moral self-critique. This is not only due to the fact that, like shame, guilt is a diremptive experience, but more specifically because in guilt I am given to myself before another as accused through an experienced transgression and as responsive to another.

I begin this chapter on guilt with leading clues to the experience, settling on a set of distinctions proposed by Karl Jaspers that support a phenomenological analysis (1). I then examine the elemental structures of guilt (2), and describe guilt as a unique type of diremptive experience that calls pride into question (3). Because Martin Heidegger also gives us an important clue to the experience of an indictment or accusation of Myself before another, I undertake a critical appraisal of Heidegger's analysis of guilt within the context of vocational experience (4). Finally, as a transition to the meaning of repentance, I examine the interrelation of shame and guilt as similar yet distinctive ways of eliciting experiences that respond to pride by soliciting repentance (5).

Guilt in Historical Perspective: Leading Clues to a Phenomenology of Guilt

It is possible to approach the phenomenon of guilt from several historical perspectives. The fact that these perspectives tend to be so varied point not only to the richness of such an experience, but also to its experiential ambiguity. For example, the classical Greek sense of guilt, *hamartanein*, conveys missing one's mark as a lacking or flaw, and by implication, a debt (as in Homer), or even as an intentional violation of norms. We see a similar sense in the Hebrew *ashmah* (loosely, transgression, wrongdoing), which is connected to the sense of the Hebrew *het* (sin), as missing the mark. In a Western theological context, guilt and sin (or the guilt of sin) are related in the doctrine of Augustine, where for him—and often against the Pelagians—this guilt is the human person's removal from God, a removal that is rooted in the Fall, and is overcome only by grace (sacrament of baptism and death [and resurrection] of Christ).[1] In the modern period, Kant determined guilt legalistically as debt, whose "religious" formulation is sin as grounded in the exercise of freedom. "Sin" is moral evil as the transgression of the moral law by adopting sensuous nature fully as determinative of the will. Depending upon the circumstances, this exercise of freedom can yield either intentional or unintentional guilt.[2] Hegel, on the other hand, adopts a dialectical-historical view of guilt in which ethical self-consciousness, in its action, becomes aware of its particular character or its own finitude vis-à-vis the necessity of destiny, such that for it, self-consciousness, human (ethical) action becomes always guilty.[3]

To mention only these historical watermarks is not to depreciate the impact others have made to this topic of guilt in the history of philosophy, but only to glimpse the phenomenon, and to suggest that there is a long and varied consideration of this fundamental human experience in the Western philosophical tradition.

More recently, research on guilt has been trained on various cognitive dimensions of this experience. The more common tendencies are reflected in investigations that include research into the psychodynamics of guilt,[4] the human developmental stages associated with the acquisition of guilt,[5] the adaptive quality of guilt to situational circumstances,[6] the social effects of guilt,[7] and the cultural contexts in which guilt emerges.[8] It is beyond the scope of this chapter to take all of these currents into account, though some do surface in the following descriptions. My task is to examine and to describe the meaning-relations of this experience as they bear on the dimension of self-givenness. To this end, I begin by honing in on a set of distinctions that the German psychiatrist and existentialist philosopher Karl Jaspers makes. I do this to provide some initial clarity in the complexity of issues that surround this lived-experience, and to draw important distinctions concerning the multilayered senses of guilt.

Jaspers's explicit concern with the problem of guilt occurred within the context of postwar Germany, as the Germans were coming to grips not only with the general aftermath of the war, but with the atrocities of the Holocaust and the role that the everyday German citizen and the German intellectual, as well as the soldiers and officers of all stripes, played in these events.[9]

Pertaining to the question of German guilt, Jaspers provides helpful structural distinctions between four senses of guilt. The first is criminal guilt, which is susceptible to objective proof (like when laws are broken). The second sense of guilt is what he terms political guilt. This guilt involves the collective person of the state—the statespersons and citizenry—who are co-responsible for the deeds and consequences of the deeds. Here, the power and the will of the victor hold the province of jurisdiction. Third, Jaspers describes a moral guilt. In this instance, the individual is responsible as an individual for all that he or she does, including the acts that he or she carries out under political or military order. Finally, Jaspers distinguishes the previous three kinds of guilt from what he calls a metaphysical guilt. Metaphysical guilt is grounded in a solidarity among all persons that makes each co-responsible for every wrong and injustice in the world, especially for those things that are committed with the individual's knowledge and within his or her presence. Here, writes Jaspers, jurisdiction rests with God alone.[10]

While criminal and moral guilt do not accrue to the individual for crimes committed in the name of the state, political guilt does so in terms of the liability of all citizens for the acts and deeds committed by their state. Yet, while a judge or jury may decide criminal guilt, moral guilt can only be assumed "in a loving struggle" between persons in solidarity. Finally, metaphysical guilt takes place on the level at which we can address the phenomenon of survivor guilt. Jasper writes: "If I were present at the murder of others without risking my life to prevent it, I feel guilty in a way not adequately conceivable either legally, politically, or morally."[11]

Correlative to each essential distinction within the phenomenon of guilt, Jaspers cites the following possible repercussions. Corresponding to criminal guilt is punishment, which presupposes free will on the part of the guilty. Related to political guilt is (collective) liability, which may entail restrictions in the arena of power as well as economic reparations—whatever is imposed upon the offending party by those in power. Moral guilt finds its effect in the concrete world initially through insight garnered by penance and renewal. Finally, metaphysical guilt entails a personal transformation before the Holy, and it is here, writes Jasper, where pride is shattered and where arrogance becomes impossible.[12]

Structures of Guilt: Accomplishment, Accusation, Demand

Jaspers's analysis, which is more complex than the occasion warrants to reproduce here, helps to underscore several things. It gives us a way of viewing the difference between guilt as a judgment by oneself or others, and guilt as a moral and religious experience before others. Moreover, while guilt can be a legal concept, it is also a moral one.[13] Further, it provides us with sharp distinctions where the experience of guilt is concerned, and it draws out implications peculiar to each one of these distinctions. Finally, his work also affords us several leading clues to the phenomenon of guilt, allowing us to identify some of its basic structures and modes of givenness.[14]

For example, we can discern, first, an experience of something being accomplished that is given as mine (or ours). Second, we can detect a temporal structure in guilt that appears to have both past and future orientations and meanings. Third, we can observe how there is an experience of being accused or indicted by some other. Fourth, it suggests that guilt harbors an interpersonal or moral demand as an experienced transgression and responsivity toward another. Finally, it implies that there are varying degrees of guilt in terms of intensity. Let's leave the appraisal of Jaspers's admirable work, and turn to a phenomenological analysis of these aforementioned leading clues.

Accomplishment as mine. Colloquially speaking, when I experience guilt, I experience guilt about *something*. Let's examine this "something." Generally, this something can be a deed done or undone, a thought had or not had, but phenomenologically understood, this "something" is what we call an "accomplishment" which is in some way "mine." Let me explain.

Guilt as an emotional experience does not arise in relation to just any occurrence that is given in a neutral manner, then to be judged objectively. Rather, the "object" of guilt is given as an "accomplishment." By accomplishment, I do not mean that I necessarily achieve something consciously at a particular point of time, or that an action has been completed. Eugène Minkowski, the French psychiatrist and philosopher, writes for example that "the givens contained in the phenomenon of accomplishment form a framework for our knowledge concerning our tendencies, concerning the consequences and the goals of our activity."[15]

An accomplishment, therefore, is a constituted sense that, in order to become what it is for me, has to be "accepted" in such a way that it elucidates not just the moment, but my predispositions and orientations toward it. Accordingly, for an object-sense to be constituted it does not have to be a "product" of an ego; simply acquiescing, appropriating implicitly, taking for granted, and so forth counts in this phenomenological sense as an accomplishment. For this reason, I can experience guilt over something that I have not explicitly condoned or over something that has not yet taken place. Such an accomplishment can originate from the designs put into play to the steps taken necessary to realize something. For example, I could experience guilt over a theft in which I have only implicitly and unintentionally become complicit—even where I might volitionally not want to be complicit.[16] In the final analysis, such complicity means that it is in principle interpersonal, and it also implies that an accomplishment in our sense within the experience of guilt is prior to volition or judgment. Hence, for Dostoevsky, I participate in the guilt of others beyond myself in the moral universe, and I can share in this guilt even when it exceeds my subjective intention.[17]

Implicit in the experience of accomplishment is not only that it bears on me in some way, but that it is in some way "mine." The mineness of the accomplishment can be understood as a work, which, while remaining mine, is integrated into a larger overarching complex such that it can be trans-subjective. As mine, I "own" it and it affects me such that the guilt-event accrues in principle to my personal dispositions.[18] This gives us another clue to the experience of guilt, namely, it does not merely occur in relation to something that is done momentarily, but it can occur in relation to an orientation where this ongoing directedness is also an "accomplishment," an "acceptance." One could experience guilt about thoughts to the extent that those thoughts express an orientation toward a way of life, as somehow defining "who I am," or again qualifying myself in terms of this or that directedness. In this regard, I can already be involved in the accomplishment for which I am guilty, for it is a matter of being aligned with whom I experience myself "to be." I am this person who cheats or who will steal (without ever having done such and such before). I experience it as possible for me; if it is significant enough (in ways to be specified below), I can experience guilt. Thus, I participate personally, "creatively" in the accomplishment over which I experience guilt—pointing implicitly to a core of freedom which is not on the level of executing a self-knowledgeable willfulness.

If the accomplishment has to be given to me in some way as mine in order for me to experience guilt, then we could still ask whether it is possible to experience guilt about something that is not related to me at all. We might think here of "survivor's guilt" in which I have done nothing, in which I am not "at fault." For Jaspers, survivor's guilt is a mode of "metaphysical guilt" because it is expressive of a lack of solidarity with other human beings in the moral universe, whereby this solidarity is violated by my presence at a wrong or a crime.

The reason survior's guilt takes place in relation to something as "mine" is because in such guilt, I also experience that it was not enough that I cautiously approached a wrong or an evil. Jasper writes: "We did not go into the streets when our Jewish friends were led away; we did not scream until we too were destroyed. We preferred to stay alive, on the feeble, if correct ground that our death could not have helped at all. We are guilty of being alive. We know before God, which humbles us deeply." The weight of survival guilt as a mode of metaphysical guilt strikes me, as mine, so deeply that is hardly something to be taken lightly (for example, I cannot rightly say that I have "survivor's guilt" when I get a job when my friends don't—which might instead be some form of braggadocio), because survival guilt has no rational answers, going as it does to the mystery of human freedom and opening up to either the intrusion of grace or the possibility of non-sense.[19] Jasper sums up: "if it happens, and if I was there, and if I survive where the other is killed, I know from a voice within myself: I am guilty of being still alive."[20] In this way, "surviving" is experienced as my accomplishment—an accomplishment that I both want and don't want at the same time.[21]

Although the sense of mineness in the experience of guilt is more fundamental than being "at fault" (and here "at fault" is more than the experience belonging to me or me "owning it"), it nevertheless foreshadows the aspects of accusation, transgression, and responsivity, which intrinsically implicate me in what is accomplished. Put differently, I am the *subject of* guilt in the sense that I am *subjected to* guilt, and I am the subject of guilt in the sense that it concerns my accomplishment.

Temporalities of guilt. To say that guilt takes place in relation to something as accomplished that is somehow mine points to the temporal orientation of guilt as past. But this does not alone determine its temporal meaning. As we will see, it also has a futural significance to the extent that the "point" of guilt is repentance, the reparation of relations with others, setting things right, making things righteous.

One can experience guilt in relation to a past event or even about a thought concerning some futural event. But in both cases, guilt takes place in relation to something experienced as accomplished. In this case, the temporal orientation is the past, which is to say, guilt is qualified as a re-action to an accomplishment that has taken place. Accordingly, even if we could imagine an abnormal experience of time in which there were no experience of the future, or if the future were "shriveled up,"[22] it would still be possible to speak of an experience of guilt, especially in the sense of its temporal orientation. But this would not be the case if the past were completely lost and I only had futural possibilities. Thus, while there is "normally" (i.e., normal in the constitutive sense of concordance and optimality) an implied future in the experience of guilt, guilt could still be functional where the future is experienced as closed down. In a related manner, an overwhelming sense of guilt might itself close down the future. We could be so immersed in the pain of guilt (e.g., Marmeladov, the drunkard in Dostoevsky's *Crime and Punishment*) that we could be captivated by and in the past such that we would only be directed toward a self-punishment or self-loathing—which might really be insidious forms of pride.

Although guilt has a past meaning-orientation, it is distinctive from other modes of temporal consciousness whose significance is past, namely, retention and remembering. The elementary temporal perspective of the past is a "retention." When we examine the elementary past dimension, we have to keep in mind that it occurs within the "living present" as a whole. Unlike a present-directed experience and unlike a protention (primordial dimension of the future), a retention does not have an intentional structure. It simply "holds on" to the present, lingering as a "comet's tail" from the present. Further, it is not capable of being crossed out, disappointed, or modified in any way.[23] The retention is a dimension of every experience insofar as it retains the past as past and allows for a continuity of experience to unfold in a harmonious manner or for the experience to be ruptured (as in a disappointment) by a new present experience. This is due to the fact that the intrinsic adhesion of the retention onto the present sketches out a futural orientation or a style of becoming. This sketching out is a protention or a "prefiguring" of what is to come.

The retended present is a storehouse of the past that is implicitly affectively significant and that can in principle come into affective relief by being reawakened through, for example, a remembering. This is the transition to an active remembering and the explicit dimension of past-temporalization (a process that I have alluded to above in other contexts). By holding onto the affective significance of the present now as retended, the retended past can be reawakened through such a remembering or by a more or less prominent affective significance that evokes a remembering. If the retended present reaches a zero-point of affective force, it is no longer "given" in any way.[24] Accordingly, we can say that guilt's relation to the accomplished past is always affectively significant.

While the experience of guilt is oriented toward the past, it is oriented toward the past in ways that differ from a retention or a remembering. First, guilt's past directedness does not operate like a retention in the sense that guilt does not automatically attend the present in just any manner that it is given. Not everything that has taken place or that is experienced as past is an object of guilt. It may be the case that something is retained with the emotional quality of guilt as it is retained, but this need not be the case. Or it could happen that something has taken place, is retained, and once it is brought to my awareness, I experience guilt about the past—even if it does not belong to my individual past, that is, in the cases of collective guilt or intergenerational guilt. So, obviously, something can be retained or remembered, yet not be a matter of guilt.

Moreover, although retention unfolds without the active participation of the ego, and a remembering takes place on a more active conscious level, retention and remembering both bear on the epistemic qualities of the experience and concern, however modestly, the acquisition of knowledge. In contrast, guilt transpires in a personal manner such that what is at issue in the experience is not an acquisition of the knowledge of something (though I may learn something about myself), but here bears the moral tenor of an accusation and transgression vis-à-vis another. When I write of the moral tenor here, I do not mean that the individual has something like an ethical duty to feel guilty; rather, the experience of guilt bears on the very meaning of the person and the interpersonal nexus.

Moreover, a retention will retain the affective sense of the experience no matter what it is, positive or negative (whether it is the pain from a ruptured tendon or the joy at the sight of a friend). An active remembering may recall the former pain, but it may issue in a new sorrow; or again, a remembering might evoke a new original laughter (like when I recall a joke that I did not completely get before), or when I remember a happy gathering and am pleased about it again through the remembering. By contrast, guilt is *always given with a negative emotional valence,* which may be accompanied, say, by a terrible unpleasantness, sorrow, grief, and so on, even *in the new experience of guilt.*

In relation to remembering that re-signifies the past, guilt is an emotional act oriented toward the past that makes an original contribution. This negative experience characteristic of guilt is "original" in the guilt and not necessarily contained in the past experience. For example, I may have accidentally dented the door in the car next to me in the parking lot, and never experienced any kind of negative (or even positive) emotion; but if guilt arises in relation to this occurrence, the latter will be qualified in the guilt experience such that the event achieves a new kind of emotional valence, a negative one, *which is peculiar to the guilt experience.*

Further, unlike a retention, guilt does not call forth a style of coherent becoming (like a guilty future way of being). Not only does guilt not forecast a new present or provide continuity with the present, the experience of guilt is given as a *rupture of a style.* I mean by this that the experience of guilt, when it arises, intervenes in the "natural" unfolding of events and calls into question what occurred or (in some cases) what may occur. (I will take this up below under "diremption.") The retention-present ensemble has a futural significance (they sketch out a futural orientation), but guilt does not forecast a future on the basis of guilt. It does not move in the same flow of the guilt event, anticipating more of the same, but calls for a self-critique, and thus foreshadows what goes against the grain of guilt (in the direction, say, of atonement or repentance).

If we move to a more "active" temporal level, we can see similarities between remembering and guilt. For example, in a remembering, the present may explicitly or implicitly call forth another remembering without my wanting to remember it; it may simply be awakened through affective association. In addition, I may try to rid myself of some instances of remembering, for example, if the memory of an event were too painful. Likewise, a present experience may be the catalyst of a guilt experience, or I may also try to rid myself of a guilty feeling. But unlike other instances of remembering, guilt is not a volitional act in the sense that I cannot actively try to experience guilt or make a past the object of guilt like I can volitionally remember (or try to remember) something. So, in distinction to the way I might struggle to remember the name of a film that I saw, one that reminds me of the film I am seeing now, guilt *comes upon me*, and it does so in such a way that I may still experience guilt while *I try* not to feel guilty.

Finally, while remembering will always have a specific object (even if that object is vague or misremembered), guilt can have both a specific "object" and a more indeterminate dimension in which I am unable to specify the object. And as we will see below, guilt has a radically *personal* dimension that is linked to the experience of vocation, and in this way, the matter of guilt cannot be equated with an object. It is interesting to note in this regard that I may still experience guilt even though I can no longer remember or have any memory of that which I am guilty. For example, I may have repressed a painful event, but am still aware of it on some level and so feel guilty; and indeed, my guilt could be the source of the repression of the memory. I am not able to treat psychoanalytic theories of guilt here, but only want to note this phenomenon in order to draw out the temporal-emotional significance of guilt which cannot be reduced to temporal significance of an act of remembering, while nonetheless recognizing the past temporal quality of guilt.

While the temporal orientation of guilt is directed toward the past, the temporal meaning of guilt is not necessarily located there. This will become clearer below when we consider the dimension of otherness in guilt. We can say here, however, that as accused, I am oriented toward the past; the experiences of transgression, and especially that of responsivity—which are profoundly interpersonal—as well as the spur to repentance, connect the meaning of guilt to the future. They do so because implicit in these experiences is the reparation of relations with others and a turning toward a "new" or "renewed" sense of Myself. It is precisely this interpersonal dimension that ushers in the futural significance of guilt.

Accusation. The experience of guilt entails the experience of being accused or indicted. The experience of accusation may concern some deed done or left undone, something experienced as an "accomplishment" on my part for which I am responsible. In order to have the experience of an accusation, it has to come from "somewhere," from some "other"; and it has to be experienced as a transgression of some kind (of a norm, law, personal boundary, interpersonal expectation, etc.). Ultimately, this goes in tandem with its interpersonal quality.

The accusation, of course, may or may not correspond directly to an actual happening, and the accusation is not sufficient for an experience of guilt, but it is a necessary component. For example, I may be (falsely) accused by my siblings of not having tended to my parents in their old age. To experience something as "falsely accused" means that while someone suspects me of a misdeed, it is unwarranted or wrongheaded. Still, to the extent to which I feel I could have done more (even if this is not what my siblings meant), I will feel accused. I can even feel guilty that I do not feel guilty (if, for instance, feeling guilty is part of what it means for me to be a good person).

As noted, an accusation comes from some "other," even if that other remains an indeterminate source or is "myself." For example, my cycling partner may accuse me of bumping him at the finish of a sprint, or I accuse myself for having treated my cycling friend poorly. But I can also feel accused without any determinate source or for any determinate deed. I can feel accused for a vague something and by some vague party (even though I can find nothing wrong)—as Joseph K in Kafka's *The Trial*. I become the subject of accusation in the double sense of the expression: I can be accused by another and am the terminus of the accusation; or I can accuse myself without being accused by another, and in a certain twist, internalize the accusation. Even if I somehow know objectively that I am not at fault, I can still experience guilt to the extent that I discover myself complicit in some way. The accusation puts me in the accusative: I am thrown back on *myself*. In being thrown back on myself in the accusative by being accused, I am stopped in my tracks; this goes against the normal flow, for example, when I am not experiencing guilt. Thus, the accusation in guilt *arrests* me, and it is precisely this experience of being arrested in guilt through an accusation that enables me potentially to get stuck in the past (as in the case of Dostoevsky's Marmeladov). Merely being arrested in the past through an accusation (real or imagined) is something that I just cannot get over provided I remain only in guilt.

For this reason, being placed in the accusative in guilt is not a mere fault-finding or finger-pointing; it weighs me down and I feel burdened by the accomplishment in guilt, *and* burdened by the guilt. This is expressed bodily generally as eyes averting the accuser (real or imagined), a casting stolen glances, a heaviness of body, tightening of shoulders and neck, flinching movements, and nervousness of gestures. Of course, I can live under the pressure of this guilt without addressing it explicitly. It may play itself out in all sorts of ways—as something to be dismissed, as a mental preoccupation, as an emotional thorn, as a physiological ailment. But if it is experienced as guilt, I will be thrown back on myself in the accusative, as accused.

By whom am I accused? It can be a vague other, a personal other, a community, an anonymous other. Or it can be an accusation that arises from myself, most fully as "Myself" who receives myself from another. Describing the meaning of this "myself" leads me in a later section of this chapter to a more explicit discussion of the vocational Myself. Before I explicate the latter, let me pick up on the former point concerning being affected, arrested, and burdened in guilt. I am arrested, accused, burdened in guilt because my deed that is accomplished as mine takes place before another as a transgression such that in the transgression, I experience the violation of a demand issuing from the other. It is to the question of the moral demand which in guilt ushers in the experience of transgression and responsivity, to which I now turn.

Moral demand, transgression, and responsivity. The interpersonal quality of the accomplishment, which comes to me as an accusation, gives me to myself as accused. In guilt, however, I do not merely feel accused; rather, I experience an indictment via a transgression of another, and this is lived as a violation of a moral demand.[25] I have not merely done something wrong before another in a neutral manner, but I have violated another in some regard. To experience something as a *transgression* means that the event, my accomplishment, is given not as an occurrence that simply happens, perhaps something that we all witness, or that can eventually be explained away. The betrayal, the offense, the violation of a norm, and so on, is something in which I am caught up in an intimate manner: I have transgressed such that I am placed in a position of responsivity with regard to another in light of this transgression. This is more than attributing responsibility (by/to self or others) when guilt follows upon a transgression.[26] Following Waldenfels, responsivity is a fundamental trait of all discourse and all doing. Here, being responsive means that I am immediately poised for a response whether or not I actually respond, positively or negatively, or whether I take responsibility for it or not.[27] Transgression and responsivity take place from a "moral demand," which issues from another, even if—as we will see—it can never be fulfilled.

Implicit in the experience of transgression as placed before another is the experience of being situated as responsive regardless of whether I can be adequate in a response. The fact that I can be manipulative in guilt (for example, by making others feel guilty to get them to do what I want them to do, to strengthen a relationship, or to redistribute emotional distress)[28] only presupposes this basic structure. It remains to clarify the quality of this demand. To do this, allow me to make a distinction between different kinds of demands and the possibility of their "fulfillments" according to the kind of givenness at stake. First, I will consider the epistemic demand, then the aesthetic demand, and finally, the moral demand.

Epistemic demand. By an epistemic demand, I mean the kind of practical or knowledge-based demand that we experience from perceptual as well as eidetic objects. For example, Husserl has described the way in which the object or the aspect of an object "calls forth" or exercises an affective allure on the perceiver in order to be constituted (or intended) in this way or that, depending on its manner of givenness. A ladder might come into affective relief as it gives itself as something to be climbed upon. Depending on the context of a project, it might solicit a tactile exploration, even a stepping on the rungs to see if they support my weight. In general, we have an epistemic (and a practical) acquisition. The most general epistemic demand is for something to be grasped in practical and thematic contexts of interests. Something is understood when it becomes a lasting acquisition in knowledge and practice, which enriches the sense of the object.[29]

Alfred North Whitehead also understood eidetic objects to exercise a demand in the sense of becoming a "lure" for feeling and the creative unfolding of reality. For example, a proposition is a lure for x to be taken as P, where the fulfillment of the proposition is its truth. However, where the "adventures of ideas" are concerned, creative emergence depends as well on false propositions (not being fulfilled) because they introduce novelty into the world.[30]

We understand by fulfillment the givenness of the object (or aspect of the object) in the way in which it is/was intended. If the ladder is given as ladder and as something to be climbed, and if the ladder continues to give itself in the manner "forecasted" by the protention and/or expectation; if it further supports my weight and allows me to climb in the manner according to the intention or solicitation, then the current perception is fulfilled by the new givenness. If the ladder is missing rungs, if the rungs break when I begin my ascent, then the perception is "unfulfilled" (in the manner of "being otherwise," "doubt," "negation," or "disappointment").

What arrives in an experience is fulfilled when it is given in the manner in which it is intended (or conforms to how it is expected). The epistemic demand is unfulfilled (i.e., modalized) when the object is given in a manner that does not conform to the way in which it was intended. While there is a basic "constitutive duet" noetically/noematically, while the demand is a shared demand, the demand can still be issued by the "perceiver." The non-fulfillment here is on the side of the object. Likewise, a proposition is unfulfilled when—according to Whitehead—the eternal object or the idea does not ingress in the actual occasion as "proposed," so that the idea becomes actualized differently in another actual occasion or not at all. While the epistemic demand which is fulfilled might lead to a confirmation of knowledge or an enrichment of knowledge; while the non-fulfillment of an epistemic demand might yield a "disappointment," "falsehood," or even issue in a new form of knowledge not anticipated, we do not speak of guilt in this regard.

Aesthetic demand. We can also speak of an aesthetic demand, which is qualitatively distinct from an epistemic demand. Here we are not taking "aesthetic" in the sense of general bodily sensibility, but in the sense of a "work," which may include "art work." For example, a painting may exercise a demand of being seen from this or that angle in order "to work," such that we are obliged to turn our heads according to it and to adjust our perspective to accommodate it. A performance like a dance may demand being seen in a certain way or participated in to be an optimal performance. What works as street theater may not work on the stage.

Whereas in the case of an epistemic demand, there seems to be more control on the part of the "subject" who explores, investigates, and in general follows out the leads provided by the object, in the case of an aesthetic demand, the subject is all the more enlisted to conform to the work in order for the object to be given optimally, as its "true" self; the weight of the demand falls more on the side of the work, and the obligatory fulfillment on the side of the "subject."

A work (of art) is dependent upon a context—be that context interpersonal, intercorporeal, historical, cultural—in order to make sense or to create its own audience. A piece of music "has to be" played in such and such a way, or else it (the work) does not "work"—though there is flexibility, since it is conceivable that a classical piece might work better arranged as rap for a particular time or audience. Furthermore, a work (a piece of glass, marks on a canvas, a dance) can be taken as more than functional and as an artwork in a particular homeworld or at a particular historical epoch, but might not have that same sense (or exert the same aesthetic demands) in an alienworld or at a different time. If it is altogether too strange, it may not make a demand in any aesthetic sense. Or conversely, what might have been a mere utensil can itself become a piece of art. The ladder which no longer functions as such can still exercise a demand on us, but if it does, then it probably does so aesthetically (as an antique, a style of woodworking, its unique placement, etc.—all while its functionality is called into question).

As intimated above, the fulfillment of an aesthetic demand places the onus of fulfillment more on us. An aesthetic demand requires us to conform to its givenness and not to bend the work to conform to our outlook. We tilt our head "according to" the painting; we place ourselves at an "optimal" distance *to it;* we play the piece of music within the range of a proper tempo. If these demands are not met minimally, the work may not give itself as such.

We distinguished between an epistemic and an aesthetic demand. In the first instance, we can speak of an "allure" or "solicitation" from the side of the object, or as a lure of a proposition. There is a constitutive duet and a co-relativity between the subjective and objective vectors of the relation. In the second instance, we can characterize the demand as a "contextual" one. That is, the fulfillment and non-fulfillment depend in part on the context and in part on our conforming to the givenness of the aesthetic object demanded by it. Let us now consider the moral demand.

Moral demand. By a moral demand, I mean a demand that occurs within an interpersonal framework. It is here that we can properly speak of moral transgression and responsivity in guilt. It is certainly possible to describe demands (as we have sketched above) or what Al Lingis has called "imperatives" on all levels of experience.[31] We have experiences of demands issuing from elemental things, the Earth as ground, the charge of erotic demands, and demands issuing from animals other than human, and so on. Accordingly, we as human persons can experience guilt in relation to these imperatives which exert their pulls on us. My point is simply that guilt is a human personal experience, and within the moral sphere, it does not issue out of the respect of a law, but from another such that the experience of transgression and responsivity take on a unique moral depth. Thus, I do not mean by "moral" a kind of behavior that conforms to preset norms and ethical theories, nor do I reduce all kinds of demands in human experience to the moral demand.

One may object that I can immediately experience a demand that issues from a standard (of behavior) or a norm.[32] But all norms, according to Max Scheler, have their foundation in the value of person as this person is given ultimately in loving. By this he means that there can be no norm of duty (Kant) without a person who posits it, no rightness of a norm of duty without my grasping the essential goodness of the person who holds it, as well as my ability to see for myself what is good, even if it is given in an exemplary manner in the other. Accordingly, there can be no "reverence" for a norm or moral law that is not founded in a love for the person who functions as exemplary of that norm or normative actions. If a norm functions as a demand in guilt, it is because it has a personal basis.[33]

We can see how this dynamic is functional even in the more superficial case of feeling guilty over something like breaking a diet. If I break my diet, and if I feel guilty, I do not feel guilty because I violated the guidelines of the book or the schedule outlined in the training manual (I may have modified it to fit my goals and needs), but because I did not live up to someone to whom I made a promise, and this includes myself (or Myself) as another. Even if it is just "myself" who made the promise or resolution (to myself), in order to experience guilt, I have to be more than myself, other than myself. For if I were reduced simply to myself in a simple identity, and if the norm or demand did not issue from myself as somehow more than this, I could simply change any rule, any commitment with no consequence. "I made the rule, but I am going to change it." Of course, we can do this any time. But in order for guilt to be operative, something more has to be in play, and this is the violation of a "demand" that issues from another and to whom I am responsive. Similarly, I would only feel guilty about a murder if the act is experienced as a transgression or violation of a demand issuing from another: "Thou shalt not murder," signified, as Emmanuel Levinas writes, in the face of the Other.[34] If I do not have this kind of experience, I will not feel guilty, even if the deed violates social norms, and even if I am fully cognitive of the fact that it violates norms or accepted standards of behavior.

This does not mean that "the code" or some other value cannot take on more significance as demand than the person. We often get the image in film noir of the hit man who has no qualms about this murder, but protects the weak, the injured, or animals (as in Philip Raven/Alan Ladd in Frank Tuttle's *This Gun for Hire*) or stops short of the hit not because of the person, but because of something like the value of music (as in Claude/Vince Edwards in Irving Lerner's *Murder by Contract*). My point is that the experience of guilt issues from a transgression of a moral demand, experienced directly as personal, or more indirectly as violating an interpersonal bond, even if objectively this amounts to the failure of protecting a pet cat. This is why Taylor is correct in her criticism of Rawls that in experiencing guilt, I experience harming another, even though I may never experience an infringement of a principle of right.[35]

It is possible to consider both the non-fulfillment and fulfillment of epistemic and aesthetic demands. But while a non-fulfillment of a moral demand can be lived as a transgression and revealed in guilt, moral demands fall out of the purview of fulfillment (let alone the problem of ever knowing how or when we fulfilled such a demand).[36] Further, to assume that we could determine the fulfillment of a moral demand would ultimately place the other person under our control. This would be an expression of pride, which might be revealed in a patronizing attitude. But if this were the case, then guilt could never function as it essentially does, namely, as a self-critique and check on pride.

Let's imagine that I feel guilty about the people I see who are hungry or homeless at Thanksgiving. My experiencing guilt has not only placed me as complicit in their situation (an accomplishment that is mine); I not only experience myself as somehow accused, but I live this accomplishment/accusation as a transgression on my part for which I am responsive and can be responsible. Let's imagine, further, that I respond by helping serve food to the homeless at a shelter. Now, I might do this just to be with these people, and in the style of Mother Teresa, comfort the afflicted without any instrumental pretension to solving their problems.

But if I somehow see myself engaged in a kind of "technology of service" as if I could respond adequately on the level of a moral demand; if I am doing this not as a response to the infinite demand issuing from the personal other, but to placate or mollify my guilt; if now I feel good about what I have done, now feel good about myself; or worse, if I expect the "homeless" now to be appreciative for what I have done; if all of this should indicate for me that I have somehow fulfilled the demand, then in effect I try to encompass an infinite movement with a finite response: I try to handle a spiritual appeal with instrumentality, I try to subsume the absolute value of the other person under relative deeds, and ultimately vault myself above them in order to control their response. It might just be an attempt to shut down the moral demand from the other by some action on our part. Accordingly, Martin Buber writes that acknowledgment of guilt and reconciliation with the one or ones offended is only valid if it is done, not out a premeditated resolution, but rather in the *non-arbitrary* working of the existence I have achieved, as I work with another to overcome the consequences of my guilty action.[37]

This is why the attempt to fulfill such a moral demand (and the supposition that I have fulfilled it) would be at root a form of pride. Instead, the deeper I go in such a response toward a non-arbitrary reconciliation with another, the more I might be revealed as even more guilty! Responding to a moral demand is not the fulfillment of a demand, but it is a being placed before another as always having to respond in some manner, of responding so as not to ignore, such that it is only revealed after the fact as non-fulfillment. Hence, we can say that guilt reveals me as accused by another in relationship to which the demand is non-fulfillable.

Degrees of guilt. While this has been implied throughout, it is worth noting that the experience of guilt admits of degrees. I am burdened with guilt, and it weighs upon me in qualitatively distinct ways depending upon the experienced demand.[38] Certainly, we can distinguish between, say, a moral and a metaphysical guilt—to employ Jaspers's descriptions. But even within each mode of guilt, guilt can be given with different gradations of weightiness and levity. The demand placed on me will determine the burden of the guilt. For example, feeling guilty about breaking a diet will probably not weigh upon me in the same way and with the same intensity as might be the case if I go on a gambling binge and lose the paycheck I had to support my family.

Here, I experience the demand issuing from the others more radically than my personal goals of going on a diet. Of course, the intensity is not determined by the "what" of the guilt. It is altogether possible to be weighed down more by the guilt of breaking my diet than by not being able to feed my family. This depends upon what Scheler would call the "order of the heart" and the implicit individual or collective value-orientation. But to maintain that guilt admits of degrees is not to follow Ricoeur's unsubstantiated claim that guilt is quantitative whereas sin is qualitative (it either is or is not).[39] This also goes to his misleading assertion that sin is ontological and collective (suggesting a "realism" of sin) whereas guilt is subjective and individual (suggesting a "phenomenalism" of guilt).[40]

What this discussion of guilt as transgressive experience implies, including guilt as a moral demand and its degrees of weightiness, is that such an experience incites both a reparation of relations with others—since the guilty deed is always more than an infringement of a right, but instead a violation of the interpersonal nexus—and a repentance of the deed, which when it goes to the core, entails the whole of the person (as we will see below). For now, I turn to the way in which guilt is a kind of diremptive experience such that pride can be called into question.

Guilt as a Diremptive Experience and as Calling Pride into Question

It is now that we can consider how guilt is a diremptive experience such that it can call pride into question. Let us recall that a diremptive experience is that experience in which I am at once identified with a more basic orientation—an internal coherence—and a challenge to that internal coherence, a challenge that deviates from it, contrasts with it, but is not sufficient to be its own independent orientation. In this way, there is a unity in difference of orientations, one against which the other is measured such that I am given to myself by being thrown back on myself. Both embarrassment and shame were characterized as kinds of diremptive experiences, but shame was depicted as radically self-revelatory because it concerns becoming who I *am*.

Guilt is also a diremptive experience because it is an accomplishment which is given as mine, and is highlighted in relation to my "better" self, put into relief through transgression. Guilt does not just touch me, it burdens me as it bears on my existence. If the accomplishment in our phenomenological sense were just a mere happening; if I only experienced the event as ultimately concordant with myself (if there were not a diremption), I would not be at odds with Myself in this way. Instead, it is this accusation and experience of transgression that throws me back on myself. Guilt comes upon me, even if and when I try not to feel guilty.

Being thrown back on myself in the accusative in the experience of guilt is a disruption of the normal, unchecked flow of experience. It arrests this normal flow, even if I continue in the same guilt-ridden action. Guilt is also an occasion for critique, a motivated self-critique before and from another. But it is more than a critique of the natural epistemic attitude, it is a critique of what we have called a "subjective" attitude. In this respect, guilt is another kind of diremptive experience that can call pride into question. In Taylor's language, which is not entirely my own, guilt would not be an emotion of "self-assessment," if guilt were merely the thought that I had harmed another.[41] We can accept Taylor's assertion because guilt is more than the cognition of an injury inflicted upon another, and is experienced as more than a fault-finding with myself. However, for us, it is most basically a diremptive experience through which we are given to ourselves in the accusative, and therefore to a self-critique. Only at higher levels do we have the self-givenness as self-appraisal or self-assessment, which for its part may or may not be rooted in a guilt experience.[42]

Let's examine the diremptive and critical character of guilt more precisely. Let's say that I have maligned another through gossip. I thought I was justified in this slander because I believed myself to be correct about what I said. After I discover that I was wrong, I might feel guilty. To the extent that I do feel guilty, I am thrown back on myself, as unjustified, weighed down by having injured another, as having acted badly toward another (which may have come into relief only because I discover now that I was mistaken). Guilt discloses me to myself through the deed, even if it is a general question like, "What have I done?" I might want to know why I feel accused, but once I experience guilt, I have taken in the accusation, and this can start a process of self-examination and self-critique. At least for that moment in guilt, I am not in the "normal" subjective flow that sustains pride. Guilt reveals me to myself as being "off," as having to set things right with another, and implicitly reorienting myself.

This can be seen in the possible courses of responsiveness. One recourse to the above is that I could set about to address the wrong the best I can through apologies, retractions, reparations, and atonement. Here the orientation is toward the other who was offended. Another possibility is that I apologize, and so on, because I cannot bear the guilt and because I want to feel better about myself. Now that I apologize, I no longer feel the burden of guilt; I can have a good conscience and feel good about myself. Whatever the case may be, these processes reveal me to myself as indebted to another, as having to be connected with another, as responsive to another, as owing another and as having to repair myself in relation to him or her. The point is that this interpersonal realization runs directly counter to the occlusion of otherness that we find in pride. It reveals me as owing to another, and in this way as interpersonal. The experience of accusation and transgression, which discloses me to myself critically as interpersonal, also points us toward reconciliation with others, and thus implicitly becomes a check to pride. Even if I just wanted to make myself feel better by doing something that quells guilt, it shows (1) that guilt has this direptive character and (2) that it calls pride into question. The fact that I would try to repair myself as it were, and live back in the flow of myself reveals this inherent quality of guilt as being oriented interpersonally, and whose temporal meaning is toward a new future—even if the temporal orientation of guilt is the past. I am revealed to myself as someone who has done wrong (or not done right), is responsible for it and to another. In this way, guilt is attuned to a dimension of transcendence.

The general significance of the "rupture" quality of guilt, then, is to allow the individual to refigure the personal style of unfolding, to create a new world with others, precisely not in the mode that constituted the "object" of guilt in the first place. Yet it does not *cause* a change. I can feel guilty about cheating another in a business venture, and still cheat her out of her savings, all the while feeling guilty about it. On the other hand, even though "I" am not the origin of guilt in the sense of making a self-conscious choice, to feel guilty is to be responsible for the guilt in a positive sense, since I must be oriented in the direptive experience in such a way that I could still experience guilt, and to this extent, it is a creative, spontaneous qualification of who I am.

Let me be clear, however: the critical function of guilt is not something that I can produce voluntarily, as if the origin of guilt could be executed as a matter of will. (Even if I want to feel guilty, I would be after that negative accusatory experience.) Guilt can only befall me in the accusative before another. For example, a mere reflection does constitute a break in our immediate consciousness of the world, and this break need not be self-critical or question the meaning of the past or course of current events. With guilt, however, there is always a negative valence that accompanies the experience, striking me with respect to what I have accomplished before another. So, while a radical reflection or hyper-reflection as described by Merleau-Ponty or Husserl might constitute a critical reflection in relation to our consciousness of the world and our natural (and naturalistic reflections on) experience, in principle, the radical reflection might "only" rest at observing or describing the experience, becoming aware of it, and in this sense being critical with respect to the constitution of meaning. By not going along in the direction of the natural, "normal" flow of world-constitution, it can hold the positing of being in abeyance in order to see *how* that very meaning is constituted and how we participate in that very meaning-emergence. Guilt, however, is morally nuanced because it concerns our personal bearing in relation to others, reconstituting the meaning of that interpersonal nexus.

I asked above, "By whom am I accused? Before whom do I stand indicted" in the experience of guilt? If we refrain from arbitrarily delimiting the reference outlined in guilt—like we might in pride—one response is that it points to Myself. But this Myself is received, in the accusative, as interpersonal. The "from whom," "before whom," "by whom" of this experience can remain vague, a mystery, an unknown or ineffable presence, what Rudolf Otto would call a *mysterium tremendum*.[43] But when it is experienced in the dynamic of repentance, it is qualified as loving, and as a personal presence that calls forth Myself in a vocational sense. In the next section, I explicate Martin Heidegger's notion of guilt. I do this not because he successfully articulates the vocational dimension of Myself or the non-self-grounding character of the religious dimension in it. On the contrary, he misses it. Yet he broaches the problematic through the experience of guilt, and in this way gives us a deeper leading clue to it.

Guilt and the Vocational "Myself"

These considerations of guilt as a diremptive experience that throws me back on myself and puts me in tension with myself before another, as the experience of being accused and of transgression, of being responsive to another and as the calling into question of pride—all this ultimately situates the problem of guilt in the context of a vocational self, or what I call the "Myself." Why? Because when I approach the other in a non-arbitrary (non-prideful) manner, I become uniquely who I am with others in the moral universe.

I explicate the phenomenon of guilt in relation to this vocational Myself in two stages. These two stages can be understood as two movements within the global phenomenon of guilt. The first concerns guilt before Myself, as an inter-Personal phenomenon, that is, as I am given to myself from another (which can be grasped in a personal register as Holy, since it is grounded in the movement of loving). The second concerns a guilt before others, interpersonally, which is intimately but irreducibly related to the former. To help get at this dimension of guilt, I deviate slightly from the style of exposition in other chapters of this work by turning first to an explication, namely, of Martin Heidegger's notion of guilt. I do this because his own phenomenological analyses serve the descriptions of guilt on this level, and help to bring the vocational signification of guilt into relief.

I begin by examining the problem of guilt as portrayed in Heidegger's treatment of Dasein's "guiltiness." I do this in three parts: I explicate the notion of guilt in Heidegger's existential and ontological Dasein-analyses; I examine critically Heidegger's notion of guilt as it pertains to the modal determination of Dasein; I relate guilt more concretely to the concrete character of the person with respect to the experience of vocation.

Dasein and guilt. Heidegger determines both ontic (or existentiell) and ontological senses of guilt. He does this, methodologically, by taking up everyday understandings of guilt, similar to what we have considered above, to the extent that they function as leading clues to the deeper meanings of guilt. He maintains that even though such ordinary understandings can be misleading, the ontological meanings can still become intelligible through them; for the very ways in which the former miss the phenomena, he contends, can still say something about the very experiences they conceal, and in this way are revelatory.[44]

Heidegger therefore admits that there are many kinds of guilt that can be adduced (e.g., in psychology, sociology, ethics, jurisprudence). But if we were to keep to them merely, we would tend to restrict the very disclosive range of the phenomenon. Further, by expecting something strictly "useful" to come out of a conscience and guilt, by thinking that they are going to tell us about what action is possible, available, or calculable; or, alternately, by taking guilt as merely getting in the way of action (and in this sense, being not useful, or as inhibiting conduct), we would miss the positive content of primordial guilt.[45]

GUILT

Before examining the primordial sense of guilt for Heidegger, let's identify the leading clue that arises in ordinary experience for Heidegger. This clue in the ordinary experience of guilt (and the conscience through which guilt emerges) is the character of the "not." In everyday experience, the "not" shows up in the reproofs like "I should not have done that," in the self-accusations for the deed left undone, in the sense of lack or failure on my part, and in the negative tonal quality and emerges in the experience—what we have referred to above as the emotion's "negative valence." Further, in our ordinary understanding, the "not" of guilt is related to an indebtedness or to a being responsible for something that arises through a deed, a willing, or an omission; it is expressed through warning kinds of conscience.[46] In this way, the "not" of guilt might be deemed "useful" to the extent it can tell us what action is or is not beneficial according to moral precepts.[47]

"Dasein," let us recall, is Heidegger's term for the human being inasmuch as the human being *exists as* the place of "Being." The expression "Dasein" means not only "existence" in colloquial German, but etymologically it refers to the human being as the "there" (or "here") of Being: Da-Sein. Thus, Dasein is a *mode* of Being as the distinctive disclosure or opening of Being.

The negative valence evident in guilt, which is expressed by the "not," however, points more deeply in Heidegger's existential interpretation to the "not" at the basis of Dasein's being; it points to a fundamental nullity (*Nichtigkeit*).[48] This nullity does not designate the absence of some present object or the lack of something being at my disposal; rather than a contingent negative, this "not" is constitutive of Dasein's very Being. More specifically, the nullity belongs to the meaning of the thrownness (*Geworfenheit*) of Dasein. Dasein is not the cause of itself. In terms that convey this sense of nullity through thrownness, we could say that this "not" is revealed as Dasein *not*-being-self-grounding.

Existentially, Dasein's guilt arises in part through its finitude, which is expressive of its thrownness. Dasein as thrown is given over to itself as able-to-be, as able to make something of itself, as it were. It takes over its ability-to-be and to-become (*Seinkönnen*) by "projecting itself upon possibilities." Dasein, therefore, has been released from itself, but also *to itself*, so that it can take itself over authentically. Indeed, Dasein is thrown insofar as it projects itself upon possibilities into which it has been thrown. But existing as thrown, Dasein lags behind its possibilities. The weight of being this thrown basis manifests itself in Dasein's mood or attunement, in this case, revealing Dasein to itself as guilty.

As a being that is thrown, Dasein understands itself in terms of its possibilities; as an ability-to-be, Dasein orients itself in an open future. But this implies that by going down this or that path, selectively, it necessarily excludes other ways, since it cannot pursue them all. The constitutive element for the structure of nullity resides in Dasein's ability-to-be as being-free for its possibilities. This freedom exists therefore only in being able to live out one possibility, while having to forego the others.[49] Dasein as a thrown projection is not able to get behind itself to master its own "nullity," and is not able to become everything. Such a formal, existential interpretation yields Heidegger's assessment that *"Dasein as such is guilty."* Dasein is basically guilty because it cannot do everything; the human being who is "there" has to neglect some possibilities because it selects others.

This interpretation is *existential* because it concerns Dasein's freedom and the possibilities it has before it on the basis of its thrownness; it bears on Dasein's finitude which here surfaces as not being the ground of itself and as the inability to take up all possibilities; even though it is an ability-to-be, it cannot be everything. The interpretation remains *formal* for Heidegger because it discerns a structure of existence that bears on every particular Dasein, universally. It only says that there are possibilities, and that there is a restrictive freedom; while it assesses Dasein's finitude, it does not investigate *how* Dasein is in relation to other modes of being and more specifically, it does not question the meaning of its own mode of being.

But if this existential interpretation remains too ordinary, and if it suffers from formality, it does not obviate a more profound interpretation. For Heidegger, it presses us toward an inquiry into the ontological meaning of nullity, a nullity that discloses Dasein as more fundamentally guilty. To be brief, this dimension concerns Dasein as a mode of Being.[50] Da-Sein is Being-*there*. As a human being in the mode of the "there" (or "here")—as disclosive of Being—it is profoundly different from things, objects, or tools—all of which have a different mode of Being. Dasein's problem is that it forgets who it is as "there" and conflates its own mode Being (its thereness as disclosive of Being) with other modes of Being (being of things, objects, tools), and in this way loses itself. It loses itself in the anonymity of Being called *"das Man"* (the "one" or the "they").

Fundamentally, *das Man* signals an anonymity of Being, not an anonymity of individuals in a mass; the latter is only a derivative consequence of the former. One way Heidegger suggests that Dasein is called forth from this ontological anonymity is through "anxiety." Anxiety discloses Dasein in its unique individuation as Da; Dasein is *unique—einzig*—in relation to things and tools, and is able to identify itself through a first-person responsible reclamation of being *there*.[51] Yet Dasein still has to take over this nullity at the core of its Being. It has to want to be guilty.

Ontological guilt for Heidegger, then, is the essential being guilty, even if or perhaps precisely because it remains for the most part undisclosed and shut down by Dasein's fallenness.[52] The call of conscience is not an arbiter or admonisher for Heidegger; it is not a social or an ethical conscience that would make us feel guilty because it tells us what is right and wrong, good or bad.[53] The call of conscience is the call of care that gives us this primordial being-guilty; it summons Dasein back from itself as lost in *das Man*. It calls Dasein *forth* to take over that thrown being which it is, and it calls Dasein *back* to its thrownness so as to understand this thrownness that it has to take up into existence. "And this means that it is *guilty*."[54] Such a call and primordial guilt, for Heidegger, is the condition for the possibility of morality in general, the morally good and the morally evil, and for being weighted down with all sorts of factical guilt. Indeed, this primordial guilt cannot be defined by morality for Heidegger.

Such an ontological being-guilty is not derived from information about my failures or omissions in order then to find myself guilty. For Heidegger, Dasein must *be*-guilty. Moreover, to be responsible ontologically, Dasein must want *to be* guilty—to be authentically the thrown basis, "there," that it is. Being-guilty in this sense requires hearing the appeal correctly; it requires that Dasein understand itself in its ownmost ability-to-be, that it take up being thrown, "there" as not self-grounding. This entails another kind of freedom, not the ontic freedom to live in one possibility among others, but rather, being free for the call as a readiness to be called. When Dasein chooses itself in this way, it has a conscience as being-free for one's ownmost being-guilty. Understanding the appeal means wanting to have a conscience, which is the very basis for indebtedness.

Conscience calls Dasein face-to-face with its ownmost ability-to-be. And wanting to have a conscience (and to assume being guilty) means to be ready for the anxiety that individualizes Dasein down to its ownmost being, to the *there* of its Being as Da-Sein. This is what Heidegger calls, in short, resoluteness.[55]

Critical examination concerning the problem of guilt. Having given this brief existential and ontological exposition of the problem of guilt in Heidegger, we can make a few critical observations. These should help to specify further what is at stake in the experience of guilt.

If, on his own account, the ontic interpretation of guilt is too formal, his ontological interpretation for us nonetheless remains too vague. Let me explain. For his own reasons, Heidegger dismisses the existential interpretation as too ontic and too formal. For example, I might regret that I cannot live out each possibility that is open to me, even if those possibilities are already circumscribed by my being thrown. I might even feel cheated that I could not freely choose my own freedom. But there is nothing in this experience that touches me so uniquely that I might experience guilt or "be" guilty. The character of the "not" that surfaces here is too superficial to do that. The fact that I have the freedom to choose a way of life, but cannot choose them all might be tragic, but this does not bear on me in a *personal* manner. Further, simply to speak in terms of one possibility over against others that I might freely choose does not take into account the social, economic, and political circumstances in which I find myself, circumstances that could foster or inhibit pursuing one possibility or another. Still less does it reflect *how* I am thrown such that these or those possibilities might speak to me or weigh on me more profoundly than others. In this way, simply speaking of one possibility in relation to others is much too abstract. This leads me to the next, more fundamental point. The existential interpretation also provides Heidegger with a platform to pursue another angle, one he obviously deems more meaningful because it is ontological.

If Dasein is guilty ontologically, it is because Dasein has conflated, perhaps always conflated, its distinctive mode of being—being *there*—with other modes of beings, like objects and tools. Wanting to be guilty does not mean wanting to persist in the forgetfulness of its own kind of being, but wanting to be awakened to itself as being given over to itself as *there;* it is something it cannot get behind, but something it must assume in the form of resoluteness. Dasein must take over being *a* null basis. This guilt bears on the call to bring the Da of Dasein out of this ontological anonymity (confusing itself with other modes of beings), so that it can realize itself *as there,* as its own unique mode of being a distinctive opening of Being; this level of guilt bears on Dasein's thrownness *as there,* and as there, it must be attentive to itself *as thrown and null*—that for which it was never responsible.

The problem in my view is this: a human being who has the being of the there (Da-sein) is given to itself as such. But Heidegger simply leaves the matter at Dasein being *a* basis, and does not explore what it means to be *uniquely, this* basis, personally. To approach the problem of guilt, Heidegger needs to pursue *how* Dasein is given over to itself, *in what way* Dasein is not self-grounding, and not simply because of *the fact that* it is thrown. And it must consider how Dasein takes up or the ways in which Dasein "originates" this way. This would lead Heidegger to the experience of personal *vocation,* but because he leaves it on an indeterminate, modal level, he misses it.

Claude Romano in his recent work, *Au coeur de la raison, la phénoménologie,* has brushed up against this matter in Heidegger.[56] While recognizing that Heidegger is not clear about the sense or senses of "possi-

GUILT

bility" that he employs, Romano interprets Heidegger generously. He contends that far from being given as a fait accompli, Dasein must determine itself according to this or that manner.[57] Its being is in the first instance a being-possible in the sense that "being" and the "possibility of being" are really one and the same thing. Because Dasein's essence resides in its existence, in its having to be, Dasein possesses its being in such a way that it "is" its being in *this or that manner* and must determine its possibilities that are most proper or intimate to it, namely, the possibility not only of determining its being according to this or that mode, but according to this or that type of Dasein.[58]

I agree with Romano that the issue is indeed the mode of being of Dasein, namely, existence, in distinction to other modes of being that are not Dasein, namely, being-ready-to-hand and being-present-at-hand.[59] But Romano also affirms that this being-able-to-be of Dasein is moreover the fundamental capacity of Dasein to determine its being in "this or that manner" and "this or that type of Dasein," in short, where questions like "what am I going to do with my life?" pertain.[60] Again, Romano is correct in principle, but is this Heidegger?[61]

I want to emphasize that Romano—correctly, in my view—does not conflate the modal/ontological and existential senses of what I am calling here "vocation." Romano's point is that Dasein is its fundamental project—the project of its being—because it cannot be in the mode of Dasein (that is, in the mode of existence) *without determining itself* in its being as conforming to a fundamental project, to the life-project or of existence.[62] And although Romano does not take this issue up in the context of guilt, his analysis says two things for us. First, this is the direction in which Heidegger *needs to go*, and Romano seems to be more subtle than Heidegger here, though I don't think Heidegger goes quite this far, even if he needs to go this far. Second, the problem of guilt needs to be explored in the context of vocation, but not merely in the ontological, modal sense of vocation: what Heidegger understands as becoming the "there" of Being that it "is," or even what Paulo Freire refers to as the ontological vocation of becoming more fully human[63]—but in what I call the personal sense of vocation. Here the uniqueness of the personal vocation is primary in relation to the universal ontological vocation, since the latter is only realized through the former.

The experience of vocation and guilt. To understand guilt more appropriately in the context of vocation, it cannot be the "ontological" call of conscience to Dasein's "thereness" and in this way to the nullity of its thrownness. Instead, we have to understand it phenomenologically as a calling to the unique person, who can only be "there" *in this way (or ways)* as irreducible to other persons: those who are called forth—ultimately I maintain, in an inter-Personal manner, as "Myself," and who take themselves up originally, creatively in their own ways.[64] It is not the more vague "ontological" uniqueness of being-there in relation to other modes of being, which is disclosed, for example, through resoluteness and the experience of anxiety, but the absoluteness, the uniqueness of *this* person, which only I personally can be and become.

If we are to avoid the overwhelming passivity[65] and merely modal character of Dasein in Heidegger's characterization, we have to understand the Myself in an inter-Personal nexus, where the vocation is determined through the response, such that the response co-determines the vocation or vocations. This does not amount to choosing between abstract possibilities, but living through them, without necessarily being able to resolve the tension between them completely. This would be an experience like: "I cannot do otherwise," "this is really what I have to do," or "I am not myself when I do this"—in other words, things which really matter, deeply and inescapably in a personal sense. Here, the finding is not necessarily earlier than the seeking; it is not a development of "possibilities," as the potential that is actualized like in an Aristotelian "telos" or goal. In this sense, my beginning is earlier than my initiative, and it is not relative to my anticipation. Vocational experience admits of a different temporal structure.

Certainly, different persons have different starting points, so there are many different meanings not just for different persons, but with respect to the same personal history. This makes it a matter, as Nietzsche would say, of living beyond good and evil. Rather than justifying the responses of vocational experiences, it is matter of "having" to live *according* to their relevancy which is to some extent beyond me, having to live with awe and wonder of them, but without having to give reasons for the mystery.

Vocational experience is not just something out there for me to comprehend; it *plagues* me before I can grasp it or escape it. What dignifies me with a sense of being home with Myself also burdens me. Otherwise, what Heidegger describes as being resolute, as assuming the nullity of my being a thrown basis could not be so heartrending or felt so deeply in tension with who I *am*. Is it any wonder that we spend so much time speaking with friends, parents, counselors, therapists, clergy, and others in an effort to figure out who I am, my place in the world, what I am to do, how I am to be responsible toward others? The matter of vocation is neither merely modal and vague (and universal) nor rational, merely a matter of choice, and fully transparent. Frankl writes: "This uniqueness and singleness which distinguishes each individual and gives a meaning to his existence has a bearing on creative work as much as it does on human love. When the impossibility of replacing a person is realized, it allows the responsibility which a man has for his existence and its continuance to appear in all its magnitude."[66] One will not be able to throw away his or her life, he continues, having "seen" this irreplaceable uniqueness of the other person; knowing this "why" of his or her existence, he or she is able to bear almost any "how."

This interpretation, which we can call a personal one (because it is qualified as loving and concerns the individuation of the human being as absolute-finite, or unique in an interpersonal and inter-Personal nexus) is not Heidegger's existential interpretation, because vocational experience is not a matter of choosing one possibility over others. Vocational experience is irreducible to a profession or an occupation. Yet, it is not formal, either, because vocational experience does not concern me as *a particular* individual (under the universal concept of humanity), or as *a basis* (as a mode of being thrown), but bears on me absolutely, uniquely, as Myself.

But neither is such a vocational characterization ontological in Heidegger's sense, for a related reason, viewed only from a different perspective. Vocational experience does not apply to me generally as a mode of being, but specifically or rather *uniquely* to who I am, Myself. It concerns *the way in which* I am not self-grounding, that is, *the way in which* I am given over to myself as Myself. For Heidegger this thrown emergence is neutral; from the perspective of vocational experience, it is "charged": I am "charged" to go this way or that, to take up this givenness in meaningful ways that are only peculiar to me, Myself; it is unique to me, absolute, even if objectively I share the same occupation as another. This would require accounting for the distinctive way (or ways) in which I am given over to myself as *there*, which is to say, it would require investigating the human being as a finite absolute, and more specifically as person. Let me relate this now back to the experience of guilt.

From the perspective of vocational experience, Heidegger's existential and ontological interpretations tend to be abstract, which is why he misses the problem of guilt. First, if Heidegger were to approach the matter of guilt through, say, loving, he would discover, I believe, not a mere thrownness, but a being given over to myself, as Myself, which places me as both finite and absolute (unique) as not self-grounding and as owing to another. I am given over to myself as Myself, as not self-grounding, but *in a distinctive way,* in a way in which I can "freely," creatively take up. Perhaps Heidegger intends to do this by depicting a kind of ontological vocation to become more fully "there." But if this were the case, it is no less consequential *how* I become "there" according to how I am given to Myself as there, uniquely, as only I can be—which is open, but not arbitrary.

Guilt before Myself vocationally (which is more than choosing one possibility and not others) is inextricably tied to guilt before another who gives me to myself as Myself, and before others with whom I become Myself. This is why even the vague, haunting question (as in Kafka) is significant: "Before whom do I stand accused"? We would say then that guilt has an irreducible *religious* dimension because vocational experience is personal as inter-Personal. I am placed before another to whom I am also responsive, who charges me with or chooses me for this or these ways such that in these ways I become Myself. This relational guilt, then, could be qualified as a religious guilt, as it originates from not living up to Myself, who only I, Myself, can become. But it is also immediately and directly a *moral* guilt because it is lived out with others as responsive to others (who for their part are also accusatively "Herself," "Himself"). This is how Jaspers can speak both of a metaphysical guilt that is grounded in a solidarity among all persons such that each person is co-responsible for every wrong and injustice in the world, and likewise a moral guilt in which I am responsible as an individual for all that I do, within a loving struggle between persons in solidarity.

This is not to say that moral guilt is reducible to vocational experiences. There are other modes of guilt that concern my inability to fulfill the demands of others, the violation of trust, having offended others, and so on. And these also relate to not living up to Myself. But there is also an experience of guilt which is related to vocational experience and which is irreducible to the violation of social and ethical norms. The guilt of which I speak here concerns the tenor of interpersonal relations such that failing Myself, I am also failing others, and that one mode of responsivity toward others concerns becoming Myself. Insofar as the Myself is interpersonal and inter-Personal, failing others is also failing Myself.

Both religious and moral senses of guilt concern Myself as before others. Martin Buber sees the import of this as well. In confronting the issue of existential guilt, Buber considers the role of the therapist in relation to the person, and just how far the conduct of the therapist can go in addressing existential guilt. The therapist is only an instrumental force to the extent that he or she helps us find and navigate the person in a vocational sense. Accordingly, Buber delineates three spheres in which the reconciliation of guilt can take place, only one of which can truly occupy the therapist.

The first is the law of society which begins with a demand placed on the guilty individual according to its laws. The fulfillment is the confession of guilt followed by penalty. The third, which is also not the concern of the therapist, is the sphere of faith and deals with the guilty person, his or her God, and the confession of sin, repentance, and penance. No one can speak here unless it be the one whom the guilty person acknowledges as a hearer and speaker representing the transcendence believed in by the guilty person.

The second sphere is the only sphere in which a therapist can be active in the general sphere of conscience vis-à-vis existential guilt.[67] It deals with three events: (1) self-illumination of darkness surrounding the guilt, (2) perseverance in the humble knowledge of the identity of the present person with the person of that time, (3) reconciliation and restoring the order-of-being injured to the best of the person's ability (given historical and personal constraints), healing the world since it can be healed in places other than those at which the injuries or transgressions were inflicted.[68]

Whereas illumination in the first case concerns legally the confession of guilt, and in the third case religiously the confession of sin, here it concerns the personal confession of guilt, which presupposes the "illumination of essence" as its "meaning of life."[69] Buber suggests this style of confession with Dostoevsky's Nikolai Stavrogin in *The Possessed,* and with Joseph K in Kafka's *The Trial*. The ultimate point in these appeals is to show that in this register, the demand for a confession of guilt is fulfilled only through a primordial confession, which amounts to self-illumination of the individual's "essential being," or what we have called the vocational "Myself." The therapist (like any other person, perhaps) is instrumental in the process insofar as he or she assists the person in overcoming his or her inner resistance to attain such self-illumination.[70] This "essential being" of which Buber writes is in no way the modal character of Da-sein, but as Scheler would say, the radically unique (neither plural nor singular) personal "good-in-itself-for-me," or Myself.[71]

How is this vocation or are these vocations grasped? Do they only come in a moment of insight to which only we have the access? Can they be glimpsed by another who knows me better than I know myself? Can they come into relief when I turn away from them, showing up who we are by who we are not? Buber appeals to Kafka's parable, "Before the Law." But in my view, this is not a matter of the confession of guilt, but the confronting of Myself, vocationally: the paradoxical good-in-itself (the Law—universal, absolute, binding), which paradoxically is for-me and me alone. It pertains solely and uniquely to me, binding on me, necessary for me, bearing on me in a way it cannot bear on others, even if it is ostensibly the "same" law. It is only from here that I can become guilty before Myself and also be guilty before others. It is only from here that it is meaningful to speak of a self-betrayal in the sense of betraying Myself, and hence an interpersonal betrayal.

Conclusion: Shame and Guilt: From Pride to Repentance

I have described guilt as an experience that takes place in relation to an accomplishment experienced as mine. Its temporal orientation is the past, but its temporal meaning points futurally insofar as it announces a possible reconciliation with others and a possible restoration of Myself. Moreover, guilt emerges spontaneously in the sense that it is not caused or necessitated by any particular event, and appears as a rupture in the way the events unfolded or would have continued to unfold otherwise in my life with others. The intervention of guilt in the otherwise natural subjective flow of events is a way in which a diremptive experience is lived. It has emerged creatively in the richness of who we are as a way of calling pride into question in part by placing me in the accusative, throwing me back on myself. In this way, it opens the possibility of critique instigated through the presence of others. Though it points to a dimension of personal freedom as a creative response to my accomplishment, guilt is not an act of volition since it takes place against my will, and is qualified by a negative valence. I am not the simple origin of guilt, since I am placed before a site of transcendence which signals it; while guilt is spurred by my relation with another, it shows up my responsibility to others for a transgression given as a violation of a moral demand. Although one can become fixated on the past in guilt, dwelling only in a self-critical response, it implicitly points toward the reconciliation with others in the presence of whom the guilt arises, toward repentance and reconciliation through critique.

Further, although I am guilty over an accomplishment that is mine, guilt can be lived as an interpersonal experience in both moral and religious registers. There is a moral guilt in the sense of a transgression of a demand issuing from a social other, and there is a possible twofold religious guilt experienced (a) as a violation of Myself (as given to myself, as not self-grounding), and (b) as reversing the movement of holiness (which, when understood as loving, is qualified Personally), realized concretely through the violation of moral demands as the injury to others. It is not by virtue of subscribing to a religion that religious guilt arises; the violation of cult or ritual could only yield at most moral guilt, not religious guilt. As Scheler, Jaspers, and Buber recognize, without religious guilt or moral guilt, the other kinds of guilt that arise would be relatively insignificant and of little consequence.

Having described two moral emotions of self-givenness that speak to pride, namely, shame and guilt, let me suggest how these two experiences compare. There is no lack of comparisons between shame and guilt in literature on the subject. In fact, it seems that when one of these emotions is treated, the other of necessity is also invoked. A relatively recent survey by Teroni and Deonna has attempted a unified interpretation of shame and guilt, cogently mapping various criteria of shame and guilt that are assumed by anthropologists, psychologists, sociologists, and philosophers in both empirical and theoretical research.[72]

According to this study, the difference between shame and guilt turns, within the criterion of context, on how behavior is sanctioned such that shame is said to be social, whereas guilt is personal; where the criterion concerns particular objects, empirical research by others suggest that shame redounds upon the self, whereas guilt is connected to specific behavior; where formal objects are concerned, the Freudian legacy holds that shame is caused by failing to live up to an ego ideal, whereas guilt is perceived as a violation of prohibitions; analyses of autobiographical stories by others suggest, in the context of action-tendencies, that shame is self-oriented, whereas guilt is other-oriented.[73]

Our phenomenological analyses have also disclosed important differences and striking similarities between shame and guilt. For example, both shame and guilt are interpersonally significant, but whereas shame is given as exposed before another, guilt is experienced as transgressive of and responsive to another. Both shame and guilt exhibit temporal orientations and meanings, but whereas shame's orientation is the present, guilt's is the past—though both share possible futural meanings, as we will see. Both shame and guilt are diremptive experiences, and they relate to the self in the form of a possible critique; but whereas shame is experienced predominately in terms of who I am and as a disorientation, guilt is given at the outset in terms of an accomplishment that is mine and as a transgression. Whereas shame seems directly to issue in a possible reparation of Myself, guilt seems to open the way more immediately for reparation of relations with others.

Yet there are ways in which shame and guilt are more similar to each other than supposed at first blush. Both shame and guilt bear on the givenness of *Myself* (not just shame). Both elicit a change in the course of personal activity (not just guilt). Both *reveal* me to Myself reflexively in the sense that they are emotions of self-givenness. Shame is as much a "Western" phenomenon as it is an "Eastern" one (though guilt seems to be more peculiarly rooted in Western experiences of transcendence and transgression).[74] Both shame and guilt resonate bodily either in terms of averted eyes or blushing, turning askance or covering up.

We could continue in this manner of citing more differences and similarities. The point I want to make, however, is that these differences and similarities take on their fullest meanings when they are considered on the level of the person and as moral emotions. That is, they acquire their deeper significance—both in terms of their differences and unity—when they are grasped as expressive of the interpersonal or moral dynamic, as creative responses to pride, and as prompting a creative movement of repentance: both point to a possible self-critique, morally understood as pride; both appeal to a possible revision of Myself, morally understood as repentance.

Their unity and difference on this level consists in the fact that shame is more directly weighted toward the repentance of my personal "being," a reevaluation of myself—past, present, and futural—in relation to or guided by Myself. In guilt, a repentance of deed and thereby reevaluation of conduct or of the momentary active person who performs the deed, is preponderant. But even the latter, namely, the revision of Myself as prompted by guilt when pushed to its core, like shame, becomes the repentance of my personal being.[75] This is why Scheler can suggest that on the level of the person, a guilt that was trained on the exclusive details of our past conduct can give way to a deeper guilt expressed in the form of a "we *then* were such a person as *could* perform such a deed." It is not merely the deed, but the internal coherence of the person who is at issue from which the deed could arise.

Such a unity of shame and guilt requires us to see them, not just in relation to pride, but retroactively, as it were, from the perspective of repentance. If shame is susceptible to repentance because it bears directly on the becoming-being of the person, guilt is also susceptible to repentance—but because the accomplishment of a deed is not the actual object of repentance via guilt, but only its motive. It is the person in the full process of becoming, reexperienced in repentance that is the "object," and out of whose roots those deeds or actions arose.[76] Accordingly, Buber can write that the reconciliation with others means that I approach the person toward whom I am guilty in the light of my self-illumination or the center from whom I am, Myself—who is also touched in repentance.[77] In this regard, repentance is founding for reconciliation.

As we will see below, one can still hold on to the past accomplishments of which I am guilty or activities and forms of character disclosed in shame; one can still hold to them in pride with satisfaction and justification. For pride tends to isolate the person from the dynamic stream of existence, and self-limits the person in its dissimulating process—and so severs our relations with existence as coexistence. Shame and guilt are pointers and emergent opportunities that call the prideful person into question. But without repentance, the non-attachment to the deed or the person as the return to Myself is impossible. In this way, through shame and guilt, repentance is a reply to pride. Repentance, which incurs into the past and goes to the personal sense of the act—to the person who is more than what I have done—reestablishes these interpersonal connections, overcomes the isolating, arbitrary, self-delimitations of pride.[78]

Repentance begins this process of re-placing myself in relation, it possibilizes a future, and can be appropriated in other ways, for example, in hope, trust, loving, and humility. Let me turn now to the experience of repentance under the rubric of a moral emotion of possibility.

Part 2

Moral Emotions of Possibility

In the second part of this work, I treat moral emotions of possibility. They are called moral emotions of *possibility* because of the ways in which our straightforward ways of existing in the world are modalized. By this I mean that they express the transformation in relation to the way things *have been* or the way things *are*, a liberation from otherwise fixed predictable meanings, and a liberation for something becoming otherwise. In this way, they have a direct bearing on the generation of our lives and of our relation with others.

The three primary emotions I treat under the heading of moral emotions of possibility are repentance, hope, and despair. The first two are "expansive" emotions because they creatively open dimensions of the person where interpersonal relations are concerned. I also describe experiences of possibility in relation to repentance and hope that are not expansive in the same way, and even in which possibility is closed down: remorse, regret, wishing, longing, optimism, desperation, denial, pessimism, and hopelessness, and in the antithetical case to hope, despair.

Because these emotions have such a central place in who we are and who we become interpersonally, they become predominate themes for existentialist philosophers and philosophers of religion, and theologians. Because they lack the self-referential quality or dimension of self-givenness (as with pride, shame, and guilt), and because they do not explicitly challenge normative behavior, these moral emotions tend to escape treatment by cognitive and developmental psychologists, sociologists, and empirical researchers. This does not mean that they are not taken up in social research, for example. Due to the possibilizing nature of these emotions understood precisely as liberation, they have become pivotal experiences for critical theorists, Marxian critiques, and liberation political theologies.

The possibilizing features of repentance and hope are intimately tied to their structure of liberation: to free from something and to free for something, and to realize personal freedom as a being bound to others. I take up repentance first because it responds directly to the dynamic put in motion by pride and elaborated upon by shame and guilt. Shame and guilt can become catalysts to repentance when I take up what

I have done and who I am in a new direction as a turn from and return to Myself. Repentance liberates the past and present meaning of the accomplishment or of Myself, with its implications for the future, and dis-posits their reality, disclaiming their existential hold through a revolution—a so-called revolution of the heart. The moral emotion of repentance moves in a direction different from that of pride. I return to Myself, not only in the sense as creatively originating who I am as given, but to Myself interpersonally as not self-grounding and toward a reconciliation with others. It institutes a hopeful relation in and through which I become otherwise vis-à-vis what was revealed in guilt and shame.

Hope liberates in a twofold sense. What is hoped-for is not tied to the motivations of the past and present that sketch out a future. Hope possibilizes a future that is not restricted to past accomplishments and expectant foreshadowings. Yet it only does so because what is hoped-for in the act of hope is *sustainable*, and it is only sustainable because a ground of hope is given without me ever intending it. The hoped-for thing or event is out of my control to produce and yet what I hope-for is sustainable by a ground of hope (that is not intended) that or who constitutes me in this relation of dependence. By contrast, despair is the experience of the loss of a ground as such, and thus goes to the very source of what could sustain hope. They are related in terms of the absoluteness of the ground that either sustains or is given as impossible. Hopelessness is distinct from despair, yet it is connected to it in a different way, because hopelessness pertains to the experience of the impossibility *of a specific occasion;* hope and the ground of hope implied in this experience are "only" suspended on this occasion, whereas despair impacts the ground as such.

Whereas hopelessness and despair might be interpreted as modalities tied to the experience of pride, the very act of hoping and being constituted as hopeful, as sustained by a ground of hope which is not my intention, runs counter to the movement of pride.

4

Repentance

> Try what repentance can. What can it not?
> Yet what can it, when one cannot repent?
> —*Hamlet,* act 3, scene 3

In a gripping work that has now become a classic reference for the dynamic of forgiveness, *The Sunflower: On the Possibilities and Limits of Forgiveness*,[1] Simon Wiesenthal recounts his unimaginable situation as a young man in a Nazi concentration camp assigned to a makeshift "Reserve Hospital." Summoned arbitrarily by a nurse at the behest of a severely wounded Nazi on his deathbed, Wiesenthal suffered the prolonged confession of this dying man, a man who as a youth had joined the Hitler Jugend and then voluntarily became an officer of the Schutzstaffel, or SS. Wiesenthal was selected as "a Jew," as a representative of the Jews, to forgive the young Nazi, Karl, for his horrendous murders.

One of the horrifying scenes recounts how this Nazi SS officer had assisted in crowding a small building with Jews, locking the doors, and setting the structure aflame with gasoline and hand grenades, then shooting a family, who, afire, tried to escape through a window. Wiesenthal left the hospital room in silence without granting forgiveness.

Whether Wiesenthal did or did not absolve him, whether or not he wanted to forgive him, was beside the point. The issue was that he *could not* grant forgiveness as a "representative" of the Jews, as a Jew "in general." In the Jewish tradition, one can only grant forgiveness *as* the person offended, *to* the person or persons asking forgiveness. Alternately, one can only ask forgiveness from the party offended: hence, one of the tragedies of murder. The radical uniqueness of the person prevents representative forgiveness, since it, the radical uniqueness of the person, entails for its part what we might term a non-representable solidarity.[2] Granted that we human persons are capable of the divine power of forgiveness (as exemplified in the expression *salachti:* "I have forgiven"),[3] only the offended person, God or human, can forgive the offense.

Figures from the Dalai Lama to Desmond Tutu, from Eva Fleischner to Herbert Marcuse, have weighed in on this dynamic of forgiveness, considering either what they would have done or what one should do in such a situation. However, what is mentioned in passing, or simply acknowledged on the way to the matter of forgiveness, is repentance. Even more compelling, then, Wiesenthal not simply presupposed that the SS man was truly repentant, but apparently grasped sincere repentance in the confession of this officer, Karl.

While it still does not change for us the situation and interpersonal limits of forgiveness—which is beyond the scope of this book and a feature of another work—it does provoke the question concerning the dynamic of repentance, its role in the face of shame and guilt, and its meaning and place in human existence. Even if repentance must precede the asking of forgiveness, it cannot be reducible to forgiveness or to the granting of forgiveness. And while we can see the ultimate place of repentance in the *interpersonal* dynamic of forgiveness, we still need to understand repentance on its own terms in order to gain clarity concerning its meaning as an irreducible human experience and emotion.

In this chapter, I investigate the meaning of repentance as a personal emotion, specifically as appropriating shame and guilt, and as a unique way of responding to and overcoming the arbitrary self-limitations introduced by pride. Repentance does this as a personal act in relation to a lived shame or guilt; it does this as the revolution of the heart, and as shedding limitations, and as reconnecting us with others, and with Myself within the "suspected Center of things"—as Max Scheler puts it—which grasped personally, is a reconnection before the Holy as loving. Repentance opens up new possibilities, a return to one's "true self" or new beginnings with respect to Myself—renewed beginnings with others, co-generating a future with others constituting a moral world. Here Scheler would agree with Marx: "Repentance, not utopianism, is the most *revolutionary* force in the moral world."[4]

Rather than presupposing repentance as it is sometimes regarded philosophically, say, as motivated by fear so as to live more under the guidance of reason (Spinoza), or theologically, as a removal of sin and way to salvation, or in a more pedestrian manner, as a style of regret, remorse, self-punishment, resolution, or apology,[5] I investigate the experience of repentance by describing its temporal structure as "reprise" (1), and its modality of possibility as dis-posited, disclaimed, and liberating (2). Because repentance can be viewed abstractly merely as an immanent change, I consider the "transcendent" social-economic context and limits in which repentance occurs (3), examining as well its relation to otherness in terms of "for whom" and "for the sake of whom" (4). Owing to these transcendent and immanent concerns in relation to others, I briefly situate repentance in the context of forgiveness (5).

Reprise and the Enduring Quality of Repentance

The temporality of repentance as it bears on the act: Reprise. Edmund Husserl's phenomenology of time-consciousness has shown the ways in which time as lived is not the experience of an objective sequential order whereby one event stands in a causal connection to another, producing a future effect determined by the past. Certainly, our past does have a bearing on our present and future lives. Investigations into the passive synthesis of association (Husserl, Merleau-Ponty, and in psychopathology, Minkowski), have shown the ways in which past or even present meanings elicit some present or future occurrence in the style of a "motivation," exercising an allure in such a way that a future becoming is solicited.[6]

For example, something "retained" can become affectively significant and reactivated "passively." To a climber, a chalk mark on the rock cliff can become passively integrated as an element in the pathway to the top. Likewise, the buzzing of a light can finally come to consciousness and reach back passively to include the first occurrence of what was not at all present in a conscious manner. In a more active manner, a present event can solicit a sedimented past that I now recall explicitly: seeing the ferns in a garden affectively awakens a hike at the beach; I recall the old growth forests in the hike that I took two years ago. I can also actively try to remember a past event, like motocross racing on snow-covered trails.

All this is not to say, however, that the past, present, and future just flow by as if streaming in a causal nexus. In relation to the temporal flow of events, remembering is an act that "liberates" the past from its otherwise fixed place; it reaches back to a past already accomplished, which is affectively significant in some way now, and accepting its pastness makes it present in a new way, emboldening it as a past in the present. The meaning remains the same, though by becoming present, it can be associated with new events. Even misremembering, when it is discovered as such, presupposes the same meaning precisely *as* misremembered.[7]

In distinction, repentance is that act, or rather, re-*action* that modifies the *meaning* of that past event or present self as it orients toward the future. It does so in relation to who I am now and to who I can become; it liberates me from the otherwise determining or motivating power of the past and present. (I develop the dimension of liberation below.)

I mentioned that repentance is a re-action. By reaction, I do not mean that repentance is "caused." Rather, it is meant to express two components. First, repentance is an act. By "act" we understand that repentance is creatively executed, belonging to the spiritual dimension of the human being as person. Second, repentance is a response: hence the "re-." As a re-action, it replies or responds to an event, to something "wrong," to the truth of what one has been doing as before another. Accordingly, it is the relation with the past in some form that constitutes this "re-." We can distinguish loving as an act proper from repentance as re-action. By loving we understand an "act" as a creative, "initiated" dynamic orientation or *movement* peculiar to the level of spirit, and not a function or an anonymous, psychophysical operation that happens passively or that can become an object in time. It is essentially futurally oriented. Yet, without the past of some kind, there is no repentance. The past is a dependent moment. By contrast, loving does not need the past in order to be loving; I can freely love someone or something I have never known or encountered before.

There is a further distinction to be made in terms of repentance's relation to the past. To say that repentance is related to a past means that repentance's relation is to an event in time or to an orientation (say, of who I am) that the past event expresses.[8] It is what we have defined above as an accomplishment.

Despite the fact that repentance is a re-action, it is not a function. Repentance is a creative, expressive, and hence "personal" temporal act as enaction because it takes up the given, constituted past or present—what I have done, who I was, or who I am—and endows it with a new significance in light of a differently charged futural orientation.[9] Insofar as repentance alters the meaning and value of that event for our lives, prompted by guilt, or who we are, prompted by shame, repentance is lived temporally as a "re-prise." It would be misleading to say that the temporality of repentance is directed toward the past or present *tout court* if one means by this that the act of repentance "ends" or finds its fulfillment in the past or present. The reprise of repentance is decidedly not a negative judgment about my past or present. To be sure, we confront the past and make it present when we are attentive to it or reexamine our past deeds. Yet, the past is taken up in repentance only insofar as it is "re-lived" *toward the future.* If there were no futural dimension to repentance, we might only experience a kind of negative valence toward a past event or to the present self—a negative valence inherent in shame and guilt.

The negative valuation of the past, however, is grounded in a positive orientation to a new possible future—a hopeful one, for reasons we will see below. Not a denial or a forgetting of the past, repentance is the full acceptance of it and my responsibility for the accomplishment and who I have become through it. I do not neglect it, refute it, or separate myself from it; instead, in affirming it, the event or pattern of action is valued *negatively* in the disavowal (though the valence of repentance itself is *positive*). Rather than assuaging guilt, my guiltiness in fact increases the more repentant I am since it is through the act of repentance that the offenses become clearer. This is nowhere more evident than in the mystics: they become more and more scrupulous concerning their own "faults" the more they turn from them; what would seem to us as excusable because it is merely "human nature" is experienced by them now as offenses against other persons and the Holy, and because through repentance they are intrinsically already moving in the direction of holiness.[10]

Repentance is more than an epistemic act that merely acknowledges what had happened or even that recalls it explicitly. The latter I could do in a very detached manner. The mere feeling of objective culpability is to be equated neither with guilt nor with repentance. For example, I concede that it was my fault that I left the back door open in winter and our pet parrot died. I cannot blame it on anyone else; I accept responsibility. Moreover, while a sense of culpability might be a necessary condition for repentance, while guilt can become a catalyst for repentance, while shame might spontaneously point the way to repentance, they alone do not make one change one's ways. I can always acknowledge an act in the past with which I am associated or for which I am "responsible"; it can be an acknowledgment in a neutral manner or can be accompanied by a terrible feeling because it may have upset others. But none of this can be equated with repentance.

By contrast, repentance responds to an experienced guilt before another or to the shame that reveals me to Myself. Even though this past has occurred and has its historical placement in time, repentance modifies the very significance and moral worth of the event as it takes its seat in the full meaning of our lives—a meaning that remains open.

The duration of repentance. I have discussed the temporality of repentance in relation to its past and a futural orientation. But I have not yet discussed the temporal quality of this act. Rather than being punctual, the temporal significance of repentance is futural and open to infinity, since I cannot live through repentance with temporal delimitations. For example, just as I cannot say, "I will love you for five years," or "I love you now; that's enough"—since love is essentially oriented infinitely (to eternity, omni-temporally, one might say, unconditionally), repentance is not undertaken with foreseen limits. We do not say, "I've already repented; I'm done for now"—like we might say in the case of an insincere confession. Instead, I am never over repentance in the full sense, since it is expressive of a change of heart; we are never certain we have done enough in this ongoing revolution of the heart—which is not to say that we always have to think about it actively.

Kant grasps the spontaneous nature of repentance, but does not develop its futural quality. For Kant our motivation for rebirth is duty, and duty demands nothing of us that we cannot do; we are always capable of it and it is necessary—the unconditioned respect for the law as the ultimate condition upon which maxims are to be adopted. Because a gradual reformation for him implies that we have an incentive other than this representation of duty itself, and that the basis of the maxims is impure, it must be effected through a *revolution* in the human beings' disposition (a going over to the maxim of holiness of the disposition). "He can become a new man only by a kind of rebirth, as it were a new creation . . . and a change of heart."[11]

For Kant the "rebirth" as the "revolution of the heart" is not an ongoing process, but punctual. Kant wants to express that when I experience something like a change of heart, it is decisive. I do not sort of want to change, and maybe do it now, maybe later, depending upon my whim or external incentives. Rather, in our terms, I am seized, say, by guilt; I acknowledge it in a flash. Or put differently, when I get this change in perspective, it comes on all at once.

Reading Kant generously, he is trying to express the change of heart by contrasting revolution with reformation: namely, there is a break with the past or the present. For us, however, we have to say that the "origin" of repentance continues to originate, and we cannot live through the act of repentance with temporal delimitations. There is a revolution of the heart, something decisive, but this decisive origin continues to originate.

Futural orientation in repentance and anticipation in regret and remorse. Given both these temporal modes peculiar to repentance, reprise and revolution (of the heart), we can distinguish repentance from the experience of mere regret. For example, I can regret carrying my fine china to a party after I tripped and fell with it, shattering all the pieces. I can regret that the china broke without doing anything about it, for example, modifying how I will carry something in the future, or what I will take to a party. Regret lacks a futural orientation. But it is more than that. When I repent, I do not experience the past as a mere infraction or as an exception to a "rule" or "internal coherence" of the way I am, no matter how many times it may occur. For an infraction, I might be sorry, I might regret. Only when the past incident is experienced as the "rule" or as exemplary of who I am—even if factually it only occurs once—does repentance become an issue. To relate this to the distinctions we saw in part 1 above, this is why repentance responds to shame and not to embarrassment. Moreover, unlike guilt, remorse is not an emotion of self-givenness. Because guilt entails self-givenness as Myself, remorse structurally presupposes guilt.

We can sharpen this description of the phenomenon of repentance by contrasting it with an experience similar to but distinctive from both repentance and regret, namely, remorse. While there is no positive orientation in remorse, it is nonetheless more affectively significant, "deeper," than, say, being sorry. In remorse, however, one dwells on or with the past, holds on to it, like a tenacious retention which is not restorative. This is one reason Vladimir Jankélévitch writes that remorse in contrast to repentance is sterile, merely a "realism"; since remorse remains non-resolved guilt, it is deprived of hope, only past-oriented, with no temporality of the future, as is the case in repentance.[12]

Let's contrast remorse and regret with respect to anticipation. It is altogether possible that I could go on a drinking binge and think, in advance, "I'm going to regret this in the morning" (implying that I am going to do it anyway, and that I know, from myself, how I will experience this action from the perspective of tomorrow). But it does not seem that we could experience "remorse" in this way. Indeed, it would be curious to say that "I'm going to be remorseful of this in the morning." This points, in part, to the depth of the experience of remorse in distinction to regret, and to our inability to anticipate remorse. In this regard, remorse and repentance are similar.

In yet a deeper contrast, we could try to imagine thinking this way with respect to repentance. What sense would it make to say: "I going to repent this in the morning!" This would belie the whole experience of repentance as a spontaneous, immeasurable act in relation to guilt or shame. Indeed, it is possible that we could experience something like: "If I go down this path, like the last time, I might feel guilty (or remorseful), like the last time," or "knowing myself, I will feel guilty, again." While this could prove a cognizance of who I am based on my past experience, while I could even anticipate having "to do penance" or make reparations, it would not be true repentance.[13] My point in mentioning these examples is to illustrate that the *futural orientation of repentance does not map onto the structure of anticipation.* So, while we are able to anticipate regret, we cannot anticipate repentance as an original relation to the past and to our guilt concerning it, or the shape of who we are, and our shame concerning it.

Let me take a final, more extreme example, that of self-punishment, where the orientation to the past exhibits a strong emotional content.

I can be severely distressed that my callous remarks on a student's paper prompted his suicide. I bury myself in the past event, and am unable to escape it. I feel powerless to do anything about it and—to recall the example from the last chapter—only dwell in the pain in the manner of Dostoevsky's Marmeladov.[14] In this respect, the past would be lived as unalterable, its significance definitive of a particular dimension of my life. By contrast, in repentance, the significance of the past is open, and we are faced with the problem of what we are going to make of it. The moral danger here is not the deed itself, but the self-loathing and despondency over it. We can recall the Chassidic tale of a man who complained to the Rabbi of Lublin that he had become despondent over his evil desires. The Rabbi replied: "Guard yourself from despondency above all, for it is worse and more harmful than sin. When the Evil Urge wakens desires in human beings, it is not concerned with plunging them into sin, but with plunging them into despondency by way of their sinning."[15] The integral dimension of possibility here is related to another act understood as a moral emotion, namely hope, as we will see in the next chapter.

Repentance as Liberation

The temporality of repentance as it bears on the act is a reprise, and the temporality of repentance as it bears on the person is a revolution of the heart. In both modes (reprise and revolution), repentance has a futural orientation. Just as we inquire phenomenologically into an act's relation to being in, say, a perception, remembering, imagining, or anticipation, we can ask after its relation to being in repentance. Here a straightforward attitude and its relation to being is *modalized* as "liberation." The meaning of this liberation is twofold: (a) the new orientation is given as positive while the past is given as negative, (b) the past is dis-posited in its appropriation such that the past no longer has an existential claim. Repentance is experienced as liberation in these modalities, as dispositing and disclaiming, and thus frees one *for* self-revision.

Positivity of the experience. The new direction of my repentance—new in relation to the past event or current person that I am—is always *experienced as "positive."* The repented accomplishment or person gets lived now explicitly as negative since it is evaluated *from* the "positive" orientation provided by repentance and my commitment to a new manner of being. This is the case even if, in light of this new directedness, the latter is regarded by others as negative: through my repentance, I might engage in acts that are seen to be socially malevolent. If I repent the past and myself, this repentance issues in a different set of acts, I will experience the new directedness as positive in relation to which the past actions or present sense of myself are valued as negative and thus disavowed. This is why repentance is given with both a positive *and* a negative valence.

Repentance as dispositing and disclaiming. Repentance is not a denial of what has taken place, nor is there a "gee, I've processed all that, now I am over it." Rather than forgetting or explaining away what I have done or who I am, when I repent, I affirm what I have done and who I have become in this limited and limiting way, but I do it in such a way that there is a transformation of its meaning in light of a new way of being. Let's say that I admire the local café's new coffee equipment, and one day I steal it. When I relate to this past event or way of being in repentance, I do not "accept" it in a neutral or straightforward manner, historicizing it simply as something that has happened or how I am; moreover, I do not deny that the event took place or that I did it "by accident." Instead, motivated by shame or guilt, I accept it *differently* in repentance: as I appropriate the past, I simultaneously distance myself from it because I have internally turned from this kind of a person who would, for example, covet to the point of stealing.

In repentance, I integrate the event or internalize myself, as it were, which allows me to get beyond it in a qualified sense; or if my repented actions count as a departure from "who I really am," then it is a return to my "old" or "former" self or my former good ways (but still "new" in relation to what is repented). In repentance the past or present is "confronted." Yet, it is more than confronted; it moves along with me in a new manner; it is taken up and given a new meaning in the wake of my new orientation.

If remembering is an acceptance in the sense of positing the being of the event and making it present, then repentance is an acceptance of the past or present whose full gesture is a being "dis-posited" and a "disclaiming": The past and present release their hold on me, and I am unburdened from their determinacy. Even if "determinacy" is too strong here (since epistemically, the past and present motivate rather than cause the future), then at least we can say that the past and present no longer have the same existential claim on me as they would have otherwise. And this is what I want to evoke by using the term "dis-posited." The past's and present's meaning is undone—not in terms of what actually occurred, but in terms of its bearing on what I can do and who I am. In this respect, repentance reconstitutes the new significance according to the change of heart; the meaning of the past is in the process of being refashioned retroactively. As repented, the shameful or guilty person is existentially "disclaimed" in light of who I can become such that it is no longer expressive of who I am. As a liberation from an otherwise fixed meaning (this is what I have done, this is who I am), repentance makes a new life possible.

The initial movement of repentance, however, is in no way an attempt to "dis-posit" or "disclaim" the past. It is nothing "I" do. Rather, the dispositing and disclaiming arise because I am attuned to a different way of being; I have already been lured in a different *manner*, a different *how* of the being of this event or the being of myself, but not away from the event or Myself as such. The liberation in the modality of the possible enables a self-revision understood as the "change of heart," although it is the change of heart first that allows the past event given through guilt or myself given through shame to present itself as "repentable" and not just as "something that happened."

Repentance as revolution of the heart. Repentance opens the possibility of a future that is not bound by the past or restricted to the meaning that is sketched out by it. Rather than positing a futural event like an expectation, the futural orientation in repentance is connected to its temporal structure as a reprise that takes up the past and present in a different light—"different" in relation to the accomplished meaning of that event. One is not only orientated toward a past or a future on the level of a contemporaneous act. This act as reaction, this reprise, has its significance as it is taken up in the person's life. I do not want to be this way any longer—as revealed through shame and/or guilt. The act is taken up in the movement of my being, who I am and can become. We witness a turning in relation to the past, a change of orientation, a change of heart. Peculiar to repentance is the phenomenon of the "revolution of the heart," a "turning around," a "conversion" expressed by the Hebrew *t'shuvah* or the Greek *metanoia*. If the experience of shame is the beginning of a revolution, as we saw above, repentance is its enactment.

The movement of repentance is a spiritual conversion on the part of the individual, that is, a turning taking place on the level of the human being as person, and discloses the futural dimension of this act: it is not just a relation to the accomplishment, since it approaches the past or Myself with a "new heart" so that its occurrence can have a new meaning in relation to a future in which I am directed differently. The temporal meaning of repentance is futural. "Subjectively" speaking, I become different in the act of repentance. "Objectively" speaking, the past becomes different. Again, this does not mean that the past changes, but its *meaning*, the *how* of its givenness as it bears on me now and who I can become, is transformed. The *repented past* as disclosed by shame and guilt, the repented person as revealed in both shame and guilt, bear on me differently now.

Thus, if "being-constituted by" signifies not only that the meaning of something has been posited, but more broadly, that a future is sketched out on the basis of the past and the present, then we can say that through repentance, I am no longer constituted by the past or present, where I am understood as *person*. This is the sense in which we can speak of repentance as "liberation." Not only is repentance a freedom from, but it is a freedom for self-revision, thus instituting a new relation to being, a *hopeful* one in which I can become otherwise.

Not being defined by what I have done or what has occurred, repentance clears the way for new perceptions and different actions. For Husserl, the constitutive notion of "normality" includes both the *concordance* of the object over time and its *optimal* mode of givenness. If there is an established mode of concordant givenness (normal), and if a new givenness intrudes on this concordance, the latter discordance is constituted as "abnormal." But if that new givenness is "richer in difference within a unity," it becomes a new optimal mode within experience itself: what was once concordant/normal becomes abnormal for experience, and what was given as discordant and abnormal, now becomes for experience discordant as "hypernormal," instituting a new norm from within experience. Over time, this hypernormality—which had been discordant with the previous concordance—can itself issue in a new concordance, and thus a new temporally dense "normality."

In the sphere of person, we would not speak of "concordance," but rather, the "internal coherence." Here, a similar movement can be detected in the moral sphere. Repentance is a discordant act with respect to the past and present internal coherence of who I am that allowed me to act in such and such a way. But just because it is discordant, it can liberate me from that internal coherence in a way that is more "optimal" for who I am. I can now recognize the past and present in which meaning is altered. Not limited to the primordial present, the noematic transformation from the present "radiates back" in the form of a reconstituted past, transforming its accomplishment of sense that stemmed from the previous accomplishments. Thus the liberating, transformative power of repentance issues in a kind of retroactive temporal lag of meaning, a *"Nachträglichkeit"* in which the past is reoriented with the present in a unity of meaning, sketching out a future with others to whom I am bound in moral solidarity.

Because repentance is such a deeply interior act, it is tempting to treat it abstractly, that is, as merely a subjective process, having only an immanent significance. In fact, it is a question whether repentance can be fully achieved if it remains confined to the immanence of the personal act. In the next section, I examine the immanence and transcendence of repentance.

Immanence and Transcendence in Repentance

Not only is repentance an immanent transformation, it is a transcendent one as well. In order for repentance to be truly repentance, it has to be what I call here a "repentant praxis." We can see this necessity expressed in the soliloquy of Claudius, the Uncle/King in Shakespeare's *Hamlet*.[16]

Let us recall that, in this play, Hamlet's uncle, Claudius, kills his brother (Hamlet's father) and marries his wife (Hamlet's mother). The uncle assumes the throne, gaining Kingdom and Queen. At one auspicious moment, Claudius expresses a subjective readiness for repentance, and there is an inkling of sincerity on his part. He acknowledges that his "offense is rank," and wonders whether such a "primal sin"—the sin of Cain and Abel, one brother killing another—can be forgiven. In the Talmud Yoma (86a), it is written that one can gauge if the individual is truly repentant when, confronted with the opportunity to commit the same sin, he or she does not yield to it a second time. Certainly, the situation is complicated when we are considering murder, since one cannot murder the same person twice. But since we are not considering forgiveness by the one murdered, the matter of the repentant heart would concern the possibility of committing a murder again, of another person.

In principle, one can repent of such an offense: "Try what repentance can. What can it not?" There is a "subjective" readiness or "intention" here. Claudius will pray, he will rely on the power of repentance, and even anticipate mercy. This "strong intent" is the "immanent moment." Yet, his strong intent is defeated by a "stronger guilt."

This stronger guilt does not relate to his subjective feeling, but to the possession of the effects of his deed—here the transcendent dimension. How can his immanent repentance help him when he still possesses the effects for which he has committed the murder: the Queen, the Kingdom, his wealth, his ambition? He poses the important question: can one truly repent and keep the fruits of the offense?

What we learn from the example of Claudius is that repentance as an immanent moment is dependent at least upon divesting ourselves of what we have gained through the offense. Repentance has to be more than an immanent intention or it is ineffective: "Yet what can it, when one cannot repent?" Repentance that bears on immanent conversion must be matched by repentance that bears on transcendent transformation. Measured charity, charity at my disposal, is not true charity and inadequate to repentance, because I retain my power of disposition over another. "Giving back to society because we have received so much" only constitutes a partial return of profit resulting from surplus value (legal theft for Marx), just enough to try to alleviate guilt. My putative charity would be based in surplus value = surplus labor, and thus my possession of another's (coerced) labor and stored labor: All of this would still remain at my power of disposition. I can keep enough of the offense to remain in control and still get the accolade for being "charitable." Marx makes an excellent remark about "credit gratuity" whereby so-called charity both presupposes and maintains the offense, and gives the capitalist praise for managed or measured (not infinite) distribution.[17] Such a putative "virtue" would be grounded in dishonesty, so-called moral goodness rooted in moral evil, so-called charity in religious idolatry.

Certainly, repentance in its transcendent mode *cannot* be reduced to external effects, as if, say, Claudius were simply to give everything back or to be made to divest himself of his possessions. It is not a matter of a quantitative recompense devoid of any internal "turning." This would be like an empty fast about which Isaiah protested.[18]

Repentance entails making recompense "in spirit" *through* deeds (*mitzvot*). In the Jewish tradition, for example, *tzedakah* (righteousness, justice, charity) must also accompany the turning of *t'shuvah,* but the "turning" has to animate the *tzedakah,* or the deeds are not "good" and ultimately ineffective. Whatever the deed, whatever the offense, repentance is carried out "worldly" in the spirit of not carrying the same meaning, the same person, or the same world forward.

That is why I cited the example from Isaiah. Fasting is not simply a matter of refraining from eating while oppressing the laborers, the putative self-affliction, or "giving back to the community" while continuing to take from it. Not being ready to repent (immanent decision, ability to change inwardly) means still clinging to the results of the offense (outward goods). Inversely, the "ability" to dispossess signals the ability to change inwardly. This points to the integral nature of repentance for which the "immanent" and the "transcendent" are only moments.

Repentant praxis entails the divestment of what we have gained through the offense, "completing" and "beginning" immanent repentance. Paradoxically, we can only repent when we have fully repented. Otherwise, we remain, as Claudius says, "to double business bound," and we "stand in pause where [we] shall first begin." As a result we wind up "neglecting both," namely, the beginning and completion of repentance. As Max Scheler remarks, the act of repentance precedes in a certain sense both its point of departure and its point of arrival.[19]

We should not, however, equate repentance, even in its transcendent dimension, with "atonement." Atonement is the active reconstitution of the interpersonal bonds that have been severed through the offense. On the one hand, atonement springs from the repentant heart, for it is only from this internal conversion that one is motivated to set things right. So, while we could account for the experience of a deathbed repentance, at least in the immanent sense, it would be impossible to speak of a deathbed atonement in the sense of performing acts that carry a religious and moral significance. For example, one might repent after having exploited others for years, and with this repentance destroy all the capital one had garnered so as to begin anew, divesting oneself of all the profits gained. Atonement, however, would entail another interpersonal dimension, say, returning to them the money stolen, or simply serving them in turn, and asking forgiveness from those whom one had exploited. Yet one could also make reparations externally without it carrying the sense of repentance or atonement.

Repentance does not have to be "complete" in order for atonement to begin. In fact, atonement, which might be accompanied by prayer and meditation, acts of justice, charity, righteousness, can deepen the repentant person and open him or her further to a more profound repentance, completing it in what we are calling here "transcendent repentance."[20]

Let me turn back to the issue of repentance in and of itself, and investigate further the freedom and the ability to repent along these two lines: (a) the attachment and the non-attachment to things, and (b) the attachment and non-attachment to self.

On the one hand, the ability to repent depends upon a non-attachment to things: it entails a willingness to let go of the matters related to the transgression. Thus, I cannot at the same time covet what I have obtained or achieved through the "offense" and repent of the deed that garnered those things, for example, objects, material wealth, fame, mastery, and so on. Not being able to repent might be expressive of the implicit love of the "offense," possessing it or even savoring the memory of it. I could be addicted to things, physiologically and psychologically, obsessed with material things that prevent me from repenting, what we could call religiously "idolatry."

But not being able to let go as a not being ready to repent might have other dimensions where it is not just a matter of my willingness or non-willingness. The depth of these problems can be concealed if we speak cavalierly of "not being free" to repent. The lack of freedom or ability to repent expressed as an attachment to things can be socially, politically, and economically significant. Here we could examine the ways in which our focus on use-value and exchange-value for the purpose of survival "demands" the sacrifice of the deeper human and personal values, as Marx has shown in his analyses of alienation and surplus value. Here, my freedom is expressed by enslavement, and the objects to which I am attached, inversely, enjoy the freedom of the market as independent of me. My attachment to surplus or alienated labor (coerced labor) and to "free" objects might be necessitated by my very real demand to survive.

Thus, private property, division of labor, stored labor (capital) can motivate the inability to repent by having to survive in such a way that I take advantage of others. One may "want to repent," have "strong intent" but literally be "to double business bound." While there could be an insight into the exploitation in which I am complicit, and while I might be truly repentant in relation to what I have done, I might not be able to repent concretely (as transcendent transformation). It might just rest with feeling badly about things and an impotence of being able to transform the social and economic structures necessary to divest myself concretely of the offenses. In extreme cases, the necessity of acting in a way that violates the repentant heart might be emotionally destructive (depression, being ill at ease in the world, and the like), or physically destructive (ulcers, insomnia). Here I am not concerned with the disorder of value-preference evident in capital, but only caution the too facile approach to repentance that neglects the concrete circumstances in which one repents and divests oneself from the things associated with the repented past. My point here is that the more attached we are to things for whatever reasons, the more difficult it is to repent.

The second issue concerning the ability to repent concerns the attachment or the non-attachment to self. Here it relates directly to pride. A fuller investigation of what I mean by loss or forgetfulness of self, or recovery of Myself, is reserved for chapter 7 on humility. Nevertheless, let me relate this provisional understanding to the example in question. As in the case of the Uncle/King, it might be difficult to separate ourselves from, say, the accolade, the sense of mastery or control, or general "power" we have gained through the offense. Seen over time, repentance might even be all the more difficult because we have become habituated to the offense; in fact, the offense might no longer be lived as an offense, but straightforwardly as expressive of who we are. Pride is expressive of such an attachment and arbitrary self-limitation. Repentance reestablishes the interpersonal and inter-Personal connections.

So, to return to the example of Claudius, the latter realizes that, yes, repentance can do anything and everything; the power of repentance is *infinite;* but it can do nothing when it is merely a subjective intention and measured out according to my own whim. Here there is no humility. The problem is that Claudius, the Uncle/King/Husband, wants to remain *in control* even in the act of repentance; he wants to measure it out, and not to yield to the divestment of his possessions as a mode of self-attachment. But putting restrictions on infinite repentance, he cannot repent. Without having to appeal to theology or church doctrine, we can note that the movement of repentance is most deeply of a religious nature because it has to follow the movement of infinity, the Infinite movement of self-dis-position in order to be realized as such. It results in a self-emptying, a kenosis, that is religiously (inter-Personally) and morally (interpersonally) significant.

To be sure, the relation between the attachment to things and to the self are intertwined. It is not the case that I can simply change the objects of my interest (avowing or disavowing the past, say), and have the "self" remain the same. In repenting of the past events, I also change. As I change, the meaning of the objects changes; as the meaning of the objects changes, I change. The whole structure and modality of the experience is modified. This explains the seemingly vicious circle lamented by Claudius. He would have to become a different person in disclaiming the results of his actions. It is not that he could disclaim them and remain the same, or be spiritually modified and have the same objects of interest.

"I" become non-attached to myself (if we can speak in this way), the more I am possessed or occupied by another (for the mystics, the Holy), and in this way recover Myself. If I am liberated from the past, from the offense, if I am no longer clinging to myself or to things in this way, it is because I am in the presence of another.

For Whom and for the Sake of Whom

Having described the modalization of repentance in terms of a liberation in which the being of the past and present is disposited and disclaimed, explicated as the ability to repent, let me now come to the dimension of repentance that has been implied throughout all these analyses, namely, that repentance presupposes a relation with others. One is implicitly or explicitly before another: an individual or collective person, elemental beings, divine beings, or as in the Abrahamic tradition, before the Holy.

I never repent in abstraction: I am repentant before someone because my offense is before others, directly or indirectly. This is another way of saying that I cannot in and of myself motivate repentance like I can a remembering, for it is before another that the event is or I am qualified in the first place as "repent-worthy."

Repentance is emotionally significant (and not merely affectively significant) because of this interpersonal dimension. Moreover, we can be repentant with respect to a particular act or with a more general situation, but most deeply, it goes to the core of Myself as relational. For example, I may not know what it was that I did in terms of a specific act, but I can be repentant regarding the general situation in which something happened so that I do not put myself in such a position again. We can be repentant for a way of being that put us into such a situation in the first place, regardless of whether or not we did anything specifically that is repent-worthy. This concerns our relation to who we are and to our style of being.

As we saw above, a putative turning toward others is not necessarily a turning to Myself, but might only be a turning from myself, positing my disvalue and thereby seeking refuge in the "other" merely because it, she, or he is other than myself. This is one reason why repentance cannot be reduced to mere self-regret, self-punishment, self-loathing, or self-effacement. This is much different from what Levinas calls metaphysical Desire in which I am first struck by and attuned to the Other, and thereby sense that I am unjustified in my freedom before the face of the Other as the trace of God.

Accordingly, Scheler writes that without repentance, the truth against the self (in pride) is impossible, and likewise, the readiness to repent is coeval with humility.[21] Repentance breaks down the barrier of pride, which restricts my return to my past accomplishments with satisfaction and justification. It is a vehicle of truth against oneself. Claudius, for example, is unable to repent as long as he remains attached to the glory of his acquisitions that he gained through the offense and offensiveness of his person; it is literally, as Hobbes writes, a vain-glory.

In this regard, I can both regret something (breaking the china) or even resolve to do better (be more careful carrying china, go on a diet) without it having any interpersonal significance. There are, to be sure, acts that might resemble repentance that do entail others essentially, but are not at all repentance. Let's take the case of apology. I can apologize to another for the slightest of offenses (bumping into someone on the street), for a personal injury (hurting someone's feelings), or for libel in which I caused another to appear badly before the public. I may be quite sorry that I injured another; but in distinction to repentance, being sorry or the verbal apology does not mean that I change my ways or that I would not do it again, unintentionally, in pursuing my course (walking the same way down the street or saying the same things about this person). Resorting merely to the internal "I statements" (like, "I am feeling sorry that you were hurt by what happened") does not and cannot change anything: indeed, I may be sorry that this other person was injured or that I was the "cause" of this injury. But I also have no intention of changing my ways. This is not to say that one should or even could repent over each and every offense; it is only to note that there are structural differences from acts that look similar, but are irreducible to repentance.[22]

When we examine the interpersonal dimension of repentance, we recognize both the "before whom" and the "for sake of whom" peculiar to repentance. My repentance always concerns another, another in some form, even if that "other" is Myself. Repentance has a religious significance when this "before whom" is infinitely absolute, or Holy. When I speak of the Holy in this way, I am not presupposing something like a theology of repentance. Rather, it is to recognize that in order for repentance to arise, there has to be some positive insight into "who I am" Myself, or who I can become, that is, into a way of being that "reveals" this past act or event as negative and repent-worthy. Such an experience originates from elsewhere, as something beyond my past or current person according to which I measure myself, or better, according to which I am measured or judged in shame or guilt.

Most profoundly, repentance is experienced in the manner of the "before whom" in a threefold manner. (1) It is experienced religiously when the event is experienced as a rupture of a relation with the Divine. Its full significance arises when an action is not merely experienced by me as bad, but when it is experienced as such in the presence of the Holy, and when repentance seeks to reestablish a connection between myself, ourselves, and the "source" of all things.[23]

(2) The "before whom" is experienced religiously when it is experienced as a violation of my way, as "who I am," as I am given to Myself.[24] This presupposes as we saw above a vocational experience of Myself, that is, myself as not self-grounding, but more specifically, as given to myself, as Myself, in a unique manner. In this way, repentance is a response both to the violation of the Holy and the violation of "Myself." Repentance before "Myself" is de-limiting in the positive sense of removing arbitrary limitations because the experience of vocation is already inter-Personal. One does not choose a vocation or vocations; one is chosen for it or them, through which the responses constitute them as such. Here repentance is a manner of returning. This is essentially different from simply

choosing a way for myself, and hence merely violating, for example, a *profession*. Where I am self-grounding, there would be no grounds for repenting a so-called violation of a profession, occupation, career, job; it is just a wrong choice or a choice relative to others. It might require a resolution, but not a repentance.

(3) The "before whom" is experienced morally when the violation has ruptured my bonds with another as finitely absolute (say, by violating a trust, inflicting harm, etc.). In this sense, repentance has an interpersonal significance. This interpersonal significance is also de-limiting as a reconciliation with other persons. It is ecologically significant when it is our reconciliation and reestablishing connections with beings other than human.[25] Accordingly, any form of violence or violation regarding another has a religious, moral, and ecological significance. Repentance as opening the future possibilities with others, as therefore on the way toward repairing relations with others, is foundational for reconciliation.

In short, repentance does not receive its impetus from the self. Although one could be repentant, for example, for stealing money from a business, this would have to be more than not having wanted to be caught; rather, it would have to be felt as having harmed another in some way, and ultimately as a before whom (an individual, collective, finite, or infinite person).

Repentance is interpersonal not only in the modality of the "before whom," but also for the sake of whom. This "for sake of whom" has two dimensions. In the first case, repentance is carried out for the sake of reestablishing inter-Personal and interpersonal bonds. I change my ways to be with others (finite or infinite) otherwise. Repentance is accordingly not merely being sorry or apologizing but a reordering of the heart. This reordering to be with others otherwise expresses the dimension of the future; in this way, it is not tied exclusively to the past or to the meaning of that past event. In the case of Karl, the SS officer cited at the beginning of this chapter, the urgency of repentance cannot be a matter of "saving his soul." Rather, it would have to be a turning from violence by reestablishing interpersonal bonds. One does not do this, however, with a "representative" of others; but in the case cited, it could have happened in the unique encounter of a person, "Simon," preparing the way for a new future quasi-liberated from the violence of the past. At least this would be part of the "immanent" moment of repentance. The question of forgiveness by those who are no longer in a position to forgive is another matter.

Second, repentance has a communal sense. It is entirely possible that I could be repentant *for* others in a qualified sense. In order for this to be the case, I would have to regard myself as integral to a community, a collective person, and experience myself as a "home-companion" with others, sharing and co-constituting the same homeworld, synchronically and diachronically. This does *not* mean, however, that I could stand in for another, as if I would "represent" another in repentance. So, for example, one individual or several individuals, collectively, could be repentant for a past or present wrong (national acts of aggression, slavery), even though I was or we were not directly responsible. While I could make reparations for past evils that others have committed, and take responsibility in this sense, I cannot repent for him or her. But insofar as we co-participate in the constitution of sense of the homeworld in relation to alienworlds, we are "able" to repent for "our" sake as for the sake of others.

It seems possible, then, that an individual person or the collective person, "the South," could repent for slavery, even though those actually repenting are several generations from the type of "slavery" in question. The repentance would be meaningful (and not merely making an apology) insofar as the South, or the North, or the United States is still benefiting from the fruits of slavery. It would be a matter of turning toward, say, equality and justice, and turning from exploitation. Affirmative action in the United States, for example, could be understood as a form of collective repentance. But if it is not, then it is merely a case of "reverse discrimination."[26] So, while I cannot repent *for* another (in the sense of representative repentance), I can repent for the sake of others as belonging to a collective person. And this means it is possible to alter, however modestly, the moral tenor of the community.

Finally, in this case, an individual or a collective person would not be seen as "leading" repentance in relation to whom others would "follow." Rather, repentance for the sake of whom would be exemplary. So, if and when a pope were to apologize on behalf of the Catholic Church, say, for existence and silence about the Magdalene asylums or "Laundries," the pope would assume a collective responsibility as an "exemplar" and not a "leader" of the church. Insofar as he can direct its course and how it acts in future instances, it is meaningful to speak of the pope repenting for the church, but always as a member of the church and insofar as the church could undergo an internal transformation. It is not a quantitative issue, that is, how many repent, but it is a matter of qualitative change. This is to say that others who wish to be integrated into this repentance actively take it on fully, but inexhaustibly, in their own creative, "spontaneous" manner. Otherwise it would be merely "representative" and ineffectual. An individual can be exemplary of repentance for a homeworld, and a homeworld can be exemplary for other homeworlds or for an alienworld within Generativity.

Forgiveness and Mercy

When I brought up the example of Hamlet's Uncle and his concerns about repentance, I mentioned that in order for repentance to be "complete," it could not remain an immanent repentance, but had to be a transcendent repentance as well, that is, it must address concretely the gains of the offense.[27] Otherwise, repentance is stymied from the very beginning, "to double business bound" standing "in pause where [we] shall first begin."

This raises the question whether and to what extent we can ever make up for all the effects of our offense: what happens when we cannot address all the effects of the past deeds, even if we wanted to do so? We can consider events that range from the violence of libel to that of murder. Are there limits to repentance? Is the liberation experienced in repentance unbounded or restricted?

Claudius asks whether the rains of heaven can wash his blood-stained hands "as white as snow." In principle, this is exactly what forgiveness does, namely, it confronts the offense and does what I cannot do, de facto and de jure. It points to another interpersonal dimension that fulfills immanent and transcendent repentance by addressing the offense that is *no longer in my control*. Repentance is elaborated, as it were, in a creative way through forgiveness *by another*, or as Claudius puts it, "mercy."[28]

Thus, in the proper sense, repentance responds to our finitude with in-finitude, from infinity. But it would be a mistake to think that infinitude (redemption) operates without our participation, or simply covers over finitude, that our actions, our "participation" (or "co-participation" as in the case of solidarity) are insignificant. If this were the case, repentance could never have been an issue for Claudius. Nevertheless, in repentance, one has to be ready to be forgiven, and to accept the forgiveness, even if there is "no effort" on our part. This is part of what it means to live in humility. But to receive forgiveness, the offended party has to grant it in a non-representable solidarity. And this is precisely the tragedy of the violence of murder, and the irresolvable nature of the situation presented by Simon Wiesenthal in *The Sunflower*.

Conclusion

An account of repentance can be intertwined with that of forgiveness. In this chapter, however, I have focused on the moral emotion of repentance, and have characterized the temporality of repentance as that of reprise, the modalization peculiar to repentance as liberation, which entails an existential dispositing, disclaiming, and revolution of the heart, and I have described the intersubjective dimension as the before and for the sake of whom. Repentance as a whole was further described as a repentant praxis that avails itself of forgiveness, provided of course that the other is there to forgive.

Having a distinctive temporal structure, repentance exhibits an interpersonal relation. Although I am not self-given in the style of shame and guilt, nevertheless, I am an issue for myself, as a returning to Myself. Despite these features that are mutatis mutandis shared by other moral emotions, I include repentance under the rubric of the moral emotion of possibility because its main contribution concerns its modalization of being as liberation. Through the shocks of shame and guilt, repentance takes up what is revealed in them—Myself—and replies to the moral movement instigated by pride. It opens the possibility of reconciliation, which as interpersonal, has social, political, and economic implications.

Repentance liberates in two ways. In one respect, it liberates me from fixed meanings of myself and of the past deed such that I could accomplish it, as they are exposed through shame and guilt. This is the sense of the existential dispositing and disclaiming. In another respect, repentance frees me and us of limits. The limits we have explicated are *interpersonal* limits. They are arbitrary, not only because they are imposed subjectively by me, but because they presuppose the isolation of the self; they exclude all kinds of otherness and make them subordinate to me, essentially severing relations—and there is no justification for this, though as we saw, there are understandable basic senses that are reconstituted as lures for pride, which is self-limiting and self-dissimulating.

Because it reestablishes relation, recovers the limitation of myself to myself, and returns me to Myself as not self-grounding, repentance is liberating. In this respect, repentance is infinitizing, and as removing limits, reconciling relations, it is redeeming. It is—as the Jewish mystics say—a process of leaving Egypt (מצרים), a process of removing spiritual, personal limitations (מצרים), making connections, or redemption. Although it is a re-action in the sense we encountered above, it is still an act in the sense of a spontaneous and creative emergence, and testimony to the freedom of the person. Although pride is expressive of freedom, lived subjectively as my will, it is constricting; although the freedom of repentance retrieves my bonds with others, it is liberating.

Thus, repentance has both religious and moral significance. Let me be clear, however. As I stated in the "Introduction" above, shame and guilt are not ready-made experiences that are imposed upon us human beings from some other source for some grand scheme. They are creative interventions, as it were, that have spontaneously arisen out of the fullness of what and who we are becoming spiritually as persons. They are moral emotions insofar as they emerge as human personal possibilities emerging out of and responding to our existential situation as finite persons. Shame and guilt most deeply affect us on the level of the person, stopping us in our tracks, possibly bringing us back on track, as it were, being attentive to who we are as persons, enabling us to return to Ourselves in the vocational sense. They are prompts to realign ourselves with Ourselves and to reconcile ourselves with others. Insofar as they break down or reestablish these relations, they have a *moral* sense; insofar as they break down or reestablish our connections with the "source" of Ourselves, they have a *religious* significance.

Repentance is possibilizing because it frees us from fixed meanings and frees us for self-revision, to become Myself for a new and different future, to return to Myself as bound to another. This is the sense in which we can speak of repentance as liberation, and how it enables us to be *hopeful* for the constitution of new meaning with others who are not in our control, yet with whom we are interrelated.

5

Hope and Despair

We saw how repentance can appropriate the past and present significance of an event and myself through a reprise toward an open future; and we saw how it can liberate me through a dispositing and existential disclaiming so that I can reorient myself through an immanent and transcendent revolution, reestablishing interpersonal connections. I treat hope under the rubric of a moral emotion of possibility not only because of its futural openness—this is shared by many experiences—but because of the modality of a sustainable future that it actualizes by being in relation to an other-than-myself. Because I am dependent upon this other who or that sustains my hope, hope can never in the final analysis be a matter of pride. I regard despair as the most profound counter to the moral emotion to hope because in this experience, the other that sustains hope is paradoxically given as not given such that this sustainability is experienced as radically shut down. As Albert Camus has shown, without the experience of some absolute, some ground, some transcendence, some other, both hope and despair are meaningless; or better, we are left neither with the moral, nor the religious, nor even the quasi-existentialism of a Nietzsche, Kierkegaard, or Sartre, but rather with absurdity.[1] Hope and despair by virtue of their shared structure are emotions that are enacted in the sphere of the person, and resonate morally and religiously.

Rather than presuppose the work done by acclaimed philosophers and theologians on hope and despair, such as Søren Kierkegaard,[2] Ernst Bloch,[3] Gabriel Marcel,[4] Paul Ricoeur,[5] Martin Heidegger,[6] or Jürgen Moltmann,[7] to name just a few, I continue with a phenomenological style of description of these experiences. To discern its structure, I draw on mundane examples by design. I do this because hope, which emerges in the face of the impossible, can contravene even the everyday situations in ways that we often take for granted, and not only those that are issues of life and death. Hope at its root is of course radically personal, radically "existential," whereas the existential bearing of despair, by its very nature, is more immediately evident and therefore is more demanding of such "life and death" examples.

After appealing to the futural dimension of hope as inherently distinct from an expectation (1), I turn to the unique possibility-structure of hope, initially discerning its modality of possibility as engagement (2). Observing that, in hope, something is experienced as beyond my control such that I am dependent upon what is other than myself, some otherness, without intending it as such (3), another possibility structure comes to the fore, namely, sustainability (4). These structures suggest that the experience of hope is essentially distinct from other experiences such as probability, wishing, longing, desiring, and importantly, denial (5). Further qualifying the temporal meaning of hope, as an awaiting-enduring (6), I take up potential counter-experiences that also relate to the modality of possibility. I describe despair as the experience of the ground of hope as impossible, such that it is *given as* impossible. I distinguish despair from other experiences that seem to rival hope like disappointment, pessimism, desperation, panic, and hopelessness (7).

Hope's Temporal Orientation as Futural

When we examine the temporality of hoping we notice that one temporal dimension stands out as essential, namely, the future. When I hope, I am oriented toward a futural open significance, most often (but not exhaustively) expressed in terms of some futural occurrence. Let me be more precise by beginning with some very simple examples.

Let's say it is in the middle of winter and I hope that it will become sunny and warm outside; I hope to go cycling. The futural dimension is evident in such acts of hope. Notice that I cannot hope that it *was* warm or that I *went* cycling; similarly, I cannot hope that it is sunny *now* and that I am cycling *now*, when I experience it as actually sunny and warm and me actually cycling. The actuality of the event in the present or the past will either be the fulfillment or disappointment of hope, but it will not constitute the temporal orientation of the hope-act. A discussion of the structure of fulfillment and disappointment where hope is concerned would take us too far beyond the limits of this chapter.[8] Suffice it to say that the fulfillment of hope depends on the manner in which the hoped-for event arrives as corresponding to the way in which the hoped-for act was directed. Such a fulfillment of hope need not be instantaneous, but can be temporally extended or historically developed. We only need note here that if a hope is realized in the manner in which the event was hoped-for, or if it does not occur at all, the hope will cease because it will have been either fulfilled in the manner appropriate to the hope, or it will have been disappointed.

Still, one may object that there are instances in which we are oriented toward the present and the past in hope. For example, let's say that I was outside in inclement weather, and while still outside I say: "I hope I am not catching a cold now," or an hour later after returning indoors, "I hope that I had not caught a cold." Although it seems that the hoping relates to the present or the past, the hope-act actually bears on an open futural significance.[9] This can be seen more clearly when we contrast hoping with wishing (I return to this distinction below). When I *wish* I had not caught a cold, I presuppose the pastness and accomplished reality of the event. I only wish it were not true or had not happened. By contrast, when I am living through the hope that I am not catching or had not caught a cold, the futural significance of this event is experienced as open for me and not as determined or completed; it is not a fait accompli. It is such an openness that relates the hope experience to the future.

Having noted that hope pertains to the future, it remains to describe its unique kind of futural orientation. Within the phenomenological tradition, it is customary to discern temporal modes in terms of time-consciousness: either as "protention," "expectation," or as "anticipation." The question concerns the relation that obtains between these kinds of time-consciousness and hope. Let me first examine whether hope is founded in expectation as a mode of time-consciousness or whether hope is a distinctive act with a different temporal structure.

Briefly put, protention is a functional, anonymous sketching out of the future that is based on a present occurrence and how that occurrence was retained as past. For example, as I take notes while reading a book, my bodily comportment is directed implicitly to what follows—from sitting on the chair, to the movement of my hands as I continue to read—all of which may be disappointed or fulfilled by the oncoming events. Now, as I interrupt my note-taking to sip a cup of coffee, I reach again for my pencil, still reading my book. The protentional threads of my hand guide me to where I last placed the pencil, and I go to grasp it, miss it, grasp it, miss it, and so forth. All this can go on implicitly while still concentrating on reading a passage. Though protention is functioning through and through taking me in this fumbling manner from one try to the next, without any explicit judgment or inference of this process—at least for the first few tries—there is no necessary engagement of hope. I may then get frustrated and turn my attention to the pencil, look around; at this point I may hope to find it again (because I need to record a thought), but the hope-act has a different orientation than that of the temporal, kinesthetic process of protention.

Hope, however, has a closer affinity to expectation. Expectation is similar to protention insofar as it is open to a futural occurrence arriving in the present, and it is also unfurled from the present and the past. Certainly, to say that expectation is related to the present and past does not mean that it is "caused" by the present or past. Rather, we would say that it is "motivated." To say that it is motivated means that the past and the present discharge a futural event or flow of events because of the alignment of sense the expected event has to the former, not because it has an objective connection to them on the order of rational correlations or natural occurrences.

Expectation is different from protention, however, insofar as expectation is an active comportment to the future. Expectation and hope, then, have this much in common: they both exhibit an orientation toward the future, and they are both carried out within the sphere of activity, not passivity.[10] For example, having observed the recent air currents, weather patterns, and cloud formations, I both expect it to be a mild and sunny day and I hope that it will be a mild and sunny day. Here, expectation and hope overlap in terms of object-orientation. However, even though and despite the fact that I expect a mild, sunny winter day, I can hope for a violent snowstorm (I want to take out my cross-country skis).

This example gives us a clear indication that expectation and hope are distinctive.[11] The question we have to answer, however, concerns whether hope is somehow a modification of expectation or whether it is a unique and irreducible orientation toward the future. To do this, let me describe the belief structure inherent in expectation.

Intrinsic to the act of expectation is the fact that it posits the existence of something futurally. Expectation is carried out in the mode of belief as an unbroken, straightforward relation to the future. When I see the FedEx person drive up to the house, I expect him to drop off a package, and when I expect him and the package, I implicitly posit the existence of the FedEx person, the package, and so on; I live in the mode of natural acceptance. This is another way of saying that when I expect something, I expect it as actual, not as possible. When I see the truck pull away, I posit or accept its actual pulling away, not its possible pulling away. Of course, I may expect that something (else) might possibly occur; I may panic in an instant that it has stopped or turned into oncoming traffic—which would rupture my expectation, or maybe instigate a new one. But in the expectation itself, in this instance, the so-called possibility is lived as actually going to occur in the mode of belief. *Expectation is not a modalization of belief;* it is another kind of belief, a straightforward one oriented in the direction of future actuality as a mode of time-consciousness. In expectation, we "count on" the futural event as it is foreshadowed or anticipated.

Further, although expectation does not exist in a relationship of causality to the present and past, it is *not completely liberated from* the past or present, either. There are features of the past and the present that "demand" or "speak in favor of" something occurring. When the "demand" on the part of things is accepted in a straightforward, unquestioning manner, the future is posited as actual (i.e., as actually coming). When such a "demand" or "speaking in favor of" is mitigated by countervailing tendencies, expectation can become modalized. In this case, something is posited as probable or likely to occur. Likelihood and probability are "impersonal" modifications of the act-structure that is carried out in expectation.

To sum up, expectation is a temporal belief-act that is oriented toward the future as a mode of time-consciousness, and arises as motivated on the basis of the present and past. Further, the actuality posited in straightforward expectation can be modalized, for example, in terms of probability or likelihood. Having understood expectation in this way, it is easier to see the distinctiveness and irreducibility of the hope-act. Before I give further specificity to the temporal structure of hoping, I first examine it as a modalization of straightforward belief in terms of its "possibility" structure.

Hope as Engagement

Expectation remains functional as the hope is carried out, even when the hope runs contrary to the expectation; likelihood is a direct modalization of expectation. But hope is not on a continuum with likelihood, say, just quantitatively less.[12] When I hope it will rain, I do not necessarily believe it "will" or "may" rain. Hope is different in kind, liberated from actuality and probability because hope is a unique modalization of belief carried out in the mode of possibility. I am not suggesting that possibility only arises with hope, but that when I hope, a unique kind of possibility structure is in play, one that has more than perceptual and judicative value.

This is one reason why we must avoid the too facile identification of the expectation of a future or guarantee of a promise, and hope, such as we find in Moltmann.[13] This is also why we cannot identify optimism and hope. Optimism has a futural orientation that expresses either a thematic or pre-thematic attitude of things working out for the best. Optimism in the true sense is not a synonym for probability (e.g., "I am optimistic that Helen will finish her project this spring"). Rather, in optimism we might hear someone exclaim: "That's okay, we will get 'em next time," or "Yes, that's too bad, but things have a way of working out for the best." In these cases, the future is posited in some positive way in a more or less indeterminate sense. Likewise, optimism must be distinguished from experiences like confidence ("I can do this") or positive thinking ("I am going to do this")—an attitude in which I am susceptible to motivational speakers, coaches, and so on, for the purposes of conditioning ourselves or convincing ourselves so that things will unfold in a specific, predetermined manner.

Let me state here at the outset that I hesitate in using the term "possibility" to characterize the hope-experience because it might fail precisely in evoking the movement of hope. "Possibility," for example, can suggest that I somehow have a predetermined, ready-made object "out there" ("a possibility"), for which I then choose to hope. This, however, might be a more appropriate way of speaking where imagination is concerned. When I imagine, I can posit a realm of possibilities and then entertain one of them. But in hoping, I do not "hope" a possibility. Instead, as I will note below, we rely on an other-than-myself that makes something possible, internally, so to speak, but I do not posit something as a possibility in hope.

Furthermore, the discussion of possibility in this context could imply that I first encounter dire circumstances and then I hope (for a different possibility) as a way of escaping them. Nothing of the sort goes on in the hope experience. Hope is initiated as a way of taking up a situation and living through its meaning "spontaneously," such that there is nothing thinglike to it. This is not to say that there is no motivation for hope, which as we will see is the ground for hope itself, but only that hope is not a rationalizing activity. Hope, we must insist, is evoked in the situation itself and emerges as part of its texture. It is not an ornament dressing up the situation or an afterthought posited in the face of trouble as an addendum. It is only after the fact that one can then attempt to analyze its structure, for example, in terms of possibility. Given these limitations of the expression "possibility," I nevertheless find it useful because it gives us a critical device—by no means the only one—of distinguishing hope from other acts like imagination, wishing, and longing, and examining the internal relation as a moral emotion to the liberating structure we saw in repentance.

With this caveat, let me continue by noting that hope lives through something implicitly as possible in the sense of liberating. In order to discern the possibility structure of hope, let me begin by contrasting it with the possibility structure peculiar to imagination. When I imagine, say, a boat sailing in my front yard, my imagining operates in the sphere of *pure, open possibility*. Anything is possible. Here we would have a kind of arbitrary possibility since it is "motivated," in the sense described above, neither by the past nor by the present, though it may borrow from the past and the present. It is completely free; I am in no way committed personally to what I imagine; there is no personal investment, even though it is "I" who do the imagining. Imagining is an act that is quasi-tied to reality: I do not posit the boat in my yard as real, but I do posit it in the mode of "as if" it were real.

We can hone in on the structure of possibility peculiar to hope if we take yet another example, this time by distinguishing it from wishing. Wishing operates in the sphere of a *hyper-factual, open possibility*. As such, the latter has significance not only for the future, but for the past as well. Let us take an example of cycling over broken glass. The moment I roll over the glass, I can at the same time wish that I had not been biking, I can wish that I had taken another route, I can wish that I had not hit the glass, or I can wish that I will not get a flat. Like imagining, wishing can relate both to the past and the future; and although there seems to be a more direct tie to a personal investment in the wishing when compared to imagining, I still do not need to have a personal involvement for the wish to be a wish; I do not have to attend to it with any personal commitment; it can be frivolous or casual and still be a wish.

Like wishing, hope is imbued with a *positive* valence. But in distinction to both imagining and wishing, hope has a unique structure as an *engaged possibility*. For example, when I live through the experience of hoping—where the object could range anywhere from escaping from prison to completing a hike, from being with someone I love to finding a piece of dark chocolate—I am invested or committed in the outcome of the situation. Of course, I can both wish and hope for the same things, such as peace on earth, a solar eclipse, or being a horse. Important to note is that it is neither the object that qualifies the experience of hope, nor the "objective" reality and how it might be perceived by others. Peculiar to the experience of hope is my disposition toward the outcome as I am engaged in it, whereas in wishing, I can live in the wishing without an actual engagement in the outcome. Hence, when I am about to undergo surgery, I do more than wish all goes well (which I could do, of course), but I hope all goes well! And although both wishing and hoping are acts that have a positive valence, I am implicitly more at a remove, as it were, when I wish than when I hope.

Of course, there are other experiences that have an engagement, similar to the act of hope, yet are distinct from the hope-act. We can examine "longing" as such an experience. When, for example, I long to see a friend who is in prison, it is more than a wish to see him; my orientation is an engaged one, maybe even emotionally charged. But this engagement lacks another essential element that distinguishes hope both from wishing and from longing: *sustainability*, which presupposes a basis of hope. Thus, I may long to see my friend literally without any hope of him ever being released.

In order to articulate this important feature of sustainability peculiar to hope's structure, let me first describe the hope-act as essentially related to an other-than-myself. I reserve the treatment of hope as sustainable until after I treat the following dimension of hope (see the section "Hope as Sustainable" below).

Hoping as Other-Related

Hoping is a way of taking up a situation not only by being personally engaged, but by experiencing myself as not being sufficient to the situation or as not in control of the situation I live through. If we inquire even further into the structure of hope, we observe that hope is an act that is related to an "outside" or to an "other-than-myself." This is a structure that is essential to all acts of hope, and constitutes one of the core features of this experience. Negatively put, this feature is suggested by the fact that when I hope, the hoped-for outcome is *given as not in my control to bring it about*.

Even the most ordinary cases of hope harbor something very extraordinary, namely, a relationship with an "other-than-myself." This is why it is illuminating to pick mundane examples. It is this sense of being connected with an "other-than-myself," even if only implicitly, that I want to trace back to its ultimate foundation. For example, if I am gambling, repairing a computer, or in a relationship, and if I *hope* (e.g., to win, to fix it, or to be with someone), I am already in relation with an other-than-myself where the hope is concerned. Alternately, if I experience myself as in control of a situation or as completely confident to bring something about, I will not hope. Therefore, no matter what the objective circumstances are, my hope implies that I am not ultimately in control of the situation, which is to say, I find myself reliant upon "something else" (put most broadly) that is able to support or sustain the situation. Accordingly, not only is the current hopeful situation not in my control, but in hope I find myself in relation to an outside of myself which or who also is not in my control.

It may be objected, however, that there are certain cases of hope where I am not supported by any "outside" of myself; I not only rely on my own abilities, but I hope precisely in my own abilities such that the hoped for event is in my control. I could hope, for example, that I do well in an interview, or even that I had done well on my exam. By "in my control," I understand, in its narrowest scope, my capacity, as who I am now, to bring about something in the living-present, however broadly this be taken. If I say, for instance, "I hope to finish this book soon," I do not mean that I cannot read, but that it is not in my power to bring it about now; perhaps I am lacking in energy and time, and it is literally "beyond me" to do it. Similarly, when I hope to do well in an interview or to have done well on an exam, an appeal is implicitly made to something that will make it so, "something" in my future or "something" animating my past actions that will make it so. When I hope in this way, I implicitly presuppose that I, myself, have no power to produce this situation now or any power to change what is already done, but I hope that something "in" what has happened will make it so.

These are perhaps trivial examples. I mention them because even in these everyday examples, we see that to experience a "not in my control" in hope points to a "beyond myself," to an "other-than-myself" to bring about something whereby I experience, however generally, a dependence upon this something other as beyond myself. Hence, hope is an act that expresses an experience of some power greater than my own as a power upon which I am dependent for occasioning the hoped-for event; it evokes a relation of dependence.

So far I have considered hope primarily in terms of object-relations. But these experiences point back more profoundly to the experience of myself and my finitude. For this reason, when I experience hope in any dimension of my life, it does not only indicate a power other or greater than me or an "outside" myself; it does not just evoke a relationship of dependence; it reveals most profoundly that I am not self-grounding. If I were self-grounding, I would be sufficient unto myself, I would be my own ground for the hope-act, which is to say, there would be no emergence of hope as a distinctive experience. The other-than-myself upon which I rely in hope is the other that "grounds" my hope and me in hope, and not just particular events that are hoped-for. The experience of hope, then, reveals the experience of an "other" who gives me to myself in the hoping as hoping, and hence as not self-grounding—in terms I will suggest below, as *sustainable,* without cause or arbitrariness.[14] That which gives me to myself is that which sustains me in my openness and my becoming as witnessed in the hope-act.

The experience of dependence upon a power of some kind other than or outside of myself, and the experience of not being self-grounding that is given in the hope-act, points to a dimension of experiencing that I call most radically "religious." Even though hope does not have its only significance in the religious dimension of experience, hope takes on its full significance at this level.

By religious experiencing, I do not mean practices or rituals undertaken within a religion or cultural heritage, or a making a petition to God. To cite Otto, religious experience is the experience of being before "an overpowering, absolute might of some kind," the experience of the presence of that "Something," that "whom or what," which Otto calls the "numinous."[15] Here, however, the numinous is not necessarily qualified as Personal, since in any religious experience, it may still remain undetermined, though in the Abrahamic tradition, and particularly as exemplified in the mystics of that tradition, it is given as inter-Personal.[16]

Here I want to restrict myself to four observations. First, there is a general characteristic in hoping of the essential relation to a "beyond" myself that is revealed in and through the experience of hope. It suggests that the interpersonal dimension is essential to hope, and that hope cannot be reduced to the mastery of the ego.[17]

Second, the experience of hope, which presupposes a not being in control and of finding myself before an other-than-myself in a relation of dependence (however generally), means that hope cannot be lived alongside pride; "I" cannot be the ultimate sustaining power of hope. This would be one reason why hope could not be reducible, for example, to desire.[18] Desiring, like wishing and longing, are acts rooted in the "I" or the "subject." Desire has no ground, or strictly speaking, I am the ground of desire; and when I desire, I am oriented toward a specific object as subject to myself. In desire, I am left to myself, as it were, and if I were left to myself, I would only wish-for, long-for, or again, desire. But by virtue of the ground of hope, which is given in and through hoping, I am not left to myself. In this way, hoping does not evolve from desire, but it can signal the eclipse of desire.[19] In desire, the "other" is the object of my desire. In hope, the other-than-myself is sustainer of the hope-act in its initiated orientation.[20] Nicholas Lash is therefore correct when he writes that it is not something like the openness of the future that furnishes the grounds for hope.[21]

Third, even if the hope-act does not have a religious orientation, the hope experience ultimately has a "religious" tenor. This is suggested by the fact that hope always already puts us in relation to an other-than-myself in all instances of hope, no matter what that hope pertains to or no matter how vague this "beyond" myself might be experienced in *otherwise everyday* acts of hope. Certainly, hope takes place in acts that are not explicitly religious. Hoping that my cell phone works after I drop it is not directly a religious act. This is because the ground of hope is not thematically intended in hope. If it were thematically intended then we might have the experience of prayer, where, for example, we are oriented toward a ground, say, to bring something about. If the attempt were to manipulate the "ground," it might be expressive of what Horkheimer and Adorno have described as Enlightenment rationality.[22] I would call it idolatry.[23]

When I take the cell phone to the repair shop and hope that the agent can fix it, I am relying upon the ability of another person to fulfill my hope. I do not have to pray to God or believe in God, for example, for this to be the case. My point, however, is that these experiences are grounded in a dimension of experiencing instituted through a primordial experiencing of an outside in terms of dependence. Without any explicit religious appeal, a hope, one as seemingly innocuous as hoping my cell phone works, already bears a religious significance "before" I could want it to be a religious act. Accordingly, when I hope for something, my hoping is oriented precisely as a specification or delimitation trained on this or that. This is why hoping my cell phone works is not explicitly a religious act. Nevertheless, since hoping puts me in a non-intentional relation to an other-than-myself—which opens up simultaneously along with the intentional relation of hoping this or that; since I am revealed in a dependence upon this non-intentional other-than-myself, my hoping with respect to the cell phone is simultaneously a de-limitation, that is, an opening; it opens me precisely to this dimension.

Of course, this does not mean that hope is always a good thing, even if hope always carries a positive valence in its orientation, and even within the religious sphere of experience. Let us examine an example from Saint Teresa of Avila. She writes: "Look at the good remedy the devil gave me and the charming humility—the great disquiet within me. But how could I quiet my soul? It was losing its calm; it remembered favors and gifts; it saw that this world's pleasures are disgusting. How it was able to go on amazes me. I did so by means of hope because I never thought (insofar as I now recall, for this must have happened twenty-one years ago) I would cease being determined to return to prayer—but I was waiting to be very purified of sin. Oh, how wrong was the direction in which I was going with this hope! The devil would have kept me hoping until judgment day and then have led me into hell." In this case, hoping was a distraction and a false humility since according to her the devil had insidiously become the sustainer of hope.[24] Nevertheless, even in this example, it points to a relation with an other-than-myself, and to the fact that hope is given as sustainable by some ground of hope.

Finally, because the moral and religious dimensions of experience are susceptible to different orders of givenness and evidence, and do not follow the logic of presentation or object-givenness, and because it is in the religious dimension of experience that hope receives its fullest significance, wherein modes of givenness such as epiphany and revelation are operative (and not the presentation of objects),[25] these modes of givenness are not susceptible to the structure of intention-fulfillment that is evident in the presentation of objects. Not only does the ground of hope not fit the category of object-givenness, since it is given without being intended, but we would have the experience of more being given than what I hoped-for, and hence an "overflowing" beyond the intention of hope. This is different from being given more of the same, like the plus ultra of an object's horizon. Instead, there is an otherwise of givenness that takes place alongside or subtending the hoping-that. Accordingly, we distinguish between the intention of hope, which is oriented toward something, and hopefulness. Hopefulness is already a relation with a ground of hope, without it being identified with any particular object intended in the hope-act. In fact, the comportment of hopefulness, which is grounded in the ground of hope, imbues and animates all I do, even when I explicitly carry out an act of hope. For this reason, hopefulness could be understood generatively as foundational for the hope-act.

Hoping therefore entails a basis for hope, which is a dependence upon another for living the situation beyond its otherwise closed strictures. But this ground of hope is only given in and through the hope-act itself. I do not first think "I cannot bring something about by myself; therefore, I will hope." It is not as if the ground of hope were somehow given first, and then I hope, or when I hope, the hope-act somehow causes the ground of hope. It is not that I hope "in order to" open possibilities or produce something. Then I would be asserting my control and having the power of disposition over another, and this would vitiate the hope-act. Again, I am not attempting to adduce when one should or should not hope, but only describing what is going on in the hope-experience.

When I hope, "I" do not "appeal" to a ground of hope; but in and through hoping, an appeal is made, or can be understood as having been made. It is not my hoping that is efficacious, but the other-than-myself which sustains my hoping. As I intimated above, hoping is a peculiar way of taking up a situation spontaneously, originally each time, such that the experience itself is the relying on another of some kind and such that it "reveals" a ground of hope out of which hoping itself becomes possible. The ground of hope is "discovered" only in and through the experience of hoping.

Hope as Sustainable

Hope is the experience of an engagement. In addition, due to the other-oriented dimension of hope, which reveals a ground of hope, possibility is also *sustainable*. For this reason, hope cannot be "merely" subjective. Without this basis or ground of hope, which is given without being intended as such, and which enables the intentional orientation in hope to be sustainable, one would be unable to distinguish, for example, a hope from a mere wish, or hoping from merely longing. Longing and wishing are differentiated by the former demanding an engagement and the latter permitting a frivolity. But both are differentiated from hope insofar as hope is, essentially, sustainable. Thus, in wishing, longing, like in hoping, there is nothing we can do; but in hope, something can be done, as it were, and this goes to the ground of hope.

When I hope, for example, that I find a piece of dark chocolate, or when I hope to become a horse, all objective criteria are held in check by the ground of hope, whatever that may be. I have lived the hoped-for event as sustainable. Somehow it can happen, despite what I expect, despite its probability, despite what others think, despite how it may look "objectively." Note also that the event of hope is essentially different from the motivation of an expectation. A motivation is given for expectation "internally," as it were, from the past and present. In hope, a "beyond" sustains the hope (precisely as the ground of hope, be it the horse-people or the Holy), but strictly speaking it is not "motivated," and even less "caused."

Let us examine the other side of what it means for hope to be lived as sustainable. When I am engaged in the hoped-for outcome as sustainable, I simultaneously have before me the contingency of that same outcome as not occurring. Although the ground of hope is the founding moment in the sense that it makes hope sustainable, to be sustainable also entails a contingency. Otherwise, the act of hope would be immaterial. Let me give an example. I am seated in a café, waiting for a friend to arrive. We had made plans to meet for a performance; my friend is reliable, and I expect him to arrive any time now. As the hour approaches, I begin to get nervous, and I hope that he arrives soon. Here, I experience that he may not arrive on time. Expectation is still functional, and in all *probability* he will arrive on time, but now an act of hope is carried out that intervenes in the situation and qualifies it uniquely. If the contingency were not given along with the positive sustainability, hope would not arise as an experience.

Notice that the other-than- or outside-of-myself I mentioned above *cannot* be experienced as a predetermining, necessitating force, be it either from laws of nature or a deity. In fact, it is in the face of such necessitating determinacy that I hope (and this means that in hope such an "other" has to be experienced as something other than necessitating). On the other hand, by noting that a hoped-for event is experienced as contingent, I am not suggesting that the event is experienced as impossible—that is, where it is given as ruled out in advance.

Certainly, something may be understood objectively to be impossible, or be experienced as impossible by someone else. But I cannot at the same time hope and experience what is hoped-for *as* impossible. For example, I might hope to survive an F5 tornado while standing in its path, even though for everyone else it would just be "suicide." For me, it is—by some means, and sustained by the ground of hope—experienced as possible to survive it even though I am aware that I probably will not survive it. There is at least a hairsbreadth of sustainability given in hope. If I *experience it as* impossible, I will not hope.

Thus, hope does not have the same rapport with impossibility as it does with some of the other features I have described, like expectation, probability, and improbability. But whereas hope may be at odds with expectation or probability while I live through both (possibly) contesting experiences, hope *transforms* the experience of impossibility such that the two cannot be lived through simultaneously. For example, I am on the coast when an earthquake hits offshore; an enormous tidal wave towers above me on the beach and I take any attempt to flee as futile; it is impossible to outrun the tsunami, and I give up. Now, if I were to experience hope in such an instance, which is entirely possible, I could not simultaneously experience my escape as impossible. Hope lives the situation in such a way that otherwise objective "limits" are no longer definitive, and their rupture is sustainable. Hope does not merely mollify the experience of the impossible; it commutes the experience of the impossible into sustainability. Hoping something does not make it possible; rather, the entire structure of possibility is transformed; it is given now as sustainable in the hoping and this allows hoping to be precisely hopeful.

In brief, hope operates in the sphere of engagement and sustainability; it takes place in excess of or in the face of expectation, probability, improbability, and impossibility, but in the latter case, it transforms the experience of the impossible and makes it precisely hopeful.

Hope and Denial

With the commutation of the experience of impossibility through the experience of hope, questions concerning denial naturally surface. When I hope, am I not just really living in denial, in denial, that is, of an impossible situation? For the sake of simplicity, let us define denial as not accepting the "facts" as they are presented, so that when I am confronted with a situation, I posit a different reality. Objectively speaking, the reality I deny may or may not be true. At issue is the fact that when I live in denial, I do not accept the reality as presented, and I do this by positing a different one. This is distinct from resignation, in which I just take things the way they are, without however having posited a different one. Further, in denial, I do not explicitly experience my positing of a new reality *as* a denial. Rather, I take my position as "just the way things are." It is only to another that I am "in denial" or it is adduced as such by the outside. Finally, denial is not future-oriented, but *present*-oriented. In denial, I assert that the present situation is such and such; there is no different outcome to be awaited, and no change of a situation. I posit the state of affairs as such, now; this is the way it is and nothing anyone can say or do will change that.

In hope, however, I do not deny the present facts, for in some sense, they are already accepted. Yet, in this tacit acceptance, hope is directed toward the future and a sustainable, possible transformation of the current situation. What is held in check, as I intimated above, is the expected, the likely or unlikely, or the impossible outcome of the situation. Further, in hope, I do not posit the futural outcome as real, for if it were real, I would be precisely in the experience of the fulfillment of hope, which, when fulfilled, would be the cessation of hope. But where hope is operative, it is functional "despite" or in the face of an outcome that might run counter to the hoped-for event. Lash, in his interpretation of Marx, is correct when he writes that unlike optimism, hope does not leave behind tragic experience, since the latter—and as we would say, denial—already "knows the answer." Whereas hope can only be carried out, he contends, in the interrogative mode because it is "mystery" that supplies the grounds of human hope and its fulfillment.[26]

Let us take the example of a person missing in action (MIA), and let us begin with the case of denial. After a time, let's say, a loved one hears word from military officials that his brother has been killed in a war. Denial would imply a negation of this situation and the positing of another one. "I don't believe it" (i.e., I *believe* something else); "he is still alive"; "he will come back home soon." Or I can catch myself in denial: "It can't be true," I say to myself. One could live in this belief posture for an indeterminate time. Certainly, the person who is living in actual denial of this official promulgation may actually be right; perhaps it is a case of mistaken identity; the brother is still alive and will come back. The point is that in denial a situation is negated and a different reality is accepted such that when I deny a particular "reality" there is no room for hope, since I have already asserted another reality.

Now, if we examine this example in light of hope, we see immediately how hope is distinctive from denial. In hope, there is not a direct denial of the situation; but I do not accept the finality of it, either. Against expectation as an unbroken, straightforward relation, against probability or impossibility, *I hope,* which takes up the situation as an engaged, sustainable one with at least an implicit ground for that hope. "Yes, I understand what you tell me, but still I hope he is alive." I do not imagine that he is alive; I do not expect that he is alive, I am not "optimistic" that he is alive. I hope, against all odds, that he is alive. Someone may think that I am just "in denial." But when I *live through* the experience of hope I do not negate a current reality by positing a different reality; I implicitly acknowledge both the negative and positive possibilities, and live the hoped-for event as sustainable. The positing of a new present reality on either side of the report (acceptance or denial) would not be the experience of hope; it might be the disappointment or fulfillment of hope as accepting a new reality, but it would not be or would no longer be hope.

Hope's Temporal Meaning as Awaiting-Enduring

Hope, I have maintained, is not itself a temporal act in the manner of protention, expectation, or anticipation, but it does have a temporal character. Its temporal character is what I call an "awaiting-enduring." This awaiting is an openness and an endurance, what we could also term a patience. By "patience," I do not mean a kind of "waiting around," but a mode of comportment that is precisely in opposition to my *actively* assuming control of the situation, that is, in contrast to what we might term an "actience."[27] In hoping, I await not only the fulfillment of hope; I endure in hope both because the hope is sustainable (by virtue of the ground of hope), and I await-enduringly due to the contingency expressed in hope. Certainly, I can give up hope, even generate a new hope. My point is that in the experience of hoping, as long as the hope is functional, ongoing, *as long as we live in the hope, this awaiting is an enduring, a patience.*[28]

Let's contrast this awaiting as endurance and patience with a similar but essentially different temporal experience of waiting-for. Waiting-for as futurally oriented is tied to expectation; more precisely, waiting-for is a modification of expectation. I cannot wait-for something that I do not also expect; but as we have seen, I can hope for something that I do not expect; I await, and while the hope is ongoing, I await enduringly. In hope, I enduringly await the return of the MIA, while I may not expect the return or even wait-for such a return.

Let's now look at a particularly complex situation involving expectation, waiting-for, and awaiting-enduringly. I am in a waiting room at the doctor's office. I have given my name, informed the receptionist that I have an appointment, and so on. I *expect* the nurse to call my name any moment now. I look at the clock, a few minutes have passed, and I patiently *wait-for* the nurse to call my name. Notice that as long as I expect the course of events to follow through according to how they have run in the past (if it accords with my expectation), I do not hope that the nurse will arrive; he will; it is just a matter of time; I wait-for the call with more attentiveness than merely expecting. Now thirty minutes have passed and he still has not called my name; I grow irritated and impatient. Notice also that while I could remain or could have remained patient, impatience is a possibility in waiting-for, something that is not possible in awaiting-enduringly.

I can become impatient in waiting-for because I assert my wanting to be in control of the situation, and this implicitly removes the relation of dependence that is essential to hope and awaiting-enduringly in hope. Waiting-for can be impatience because it allows the expression of my being in control, or negatively put, of my not wanting to be dependent or reliant upon anything else, either actually or virtually. Thus, the moment I want to take over the situation, or feel it necessary to take control of the situation—and maybe well I should—is the moment I am no longer in the hope-experience.

In contrast, I remain patient in awaiting-enduringly because of my tacit dependence on the other-than-myself, the ground of hope, in hoping. In some sense, I have to let it happen. But I also hope, in patience, because in and through the hope-act, the ground of hope gives the hope as sustainable. I can "await" in hope, enduringly, since I am not left to myself. By contrast, there are no grounds for impatience; there might be grounds for anxiousness, uncertainty, and so on due to the contingency mentioned above, but in the hope-act itself, there can only be grounds for awaiting-enduringly.

It is true that I could become impatient with respect to something that was hoped-for, but at that moment, at the moment I become impatient, the hope-act has ceased. Impatience therefore can be a sign of disappointed hope. Hope has become something else at that point. Maybe the hope just goes away; maybe it becomes hopelessness, or even despair, maybe I just "wait-for." But, again, as long as the hoping is functional, there is patience where the fulfillment of hope is concerned.

I ask the receptionist if it will be much longer, and I am told that the doctor had an emergency, she will be back eventually, but it may take a while. Now it is not clear that I will get my appointment since I have to be somewhere else. I don't expect the doctor to show up in time, but a hope arises, namely, that the doctor will get here before I have to leave. This hope is the intrusion of patience in the situation, and immediately colors it differently; the tenor of my comportment in this situation is modified precisely in terms of hope. I hope the doctor arrives in time for me, even if it runs contrary to everything I expect or wait-for; I really do not believe the doctor will arrive in time, but I hope so. As long as I hope, I will remain there in the doctor's office. I endure it, I tarry with the situation; I do not leave.

This exposition of the temporality of hope as an awaiting-enduringly rejoins the initial discussion of hope as a futural orientation, yet as structurally distinct from an expectation. Hope *liberates* the future from past and present, and even from what is to be expected. Thus the future given in hope is not just an anticipated or promised future, but a liberated future which entails an awaiting-enduringly. Hope commutes the impossible to the hopeful. It does so because as a moral emotion of possibility, I am not only engaged in the hoped-for event, but more significantly, because the hope is sustained by a ground of hope given in the very execution of the hope-act. I am given in relation to something other than myself in a relation of dependence, where what is hoped-for is not in my control, having in the very hoping, eclipsed pride. These essential characteristics of hope distinguish the experience from other experiences like imagining, wishing, longing, or negatively, denial. It is a feature of hope that we cannot simultaneously experience hope and the impossible *as* impossible; if this were the case, the latter would be precisely the experience of despair.

Despair as the Impossible Ground of Hope

In this section, I continue to describe the experience of hope, but now by focusing on the experiences in which the sustainability of a futural openness is rivaled, and in an extreme experience, shut down. I do this by elaborating upon experiences that seem to challenge hope, namely, disappointment, desperation, panic, hopelessness, and most profoundly despair.

In contrast to the ancient and modern traditions, the contemporary concern with hope seems to have emerged along with existential issues that challenge hope, experiences such as absurdity, anxiety, and fear. Of course, we are all familiar with Hesiod's account of Pandora opening a jar that Prometheus and her husband, Epimetheus, had warned to keep shut, releasing not only all sorts of ills that plague humankind, but Hope, which discourages mortals from general suicide.[29] But Aristotle, in discussing courage, fear, wishing, and so on, never mentions hope as a virtue, since virtue is a disposition of those already perfect.[30] For Augustine, on the other hand, hope is contrasted with fear, and like love is essentially grounded in faith; hope, for him, only has an object that is good.[31] Similarly taking the object of hope as a *"bonum futurum,"* Aquinas regards hope as a theological virtue since as a character of spirit, it reaches the supreme norm of human activity.[32]

The modern period, rationalists and empiricists alike, gave scant attention to hope, though most never failed to weigh in on the issue. Spinoza's *Ethics*, for example, characterized hope as an inconstant pleasure, as a confidence with an element of doubt, and posits a traditional opposition between hope and fear.[33] Locke, for his part, posited hope as the mental pleasure one gains by thinking of a probable future.[34]

Without citing similar treatments by the likes of Hobbes, Descartes, Hume (who tended to treat it only incidentally), or Kant (for whom hope became a more prominent concern), it is safe to say that not until the advent of existentialist thought and related concerns, which arose in critical theory, in the philosophy of history, and eschatology, did we see a fresh undertaking with respect to hope. Figures like Kierkegaard, Marcel, Bloch, Ricoeur, Moltmann, Lash, and Schumacher are representative of this new appraisal and climate of hope.

What I find interesting is that these later "existentialist" authors did not take up the traditional philosophical and religious view of hope as contrasted with fear (which, by the way, is also found prominently in the Abrahamic tradition of mystical literature), presupposing its relation to faith, charity, and so on. Instead, they were driven to address the issue of hope through experiences that in various ways ran counter to hope, experiences like despair, anxiety, or the absurd.

I follow this basic movement by examining five experiences that run counter to hope (or in some instances, that only seem to do so). I do this, first, by noting the cases in which hope simply is not operative, then, by treating the significances of both desperation and pessimism. This is followed by a description of the experience of hopelessness, and finally, by treating the experience of despair. Here despair is shown to constitute the most profound challenge to hope among these experiences and to be foundational for the others, even though it, despair, is disclosed ultimately as founded in hope.

Inoperative hope. Let me begin by considering instances in which hope is simply not or is no longer operative. There are at least three instances in which hope is inoperative: (a) hope simply does not arise, (b) hope is fulfilled, and (c) hope is disappointed.

In the first case, hope may not arise at all, for example, when things are simply expected to run their course in a certain way. For instance, I am certain that the sun will rise tomorrow morning. Since certainty is a straightforward belief posture, hope never becomes an issue. Such a certainty can extend to all aspects of our lives; we can even experience certainty in the form of an obedience to a higher will. In such a case, hope could not be operative. I could assert, without the intervention of hope, a kind of absolute, unquestioning conviction that God will handle everything, cure every ill, and so on. Here God would not be the ground of hope, but the controller of world destiny. Because everything would somehow be determined for me, and I would experience it *as* determined (such that the opposite is not only impossible, but any other possibility is in effect impossible), the experience of hope would not be able to arise; here it would be eclipsed by an experience of necessity.

Second, a hope may not be operative in the sense that it is no longer functional, that is, the instant it becomes fulfilled. The hope-act is fulfilled when the hoped-for event arrives in the manner in which the hope-act was directed. A fulfillment of hope may be instantaneous, or the fulfillment may have a temporal duration. In either case, when a hope is realized, the hope will cease because it will have been fulfilled in the manner appropriate to the hope.[35]

Third, hope may not be functional in the sense that it is not realized and hence its directedness is disappointed. In perception, the non-fulfillment of an expectation takes place through the presentation of something new that stands in its stead (i.e., a new perceptual object); but the disappointment or non-realization of hope is not supplanted by a new hope. For example, I hope at the beginning of the basketball season that a particular team will win the series title. The season is over, a different event arises (i.e., someone else wins), and my hope is not fulfilled. In this instance, the hope ends, but it is not because a new hope has arisen in its place. I can of course still hope, even if the hope is not fulfilled; but then it has the quality of being "not yet" fulfilled. I still have hope. The disappointment of the hope, however, is the cessation of the hope-act, without a new one having had to take its place. Note also in this regard that whereas I can have a mistaken perception, I cannot have a mistaken hope. Since hope is a modalization of the very belief structure that we find in perception, it is the ability to arise in the face of a "contradiction" of fact or even a perceived "impossibility." To hope that it will rain on a sunny summer afternoon is neither correct nor incorrect, neither true nor false.

Desperation. Let me turn to another experience that seems to test the hope experience, namely, desperation. If we were to base our assessment of this experience on the etymology of the term, we might conclude that desperation (Latin: *desperare*) is antithetical to hope: someone in desperation, someone desperate, is someone who has given up hope. But if we examine the experience of desperation, we find just the opposite to be the case. Let's say I am climbing a mountainside with all my equipment secured and suddenly the rope breaks. I start reaching for something, anything; I recklessly flap my arms "in desperation." What I experience here is not the lack of hope, but precisely hope taken to an extreme. Desperation is, as it were, a last hope.

Here is what makes *hope desperate*. I noted that hoping is an experience of the hoped-for event being out of my control, and this implies the relation of dependence. When it is sunny out and I hope it rains, there is nothing "I" can do; in my hope, I am immediately, even if implicitly, in a relation of dependence on some other that/who sustains my hope. By contrast, there are instances in which I take control of a situation, for example, in desiring, in willing, or when I am just confident in my own abilities. My efforts are enough or should be enough to master the situation or to bring something about. I do not hope. Desperation, however, is a mode of hope that tries to force the issue; it tries to speed things up by my intervention. It would seem therefore that desperation is not at all an awaiting-enduring, as I characterized the hope experience, nor a relation of dependence. It would be easy enough thereby to say that desperation is actually the negation of hope.

Why we cannot come to this conclusion is that our actions in themselves are not executed in desperation as sufficient to produce the results. They are set loose precisely "in a hope." When we are desperate, it is not really that we think our last-ditch efforts will be efficacious to bring about the event; I "know" I cannot fly, but I hope that something in what I do will arrest my fall. I don't think flailing my arms about will actually sustain a new grip; I do not expect that grabbing the rope will stop my fall, since it is severed and not attached to any secure point; that's why I am falling. But I "hope," in desperation, that something in what I do will work. We can all think of all sorts of examples that might provoke desperation, from the distressed lover to the cancer patient. All causal connections, the finality of objective relations, and the run of external circumstances are all put out of play and recast in the spirit of hope: "I'll try anything" in desperation (i.e., in an extreme hope) that it will work. What makes hope "desperate" in such a case is that desperation verges on impatience, but rather than being a true impatience, it is a reckless awaiting; it is a hope that asserts an "I have to do something even though 'it' is beyond what I can do." This is why we often think that people who we call "desperate" do "foolish" things—at least it looks that way from the outside. For the person who is desperate, however, the efforts have an internal even if idiosyncratic logic because they are sustained in their own way.

What makes *desperation hope* is that there is a simultaneous "recognition" that the occasion escapes me, that there must be something more internal to what I do to make what I do work. It is only when, for example, desperation is eclipsed that the temporal feature is no longer an awaiting but an expecting or a waiting for, anticipating, and so on, that the hope-experience, in this case desperation, ceases.

To help make this clearer, let's take the "efforts" we witness in desperation and remove the element of hope (thus no longer being desperation at all). Here, we would have what I would call "panic." While desperation retains its futural orientation, panic can be expressed as a "freezing up" or as an "overreaction" and accordingly a denunciation of futural significance. We have mere reactions to a present that are fixed upon the present. True, in panic I also experience the situation as out of my control; but this is not an other-relatedness. As opposed to the hope experience there is not even an implicit experienced relation of dependence in panic; it does not even revert to the self (as in the case of confidence). We might think of the example of hitting black ice while driving and skidding out of control; we might think of having to sit for an important exam and not knowing the answers; we might think of someone involved in a hit-and-run accident. Needless to say, the same event can provoke either panic or desperation; they might even share external characteristics and patterns of actions. But whether it is "panic" or "desperation" could be read off from the "reply" to the event. Thus, in the case of hit and run, one may just stop and stare in panic, one may flee the scene of the accident out of panic; I can therefore be seized in panic by doing nothing or doing something (i.e., fleeing), but in either case, there is nothing purposeful in the panic, no futural openness, no enduring or reckless awaiting, no sustainability of an outcome.

Let's say, on the contrary, that the fleeing is done in desperation. In this case, the tenor of the action would be different. One might flee in desperation "in the hope" of evading persecution, "in the hope" of getting help, and so on. But as opposed to panic, we could see the desperate person also trying to do something to assist or to save the injured person rather than fleeing (i.e., giving him CPR), even if the person did not know what she was doing—precisely because desperation contains an element of hope whereas panic does not.

Pessimism. Pessimism is another experience that would seem to challenge the experience of hope. However, rather than running contrary to hope, pessimism is really opposed to optimism. Optimism, we saw above, posits the reality of things such that they will work out for the best. Pessimism, for its part, also takes a stand on reality; and like the case of optimism, we have to distinguish between pessimism used in the sense of probability, and pessimism in the authentic sense as a relation to being and independent of probability. For example, even if things are highly probable, I can still remain pessimistic. Let's take the example of completing a project. We could certainly give up hope that something will get done. But this is not pessimism. In pessimism, we take the circumstances in general as things not working out. Or we could take it one step further: "Yes, I will complete the project, but it won't be any good."

If we now contrast this with hopelessness (which I take up under the next subheading), we see that in the latter, there is the experience of no ground of hope *in this instance*. In pessimism, there is simply no "ground of hope" at issue because I go along with the movement of being in this way (namely, negatively). Thus, with respect to a particular project, I can be hopeless now, but generally, I am not pessimistic. I can be both hopeless and pessimistic, however, because these are two different kinds of experience.

Accordingly, in the cases of both optimism and pessimism, we are concerned with a general attitude, a *Weltthesis*, a style of comportment and positing; it is a casting, a coloring of a belief posture, though it can pertain to specific spheres of experience: Things are just going to turn out badly. We make such an assertion about the reality of things independently of a ground of hope or even with the negation of a ground of hope. Thus, because hope does not operate on the same level of optimism/pessimism, I can, for example, buy a lottery ticket in the hope (even desperate hope) that I will win, but be pessimistic that I will win. Or pessimism can pertain to more specific spheres. For example, I can be pessimistic about my interpersonal relations ("Yes, I will meet someone in my life, but it won't turn out well"), but be optimistic with respect to others, for example, my business affairs. This is one reason why, as we will see below, pessimism cannot be tantamount to despair.

Hopelessness. As experiences that run antithetically to hope, I examined cases in which hope is not or is no longer operative. I also examined the experience of desperation, which seemed to be antithetical to hope but turned out to be a mode of hope—an experience that can be contrasted with that of panic as well as pessimism, which runs contrary to optimism, not hope. These instances, however, have not developed a contrast with hope to its fullest extent. To do this, it is necessary to examine two further cases, namely, hopelessness and despair. First, hopelessness.

To elucidate this deeper contrast, it will be helpful to recall the dual structure of the hope movement intimated above. On the one hand, when I hope, say, that I catch a taxi in pouring-down rain, I am directed in an intentional relation to something specific that can be fulfilled. "I hope that. . . ." But in the hope experience, I am simultaneously, intrinsically, and implicitly in a relation of dependence on an other-than-myself that/who sustains this hope. This is a relation to "otherness" that functions as a "ground of hope." This relation goes beyond the intention-fulfillment structure since this other-than-myself as a ground of hope is already beyond what I could intend; it already subtends my intention (my "I hope that . . ."). Such a ground of hope—whatever it may be—renders my hope sustainable. The latter expresses experientially that I am not self-grounding. Thus, in the single experience of hope we have a bifurcation of orientations: in and through the hope experience I am oriented toward a specific hope-event, and a ground of hope is given (not intended) that/who sustains that hope. Let me add, further, that it is because this ground of hope is given in this way, that I can be *hopeful* or have a *hopeful* disposition without carrying out any specific act of hope through which I would be oriented toward this particular hoped-for event. In this case, hopefulness is understood as revelatory of the ground of hope.

Let me now treat the instance of *hopelessness*. Similar to the manner in which I intend a hoped-for object or event, I reserve the term "hopeless" for the occasion in which I am oriented toward something specific: "I am hopeless that . . ." or "it is hopeless that. . . ." Let's say I am working on a car, trying to build it from scratch, something I have never done before. Initially, I had thought I could build it (let's say without any hope-experience being in play at all—I was just very confident), but now I suddenly experience the situation as hopeless. Of course, one possibility is that after I am stuck or frustrated, I now hope that I can fix it. But let us suppose that even now the hope-experience does not intervene; I simply experience hopelessness with respect to the whole car-fashioning event.

I insist on the hope experience not intervening here because it is important to distinguish hopelessness from the disappointment of a hope. Disappointment, as we saw above, is the cancellation or nonfulfillment of a previous hope. The experience of a disappointed hope *must* follow upon the actual experience of hope. For a hope to be disappointed, then, a specific hope-act has to be carried out, which is then not fulfilled or otherwise negated. Notice that a disappointed hope stops at the present and does not extend into or say anything about the future; the hope that I have now is disappointed, now. Here, the ground of hope is still intact, and I can experience a hope with respect to the same situation at a later time, even if the hope is disappointed right now.

It is true that hopelessness *can* follow upon the actual experience of hope (and as we will see, hopelessness as a structure will presuppose the possibility of hope). But unlike the experience of a disappointed hope, which presupposes the execution of a prior hope-act that is then negated, hopelessness does not depend upon the prior execution of a specific hope-act directed toward a specific situation or event. Also in distinction to a disappointed hope, hopelessness extends beyond the present, but speaks to the futural horizon of possibility with respect to that experience.

Hopelessness is not a cancellation of the specific hope, but the immediate and direct experience of the impossibility of the event *as* impossible. Previously, I described hope as the conversion or transmutation of the impossible into a situation that is precisely hopeful; the contradictory, the unlikely, and indeed the impossible are commuted into the "sustainable." For me who hopes, no matter how difficult the situation looks to others objectively, I cannot at the same time hope and experience this situation *as* impossible. I could agree with others that indeed "it *looks* impossible," or "it *seems* impossible," but when I hope, I experience the sustainability of the hoped-for occasion in the face of what is otherwise impossible. I do not actually experience the impossibility of the situation as such. The protagonist in Bresson's *A Man Escaped* is indeed faced with a situation that *appears* hopeless, and by all calculations of most all the other prisoners, it is. But if the protagonist were to experience it only as impossible, he would not try to escape; he would give up. Accordingly, without any other prior hope being carried out that would be susceptible to disappointment, hopelessness is the experience of the impossibility of the situation *as* impossible. Hopelessness, then, has its own structure, is not related genetically to the disappointment of a specific hope, and is the experience of the impossible *as* impossible.

When we look more closely into the experience of hopelessness, we note two things. First, we note that there is both a specific directedness in relation to which I am hopeless and the experience of the non-participation of a ground of hope *in this instance*. In the car example, the situation is just hopeless; I forget it and turn away, sell the parts, give up. The experience of hopelessness is geared to *the specific event*, but it does not impinge decisively on the ground of hope. Hence, I go on, perhaps to something else; the structure of the ground of hope is still intact, as it were, only in this instance, crossed out.

Certainly, there can be different degrees of the experience of hopelessness. In this respect, such an experience can be more or less frustrating, more or less severe. But what unites these experiences and makes them all precisely an experience of hopelessness is that hopelessness is a specific orientation to a situation that in its specificity is experienced as impossible. Further, in this case, sustainability, which goes to the ground of hope, is *implicitly* and simultaneously suspended, without the necessity of any actual, prior hope-act. Again, just as in the experience of hope, what we experience as hopeless is not determined by the particular reality of the event in which hopelessness is experienced. What might be for me hopeless, might be for another a matter of hope. Rather, it has to do with the tenor or quality of the experience.

Second, to say that hopelessness, unlike a disappointed hope, can occur without any specific execution of the hope-act does not mean that hopelessness does not presuppose a particular experience of hope. In and through the experience of hopelessness, the ground of hope (and hence the sustainability of hope) flashes forth through the conduit of hopelessness *as* cancelled in this particular instance; hopelessness is an opening through which sustainability appears *as* immediately suspended in this instance; it is an experience through which the ground of hope is revealed as ineffectual, as crossed-out in this case. The impossible is given now as impossible. Thus, the moment hopelessness emerges, the "possibility" of hope emerges—not as a choice or an option from which I select—but as a structure of experience; it emerges simultaneously with hopelessness, as does the ground of hope, but in this experience of hopelessness, the relation of dependence is cut short, shattered, and it stops as a mere "out of my control." I experience or live the impossibility of the situation as impossible.

We have seen that, phenomenologically speaking, hopelessness is characterized as the experience of impossibility *as* impossible. But not every experience of the impossible *as* impossible is the experience of hopelessness. For example, I can experience the mathematical impossibility of ever getting a "19" hand in cribbage without ever experiencing the situation as hopeless. It is just a simple realization, a statement of fact; this could hold for any logical contradiction. The question, however, concerns what accounts for the difference between experiencing the impossible *as* impossible when it yields hopelessness, and the experience of the impossible as impossible when it does not.

A very obvious and easy answer would be to say that hope is indeed the key ingredient: the experience of the impossible as impossible is given as "hopeless" precisely when I have first lived through a hope-act that pertains to this event: if I do not first have a hope in this specific respect, I will not experience hopelessness. My observation, however, is just the opposite, namely, hopelessness is not dependent upon the execution of a prior hope-act. I do not suggest that hope *cannot* arise prior to the experience of hopelessness, only that hopelessness is not essentially dependent upon a prior execution of the hope-act in this specific regard.

Let's begin with a new example. Let's say that I am building a model pirate ship. I have all the instructions before me, all the pieces, the glue, and so on. I am confident I can build this ship. Notice here that no hope experience is involved; I simply begin my new task, building the ship. Everything runs according to plan and I progress from day to day—until I examine a photo of the rigging! I look at the complicated design, glance down at my spool of thread, and without any intervention of hope, I experience the situation as hopeless.

One could object, however, that I really go through various phases, even if I do not notice them. I look at the rigging, and I implicitly experience something like "I *expect* to be finished soon," "I am *certain* I can do this," or "*maybe* I can do this," "I can *probably* do this," "it is *improbable* that I can do this, but I will try anyway," and then, "it is hopeless; I give up." Again, one *could* always experience a hope: "It is really beyond me, I cannot make heads or tails of it, but I *hope* I can do it." While my overall contention is that such a hope experience does not have to be present, here I wish to emphasize that there is not a sliding scale or a mere difference of degree between, on the one hand, certainty, probability, likelihood, improbability, and on the other, hopelessness. Hope, as we have seen, is a modalization of straightforward belief (unlike expectation and certainty); hope can persist in the face of countervailing expectations, probability, and improbability. When it comes to the impossible, the latter is commuted and transformed as sustainable, and in this way, as liberation, a freeing from the impossible.

The situation is somewhat different with respect to hopelessness. Hopelessness will not run counter to an expectation; it will not go against a probability; it will go in the direction of an improbability. But this in and of itself will not be the experience of hopelessness. We come back to our formulation: hopelessness is the experience of the impossibility of the situation *as* impossible. This is why hopelessness is not more or less a probability. The experience of the impossible is something different, qualitatively distinct from probability or improbability. It happens uniquely, and does not depend upon the evolution of these modalizations of belief.

Nevertheless, something has emerged from this example and these considerations that speaks to the issue of hopelessness, namely, that the experience of hopelessness depends upon a temporal unfolding of events, and more specifically, from a genesis of an endeavoring of some kind. We observe that I only become "hopeless" with regard to something toward which I am striving, with respect to something I want to or try to achieve or I want to happen. I can experience hopelessness in assembling the model ship because I endeavor to assemble it. When

I experience it as impossible, I become hopeless in this respect. Hopelessness presupposes, we might say, a "project" both in the sense of an endeavor, a trying, and in the sense of a futural orientation, a "projection." Without this feature, experiencing the impossible as impossible would not yield the experience of hopelessness. For example, the knowledge in and of itself that it is impossible to find an end to *pi* is not necessarily the experience of hopelessness. But if for some reason in my youthful ambitiousness or in my naive self-confidence I try to find the end of *pi*, but then found out for myself I could not do it, I could experience hopelessness, and then just give up. All this can take place without initiating a specific act of hope in this regard.

Someone may still object: "Yes, but in this 'trying,' we can detect a hope-attitude, a comportment of hope could still be implicit." If this were true, then hopelessness would demand the cherishing of some hope pertaining to the eventual experience of hopelessness. It would be difficult to settle this case without further inquiry into the nature of trying. I will say here, nonetheless, that the reason trying apparently harbors a hope has to do with the efficacy of the ground of hope *that is always given or operative* even in hopelessness; it does not have to do with the execution of the specific hope-act preceding the experience of hopelessness. It is true that there is a temporal unfolding, a futural orientation that precedes the experience of hopelessness; this appears to be essential. But let us recall the earlier analyses in which it was shown that even though hope does have a futural orientation, it is irreducible to other futural orientations, orientations like protention, expectation, and anticipation. This is to say that one can be oriented toward the future (e.g., in an expectation or in a "likely to occur") without this orientation being a hope-experience. Rather than embark on this course now, let's see if we can be still more precise with respect to what it is in the experience that we called an "endeavoring" such that it must precede the experience of hopelessness.

What we sense when we appeal to temporally unfolding experiences like endeavoring or trying that precede hopelessness is some kind of first-person investment or engagement in the situation. For example, when I am trying to build the ship, when I am trying to find the end to *pi*, I must be engaged in the outcome in some way if I then experience hopelessness. True, the hope-experience, as we saw earlier, does exhibit this quality of personal engagement; there are, however, several other experiences that also share a first-person investment or engagement, but they are nevertheless not a hope-experience (they lack the givenness of the ground of hope that makes hope the experience not only an engagement, but a sustainability). As examples, we can recall wishing, but more importantly desiring, and especially longing. Let's revisit the experience of longing.

Let's suppose that I had expected to see a former classmate later this evening, but find out all of a sudden that he suffered a terrible stroke and was taken to the hospital. He is no longer able to communicate, it is not even clear that he understands what one is saying; the doctors assure me (and I fully believe them) that he will never recover. I remember the penetrating conversations we used to have, the adventures we used to share, and I *long* to see him the way he was and to converse with him again. Notice that I do not *hope* to see him as his former self; in this case, and for whatever reasons, I have no "ground" to sustain this hope. I simply long for his former self; I long to speak with him (in addition, perhaps, to wishing I could speak with him or "desiring" to speak with him). Now I do not even visit because I "know" it is precisely *hopeless*. I experience the impossibility of the situation *as* impossible. While a disappointed hope would simply end at the non-fulfillment in the present, hopelessness—*from where I am now*—projects itself into the future so that it closes down possibilities forever *in this respect, in this specific case.*

True enough, maybe later I could cherish a hope that he will get better. In the case of hope, I am not only engaged in some way (like in a desiring, a wishing, or a longing), but it is given to me as sustainable: I hope. I could, of course, then reexperience hopelessness, and so on. My point is that I do not need first to experience hope in this specific instance in order then to experience hopelessness of the same.

To conclude, then, what makes such an experience hopelessness is not the specific execution of a hope-act that precedes this hopelessness, but the ground of hope, which emerges in and through hopelessness as canceled out in this instance, but remaining operative overall. Hence, I *could* hope, later. In fact, I could hope later or have a different hope because hopelessness does not bear on the ground of hope *as such.*

Furthermore, in hopelessness, the possibility horizon is given as impossible, all the way *into the future.* Impossibility is experienced *as* impossible, that is, it is extended in this specific case unendingly into the future; accordingly, the modality of possibility shows up as impossible here. Yet the ground of hope is still operative as such, since only as manifest in this particular instance is it impaired. Accordingly, to experience hopelessness does not mean that I necessarily experience "hopelessness" in every dimension of my life, but just in this case.

In sum, what makes hopelessness distinct from a disappointed hope is that whereas disappointment is confined to the present, hopelessness extends to the future. This yields the peculiar sense of impossibility. Whereas a disappointed hope must correspond to a specific hope-act that is then negated, even though the ground of hope persists, hopelessness is not necessarily preceded by a hope-act. Thus, if we inquire into the difference between the experience of impossibility as impossibility that results in hopelessness and such an experience that does not, we conclude that it is not the specific hope-act that differentiates them, but the modality of possibility that allows us to be engaged in some way, an engagement that is also functional in a longing, a desiring, or a wishing.

Hopelessness pertains to the experience of the impossibility of a specific occasion; hope and the ground of hope implied in this experience are "only" suspended on this occasion. Because it is efficacious on the level of the particularity of the event and does not impact my being as such, the problem of suicide cannot arise in experience of hopelessness. The situation is different, however, when we turn to the experience of despair.

Despair. It is in despair that one experiences the loss of a ground of hope *as such*. Whereas hopelessness is geared to the specific event, despair is oriented toward the ground of hope; whereas hopelessness leaves the ground of hope intact, as it were, fixating on this particular event, despair experiences the loss of the very ground of hope; whereas in hopelessness I experience the *event* as impossible and this only impacts the ground of hope in this instance, in despair I experience directly the *ground of hope* as impossible. This reveals the inherent paradox or contrariety in the structure of despair.

I say that despair harbors a paradox or contrariety because despair is at the same time an openness to the ground of hope and a loss of it. Just as the experience of hopelessness is an opening through which sustainability reveals itself as ineffectual in this instance, in despair the ground of hope reveals itself as the utter loss of any ground of hope. Realizing this does not discount the experience of despair, but acknowledges its internal contrary structure—contrary because it is the process of affirming a meaning that is lived as not given. If Camus is correct in asserting that the absurd—the human experience of fundamental indifference, the radical contingency of meaning in the face of what he calls the irrational, without appeal—runs contrary to hope, then we must add that it also runs contrary to despair. For us, however, despair must be more than the mere absence of hope, more than the experience of the absurd. As Camus himself trenchantly remarks: "Being deprived of hope is not despairing."[36]

More than the absence of hope, despair too presupposes the positive orientation of hope (and the meaning given in it), but is oriented toward the lack of its meaning. There is now given an unbridgeable distance between me and any ground of hope. Despair, as opposed to hopelessness, even to Camus's description of the absurd, is the experience of abandonment as ultimate and decisive. The experienced non-ground of hope is given as the impossibility of any ground, explicitly. In despair, "I" withdraw from the ground of hope (and I withdraw from the experience of not being self-grounding) in turning affirmatively toward the self. This is another way of describing the experience of being abandoned (to oneself). But the experience of being abandoned is itself revelatory (which presupposes some ground not there, rather than a mere nothing). Thus, although there might very well be many vehicles for despair (not getting the car fixed, credit card debt, addiction, a terminal illness, denial of forgiveness, etc.), strictly speaking, one does not *despair* over them; rather, they are that through which despair arises and therefore serve as catalysts for despair.

Within the structure that Kierkegaard has described—which is not exactly my own—he is correct in tracing the intensification of despair, and that ultimately despair goes to the ground of being itself, even if the individual does not know it explicitly as such.[37] In his terms, despair takes shape before God as a will not to be oneself (weakness) or as a will to be oneself (defiance), which as before God is sin. This is further intensified for him as the despair over sin, despair over forgiveness, and despair over Christianity. This is also why Kierkegaard is able to agree with Mephistopheles's statement that nothing is worse than a devil who despairs, because such a despair is testimony to the possibility of repentance and grace *as* not possible.

I experience in despair a not-being-in-control, a beyond-me, but in distinction to the hope-experience, this beyond-me is now lived as a void. The opening of the ground of hope that is given in the experience of hope is given in despair as groundless. I do not just give up doing this or that (hopelessness), but I give up altogether. I may *wish* things were different, but I cannot hope. It is not just that this one particular thing is not sustainable; it is not just that all things are lived as impossible; rather, there is no sustainability. Thus, we recognize a qualitative difference between hopelessness and despair. Between them is not a difference of degree, but a difference in kind. Even if I experienced hopelessness in every particular instance, the sum of these experiences would not equal despair because the ground of hope can still function guidingly. In despair, however, the ground of hope itself is experienced as groundless, and this is why every dimension of my life would be experienced as without hope. Only in despair (i.e., "only" when concerned in relation to hopelessness) does the possibility of suicide arise.

This is not to say that hopelessness could not "spur" despair or become an opening for despair. But then a qualitative leap is made, an "insight" is stirred into the groundlessness of all hope. Hopelessness, however, is not a prerequisite for despair. In despair, the ground of hope as such is given as impossible; it bears on the ground of hope directly. This reveals an ultimate contrariety in the experience of despair. The ground of hope is experienced as impossible and grips me at the deepest level of my life. Yet, it is not entirely accurate to say that despair grips me at the level of my *life*. More precisely, despair grips me at the level of my *spiritual* being. This is why mere "life" may not matter to us anymore in despair; despair goes deeper than the vital sphere. As such, despair must be seen as qualitatively distinct from something like "depression" which may have a psychophysical root.

This is more precisely why despair, which strikes the ground of hope itself, opens up the possibility of suicide, where suicide has to be understood not just in a physical sense, but a spiritual, historical, purposive sense as well. Let's take the example of Andrei Rublev in Tarkovsky's film of the same name. Already enjoying a reputation as a great icon painter, Andrei Rublev seemed satisfied with his vocation and his commissions. However, after witnessing a brutal massacre at a cathedral, he experienced the absolute futility in any creation. The only response for him was despair, which took the form of ceasing to create (paint) and ceasing to speak. In refusing speech, he repudiated intersubjectivity; in refusing to create, he rejected his vocation and severed the connections to the Holy as a creative, expressive force. Though Theophanes appears to him in order to persuade him that these refusals are mistakes, Andrei does not live them as mistakes. No argument can persuade him, since nothing that comes from another level, nothing anyone says can assuage this despair—only something stemming from the same dimension of experience can overcome it. It was not until the young boy successfully fashioned the "bell"—practically ex nihilo since we come to learn that he did not really have the secret passed down to him—that Andrei was *called* to himself, reengaged community, and began creating according to his unique style.[38]

Not only is pessimism distinct from hopelessness (since the latter concerns this particular instance in which the ground of hope is called into question and pessimism is a more general attitude that things will go poorly), pessimism cannot be figured on the same level of despair. Despair points to a fundamental level in our existence such that we cannot "go on" in any real sense. In pessimism (even in the attitude of pervasive "doom and gloom"), I assert that things will go badly no matter what, but they still "go on," and I still go on. So even if every particular sphere of my experience is colored by pessimism, the ground of my existence is not at issue.

In relation to the structure of otherness, therefore, despair reveals the ground of hope as groundless. This has implications for its modality of possibility as liberation. As in the case of hopelessness, despair lives impossibility as such. But whereas in hopelessness, the impossibility pertained to the specific event (while the ground of hope was canceled in this particular instance, but was generally still operative), in despair it is directly the ground of hope itself that is experienced as impossible. This is why there is the experience of no recourse, no sustainability; every avenue is closed off. This absolute distance from the ground of hope is the experience of being abandoned, being alone, and being left to myself in the present.

I have considered the experience of despair and contrasted it with hopelessness from two of the three structures I had described in the hope experience, namely, from the perspective of otherness and from the modality of possibility. In the case of despair, we have seen that it does evoke an experience of otherness as the ground of hope—which is revealed in despair, but precisely as groundless. Related to the modality of possibility, it is not just this specific event that is experienced as impossible, but the ground of hope itself.

It is now a matter of turning to the temporal structure peculiar to the hope experience in examining the phenomenon of despair. Hope, I pointed out previously, has an exclusive futural orientation, whose temporal modality is to be understood as awaiting-enduringly, which is to say, as an enduring patience. By contrast, despair is oriented on the present. When I despair, I experience the future as closed to meaningful possibilities that should otherwise be there. Through the experience of being abandoned to myself, I experience being abandoned to the present. In despair, however, neither the future nor the past offer anything to the present. There is no "point" to it; there is no way out. I am unable either to escape toward the future or to retreat into the past. In despair, I am not so much consumed by the now, but by the absence of the future and the past in terms of how they could redeem the present. It is in this way that despair confines us to the present and functions as a kind of imprisonment (whereas hope is experienced as a liberation of the present from its fixity). Past and future are constricted to an overwhelming experience of a fixed present.

Conclusion

Having described these characteristics of the experiences of hopelessness and despair, we can formulate their interrelation and see the radicality of despair vis-à-vis hope. It is possible, for example, to experience specific things as hopeless, and yet not be in despair. However, it is not possible simultaneously to experience things as hopeful all the while being in despair. Let me give a rather poignant example. It was related to me some years ago that when close family friends were arrested by the Nazis, they eventually gave up hope that they would ever escape imprisonment or death—this situation was hopeless—but they (and many others) remained "hopeful" (i.e., they did not despair). They could only remain hopeful in the hopelessness of the situation because a ground of hope sustains that orientation.

Such an experience can only make sense if several things hold. First, what I am terming hopelessness and despair must be distinctive experiences. Second, hopefulness and despair are both, each in their own way, implicitly oriented by a ground of hope. Third, in hopelessness the ground of hope can still be functional "overall" or in the depth of one's being such that one is not in despair, but can be negated in a particular or particular instances, thus allowing for cases of hopelessness. Fourth, despair impacts the ground of hope as such, in which case the latter is lived as impossible. Fifth, hopelessness is therefore founded in despair. It is, however, only through a hope occurring "on the same level" of that despair that the latter can be overcome by hope. Of course, Camus has pointed out another experience that would presuppose neither hope nor despair, namely, the experience of the absurd (which for him demands acknowledging the arbitrariness and indifference of meaning and accepting it in an exclusively humanist context). Although there are various presuppositions that Camus makes about the absurd that I would have to challenge from my perspective, his basic characterization of the absurd only confirms the relation I have described between hope and despair.

Allow me to conclude on the following notes regarding hope, despair, and repentance. First, although there are many experiences that run contrary to the experience of hope, despair is to be understood as the most profound challenge to hope because it bears precisely on the ground of hope and the modality of sustainability and liberation from the impossible toward a more open future. Second, hope nevertheless founds the experience of despair, since in and through it, the ground of hope is revealed, even if thereby revealed as negated. This is why despair gives itself in a contrary fashion, and why even though hope accompanies despair, the experience of hope does not depend upon the experience of despair.

Third, hope is not sustainable alongside pride, since in hope there is a relation of dependence, most profoundly revealed as a ground of hope—where this ground is not intended, but given in the very hope-act.

And this tells us something about ourselves as human persons, namely, that even in the most mundane of hope experiences, hope implicitly opens us to the sphere of absolute experiencing already given, before we could mean or will it.

Fourth, repentance, hope, and despair as creative acts are moral emotions of possibility. Where repentance and hope are concerned, there is not only a dispositing and disclaiming of a past and present hold on me, but there is a liberation for revolution as returning to Myself, for reconnecting with others, and a liberation from determinacy as the hoped-for future is sustainable in this movement of hope. Both, furthermore, presuppose a relation to otherness as not being self-grounding, and in their very lived relation, challenge the movement of pride.

In the next part of this work, I explore moral emotions of otherness: trust, loving, and humility. These are founding interpersonal emotions in the sense that they have a positive, direct bearing as openness to others, and realize in the moral sphere existence as coexistence.

Part 3

Moral Emotions of Otherness

In this part, I investigate primarily three moral emotions under the heading of the emotions of otherness: trust, loving, and humility. While other moral emotions that have been described here also have a bearing on otherness, these emotions, trust, loving, and humility, are emotions that are directly engaged with "otherness" in a way that is exemplary. Further, I treat these three in varying degrees because they each express movements that call pride into question in and through their revelation of the interpersonal sphere of experience. Further, they also provide us with distinctive ways of engaging with modernity and postmodernity, ways that have not adequately been treated in customary expositions of our contemporary social imaginaries that exclude the emotions. Indeed, although it is presented in the language of "moral theory," I think such an inclusion of the moral emotions is the leading insight of the "ethics of care," and why thinkers such as Annette Baier appeal to loving and trusting as phenomena that need to be reintegrated into such a discourse.[1]

Trust is particularly significant as a moral emotion of otherness because it is directly an interpersonal relation, and is foundational for social existence. But more than that, in trust freedom is realized not as my ability to remain independent from others, but as being bound to others, so much so that an essential feature of trusting is interdependence and vulnerability. Whereas pride presupposes freedom and transcendence in the sense of excluding the contribution of others, trust presupposes freedom and transcendence in the sense of proffering myself to another in an open future, and being bound to them in this social and temporal movement.

In what follows, I attempt neither to assert when we need to trust, nor to ascertain objectively who is a trusting person, if it is wise, reasonable, or appropriate to trust in certain circumstances, or when a betrayal might be mistaken for trust. Rather, I describe the essential structures of trust in terms of trust's modes of givenness, how it is a significant feature of interpersonal existence. There are some that seem related to trust but are of a different mettle (like reliability, calculation of risk, deciding to trust). There are also other experiences that are related to but are often confused with trust in the order of execution and dependence (e.g., presupposing that mistrust or distrust must precede the trust act).

The second chapter in this part is devoted to two main moral emotions: loving and humility. I reserve a fuller phenomenological treatment of loving for another work, one that examines its relation to hating and that articulates the relation between erotic love, sexual love, and agapic love.[2] Such a context will enable me to show not only how acts of generosity, charity, and gift-giving are rooted in loving, but how some of our Western notions of charity misleadingly separate charity from justice.

Nevertheless, I take up loving here both to note the place of loving in the moral emotions, and to suggest the ways in which normative experience arises in the very movement of loving. I do this as well because loving is so closely allied with and serves a phenomenological description of humility. Humility can be characterized as who I "am," as I am given to myself in the dynamic movement of loving, but where the experiential weight is on how I spontaneously receive myself as who I am from another, ultimately *as* Myself. This is significant for elucidating the interpersonal and inter-Personal dimensions of humility.

Loving and humility are "broader" experiences than trust because while the former are both interpersonal, qualifying them in part as moral emotions, they extend beyond the interpersonal to other kinds of otherness, as we will see. Of course, there are indeed other emotions of otherness, and not featuring them here is not to say that they do not occupy an important place in our lives.[3] Wonder—to take just one example—while a powerful experience, need not be a moral emotion or interpersonal at its core. Wonder or amazement as *thaumazein* can arise as such without any interpersonal dimension, for example, when struck by the strangeness or mystery of the world; as Plato to Husserl, Heidegger, Arendt, and Merleau-Ponty have suggested, it might be the very beginning of the philosophical attitude, and thus an emotion founding reason. But this does not necessarily make it a *moral* emotion.

Of all the emotions of otherness, loving and humility are essential to this work because of their obvious relation to pride. Where humility is concerned, I distinguish it from the experience of being humbled by, of humbling myself, modesty, and especially of humiliation (relating the latter instead to debilitating shame). I also show the peculiar relation humility can have to affliction. Humility shows itself to be a unique kind of self-givenness that is unlike the self-givenness that we found in pride, shame, or guilt. Moreover, we will see that humility is foundational for pride, even if in the history of the person, humility can function as a response to pride.

6

Trust

Trust is a fundamental experience evident on many levels of our lives. We not only trust someone at a particular place and time, say, when we are involved in a transaction, but in more encompassing ways: we trust a lover to be faithful, we trust a friend to be true. More basically and implicitly still, we trust as we walk among others along a crowded street; we trust when we eat in an unfamiliar restaurant, or even when we ask a question or engage in dialogue. While trust is evoked in a variety of contexts—religious and theological, philosophical, sociological, as a feature in psychology, feminism, risk analysis, political thought, as well as in science[1]—this chapter advances a phenomenology of trust in the more encompassing project of a phenomenology of the person, and intervention into the matters of our social imaginaries.

I begin this chapter by describing the phenomenon of reliability in order to highlight the distinctiveness of the trust experience. Turning to trust, I explicate how the freedom and transcendence of persons are presupposed for such an experience (1). Observing that the past is not an essential component of trusting another (as it would be for experiencing something given as reliable), I describe the temporal meaning of trust as a "proffering" (2). This implies a different sense of freedom, namely, trust is lived out as a process of being bound to another, whose essential feature is vulnerability (3). Contrary to many prominent interpretations of trust, these fundamental characteristics of trust enable me to determine its independence from anti-trust, mistrust, and distrust (4). Trust as proffering and as vulnerable before another suggests another significant feature to this emotional experience, namely, trust is generative of trusting and can be experienced by another as an imposition (5). After distinguishing trust from the relation to something or another person in commitment (6), I clarify how trust can be lived out unconditionally in specific modal circumstances (7).

Reliability as Practical Functionality

We can speak of trust in a variety of contexts. We might say, for example, "I trust you are well." We also speak of setting up a "trust fund" or putting something "in trust" for another. When climbing a rock cliff, we might say that "I trust my footing." We say that we trust this or that institution. We might even find ourselves saying, "I don't trust myself." We might find ourselves speaking of trust when picking up that "trusty" pen that we habitually use to write a special letter, and that never lets us down. But in order to give trust its sharper, phenomenological contours, let us not depend upon these ordinary usages simply, even though they might give us some clues to trust's phenomenological content.

In the examples just mentioned, what is in play is not necessarily trust at all. In the first example, it is a synonym for expectation; the latter cases are examples of what I call here reliability. I understand reliability as a particular relation of meaning that unfolds concordantly over time, that exhibits a typical structure, or that is familiar or given as something we can count on. Something is not reliable when the concordance is disrupted or when it is experienced as somehow atypical or unfamiliar.[2]

In citing this aspect of reliability, we have already passed over a more fundamental feature, namely, that reliability is extended temporally. Reliability is something that unfolds over time. For example, if I count my pen as reliable, it is because it has given itself as something I can count on again and again; it has a temporal density that extends from the past. If I test drive a car for the first time, I do not experience it immediately as reliable. It is true that I may like Toyotas, and that I experience this particular car as reliable *because* it is a Toyota, but then the experience of reliability has shifted from this particular car to the general make of the car with which I have had good (past) experiences. When I experience something in an originary manner, however, I do not experience it as reliable, or as unreliable for that matter. Accordingly, we can ascertain that the past is essential for the general sphere of reliability. The car has performed well in the past, and I can count on it now; others have had good experiences with the car, and for these reasons, I share this basic comportment. What I experience "now" calls back into the past and retrieves the experience, as it were, requalifying the same thing now *as* reliable.

Moreover, something is experienced as reliable when it corresponds to my *expectation*. On the basis of the present and the past, a futural horizon is sketched out that prepares us for the experience of reliability. I *anticipate* the thing according to the style in which it has been given. If the thing gives itself in the way in which it was sketched out futurally, I can count the thing as reliable. Reliability, then, is a *straightforward* mode of experience that is *motivated*. When everything runs its course as it should, something can be experienced as reliable. There are no major disappointments, no major ruptures in my everyday belief posture. My orientation toward the thing remains unbroken; I live in the basic mode of certainty and its possible modifications.

Notice that reliability is more than the fulfillment of the anticipation. As I descend the staircase, even though I implicitly expect (or protend) the regularity of the steps in certainty (or modalized as probability), I do not *necessarily* experience them as reliable. Reliability includes something more; it is not mere certainty, but a *practical* mode of straightforward belief. Accordingly, reliability is not a probability, which is itself a modalization of expectation. For example, when I go to start the car on a cold day, my intention toward the car is that it will work, it will turn over: it is reliable. As reliable, I do not approach it in the belief posture of probability. Or again, if I put the key in the ignition with the attitude that "it will *probably* start," I am no longer living the car as reliable. Probability is a mode of expectation. Reliability, however, is not a mode of expectation, even though expectation figures in the experience of reliability. It is a practical mode of straightforward belief.

This practical modality of reliability gives us a main leading clue to the experience of reliability in its distinction to trust. In reliability, there is the experience of the *functional* character of the thing, which may include its instrumental character and its general use value, but in any case, all of this in the context of *practicality*. Moreover, the experience of reliability presupposes that something may change in the regularity of givenness; its functional character can be disrupted, most often in terms of a mal- or dysfunction. For example, the Swiss or German rail system is experienced, by most of us anyway, as reliable, whereas Amtrak, the U.S. rail system, tends to be experienced as unreliable. When something like my pen is experienced as reliable, it is experienced as something that will work not just now, not spottily, but consistently whenever I turn to it to write, even though in principle something could go wrong.

We experience not only things, objects, or tools as reliable, however; we often experience people as reliable. For example, the bank employee is given as reliable when she is punctual at work. But notice how the person is regarded, namely, she is regarded in terms of her function as an employee. One may object that reliability goes beyond mere use value. For instance, a person may be taken as reliable, namely, as a reliable guest. In this case, what we mean is not only that the guest shows up on time, but for instance that he is grateful for being invited, that we can count on him to be conversational, for him to bring wine, or just in general that there will be no surprises with him. One may even marry someone because he or she is reliable (he or she is a good "breadwinner," will not drink to excess, etc.). For a thing or a person to be reliable, it/he/she must exhibit a typical style of behavior and "behave" in a dependable manner.

Accordingly, if I were to feel that "I can't trust myself around cake," I am not referring to a trust experience, but rather, I mean really that I am not "in control" of myself in the sense that I may act in a way other than I think is proper for the occasion. I am in fact quite predicable to myself: I know that I am bound to act in a certain way; I probably should not give in to my appetite (given my health, my goals, my fast), but I know I will. Alternately, self-confidence is not a kind of trust, but a mode of reliability, a self-awareness of my own ability, like we saw above in chapter 1, as an ability-to-do or as an ability-to-be.

Certainly, trust and reliability can overlap in particular situations. And it is true that reliability does not capture the most profound dimensions of the person; this is in part my reason for mentioning it here. What I want to emphasize is that reliability, whether it pertains to things or persons, occurs within the context of practicality and functionality. It is a mode of experience that is operative on the level of practical intelligence, which is to say, any being (psychophysical being) capable of practical intelligence is capable of experiencing reliability.

Trust as Interpersonal

Having briefly described reliability for the purpose of highlighting the uniqueness of trust, let me note at the outset seven major characteristics of the trust-experience that I explicate below: (1) the relation of trust to the freedom and transcendence of myself and another, (2) the temporality of trust as proffering, (3) trust as binding me to another as vulnerable, (4) trust, distrust, and mistrust, (5) trust as generative of trusting and as an imposition, (6) the relation between trust and commitment, and (7) the modal specification of trust.

Freedom and Transcendence

Trust involves freedom both on the side of myself and on the part of the other. In the interpersonal sphere, this freedom is expressed as my giving myself over to another in his or her freedom.

First, I cannot be compelled to trust, nor can I be forced to trust another out of fear. Trust is a *freely* given and giving act, and it is oriented toward those who might be either trustworthy or who might violate that trust. I do not trust someone who is compelled to do what I want or who is enslaved for any reason. In fact, enslaving someone—materially, emotionally, monetarily, physically—is the evidence of a lack of trust on some level. On the contrary, trust is a relaxing in or giving myself over to the other precisely in light of the transcendence of the other. Accordingly, let us understand by freedom here not a "freedom from," but more profoundly, the freedom to give myself over to another.

This sense of freedom will become clearer when I take up the character of trust as binding me to another (3). Here let me only say that it is not my freedom that "allows" me to trust another as if it indicated a neutral possibility or a place of retreat. Rather *I find myself trusting when this freedom is realized as being bound to another.* This is why we can speak of a "bond of trust." This freedom also presupposes that I can see deeper spiritual values and honor them over more superficial ones. To prefer the superficial to the profound would constitute a restriction; as contrary to freedom, this restriction seemingly paradoxically arises from not wanting to be bound by deeper values, from wanting to level the playing field of values, as it were, which ultimately means not wanting to be bound to other persons. In a religious register, this notion of freedom is one that we find legion in the mystics of the Abrahamic tradition, where freedom is characterized most profoundly as the freedom to be bound by the will of God. This binding is expressed in solidarity with the Holy and with others in the task of world redemption. It is symbolized biblically in the "binding" (*akedah*) of Isaac (not the misnomer "sacrifice" of Isaac) in the Judeo-Christian tradition.[3]

Trust accordingly is most deeply an interpersonal act. I mean two things by this. (1) Trust is inherently a social act; by its very execution, it implies sociality since trust only finds its fulfillment in a possible other, and most profoundly, in a person or community of persons (as do acts of loving, sympathy, commanding, etc.).[4] When we do speak of trusting something like an institution (e.g., the federal government, the church, the schools, etc.), our trust is directed toward the collective person. This can be distinguished from other acts that are essentially singularizing ones, like reflection, examining one's conscience, self-esteem, and so on.[5] Strictly speaking, even if a person were factually alone, the individual could never be conceived as separate or isolated, even though one can have experiences of exclusion or being ostracized from a group; in fact, even isolation presupposes an intention toward others. (2) Trust is interpersonal in the sense that at its core it is oriented toward the other as a creative "center" of acts—acts that can be carried out freely, "spontaneously."

Second, trust is implicitly an orientation toward the other as transcendent and free, and who can do otherwise than be faithful to my trust. If I say "I trust Mt. St. Helens will not erupt," I do not experience a betrayal or violation if it does erupt. In this way, I do not meaningfully speak of trusting the sun to shine or my pen to write (unless, of course, I experience the pen or the sun to have these qualities of personhood).[6]

Let's say I am climbing a rock face. I have on my climbing shoes, and I am familiar with the path. Halfway up, I find a solid placement with my right foot and a solid grip with my left hand. I rest for a moment, I "trust" my footing and my grip; the rock face is firm beneath my right foot and my left hand. Now, the rock beneath my foot slips, or my fingers get tired and they lose their grip. Do I experience a violation of trust? Did the rock betray my trust? Did my fingers violate my trust in them? I don't think we can meaningfully speak of violation or betrayal in this instance, and likewise of trust in a genuine sense. Certainly, the rock face did not betray me. I may have poorly assessed its stability, but it does not violate my trust. Can we say the same thing about my fingers and their grip? We might say "my fingers let me down" in the sense that I *expected* them to do more or to be able to be stronger and sustain the grip. But strictly speaking it would be curious to say that there was a bond of trust. Here, trust might only be meaningful to the extent that we impute some otherness to the fingers such that they are capable of freely withdrawing support. Thus, not only does trust presuppose freedom on the part of the other, it also presupposes freedom realized as being bound to another.

One of the main distinctions between pride and trust can be seen in this light. Pride as we saw presupposes freedom and transcendence of the other, but does so by excluding them, which is to say, the contribution of meaning made by others. Pride remains self-centered in this regard. By contrast, trust presupposes the freedom and transcendence of the other person in the sense of giving myself over to others, including them in shared meaning, presupposing their freedom and transcendence. In this regard, in trust I am already given over to another such that and as a consequence, I am "de-centered," "dis-positioned." This happens without any intention to a dis-position, since in fact, such an intention would belie the trust act. Rather, I simply trust, and in the process, the position of the otherwise self-centered "I" is de-centered. But this would happen whether or not there were ever an experience of pride in the first place, since trusting is foundational and not dependent upon pride (or distrust or mistrust)—as we will see below. Trusting in this sense is original in the constitution of interpersonal relations, social relations, and intercultural communication; it is one reason why trust needs to be reintegrated into the configurations of our social and power relations.

Furthermore, reliability and trust are qualitatively distinct and reflect different orders of experience. Certainly, I can also rely on people. I can rely on the babysitter to be on time, to watch the children while I leave the building, and so forth. But here there is an assigned function that is predetermined as a kind of duty. It is regulated in advance and by the past. The sitter may turn out not to be reliable, so in this sense, reliability is not predetermined. But then again, reliability does not go to the core of interpersonal experience since it remains on the level of functional practicality. Just because I find someone extremely reliable does not mean this reliability will shade off into trust. I do not say: "I find him reliable, therefore I will trust him." Rather, in trust, I "see" the person in a different way than merely as reliable.

Notice that while I *do* want a sitter who is reliable, I do not leave my children with someone who is *merely* reliable. I leave my children with someone I trust—who will be honest, take care of them in an emergency, will not inflict harm, and so forth. Presumably, someone who is trustworthy (who will care for the child) will also be reliable. But it may also happen that a trustworthy person (say, who will always have the children's best interest at heart) may not be very reliable (e.g., not show up on time, forget the appointment, not be available when she says she will be). I take up this point further below under the modal determination of trust.

The Temporality of Trust as Proffering

While reliability is experienced only by virtue of a full temporal expanse that includes the past essentially, this need not be the case with trust. To be sure, we often speak of our "building up" trust in someone. There is a similar phenomenon that we will observe when we entertain a generative context of trust below; building up trust, however, is not essential to the trust experience, even though it can occur in the context of trust. The simple point is that we do not need to be involved in a buildup of experiences stemming from the past in order to trust another, whereas this dimension of the past is essential for reliability.

For example, I can trust someone whom I have never met to watch my computer in a café while I get a refill; I can trust someone with whom I am not familiar to watch my jacket or my purse while I use the restroom. I can trust someone I have only nodded to at a concert to "keep an eye on the kids" while I get drinks at intermission. While reliability is a relation of familiarity, this is not necessarily the case with trust.[7] It belongs to the essence of trust to be able to live through a trust act with a *complete stranger*. Indeed, at times our lives may depend upon the trust of such a stranger. Trust does not depend upon the past, but on the givenness of the person in the present, an insighting (that may be accurate or not) of the person from an originary encounter. Even if one has been betrayed in the past by the same person, it is *possible* to trust this person anew, without any "proof" from the past.

It is likewise phenomenologically improper to speak of "earning trust."[8] Holmes and Rempel, for example, assert that one must "earn trust" by being "perceived as motivated to moderate their own self-interest." They mistakenly presuppose, first, that trust is played out on the level of self-interest (i.e., as a perceived sacrifice of self-interest), and second that it is a matter of earning trust. The sense of this earning would amount to what we mean by reliability.[9] Trust, however, is an orientation to deeper possibilities (like loving), exposing myself to unforeseen dimensions of the person. Hence, there is a decisive orientation toward the future. Otherwise, it would not be possible to trust again. One can trust (again) on the basis of a new experience—for example, by virtue of an insight into the internal coherence and directedness of the person—whereby trust is re-executed, freely; reliability, on the other hand, is dependent upon the past. In fact, a new trust might run contrary to the past. Not trusting because there is no "proof" would be tantamount to wanting testimony and security in advance in order to trust. Perhaps such proof might be important at some level and in some circumstances; in our lives, perhaps there is a moment in which we have to have this kind of security, either politically or personally. Nevertheless, it would not (yet) be trust, and only limited to a search for reliability. Therefore the expression of "earning trust" is not really a matter of trust at all and is, phenomenologically speaking, contradictory. Al Lingis correctly notes, for example, that there can never be a demonstration of trustworthiness, since in trust we are oriented, in openness, toward transcendence, which is not known. All there can be is evidence of untrustworthiness.[10]

Trust is interpersonally temporalizing and one of the foundational elements in social existence. It enables us to move into an open future with others as interpersonal becoming. I trust the person, now, whether or not that trust will be fulfilled, and it is still a trust act whether or not it is fulfilled. But while trusting entails the possible fulfillment of that trust, *it is not however a mere expectation;* nor is it founded in an expectation. It does not get modalized, for example, into a probability or improbability. *It is a unique act that has its own bearing on the future.* This is not to say that trusting does not influence our expectations and anticipations.[11] It does. But this recognition says instead that these perceptual and epistemic motivations *are founded in trusting,* and not the reverse! It is easy to find examples of expectation where no trust is involved (the expectation of sunny weather, the anticipation of the outcome of a basketball game). Interpersonally speaking, there can be a coincidence of trust and expectation where the latter is guided by the former. For example, if I trust my children to act well at a family gathering, I will ipso facto expect them to act well. Unlike reliability, however, trust does not completely coincide with an expectation. (Expectation does not exhaust the meaning of the interpersonal futural orientation.)

Trust has a unique temporal structure that I call a "proffering." In trust, I proffer myself to another in an open future and toward that which the trust is directed, as being bound to this other person. I understand "proffer" here in its literal sense as pro-offer. Trusting is the temporalizing movement of "offering-ahead," allowing the trust to go before me or pointing the way forward, as in a *pro*lepsis. This temporalizing movement is, as well, a pro-offering in the sense of a "great offering"; I give myself over to another in trust toward an open future. In this respect, proffering is a "bearing forth," a "gifting"—expressive of its probable etymological sense as a *"pour-offrir,"* as they say in French when presenting a gift.[12] Proffering is distinct from the expectation we might find in reliability or in a perceptual act, and is even distinct from the "awaiting-enduringly" we find in hope, which is itself distinct from the active waiting-for that we find in anticipation.

What about being a trusting person; does this not presuppose a buildup of experience?[13] When I describe trust as not entailing a dimension of the past, I address the issue of trust from the perspective of a static phenomenology. Within a static phenomenology the orientation of trust is toward the future and not toward the past. Essentially, it does not rely on the past—certainly not in the manner of reliability.

Does being a "trusting person" presuppose a buildup of experience or presuppose the goodness of people in order then to trust? The issue for me is to inquire into the basis of those presuppositions, how those experiences get built up, how a person can become trusting in the first place, which requires an inquiry into "the how" of the trusting movement, an investigation into how trusting proffers "in an originary fashion." The phenomenon of the trusting person entails inquiring into the "genetic" accomplishments of trusting, how it is acquired, how trusting gets sedimented into the very life of trusting acts and how it becomes a stable predisposition for trusting a person in the present situation.

For example, generatively speaking, when we inquire into how a place or space plays a role in "trusting," we consider how I might trust this very same person, a "stranger" in one place (e.g., a synagogue on Yom Kippur, a cycling race, a café), and not another (in a school yard, in a subway). Even the place appeals to a certain normative familiarity and unfamiliarity that can qualify the person as "stranger." But also note that "stranger" is not a neutral term here. Ultimately, we cannot speak cavalierly about "place" or "situation" or "context," since we have to investigate the normatively significant geo-historical "places" according to the "home" and the "alien" to see how trust gets qualified generatively.[14] Then, of course, we can understand how the past plays a role in trust, because trust would take place in a normatively optimal and familiar homeworld or even in a normatively unfamiliar and atypical alienworld. However, to say that trust can unfold or not in a normatively significant lifeworld as home or as alien is substantially different from saying that there has to be a buildup of (positive) past experiences in order to trust. There are essentially constitutive dimensions where mistrust or distrust are concerned. It is only when we mistrust another that we appeal (implicitly or not) to past experiences. Such an appeal is not an essential element of trust, only of a not-mistrust.

With these qualifications, I maintain in the final analysis that we trust the person, not the place. It would be accurate to pronounce, for example, that one does not trust Pinochet's Chile. But in this case, we do not merely mean "Chile" absent of the persons or leaders; we mean a certain socio-geo-historical climate in which certain persons carry out political policies, acts of violence, and so on.

In short, the temporality of trust as proffering is tied to interpersonal temporalization. In the next section, I articulate the interpersonal aspect of trust in terms of how we are bound to another in trust.

Trust Binds Me to Another as Vulnerable

When I trust, I do more than merely live in a straightforward belief attitude; I invest myself "personally" in the other person, and therefore in what the other person says or in how the other person acts; I give myself over to him or over to her "word." *Trust binds me to another.* Accordingly, even if trust pertains to the acceptance of scientific truths, trusting itself still resides in the moral sphere because in this case it is that through which one scientist is bound to another.[15] The binding character of knowledge is rooted in the binding character of trust. This sense of binding and being bound to another points to a moral sense of "normativity" that informs our interpersonal, practical, and epistemic activities.

In trust, I am bound to the other directly, without requiring the mediation of a third person or something like a contract; I live in and through the trust with another immediately.[16] The relation of trust, in fact, may remain completely invisible to a third party. To force trust putatively to be accessible to all by making it "objective" would only mitigate the very relational intimacy of this bond, even in its transitive mode. What this attempt could yield, however, is something like a "social contract" or a contract between individuals. However, not only would the latter presuppose trust, and the bond animated by it, but it could have the adverse effect of alienating individuals from one another in the very attempt to unite them because the contract (in distinction to trust) tends to set individuals off from each other in a controllable and predictable manner.[17]

Trust, as an interpersonal act, which is revelatory of the moral sphere, is qualitatively distinct from an epistemic act. Trusting cannot be equated with a mere presupposition, presumption, or assumption. By the latter experiences, we understand taking the being of the thing or event for granted in a straightforward "belief" attitude that is operative on all dimensions of existence. For example, I can presuppose the meaning of the educational system, and live in this system without question; I can make implicit epistemic assumptions about the correctness of a theoretical problem or a life situation; I can presume that the advice someone gives me is correct.

It is therefore not entirely correct to say that we are "naive" in trust. It is true that in trust we are bound to what is beyond that which is actually given in the present. However, while naïveté may be motivated by something actually given in experience (a perception, an idea, etc.), it may also arise without any such motivation. It can, for example, arise through an uncritical belief without any prior experiential basis.

Something different is going on in trust. Trust always occurs on the basis of some givenness, some insight into the other person (which may of course be "right on" or "off"). What is given is the whole person in light of this or that modality, fully, but not exhaustively. When we are bound to this person in trust on the basis of this givenness, we expose ourselves to more than what is given. This means two things. First, exposing ourselves or dis-posing ourselves by being bound to another in trust reveals us as *vulnerable*. Vulnerability is essential to the trust experience.[18] It is not, as Morton Deutsch mistakenly assumes, a "confidence that one will find what is desired from another, rather than what is feared."[19]

Second, we cannot conflate the moral dimension of trust and the essential element of vulnerability with the epistemic dimension of judgment or assumption—which allows for the possibility of naïveté. So, while it is more apt to say that I am naive in a judgment or an assumption, properly speaking, I am vulnerable in an act of trust. I only *believe* what someone says because I trust her. In a similar way, even our systems of knowledge are based on trust.

When we hear third-person remarks like "You trust *that* person? That's just stupid" or "You're really naive!" the presumption is that we could have prevented the trust (or the trust that might be betrayed or was betrayed) by being more critical. Perhaps it expresses a desire to reduce trust to reliability. In any case, the attempt not to be gullible is the spurious attempt to mitigate the vulnerable aspect of trust. Yet, if I try not to be vulnerable (or gullible, under the guise of not being naive, say, by trying to figure out all angles in advance, by projecting the other's self-interests, and so forth), I will never trust. Contrary to Russell Hardin, it is impossible to start trusting by being skeptical.[20] To be more precise, we have to distinguish between the epistemic character of *gullibility* as a readiness to believe (and skepticism or perhaps cynicism as an unreadiness to believe),[21] and the moral character of *vulnerability* in trusting through which I dispose myself and am bound to another.

To look only for what will in advance stop me from being vulnerable is to try to discern what is not loving in others, ultimately, to discern what is evil in others. Trusting by its nature cannot seek the "negative."[22] When I trust, I do not essentially experience the possibility of betrayal. To do so would already be to hedge my trust and hence not to trust at all. When I trust, I dispose myself to another "completely" or "fully," even though he might betray me or mislead me, intentionally or unintentionally. If I am worried that I might be betrayed, I will not trust.[23] Although we might find ourselves saying such things, it violates the sense of trust to say something like: "Ok, I trust, you, but don't let me down!" or "I will give you a second chance, but don't blow it." This might be an understandable defensive reaction, but it would not be trust. In order to describe the founding structure of trust in relation to mistrust and distrust, let me make the following distinctions.

Trust, Distrust, and Mistrust

Trust is a "positive," non-modalized experience that is interpersonally formative and that without which sociality would be impossible. It is foundational, primary, in the sense that it does not need anything to supplement it in order to be trust. For example, it does not require mistrust or distrust in order to be carried out. Mistrust and distrust, instead, are modalizations of trust and that first presuppose the trust experience. I don't start out distrustful or mistrustful, even though it is certainly possible that I become "distrustful" or meet every situation in a suspicious manner. Developmentally speaking, a child trusts first and foremost, and only learns distrust and mistrust as acquired postures.

I distinguish between distrust and mistrust in the following ways. I reserve the expression "distrust" for the direct relation to the individual or collective person as such. For example, I distrust James around my workshop because I have seen how he steals my bike parts every time he visits. In distinction, I use the expression "mistrust" where it refers to a type. Thus, I am mistrustful when it comes to this breed of dog (not necessarily this dog in particular), this kind of person (one who smokes, texts, and wears earphones while driving), this type of profession (the "Washington politician" is a common U.S. favorite).

One could distrust the Ku Klux Klan, not in the sense that this refers to a type of person, but in the sense that the KKK is a collective person. A member of the KKK could mistrust the "Catholics" or the "Jews" or the "blacks" experienced here as a type, but could also distrust them as a collective person. In the same way, one could distrust a tabloid, *The Star,* as expressive of the collective person, or mistrust the tabloid as not trusting any newspapers of this ilk.[24]

It might be tempting to say that we distrust a "stranger," or the "alien," or the "Other," because the stranger is an individual, and the stranger in this sense seems to point to the uniqueness of the person. However, I maintain that we would only *distrust* the unique persons (for instance, Sally, Bob, James), and this on the basis of past experience. Instead, we would *mistrust* the "stranger" because the "stranger" or the "other" is already a type. A type is generated because of the concordant or familiar structure it exhibits, relating to a past and pre-delineating a future in the same style.[25] What one mistrusts as "stranger" goes to the heart of the stranger as the familiar style of the unknown or unfamiliar, and we are able to recognize it and mistrust it in this way. This all holds for mistrust if the alien is encountered as exhibiting the "familiar style" of the alien, and thus already integrated into the familiar as mistrusted. It would not hold if the encounter is what we would call an interpersonal one in which distrust would become a possibility. However, if it were interpersonal in this way, such a distrust would only emerge as a possibility on the basis of a more foundational interpersonal trust which paved the way for the negation in the form of distrust—refusing (for "valid reasons" or not) to be vulnerable before another.

The reason so much of the contemporary literature on trust points to the dialectical interplay of trust and "anti-trust," as Annette Baier has put it,[26] is because there is an implicit *conflation between trust and the ruling out of mistrust*. When there is a conflation of the two, one argues that the only way an individual can trust another is to rule out mistrust, namely, to secure myself against mistrust. Logically, it may be the case that two negatives are a positive, but experientially, we cannot make the same claim. Empirically speaking, we could never make such a leap to a trust, because there would always be more concern, more probable deceptions, suspicions around the corner. One cannot trust via a negation of mistrust because these are a priori phenomenologically distinct movements, occurring on different levels of personal existence. Trust is an integral dimension of comportment. Accordingly, one cannot trust through a concern about being betrayed. One cannot remove the component of vulnerability, essential to trust, in order then to trust.

Hence, we must be careful when we contend that the possibility of betrayal (or the experience of the possibility of betrayal) is essential to trust. I cannot simultaneously experience that I will be betrayed by this person and trust this person. The trusting person inhabits a different "world" than the mistrustful person, the distrustful person, and the suspicious person.[27] When the dancer is launching herself into the arms of another, she is not simultaneously distrusting or anticipating a betrayal. It is all the more evident here how trusting is a resting in, a relaxing into, and even an intimacy and a being supported by another. Certainly, we might greet another with suspicion, we might be cautious or tentative, but then we are simply not describing the trust experience.

Rather than the possibility of betrayal, distrust, or mistrust being essential to trust, it is *vulnerability* that is essential to trust. This is the case, first, because we dispose ourselves or give ourselves over to another and are bound to the destiny of another in trust as proffering, and second, because the other person is never within our grasp, is not "knowable" in Levinas's sense, is not "objectifiable" in Scheler's sense. This goes to the self-revelatory character of persons which is fundamentally "improvisational." Again, my task here is not to decide when someone should or should not trust, or to decide what a "reasonable" or "appropriate" trust would be according to the circumstances, but to discern the meaning-orientation of trusting in the emotional sphere of the person.

In being bound to another in this act of trust, we become precisely vulnerable. In so doing, we prepare the field of social existence. I mentioned above that trust is revelatory of interpersonal relations and of the moral sphere, opening up a social space. One can see this perhaps even more clearly in the opposite example of someone who is constantly suspicious of others, who tries not to be susceptible to betrayal, who is always distrustful, or seeks negative possibilities in others as a way of forestalling vulnerability. Rather than being expansive, this movement contracts, and in general retracts from the social sphere. One tends to isolate him-

or herself and sequester him- or herself from the company of others. Trust therefore is a basic condition for the constitution of a social world.

It is equally mistaken to believe that we "decide" to trust. We do not trust on the basis of a judgment; we do not test reality for the presence or absence of trustworthiness.[28] Richard Holton is correct in maintaining that in order to trust someone—for example, he will catch me if I fall—I do not have to believe that he will catch me.[29] True, we do make poor judgments, take unnecessary risks, and make risk assessments. But all this already comes too late where trust is concerned. In this respect, I also concur with Bernd Lahno that trusting is qualitatively different from rational belief and calculation, and that our experience of trusting is not met in terms of minimizing risk.[30] But I do think that there is another distinction to be made, namely, between trusting and a putative decision to trust. Making a decision to trust would be like signing a contract—all participants already presuppose an underlying direct relation of trust.

Certainly, this is not to say that one should not be critical or that we do not make assessments. My point is only that being critical or even deciding to trust is not a moral act and does not occur on the same level as trusting. After the fact, I could reflect on a situation and conclude that I was naive, but this would be something added on to the trust experience. To trust is to be vulnerable; to make a decision is to open myself to wrongness or naïveté, even if it has dire consequences that affect my welfare. Making a so-called decision to trust really means deciding no longer to decide; and this ultimately entails allowing myself to coincide with the social movement of existence by being bound to another. Put differently, making a decision to trust would already presuppose a trust which nullified the necessity of making a decision about it in the first place. Although I become vulnerable in a trust act, the fact that I am vulnerable is not the overriding issue. If it were, I would never arrive at trusting; I would be concerned with being vulnerable. Instead, I trust. The vulnerable aspect, which is always already present in the trusting, becomes especially pronounced or exposed in a betrayal.

It is vulnerability, which is not exclusive to trust, but is essential to it, that makes us susceptible not to a mistake, but to betrayal. A betrayal is a violation of personal bonds established in trust (though not just trust, for they are also evident in loving). Thus, another kind of evidence of trust, an evidence that occurs retroactively, is the fact that I experience a rupture of trust as a betrayal; betrayal takes place only when trust is in place. This is why we experience a betrayal, personally, as worse than a mistaken assumption. Unless we are speaking loosely, to be wrong vis-à-vis an assumption is not the same as being betrayed vis-à-vis a trust. To trust a person as a good human being and to assume a person to be a good human being are two qualitatively different experiences.

Trusting is an orientation to another before whom I am vulnerable in that trust. This is expressive of our relation to finite persons as well as to infinite Person. Just as loving, worship, prayer, humility, self-sacrifice, and the like are included as religious acts, trusting can also be understood as a religious act. (It is interesting to note, by the way, that this aspect is rarely, if ever, cited in the literature.) Vulnerability in the religious sense can be expressed as dependency, finitude, or creaturehood. By "religious" I do not mean following a catechism or making a profession of faith. I mean a kind of experiencing that lives from, however implicitly or broadly, the dimension of the Holy. Because infinite Person (the Sacred) can reveal itself, for example, though personal acts of self-revelation—in the Abrahamic mystical tradition, prayer (Saint Teresa of Avila), prophetic ecstasy (Rabbi Dov Baer), or unveilings (Rūzbihān Baqlī)—such modes of givenness constitute the basis of trust.[31] Furthermore, in seeing the sacredness of the other person, we bind ourselves to the other in the movement of trust, making ourselves, implicitly, even more vulnerable in the process, but also opening up the sphere of deeper interpersonal possibilities.

Trust as Generative of Trust and Trust as Imposition

Let me describe two ways in which trust is generative and then examine how this implies trust as imposition. In distinction to both loving and reliability, trust functions transitively. By observing that trust can be transitive, I mean that trust operates beyond the immediacy of the experience, passing over to effect another experience of trust. In this way, trust can be generative of trust, without it being a way of "causing" trust or manipulating another to trust, which would be a kind of moral deception.

First let's contrast this movement with that of loving, whose generative nature is intransitive. Loving is an immediate relation, not restricted to but most profoundly between persons. By "immediate," I mean that I do not love another person (individual or collective person) *because* someone else loves that person. I love Betty immediately and directly. But I do not love Charlie because Betty loves Charlie and because I love Betty. I may indeed love Charlie, but not because Betty loves him. This is something that would have to occur between me and Charlie, immediately. To be sure, loving does and can function as an invitation in this instance. Perhaps I do not see anything special in Charlie right away. But Betty's love for Charlie "points to" or elicits the lovable character of Charlie. If I "look more closely" or dispose myself to this other person, he may flash forth as lovable. The lovable character of Charlie is something I have to see or experience for myself. In this sense, Betty can "help" me love Charlie, but only in this sense. In any case, my relation with Charlie constitutes a new immediate relation. My relation to Charlie is just as immediate in loving as my relation to Betty and Betty's relation to Charlie. Even within the religious sphere, I love Charlie "because of" Charlie's intrinsic value, not because God loves Charlie.

The situation can be somewhat different in the case of trust. Let's say that I am going to have surgery and need a specialist. I trust my D.O., Dr. Jim, my primary care physician. He recommends to me a surgeon whom he trusts. Now, trust *can* have the same structure of invitation as loving does; it can elicit a new immediate and direct relation: because of my doctor's trust in the surgeon Dr. Carol, I might be able to see something trustworthy in Dr. Carol. But there is more here. I do not know Dr. Carol, and for all I know, she could just be a fake; she could steal organs and sell them on the black market. But because I trust my doctor, and he trusts Dr. Carol, I trust the surgeon, Dr. Carol. On the basis of this trust, I am willing to undergo a delicate surgery. I can feel in "good hands" (I trust Dr. Carol) based on my trust in Dr. Jim. This element of transitive trust might even be more accentuated when we, say, are visiting a foreign country. I do not necessarily have to feel Dr. Jim's trust in Dr. Carol (it may not even exist). But my trust in Dr. Jim motivates my trust in Dr. Carol. In this case, I trust Dr. Carol directly, but as *mediated* by my trust in Dr. Jim. In distinction to loving, then, trust can be both an immediate relation and a mediate one.

Let me pass over to the second sense in which trust is generative. As implied above by the element of freedom in trust, trusting does not occur if I at the same time dominate or enslave another, or do not take the other in his or her transcendence, either in the direction of confirming or violating that trust. But is there not a difficulty in all of this? Is it not the case that while I may not intend to dominate another, I may unintentionally (perhaps for socio-historical reasons) actually dominate another in my trusting? I want to make two points here. First, the generative nature of trusting discloses another aspect of trust's interpersonal temporal orientation toward the future. Second, because trust is generative of trust interpersonally, trust *imposes* on another, without this imposition necessarily being domination.

Allow me to begin with an example. I am seated in an airport, and over the loudspeaker sounds the familiar warning that "unattended luggage could be destroyed for security reasons." Unable to carry my bags to the restroom, I turn to the person seated next to me, asking if she could watch my bags for a moment while I hobble to the restroom on crutches. I leave my passport, my camera, my work, and so forth in my bag, and I even leave myself open to the possibility of being branded a terrorist. The repetitive announcements reinforce: "Be on your guard!" "Be suspicious!"

On the one hand, when I say "excuse me" to the person seated next to me, I single this person out as trustworthy, and my trust is generative of her trustworthiness, and perhaps even of trust in herself. How many times in our own childhood has the trust of a parent or a teacher generated trust in ourselves, even when we did not consider ourselves particularly trustworthy? In this respect, trusting is generative of trust.

Yet the generative nature of trust should not be taken as simply neutral. Trust as generative of trust is *imposing*.[32] Let me clarify this nature of imposition by stating it in starker terms. Is it not really the case that one's trusting may not (also) be experienced as a kind of domination over the trusted, even though the one "trusting" did not intend it in this way? In fact, perhaps this trusting on my part would not be taken as trusting by another, in this case, the woman in the airport, but as yet another obligation in her life as, say, a mother, a spouse, or more generally, a woman. Perhaps her friends or her family had always burdened her in this or in other ways. Here she is, finally escaping from all of that (the woman in my example is relaxing and reading a novel), and a man asks her "to do" something for him. It could give rise to a range of infelicitous emotions ("do I always look like I can be bothered" "do I always give off these vibes," etc.).

To respond to these sets of issues, we can say that, yes, trusting does point beyond itself and bear meanings that go beyond the act of trusting, and that a phenomenology of trusting needs to treat the phenomenon of being trusted as well. But there is also a distinction to be made between *trusting* someone (which I clarify as imposition) and *presuming* upon someone (which may take on the qualities of domination). Both may occur in the same event but could be felt differently by different people in varying contexts. Olli Lagerspetz understands trust as an implicit ethical demand in the way that a person exerts a power on us by his or her very presence, and differs from the force of an object which is merely mechanical.[33] Still, trusting does not essentially entail something like exploiting someone else. I mean by this that I do not trust someone in order to take advantage of the other person. I do not even trust the other to get the other person to be "trustworthy." This would vitiate the very trust act or, more generally, the trust event. It would be like trying to love someone to get him or her "to love me back."

Trust, however, can be understood as an imposition. There are two ways of understanding this imposition. Let's begin with another example. Let's say my children are going to a high school party—some kind of celebration—where I know there will be drinking, but I trust them not to drink and to drive. I trust the older one to drive the younger one, to stay sober, to come home early, in short, to be a responsible young adult. Now, it is incorrect to say that I trust because *I know* what my children will do or because they are perfect children, and so forth. They are subject to temptations of youth like everyone else. Maybe they have given me their "word." But *I do not trust because I believe their word.* Indeed, what would be the basis of the belief? *It is just the reverse. If I believe them, I believe them because I trust them,* and to this extent, I bind myself to them and remain, in trusting, even as the parent, vulnerable before them. *The epistemic character of belief is founded in the moral character of trust* such that it is trust that is founding for belief. Thus, there can be beliefs, expectations, and commitments attached to trust, but the nature of trust itself is not a belief, expectation, or a commitment.

My trust in the children, while exposing vulnerability, *is also most certainly an imposition* to which they respond in some way. It may generate trustworthiness in themselves, it may make them feel guilty ("my parents trust me, but I am not worthy of this trust—I will drink and feel guilty"; or "my parents trust me, I really want to drink, but because of this trust, I will not"; or they could lament, "why do they have to trust me; if they didn't trust me I would have an excuse to do whatever I want"). In a broader sphere, such a trusting could also impose on them the spirit of trusting ("my parents trusted me"), and now they live this essential possibility as a reality for themselves toward their own children.

These examples point to the felt imposition of trusting from the side of the one being trusted. There is also an imposition in the example of the woman at the airport, but it is accompanied by different meanings, meanings that are predominately negative and that can be experienced as exploitive. This leads me *not* to distinguish between trust and imposition, but (1) to understand imposition as a feature of trust and (2) to distinguish between trust as imposition, and a different act that presumes upon another. In the latter instance, one can presume upon another without any act of trust. It also requires us to distinguish between trust as imposition, on the one hand, and control, domination, exploitation on the other.

It is within this context that we also have to question the language of "motivation" when understanding trust. At issue here is not Baier's treatment of the motivation of trust as goodwill, or McLeod's understanding the motivation as moral integrity.[34] Strictly speaking, motivation belongs to the perceptual and epistemic spheres, characterizing, instead, reliability. It is internal to the process of time-consciousness and the syntheses of association. That is, given a present givenness and its retention, a futural expectation is motivated (not caused); a similar aspect or uniform object might be motivated by the appearance of (previous or simultaneous) similar aspects or uniform objects.[35] The concept of motivation belongs here. In fact, it is no coincidence that McLeod, like others, invokes the role of "expectation" when describing the motivation of trust, or again, "optimism," which still lives in the attitude of reliability: expectation, motivation, optimism, reliability all belong together.[36] But in the moral sphere, which pertains to trust, it is fundamentally improper to characterize what is happening in the trust experience as a motivation.

Instead, we have to be attentive to a *moral invitational lure* on the part of the other that elicits however implicitly a trusting act or comportment, which is peculiar to emotional existence. On the one hand, Lawrence Becker makes an important distinction between cognitive and non-cognitive modes of trust, especially where political philosophy is concerned.[37] What he means by this is that while many have presupposed trust as an epistemic act, it has more basically affective, non-epistemic features that amount to a sense of security or reliability. In the end, however, he shares similar problems as others. Just because the judicative, epistemic sphere is cognitive does not mean that non-judicative, non-epistemic kinds of experience are non-cognitive; he does not observe the essential distinctiveness between reliability and trust, and further, does not regard vulnerability as essential to trust.[38]

One could object: "But the one being trusted, can't she or he still experience this as exploitation, being presumed upon, even if the one trusting had 'no intention' of this, while trusting?" This is certainly possible. But this is because we are in a field of interpersonal and historical meanings, and because the generative context is overdetermined. Allow me to clarify this with another example.

I remember being new to Chicago, and being instructed after a nearby assault and robbery how to walk at night in the city, namely, to walk down a street at night in the middle of the street. If I had to go to a sidewalk, I was told to avoid unlighted areas; if someone were behind me, I was told to cross to the other side; if the person behind me crossed, I was told to cross the street back to the other side; if the person crossed again, I should run and yell fire. Now, it may be that the person behind me was the one afraid to be alone on the streets and wanted some security in company. Maybe he was new to Chicago; he thought (mistakenly) I was a native, trusted something in my saunter, and was keeping close to me, "just in case." Nevertheless, his trusting was being more than "imposing" upon me, it was frightening. But in this instance, I did not experience the other person *as* trusting me; I experienced this person as following me, as harassing me, perhaps with intent to harm, even though, for his part, he may have been simply "trusting." In fact, it would have probably only have made matters worse if he had said: "Hey, don't be afraid, I am only trusting you; I am really okay, a nice guy; you can trust me." For someone to keep on following me in a situation like this would be insensitivity on his part, to put it lightly. But what if he were more afraid than he thought I was? What if he had some kind of disability, was lost in the city, and was simply appealing to the kindness of strangers, a stranger who might have reminded him of a family member? Should we not say that the person behind should just know better, that he is responsible, period? Should we say that it is his responsibility as a human being in our society to take responsibility for the social relations in which he finds himself; that it is his responsibility not to be insensitive, to think about the fear he might provoke in others in such a situation? Would we not say that there could still be an experience of trust, but that it would not manifest itself in such a compromised and insensitive manner?

I take this extreme example to suggest that it is not trusting itself that is exploitive, dominating, but the sociohistorical and socioeconomic dimensions of our lives that allow other meanings to accompany them such that "imposition" (in the manner taken here) can also become felt as domination, control, or exploitation. Where a static analysis is insufficient to handle these issues, I believe a generative approach to trust can reveal such historical factors and complex nuances. Still, the benefit of a static phenomenology of trust, undertaken on the level of a one-to-one living-present relation, can nevertheless disclose the essential character of trust as imposition, and this has been the point of such a description. Having discerned these interpersonal, temporal dimensions of trusting, namely, proffering and generative trust as imposition, let me now turn to the difference between trust and commitment.

Trust and Commitment

In much of the contemporary literature on trust, the latter is either associated with commitment or seen as a kind of commitment. In commitment, I actively join my destiny to another, to a community, to social norms and ideals, or to a task. When I am committed to something, I tie myself to it even though I may give up on my commitment and not see it through. This is an action that is generated from my side. Another person, for example, cannot violate my commitment. Only I can break or go back on my commitment. Commitment, then, stems from the individual in question and can only be broken by that individual. While I can be oriented toward another in commitment, it is not necessarily an interpersonal act.

Let's compare this to trusting. Trusting, in contrast, is essentially interpersonal. For example, when I trust another, not only am I bound to him or her, I cannot break or violate my own trust. Only another can violate my trust, say, through a betrayal. One may object that I can betray myself and that this means that trust is not essentially interpersonal. But as we saw above, I must have a sense of Myself in the broader vocational sense in order (in this case) to experience something like a self-betrayal. Myself is the site of an inter-Personal relation which I can betray because it is inter-Personal. The inner armature of any interpersonal trust is this vertical trust that comes from and within the inter-Personal nexus, and which is itself generative of trust.

Such a generative trust bears on the individual person in terms of vocation and on the collective person as solidarity. The Abrahamic religious tradition has expressed the latter in terms of "covenant," but perhaps more descriptively as the reparation of the world (*tikkun olam*) as the process of redemption or removing barriers—a process to which each unique person contributes in a way that only he or she can in order "to gather the scattered sparks of holiness" or "to establish God's presence on earth." As the basic bond forming sociality, the inter-Personal bond lies behind the trust that occurs between and among persons. With respect to myself, I can betray Myself not because I trust Myself, but because I stand in an inter-Personal relation as not self-grounding. I betray myself when I betray another's trust in me as who I am. By contrast, I cannot break another's commitment to me.

Notice also that commitment and trust do not necessarily coincide in other ways within the interpersonal sphere. For instance, I can be committed to someone who is in drug rehab and trust this same person. In both trust and commitment, I make myself available to another and am open to other possibilities that I do not know in advance. But it is also possible that I commit myself to helping someone see the process through to completion, even though while I remain committed, I may no longer trust the person (e.g., to keep to the program). Peculiar to this interpersonal nature of trust is the fact that one does not and one cannot trust out of one's own self-interest, while I can be committed to another (or to a norm or ideal) out of self-interest. For example, I could be committed to another in an abusive relationship, for the sake of the relationship, for the sake of "the children," for economic gain, and so on, but still not trust the other person. Trust, as being bound to another immediately and directly as a *vulnerability, rules out the motive of self-interest.*

Further, being bound to another in trust cannot be reduced to an

"I bind myself to you." The latter would be an activity that I do, and it would be synonymous with commitment. Being bound to another is nothing "I" do, but it takes place in the trust act as a realization of my freedom in the moment of vulnerability. So, while it is correct to say that I can commit myself to social norms or that I can share a commitment, strictly speaking the latter is not a basis for the former, as is sometimes maintained in the contemporary work on trust.[39] Children trust parents or guardians without making judgments, having assumptions about or reflecting on commitments to social norms. They trust *another* directly. Accordingly, it is not at all evident that we trust those who have the capacity to make commitments, or that trusting is itself a learned capacity.[40] Aside from the common conflation of commitment and trust as learned, it is rather mistrust and suspicion that are "learned."

The strictly interpersonal nature of trust also means that trust is foundational for commitment. For instance, we do not build social relations through an "I commit to this or that," or "I commit to you and you . . . ," and so on; rather, these relations are established on the basis of *a primordial trust that enables us to make specific commitments;* trust cannot be not founded on a commitment to social norms. Trust is not a "serious commitment" which stems from an "ego ideal."[41] Interpersonal trust does not need commitment in order to be operative, but we can say that it "should" entail commitment to another such that there is a disorder of the heart when commitment does not accompany trust.

To summarize: commitment need not be interpersonal; I can commit to objects, ideals, and to others; it unfolds on the level of the ego in the active register and from the self. Trust, on the other hand, is strictly interpersonal and can be pre-judicative or pre-egoic. To maintain that trust is dependent upon the commitment to ideals or shared norms would ultimately be to found the moral dimension of our lives on epistemological engagements and to presuppose interpersonal relations under the rubric of the "social." Trust and commitment, however, are two distinctive lived-orientations.

Modal Specification of Trust

We find trust to be operative on two levels, on the level of the person as person, and on the level of the person in a modal specification. In order to see the uniqueness of trust, let's contrast it briefly with the unconditional nature of loving. Loving by its nature is unconditional or open to infinity. It is open to infinity in three senses. First, loving is oriented to the fullest possible becoming of the beloved (toward ever deeper values and boundless fullness). Second, it belongs to the nature of loving not to have any temporal restrictions on the love. It makes no sense, for example, to say "I will love you for five years and no more." Further, I can love another after the beloved has died. In this respect, when I love, loving is open to eternity, even if factually, loving may be cut short. Third, I love the person as such, independently, say, of her occupation. I love Dorothy, who is a teacher, but not simply in the context of her teaching. I do not love her only insofar as she is a teacher. In these respects, loving is unconditional and not restricted to particular contexts or specifications.

Let these brief comments suffice in order to situate the phenomenon of trust. I mentioned above that there are two levels of trust. Like loving, trust can bear on the person as person. This trust is expressed as an openness toward the other person that is unspecified in advance, as a vulnerability before the other person as such, and as a relation that is not determined by this particular set of circumstances. This is what we might call a primordial interpersonal temporalizing trust. It is no coincidence that children are the most vulnerable in this regard.

Unlike loving, however, trust is also given in terms of modal specifications. Let me begin with the following example. I leave my children at school in the care of the teachers. I trust the teachers not simply as persons, but as persons *as* teachers, *as* caretakers of the children. I trust them with respect to their teaching and with respect to the care of the children. In loving, I love the person, George, whether or not he is a teacher, was a teacher, and is no longer one. In loving there is *no with respect to*. . . But if I trust George as a teacher and he reveals himself not to be a teacher in its full sense, I may no longer trust him.

We might be tempted to say that trusting is "context-dependent" or "situational." I think these characterizations, however, are ultimately misleading. It is more accurate to characterize trusting as a modal specification or determination. I trust the person *as* a teacher and all that this implies. The reason trusting is not essentially context-dependent is because when I trust the person *as* teacher in this modal determination, I can trust the teacher as such *in every and all contexts*—according to this specification. Thus, the specification does not arise from the ready-made context, but from the modal (as-structure) of teaching which qualifies the person in this *way*.

It is also true that while I may trust the person as a teacher, I might not trust the same person as a mechanic or as someone to watch my pets. But this does not mean that the trust is "conditional." In fact, if I trust the teacher, I trust him or her "unconditionally"—within this modality. Here, trust is essentially open-ended and cannot abide pre-imposed limits, be they situational or temporal. Likewise, I do not live through the trust act as an "on the condition that." For example, just because my child is no longer in the classroom or the school with this same individual, I do not stop trusting the person as a teacher. My trust does not end just because the situation in which the trust arose is over. Trust is not pragmatic in this sense; it does not reside in the sphere of functional practicality.

Even if this is not the deepest kind of trust one can have, the fact that one can trust in this way tells us something about such a phenomenon, namely, that it is open to modal specifications. Further, that such a distinction along the lines of modal specification can be made shows it is distinctive vis-à-vis loving.

Conclusion

Allow me to conclude this chapter on trust with the following observations. First, unlike a straightforward perception and judicative acts, as well as reliability as a matter of practical functionality, trust is not essentially motivated by a past. While reliability could easily be viewed as "built up" from lower-level intentional formations, trust exhibits a different temporal structure already with respect to its dependence upon the past. This is not to say that the past cannot play a role (e.g., when the "familiar" is considered in genetic and generative contexts), but that in trust the past is not essentially a constitutive moment since trust in a complete and unknown stranger is still a possibility. Instead, trust is oriented temporally toward an open future as one of the constitutive features of interpersonal sociality. Its futural temporal structure is a proffering. So even though I can expect without a trust, but not trust without an expectation, being-bound to another in "proffering" is itself a unique structure of interpersonal temporalization and is qualitatively distinct from the temporal structure in which the time constitution of objects unfolds. Spatially, trust is socially expansive, and this can be seen in direct contrast to mistrust and distrust which are movements toward isolation, separation, and individualism.

Second, and on a related note, the "trusted" does not share the structure of an object, nor is the trusted "intended" like an object. Trust operates on a wholly different order of givenness because here the trusted is given in its transcendence as "free," as "mystery," and as non-objectifiable in principle. Most deeply, trust concerns the level of the person, and as such it has its own kind of evidence, "modalization," disappointment, and so on. Moreover, I cannot make the "trusted" as such available to intersubjective/objective adjudication or verification like I could an object, and I cannot make my trusting open to scrutiny like I might my intentions in a contract. However, we have evidence of trust in the fact that we can trust without having to have past evidence in order to trust. But this requires that one inhabit the trust act in order to see its kind of evidence.

This is why, third, it is vulnerability that is essential to trust—not distrust or mistrust—and that makes the one trusting susceptible not to a mistake, but to betrayal. The trusting person and the mistrustful person inhabit two different worlds. As we saw above, to trust a person as a good human being and to assume a person to be a good human being are two qualitatively different experiences. When we expose ourselves to "more" than what can be given in and through being-bound to another in trust, we become vulnerable and susceptible to a violation of that trust. This also has an entirely different structure from a disappointed judgment or being naive or gullible, and is not a higher-order variation of the latter. Accordingly, there is nothing to strip away from vulnerability to disclose a more putatively basic "naiveté." Our systems of knowledge are based on trust, since we only believe what someone says because we trust him or her. This is one reason why I do not originally "decide" to trust.

Fourth, being bound to another in trusting another is an interpersonal structure that is qualitatively different from intending another person, either as an object, or apperceptively as in "empathy." I am already ahead of myself in this being-bound to. This binding character constitutes an interpersonal normativity in the social sphere, whose rupture turns up as an experienced violation. Here the freedom of the other is presupposed in trusting, and my freedom is realized interpersonally as being bound to the other.

Being vulnerable as being bound to another in trusting implicitly goes against pride, because in trusting, I am not in control of the situation; the person is not regarded pragmatically as merely reliable. The interpersonal self-disposition is an implicit counter-movement to pride, since I do not shape the interpersonal relation according to my whim, displacing the contributive dynamics stemming from another. Trust is founded neither in a volitional act, nor a prideful act, nor do I trust to preserve myself. In trust, I proffer myself in the presence of this transcendent, free other, in the presence of whom I am bound to their destiny, even if for that moment or in that mode. In this regard, trusting is tied to loving and humility.

7

Loving and Humility

> What I aim to do is not so much learn the names of the shreds of creation that flourish in this valley, but to keep myself open to their meanings, which is to try to impress myself at all times with the fullest possible force of their very reality.
> —Annie Dillard

I treat the moral emotions of loving and humility in this chapter. While the phenomenon of loving has been evoked throughout this work, both because it is so fundamental to interpersonal experience, and because it is a way of highlighting the peculiar qualities of other emotions, I give only a brief treatment of it in this chapter. While a fuller treatment of loving is reserved for a complementary work, as I mentioned above, loving is so tightly intertwined with the experience of humility that I begin with an exposition of it here. Following this section on loving, I take up the phenomenon of humility. In particular, I interpret its founding character in relation to pride (1), describe its peculiar style of self-givenness (2), and distinguish humility from being humbled, humbling myself, and modesty (3). Because of the common conflation of humiliation and humility, I pay special attention to the problem of humiliation as a distinctive experience more akin to debilitating shame, and then examine the relation of affliction to humility (4). The final section of this chapter takes up humility's unique temporal modes of givenness (5).

Loving

Loving and hatred, as with all acts of the emotional sphere, have their own style of evidence, their own field of modalizations and deceptions; having their own sphere of evidence, they cannot be adjudicated outside of that sphere, say, by the perceptual presentation of objects or by rational judgments or proofs (e.g., "reasons" why I love or trust someone—which always only come after the fact). I have alluded to this unique sphere of evidence by describing this mode of personal givenness as "revelation" in distinction to the mode of givenness called "presentation" (of objects or ideas), as well as in distinction to that of manifestation, disclosure, display, or even epiphany.[1]

I had begun this work by inquiring into the extent to which the emotions have a distinctive structure; and we have seen the different ways in which the moral emotions do indeed have their own style of evidence, cognition, and modalizations. For this reason, an exposition of loving cannot begin with the presupposition that loving is blind, that it is a sentimental, aimless, feel-good mood, a state of mind, ideology, instinct, intellectual assessment, or value judgment—for these presuppose loving is either non-rational, and lacks evidence, or is a kind of judicative process. At its core—and this needs to be clarified below—loving is a creative, initiated, improvisational act, a dynamic orientation or *movement* peculiar to the level of spirit, revelatory of the human being as person. As given in and through the movement, the person is transcending, in the qualitatively distinctive (unique) directedness of becoming.

To say that loving is an act or is creative in this sense means furthermore that even if loving is *responsive* to another loving—since loving can serve as an "invitation" to love—even the responsive loving is never caused or the result of being loved; nor is it a trigger condition, say, to a happiness, grief, or enjoyment already felt.[2] I can love as a "response" to another who does not intend anything at all; or I can love in my turn from what calls me as an invitation to goodness. But even here loving is an original, initiatory act, not a causal reaction. Social psychological attempts to measure love, or, through brain scans, to detect a surge of dopamine, associating "love" with the hormones oxytocin and vasopressin, completely miss the movement of love as act originating from the person.

Loving can be oriented toward anything, from persons, to ideas, to a utensil, to the natural environment; we can love wisdom, beauty, truth, and we are oriented toward and by the love or hatred of these matters that exhibit these values.[3] While loving can be oriented toward anything as bearers of value, loving is most deeply realized as "inter-Personal" and as interpersonal. The love of the object, too, can be inter-Personal and interpersonal when in its specificity or delimitation toward this object, it simultaneously de-limits. But then the object no longer functions as mere object, but as "icon."[4]

My point in mentioning this here directly is that loving is that movement which "allows" the other to become more fully who he or she is, or what it is in the direction of its deepening or enhancement. In Max Scheler's terms, loving only occurs when there issues beyond what is already given a *movement* toward "higher" values that are higher still "in" the beloved, yet a movement that is fully *indifferent* as to whether this higher value is already in existence, unperceived, or ought to exist.[5] But—and this is essential—loving as we will see below is not an attempt to fix an objective, "to better" the other person, to implant a teleological purpose, or to form another in our image. It is the movement of loving itself that ushers the spontaneous emergence of the "ever-higher" or the "ever-deeper" as if streaming out of the beloved of its own accord without any sort of effort or wishing on the part of the lover. In this way, we can say that loving and the personal revelation in loving can be felt as a "nonviolent insistence" or as invitational lure.[6] It is related but irreducible to the kind of "felt imposition" that we discovered in the case of interpersonal trust. Loving as a loving response (which is itself spontaneous, not a causal reaction) can be understood as acting "as from another," and in the case of vocational experience, as from holiness in the world.[7]

The givenness of the beloved in the loving—which co-originates as a free self-revelation on the side of the beloved (and in this respect is not arbitrary or random)—always lets the loving-movement "peer out a little further beyond what is presently given" in the direction of depth (and in this respect is creative, open). This implies, moreover, that loving as an act is not "fulfilled" in the way that a perception or judgment is fulfilled in the latter's intending; nor can I summon love from another, like I can ask another to look at the same perceptual object. The "higher" value does not have to be given in loving in order to love, and even if *a* higher value were "realized," loving is a dynamic transcending, so in this sense, it would never come to an end in a final givenness. Although I can love a person, a pen, or a tree, and so on, I do not love them as an already fixed beloved. Scheler tries to evoke the dynamic, spontaneous movement of loving that befits the lover and the beloved by describing loving as a movement toward another as bearer of value, since in loving, I am oriented neither passively nor actively toward the beloved in the manner of a sense-bestowal on an object, whereas the latter would instead be the telos or "effort," as it were, of a perceptual or judicative act.

As we saw above in the genuine sense of interpersonal (and not subject-object) shame, another person can disclose my own depth of possibilities in the very movement of this other person's loving, a depth of possibilities that may have been hidden from me or removed from what I could "know" of myself (outside of a genuine self-love).[8] Unlike the always-more-to-see of an object, the movement of loving gives or reveals the person in a concrete creative sense in the direction of the "perfection" appropriate to him or her (in the case of persons), and in principle, beyond all limits, without achieving a definitive character or being predetermined.[9] Whereas in sensual objects, it is the increased variety that expresses the unending character of the process, in the cases of spirit (persons, for example), it is the increased depth, or infinitizing de-limitation, which is to say, the co-participation in the movement of holiness, a co-relating or historical redemption. Scheler uses the provocative expression of the "good-in-itself-for-me," as we have seen, to evoke the sense that this "ideal value image" is not drawn from empirical values or established on that basis, and further, that it is given and only given in this qualified sense in the movement of loving.[10]

In the openness to the deepest possibilities that something can be, according to its own sphere of existence, loving discloses possibilities that may have not been given before, but flash forth only in and through the movement of loving; only in this sense is loving "creative of existence."[11] The givenness in loving (in the case of persons, what I call "revealing") is creative since what is revealed in the movement is itself expressive: what is revealed is not merely discovered, because it is an opening or infinitizing or de-limiting movement. We can say that creative activity as expressive movement "reveals God"—but not in the sense that God is already there and predetermined, and only disclosed. Rather, expressive activity reveals God in the sense of the "laying down of being"; it is the participation in the ongoing co-creation, which is expressive and expansive; it "only" looks necessary and becomes "essential" in the revelatory process itself.[12] Hatred, on the other hand, is an act that is destructive in the sense that it closes down possibilities, is the preoccupation with lower possibilities, and the givenness of disvalue; and this is why hatred is not "blind," but is blinding, namely, it diminishes possibilities, dulls our feeling for such values and our power to discriminate between them.[13]

While loving is a dynamic orientation as movement, there is no sense of "effort" or exertion, or of a counter-exertion in hating. In part, this is why loving and hating can be seen as not following the coordinates of intention and fulfillment such as they would take shape, for example, in a perceptual or categorial experience. As mentioned above, there is no "object" in loving, no striving toward a goal, no teleological end point. Accordingly, love cannot be "satisfied" like a perception can, even if there is "always more" to be given in loving, more as an overfull "abyss," in distinction to the "plus ultra" of a perceptual horizon that functions as a system of referential implications. Only if we were mistakenly to take love as a duty would there be the possibility of a fulfillment of an intention. Similarly, while there is a striving inherent in benevolence, there is no such striving in loving or hating.[14]

The love of a person is an opening to the person *as given in his or her uniqueness*. In loving as in trusting, I am immediately "beyond" myself without trying to go outside of myself. Loving is the process of living in the presence of this radiance that we call the person, not the attempt to possess what is radiating in this personal manner. Loving can be characterized as letting the other become such that he or she "can" realize him- or herself.[15] This can be understood as an openness to possibilities that are not given outside of that loving, and that lie in the direction of the becoming-being of the person. In this way, the person is *revealed* in and through the movement of loving, but never presented like an object over against an intending (like an "I plan on these possibilities for you").

On the other hand, it is entirely possible for us to see nothing, to deny this givenness, or to redirect revelatory loving as hatred. What is important to note here, however, is that the hating as negation always takes place on the basis of the positive revelation given in loving. We are thus always cognizant of more than either negligence or hating would seem to suggest.

Being open to unanticipatable dimensions of the person, I can be so dedicated to the person that I do not give a first or second thought to myself. Not only is this expressive of the personal vulnerability in the face of another that we found in trusting, but this immediate and direct orientation toward the other in love can be expressed as an irreversibility in loving as being self-less or self-sacrificing, without having the self as the object of the sacrifice. Loving is only considered after the fact as a loss of self, but I do not try to lose myself, and therefore "love" (see below, under "Humility"). The positive, founding movement of loving is correlative to the irreplaceability or non-representational character of the other person; loving itself carries this irreversibility in its very movement. For example, I do not love someone in order to get them to love me back; I don't care for a child with the proviso that he or she will do something for me later.

Loving is not the same as preferring or rejecting, for preferring or rejecting are unique emotional modes of cognition in which a comparative relation is given. Loving, however, is not an apprehension of value, as a preference or a rejection of value, but a movement toward something as bearer of value, a movement that first allows that value "to flash forth" in and of itself, on the basis of which it could be preferred or rejected. Only on the basis of loving, through which values are disclosed, can one prefer—without choosing between—for example, cycling to climbing as physical activities. A volitional act may choose between cycling and climbing; an evaluative act or a judgment could further appraise a cyclist or a climber as deserving respect; but again, respect is not fundamental since it is founded in loving. Loving, accordingly, is the movement that opens up dimensions of value in the other in the direction of a deeper enhancement, allowing the other to become more fully who he or she or what it is, whether or not the higher or deeper value actually exists. This is one sense in which loving, as the movement toward another, is founding for other modes of cognition and any knowledge as consciousness of something, and thus for the possibility of respect.[16]

Just as I do not love another in order to draw out deeper possibilities in him, I do not first see the value of something, and then love it; in loving we are unconcerned about the so-called existence of higher values or the process of opening further possibilities. For loving is experiencing the other in the uniqueness of who she *is* and becoming, and not what *I want* her to be. She is not my "project." Nor do I love another because I have invested so much time in him. This idea would constitute a banking concept of love. The genuineness of love, asserts Scheler, can be seen by the fact that we do indeed see the shortcomings in the beloved, but love him all the same, though love opens me and the beloved to values higher than those which "interest" would discern. If this were not the case, then love would come to an end once the fault became evident or the possible higher value were not actualized.[17]

Rather, loving is an opening to infinity, which is ultimately in the direction of holiness, and is lived without the patronizing attitude of "trying to make the beloved better," or to change the other person according to my idea or my image, which is a more insidious form of pride.[18] The statement "become who you are," where this sense of being is dynamic, is not the same as "you should be such and such." Loving someone as she is therefore is not the same as "I love you for the value that I discern you to possess," for this would deprive loving of its inherent *movement:* namely, as the movement in which each thing, each person that is a bearer of value, is susceptible of the highest value or depth of value peculiar to its nature and fullness.[19] For a Jew to love a Muslim means for the Jew to live in such a way that the Muslim becomes the best possible Muslim he can, according to the way of Islam. It is not an attempt to convert the other to my own way, or to be evangelical in the customary sense of the term. In a related manner, I do not love another out of reverence for a norm. As we saw above, there can be no "reverence" for a norm or moral law that is not founded in a love for the person who functions as exemplary of that norm or normative actions. If a norm functions as a demand in guilt, for example, it is because it is grounded in the person given through loving.

In every instance, loving is oriented personally (from the side of the person as person) toward the beloved as an opening to the depth or richness of its intrinsic value, which entails an opening to its own possibilities that cannot be anticipated in advance. Because the person, as revealed most deeply through the moral emotions, is the dynamic source of her own intrinsic normativity, loving, in its creative spontaneity and "flexibility," as it were, bears its own intrinsic normativity, instituting its own normative demands vis-à-vis the beloved.[20]

I mentioned above that an object is most fully itself in loving when it is not lived merely as object, but as "icon." When we use an object as a use-value, we certainly want it to be useful. But when the useful object is "caught up" in the movement of loving, the object is not limited merely to the useful; it opens up to the personal as well, and thus of service in the fullest sense. I call this the process of de-limitation, for example, when the useful or technical is not restricted merely to the useful or technical, but opens up as integrated infinitely, without measure, to the absolute finite (persons) and the absolute infinite (holiness). Only in such an orientation is there the possibility of the "redemption" of the useful or technical.[21] To love a fountain pen is to love it within or through the sphere of utility; while the range and depth of its possibilities as pen are delimited by utility and being of service in its instrumentality, say, as writers, loving here does not mean to compromise its functionality for the sake of profit. Only if the pen were taken as a work of art would its functionality be eclipsed by aesthetic value; even here, however, it would not be subordinated merely to exchange or surplus value.

In the sphere of sensibility, for example, we can love coffee. Such a love of coffee has its unique type of givenness (distinct from the love of God or the love of another person, though as loving, it is still different from merely enjoying or liking a cup of coffee). But to love coffee in the sense loving is taken here means that coffee is given in a de-limiting sense; it means to bring out its fullest "potential"—that may not be given in advance—in terms of what it can offer, since it is *fully* what it is, but not exhaustively.

For the farmers who grow coffee, this may mean to plant and care for special plants in particular ways, only to pick ripe cherries, or to wait for a certain sugar content, or even to process the cherries and then dry the beans in ways that may eventually bring out different aromas; for roasters, it may mean roasting beans with an attentiveness to their "optimal" point of caramelizing, and exo-thermatic heating of the bean, and not a uniform charring of the bean. For baristas, it may entail preparing the brews in pourovers, siphons, aeropresses, French presses, or espresso shots that maximize complexities of aromas. It may mean participating in the social conversations and exchange of ideas that "coffee" elicits; it may entail being sensitive to the very farmers who produce the plants in the first place in terms of their economic and spiritual well-being. In this way, the love of coffee is de-limiting, which is to say, it is fully in the sphere of sensibility, but opens up through this to the interpersonal dimension.[22] It may sound extreme, but it is not far-fetched to say that we can *love* coffee iconically in this dynamic, de-limiting sense. As Teresa of Avila suggests, when God is among the pots and pans, they are lived differently, such that even doing dishes can become prayerful activity or the experience of holiness.

This is much different, for example, from treating the farmers as mere producers of a caffeine substance, or forgetting the farmers altogether, dismissing the matter of aromas and tastes, selling and buying inferior beans in packages or open bins long past their roast date, that is, when they are completely stale and tasteless. Loving does not limit the range of possibilities by restricting the personal to the vital or the vital to the serviceable. This would be to close down possibilities, moving in the direction of lower values, and thus move in the direction of hating, and ultimately to reduce spiritual value to surplus or exchange value.

Having examined loving in terms of de-limitation, let me now turn to the temporal character of loving. Viewed in terms of its temporality, loving, like trusting, does not need the past in order to be loving. As freely enacted, I can love someone or something I have never known or encountered before. So while loving's temporal *orientation* can be to the past, present, or future, its temporal *meaning* is presencing. I invoke the sense of presence here because one loves another *as* who or what he, she, or it *is* "now" without trying to impose external norms. Loving is not a "do this and I will love you," but "I love you, and become who you are." Nevertheless, I use the gerund "presencing" to characterize the temporal meaning of loving because of the implicit dynamic future movement in loving, as creative of new norms and openness to new possibilities within the very movement itself. Loving is precisely redeeming in the sense of liberating the "limits" of the present-now.

Loving is given without temporal limitations. As we saw above in relation to trust, it makes no sense in terms of the experience to assert, "I will love you for five years," or "I love you now; that's enough"—even if the love does come to an end. This is because the loving in its very directedness is moving toward infinity (toward eternity, omni-temporally, one might say, unconditionally). If loving goes unto infinity, going beyond the limits of death, it is because loving goes to the core of the spiritual being. Accordingly, Frankl can write about his wife who he did not know was dead or alive after they were forcibly separated in the camps: "Love goes very far beyond the physical person of the beloved. It finds its deepest meaning in his spiritual being, his inner self. Whether or not he is actually present, whether or not he is still alive at all, ceases somehow to be of importance."[23] There is futural meaning in loving because loving opens possibilities such that these limits cannot be forecasted. It constitutes a loving community that goes beyond the synchronic community and extends over the generations, encompassing those no longer living.

I mentioned the possibility of a genuine self-love in distinction to pride above in chapter 1. Self-love was depicted as an openness to who I *am* as given to myself, in other words, as Myself, without the arbitrary self-limitation that would posit me as self-grounding or restrict me to an ethical solipsism. As the creative generation of who I am, according to how I am given to myself, self-love is a responding that co-determines Myself, which is the experience of "vocation." Whereas the narrative "self" can be given historically through my own and others' interpretations, the narrative self is not the vocational Myself; rather, corresponding to the dimension and core of the person, the Myself is vocational as an inter-Personal relation given through loving. In this respect, as we will see, humility is given with a demand and an urgency that originates outside of myself and co-originates with me, Myself: I "must" love Myself. But in pride there is no such urgency or demand because in pride such a putative demand would only be dependent upon my subjective interest and time. Pride is "merely" a love of self—not a genuine self-love—which purposely sees everything, even myself strictly through my eyes, as it were.[24] Genuine self-love is not the same as letting my "self-worth" get in the way of my responsibility toward others, for self-love is a de-limitation in the positive sense mentioned above: already a reception of and an openness to the interpersonal nexus.

Loving and humility are intimately related, and I understand their difference in terms of experiential emphases. Loving is an immediate and direct opening to another—any other—in the integrity of what it is and toward the fullest realization of what it is with respect to its own sphere—be it a person, a tool, a work of art, living beings other than human, or inorganic object. Here the focus is on the other, and is characterized as a movement, in one respect, originating from the beloved as invitational, and in another respect, toward the other as an initiatory movement of the lover. Humility is this openness and dynamic movement, but where the experiential resonance is on how I spontaneously receive myself as Myself, that is, as who I am from another. Both loving and humility are equally radical, but humility is a spontaneous actualization, where the experience is lived in its emphasis on "Myself."

Humility

Humility is commonly taken as a virtue, especially in the Christian tradition. It is possible to understand humility as a virtue in our context of the moral emotions, but not if we mean by this an innate character, an impersonal or natural pole of action that is directed toward prescribed rules, some incidental adornment of temperament, states of moral perfection, or products of self-will. Rather, if treated as a virtue, humility would have to be understood as a quality of the person him- or herself, not there for predetermined action and works, but as a living force, directed toward the good such that it is personal and unique, and that is oriented toward the enhancement of responsibility.[25]

However, I hesitate in treating humility as a virtue if it were to imply the development of a "virtue ethics," as opposed, say, to a consequentialist or utilitarian ethics. Hence, the task here is not to describe, for example, humility as a virtue (or chastity, temperance, courage, loyalty, pride, etc., as virtues), if it means presupposing the very meaning of person that we are trying to elucidate. Instead, the attempt is to describe humility as a moral emotion of otherness as it points to and helps to elucidate the meaning of person. I take humility as a moral emotion because of the way in which it is inherently connected to loving, namely, as the way I receive myself in loving. In what follows, I address the foundational character of humility, and then approach the question of self-givenness in humility. This is followed by a differentiation between being humbled, humbling myself, and modesty. I then distinguish between humiliation, affliction, and humility. I conclude this chapter with a consideration of the unique temporal modes through which humility is lived.

The Foundational Character of Humility

I opened this work with the experience of pride. Let me now briefly examine humility in this context. Humility is a fundamental moral emotion in the sense that it is interpersonally founding and not founded. As we saw in the "Introduction" above, the relation of foundation is such that the "founding" dimension is independent and can exist on its own without presupposing something more basic; as founding, it can provide a potential basis for a different act or object to come into being as founded, by something adjuncting the founding level. To say that something is founded means that it requires a more basic dimension in order to be lived or given; as founded, it is "higher," and "built upon" founding levels, although together with the latter, the complex forms a new unity of act and sense.[26] The relation of foundation is an operative concept. It is operative in the sense that it can apply to a variety of contexts, and depending upon the context, what specifically is founding and founded shifts. For example, the relation of foundation can apply to acts generally such as objectivating and non-objectivating acts, as we saw above (thus, emotional acts are not founded in epistemic acts); and it can apply to a particular set of experiences, as we saw in the case of trust and anti-trust (thus, trust is foundational for and not dependent upon anti-trust in order to be executed).

As examples of founded acts that we have encountered, we can include shame and guilt. They can be qualified as founded acts because they are kinds of diremptive experiences, and as such, they depend upon this diremption (a more basic orientation, and an orientation that calls it into question) in order to be given. Traced all the way back, they can be interpreted as responses to pride.

To say that humility is foundational means from one standpoint that humility is given without further justification. We might deduce or infer "reasons" for humility from a clinical standpoint, or we might be able to show what areas of the brain are stimulated when one experiences humility (provided that we are able to identify objectively that this is indeed the experience of humility when we are examining the areas of the brain that are being affected), but this only pushes the problem back one step further. Humility, like trust, is a fundamental, original experience emergent on the level of the person that cannot be traced back further in terms of reasons for it, and psychological or neurologically based causes of it. This means in turn, as we have seen in examples of other emotional experiences, that the verification of the experience is internal to the kind of experience it is, susceptible to distinctive orders of evidence.

Further, in relation to pride, to say that humility is founding for pride and not the reverse means that we can experience humility without the experience of pride, and further, pride as founded presupposes humility as a reversal of humility. This is the case even if humility, historically or in the life of the person functions as a "reply" to pride. Let me explain. Although we began this work on moral emotions with the dynamic set in motion by pride, humility is foundational in the sense that it can in principle take place without one first experiencing pride; even though humility can furnish a reply to pride, it does not exist on the basis of pride. We can ascertain this because pride is self-limiting—in the ways that we have described above—and as such, in and of itself, it could not open to otherness and "found" humility. Thus, it is not a matter of imposing an outside standard on pride and concluding that it is "wrong," but observing how pride is essentially self-dissimulating and self-limiting. Pride is a reversal of humility such that pride is founded in interpersonal acts, in order for it, pride, to come into being at all; without the interpersonal relation, and the essential openness in emotions like loving and trusting, there could be no pride; and there would be no possible experience of pride if I were reduced to my "sphere of ownness" (which is another way of saying that the sphere of ownness is only gained, intellectually, by abstraction). Pride arises, therefore, by dissimulating this interpersonal dimension, and obfuscating loving and humility as the actualization of the accusative Myself. Whereas humility is essential for interpersonal relations, necessary and independent of pride, pride constitutes a reversal of interpersonal relations and is by no means necessary, and is dependent upon loving and humility.

Allow me to focus on humility. The perspective on pride as putatively founding for humility, and the perspective on pride as an historical a priori founded in humility, can yield two different descriptions of this experience. In the first instance, we would have a characterization of humility shaped by pride. That is, if we presuppose the self-dissimulation of pride (which yields the person as if isolated, self-sufficient, and self-centered), then humility could be characterized as the "loss of self." In the second case, if pride is interpreted as a historical a priori and humility as foundational, then humility is to be characterized as a *recovery of self* because it is the actualization of interpersonal relations. I develop these possibilities, each in their turn.

If we were to presuppose the sense of myself as it is given in pride, namely, as isolated, self-centered, and the constitutive source over others—if we were to presuppose this dissimulation, which is a self-dissimulation—then humility could be interpreted as merely a de-centering of self, a loss of self, or a forgetfulness of self. This would be the case because what we presuppose—misleadingly—is that the self *is* independent, the major source of meaning, self-grounding, and ultimately, "secular." If this were the case, then humility could only be a de-centering of this presupposed center, a dislodging of the putative "starting point" of meaning. Then any attempt to counter pride could only be the negative attempt of the so-called forgetfulness of self. Yet, if pride were our ontological starting point, what would be the motivation to overcome pride in the first place? Still, presuming it could be such a starting point, then such a movement of overcoming would have to assume the *disvalue* of the individual person, myself; as a result, "I" would be something to negate. In short, such a movement of overcoming could only be carried out as self-hatred. Starting with the subject as he does, it is no coincidence that Descartes characterizes humility as a matter of despising ourselves, and as contrary to esteeming ourselves.[27] If all this were truly the case, then in the final analysis, others, the world, and so on, could only then be the repository of my self-negation guided by self-hatred.

However, if pride is not an ontological, original condition of the human person, but has become a structure introduced historically into human existence by human persons, which is enacted each time anew "originally" as it originates at each epoch, each period, in each person, then the implications of pride and the implications of the emergence of humility are different. Pride as self-dissimulation is not essential to the human person in the sense that it, pride, would be an innate characteristic of what it means to be a human person and before there were ever humans. Rather, it has become historically an essential possibility for us that "essentially" need not be. Nevertheless, historically, "really," it is a matter that we cannot sidestep.

If we begin with this historical precedence of pride—pride as an historical a priori for human persons—then we are able to qualify humility in terms of its integral movement, and pride as a reversal of humility and of interpersonal acts more generally. Humility is directly and fundamentally interpersonal, given in and through an other-orientation. In terms of its relation to pride, historically speaking, humility can be understood as a *recovery* of the interpersonal dimension—a dimension that pride obfuscates through its resistance such that humility is not first a de-centering of the self. In this sense, humility is not first and foremost a self-forgetfulness, but vis-à-vis pride, a re-position of Myself, and a recovery of the interpersonal dimension that is implicit even in pride, and as a result, a dis-position of the prideful self. Thus, if humility is how I am self-given through being given over to another, as having been called forth by another; if we gain Myself through a "moral reduction," as intimated above in the first chapter—pointing toward humility—but initially followed out in the chapters on shame, guilt, and repentance—if this is the case, then we can understand humility as a recovery in the sense of realizing Myself as interpersonal.

Trying to escape myself by being humble, trying to lose myself in a project does not constitute humility because I am still encumbered with my-self. Here, "I" would still be the point of departure and the point of return. Although there is a loss of the self-dissimulating self in humility, a "loss" nourished by devotion and service, being humble is not undertaken as a project to lose or to forget myself in another.[28] The latter might simply be a case of what Nietzsche identified as a false altruism, as we saw in the preceding chapters. Likewise, Saint Teresa of Avila writes that we should not try to still our own mind or forget ourselves by our own means; not only would this leave us "simpletons," in her view, but it would attempt to place God at our power of disposition, or at the very least, express our expectation of favors for our efforts. Instead, "self-forgetfulness" of this sort comes as a result, interpersonally, of God occupying us *in another way*, not by what we accomplish. For her, although I can practice a non-attachment to things and to my own desires, such occupation is interrupted by the person of God, and not by my own efforts. This is why she writes: "And I say again, even though it may not be understood, this effort to suspend the intellect is not very humble."[29] Hence, it is better to respond from love and service, she writes; and if the presence of God can be likened to a flame, then it is better to place gently "a little straw there with humility" rather than stack up cords of wood with our strivings to attain spiritual delights.[30] Similarly, Annie Dillard writes: "The death of the self of which the great writers speak is no violent act. It is merely the joining of the great rock heart of the earth in its roll. It is merely the slow cessation of the will's sprints and intellect's chatter: it is waiting like a hollow bell with stilled tongue. *Fuge, tace, quiesce*. The waiting itself is the thing."[31]

The point of mentioning Saint Teresa and Annie Dillard here is to suggest in different registers how humility is not a matter of self-concern, and how there can be a non-attachment to "self" without this non-attachment being a self-occupied concern with forgetting myself. So while there is a de facto self-effacement in the movement, I am neither starting point nor theme. (We can recall the discussion of attachment broached above in the chapter on repentance.) Through the positive movement from and toward the other, as an attitude of devotion and service, there is an acceptance and reception, the acknowledgment of gift, and "*therefore*" a self-forgetfulness, and "*therefore*" a response to pride. Yet what is self-given in the movement of humility arises spontaneously as Myself, that is, Myself as oriented toward things without attachment, toward Myself as not self-grounding, as essentially interpersonal, the reception of Myself in the accusative.

By contrast, in humility, there is no expectation of merit, and there is no expectation of return; in fact, as we will see below, this temporal mode of expectation is not functional *in humility*. This is not to say that I do not, as a human person, expect anything, for example, as I move around an object while being humble. Rather, as living humbly, there is nothing to expect. Or, to expect nothing in humility means in the moral sphere that *I deserve* nothing, which is why everything in humility is received as gift.

There are no "just deserts" in the twofold sense of this expression. First, humility is not a matter of *justice* in the sense of a third party adjudication. This is not to say that measuring out justice is unimportant in many situations in our lives; it is simply not humility. Second, I do not dispose myself to another expecting something in return, with the attitude that I *deserve* this or that. Such a reception or acceptance, with no "just deserts" that qualifies humility, presupposes our freedom to do otherwise, that is, our freedom to take something as deserved (pride).

This is why Jankélévitch correctly writes that where there is no freedom, there is no humility.[32]

In presentation (like in a perception), even if I am engrossed in things, enjoying things, or working on them, there is an expectation of a fulfillment through what I intend. I may live in and among things, but I also expect something from them, and ultimately to receive something of or for myself from them. Like Odysseus returning home from his odyssey, there is and can be no humility. I remain encumbered by and with myself in the sense that I expect a return on my efforts, I merit something. But in humility, as in loving, there is no expectation of return. I do not expect that there is still something to be gained—myself ultimately. If we can understand pride as living *from* the subject or self *in* the world (as excluding the contribution from others and the world) for the self, then we can understand humility as who I am as being oriented by or *from* others *in* the world *toward* others: humility is a *self-givenness* as Myself (reception, acceptance), as giving myself over to another as issuing from another (devotion), while meriting nothing from this.

It is not the case that the humble person is pathetic or feeble. Quite the contrary; there is an integrity, "force," and strength in humility; but the point of the integrity, force, and strength arises through the spontaneous acceptance of Myself in its movement toward and reception from others. Humility should not be confused with abasement. I do not focus on myself in order to be humble. It is quite the opposite. I am too engaged in the reception of what is given to be concerned with myself. It is a question of overabundance. The point is affirming or accepting, not negating. Thus, if a figure like Moses can be recognized as humble, it is not because he was a stutterer, not because he was in any way obsequious, but because he immediately responded to a presence "on high" with "*hineni*," in a radical openness, accepting what is given, even if with trepidation. It is because, further, he recognized his own accomplishments, great or small, as a result of God's intervention, presence, and glory. Humility as the spontaneous self-givenness (as Myself) is from a different perspective the loving movement as other-oriented. Here, loving and humility coincide in their experiential unity, and ground what Kant introduces as respect.

I used Moses as an easy example, but one can find countless examples of humility on all dimensions of existence, in figures that are less and more obvious. If examples of humility come effortlessly to mind where the figures are "religious," then it is due to the nature of the experience, not the fact that they belong to a type called religious. We could even go so far as to say that it is difficult to find examples of humility that are not religious in their internal meaning. This is not because these people identify "God" or "religion" as a theme; rather, it is due to the very movement of humility which is reflected in the irreversible, non-anticipatory infinite movement. Jankélévitch writes: "Mysticism, which is the experiential philosophy of mystery, is therefore quite naturally the philosophy of humility."[33] Humility has the tenor of the religious without it having to be explicitly religious, and without presupposing theological doctrine. Further, if one finds humility in the mystics, we find it there in an exemplary way; it is in their service toward others and toward God that humility is deepened, and as living it out toward the infinite in an infinite manner, they exemplify humility.[34]

Certainly, this is not to reduce humility to the level of religious experiencing, since humility and pride can and do occur distinctively and irreducibly on the moral level of experience, for example, interpersonally. Just as pride can be understood as a mode of religious idolatry, so too can pride be understood in the mode of revelation as moral idolatry (for lack of a better term) without *explicitly* involving the religious or the question of epiphany.[35] This is all given within the sphere of human personal experience as revealed through the moral emotions.

The Question of Self-Givenness in Humility

Having examined the emotions of self-givenness above, we found an unequivocal self-givenness (which some investigators take as forms of self-assessment or self-judgment) in the experiences of shame, guilt, and pride. These emotions of self-givenness are conducive to a phenomenological analysis, not only because "I" am given to myself in these very experiences, but also because I can reflect on this self-givenness and describe it as it is taking place. Here, I become an explicit theme of the experience, even if—as in the case of pride—such an experience amounts to a self-dissimulation. Humility is usually treated alongside pride, shame, and guilt because it is seen either as marking a point of contrast with pride or as residing on a continuum with shame and guilt.[36] How are we to understand the experience of self-givenness in relation to humility? In this section, I examine the sense in which humility clearly is not a self-givenness like we find in the cases of pride, shame, and guilt. But I also describe the distinctive way humility is a unique kind of self-givenness.

Let's begin with an example. If I were to present a group design project as my own work, it could make sense to reflect on it and think, "Wow, I am really being prideful right now" (and disdain it or embrace it). If I look at the way that the other team members and the judges look at me for grandstanding, it might make sense to feel shame, and to describe it as such in that very experience. Further, if I take all the credit and the prize money for the winning design, I could experience guilt and describe this experience as it is taking place. But when describing the communal effort that went into the design, where the focus is on the design and the cooperation—and not myself—it does not seem possible at that very moment, reflectively, to describe myself as experiencing humility. "I" in some sense disappear as a focal point in the very experience of humility, which is one reason why humility evades the same kind of first-person-present description that we find in the earlier emotions of self-givenness, for example, pride, shame, and guilt. Nevertheless, the difficulty of describing humility as I experience it in a first-person-present experience is also a clue to the very experience of humility. It is a clue insofar as this difficulty corresponds to what can be loosely described as a "loss" or "forgetfulness" of self.

Because humility is given as I am disposed toward an "other," I do not find myself as humble in the first-person experience, now. Yet, as we saw above with respect to shamelessness, humility can be given from a first-person plural perspective, or from an I–you perspective (perceiving humility in someone). In this way, another can become exemplary of humility for me. Or humility can be given in a memorial experience with regard to myself as the person of my own past, whereby I am able to identify some act or attitude as humble.

Let us now examine the way in which humility is a kind of self-givenness. Phenomenologically speaking, the reduction is not a remaindering, or finding something left over after putting my prejudices out of play, but a liberation; through the *epoché* and reduction, the "phenomena" are liberated. The style of "liberation" of the reduction is operative in the merely epistemic as well as in the moral sphere, as I suggested above in the chapter on pride, though in different ways. In the "moral reduction" of humility, I am "reduced"—to Myself. This reduction to Myself is a de-limitation, which is to say, it is expansive, interpersonal, such that I am given to myself as Myself, as not self-grounding. Humility is a being revealed to myself as Myself: as related to another, as accepting from another, as accepting the givenness from another and contributions from others. Accordingly, the eclipse of self-givenness where I am an explicit theme (like we find in pride, shame, and guilt) does not mean that there is no self-givenness in humility. It is possible, for instance, to receive myself as a recovery of Myself, since humility is the way I am self-given in the process of accepting or receiving without merit or "just deserts."

Thus, in distinction to pride, humility is a recovery and realization of myself, precisely as Myself. But as foundational for pride, humility does not reach its deepest sense first as a "recovery" of the interpersonal from pride. As foundational, it is the experience of Myself as interpersonal without having to have been a recovery. It is a reception of myself in the presence of things, a reception of myself as Myself—outside of my expectation or what I would anticipate as a return (a point I will examine in more detail below in the section on temporality). As humble, I receive Myself, accepting in openness Myself as self-given. This seeming paradox evident in the peculiar non-self-givenness in the style of a thematic self, and this radical self-givenness as Myself, is the way in which I interpret Jankélévitch's statement that for the humble person, "his presence is in effect indiscernible from his absence."[37]

Hence, humility is already "vertical" as both interpersonal ("moral" in a broad sense) and inter-Personal (religious).[38] This Myself is not something we impute to or impose upon our descriptions; rather, we find in these very experiences themselves this Myself—for example, in the experiences of shame, guilt, repentance—experiences that are already more than themselves as merely psychological or theological phenomena. It is this dimension of Myself that I explore critically in phenomenological descriptions by making "Myself" thematic, reunderstanding the experiences (i.e., shame, guilt, repentance, even humility) with which we started.

Not only am I not the "object" of the experience, I am not the motivation of the movement—even though it is none other than "I" who am humble. I am not the object of the experience of humility in the sense that I am not the thematic terminus a quo and terminus ad quem. This is one reason why I did not take up humility as a virtue that I could attain through self-will, willing the negation of myself to get to the other, to improve myself (which presupposes self-hatred in some form, not genuine self-love). I am not the motivation of the movement of humility in the sense that this movement is initiated from the outside, from the other, and not from myself. For example, I am drawn toward this profession; I devote myself to understanding this text; I am engaged in pursuing that idea which "I" am trying to realize; I am caught up in a conversation with this student. Because humility is the way in which I am "self-given," for example, in loving, the humble person is completely absorbed in the attentiveness to others, to the tea, to the process, the music, and so on. In this respect, the non-reflection on myself in the experience is a by-product of humility, but not the goal. This is also why I cannot both try to be humble and be humble.

In comparison to pride, therefore, the humble person accepts the contribution of others to the meaning constitution of the world, and to Myself. We see this spontaneous acceptance in humility that qualifies the person as humble. One can find these examples everywhere, of course. I am struck by the interviews with the jazz musician John Coltrane. Whenever he received praise, he was given to say things like, "I am very fortunate—I work with very fine musicians." When questioned about his long solos (they could go on for three-quarters of an hour), he responded that he was trying to explore all the avenues that the tune offers; but when playing opposite another group, he acknowledged the importance of cutting things short. If the playing hits a point in which things are no longer spontaneous and become contrived, then it is easy to stop and bow out.[39] I am also reminded of the difference in responses between Kirill in Tarkovsky's film *Andrei Rublev,* who is the epitome of pride—wanting full accolade for what he is not—and the young boy who left to his own devices and who quite abandoned, fashions out of sheer creativity a spectacular bell for the Grand Prince. When prodded to take the glory of ringing the bell (to see if it actually was successful), he silently runs away, and allows one of the many workers and assembly crew who contributed to its making to have the honor.

Unlike pride, humility is the experience of the non-self-grounding character of who I am. Further, unlike other emotions of self-givenness, namely, pride, shame, and guilt, however, I am not self-given in a thematic way in humility. And unlike shame and guilt, I am not given to myself in a direptive experience. Nevertheless, I am given as having received Myself.

Humility has been characterized as a mode of self-givenness as who I am in loving or being oriented toward another. As a way of clarifying this, I have examined the limits of this self-givenness in humility. Because humility from the perspective of pride as called into question is a recovery of Myself as not self-grounding, as interrelated, and as interpersonal, and only thereby a forgetfulness of the self in which "I" am not an issue in humility, it is possible to distinguish humility from experiences that seem to be similar to humility, but that are essentially distinct, precisely where I am an issue. To this end, I describe below the experiences of being humbled, humbling myself, and modesty, all of which are distinct from humility. This set of issues relates to the problem of self-givenness because in these cases it is precisely an issue of how I am given in them.

Being Humbled, Humbling Myself, and Modesty

In order to discern stricter contours of humility, and to avoid common ambiguities associated with this emotion, let me describe the experience of being humbled, of humbling myself, and of modesty. We will see that in each of these cases, I come into a certain prominence in the experience, something that is not the case in humility.

Being humbled. The experience of being humbled presupposes the constitution of something like an "emotional level," akin to what Merleau-Ponty has called the constitution of a "spatial level." That is, being humbled presupposes something in relationship to which I now experience myself as lowered. For example, I may think of myself as an accomplished rock climber, but when I climb with others, and I see how good they are, I could feel humbled. This need not take place before a personal other. For instance, I could try to climb an apparently easy path up a rock face, but struggle making the climb; I may even give up. In this case, I could realize that my efforts to overpower the rock face did not work, that I do not know how to read the rock cliff, or that I am no match for the rock face (as if I were in a competition with it). In these ways, I might experience myself as humbled by the rock face without having to impute any intention to it or of it wanting to humble me.

In all instances of being humbled, the experience is accompanied by a negative valence.[40] Certainly, this is not the strong negative valence that we encountered in shame, but it is negative nonetheless because the discrepancy from one emotional level to the next is an abasing one. Even if we might feel positive about being humbled, this is not an original positive valence unique to the experience, but a positivity as a reaction to the negative valence.

For example, I may take pleasure in being humbled by the rock face (it may disclose my place in the universe), or in being humbled by another person for some reason, but then we are witnessing two levels peculiar to the experience. First, there is a spontaneity in this being humbled (which is given with a negative valence), and then there is a positivity associated with the negativity such that I may even delight in being humbled. This is why being humbled cannot be equated with masochism. Masochism wants to will being lowered, and in this sense it insidiously wills to be or to remain in control in the submission. Being humbled, experienced originally, is something by which I am caught off-guard and is not willed; I experience myself immediately as not in control or as having to release my control or mastery. Certainly, being humbled may lead to new insights that I have gained into myself; however, it could just as well motivate other responses; for example, it could just make me angry, prideful, or reactionary.

It can certainly occur—to draw upon Hegel's so-called master/slave dialectic—that an individual is humbled and must humble himself, but then realize that his ostensible "inferior" position is actually superior. In the case of Hegel's dialectic, for instance, the lord depends upon the consciousness that is in bondage, and in this sense the latter eventually realizes his superiority in being or having been humbled. But again, this is a further development of the experience of being humbled, which at this time is no longer simply being humbled. If I realize my superiority in being humbled, I am realizing something else about the experience, and I undergo a transformation of the experience in the very process. Accordingly, the initial negative valence is modified. I grasp myself in an overarching movement of being in control. I am no longer simply subdued, but I am exercising my will, or my freedom, or my power.

Humbling myself. Humbling myself relates to my egoic activity, and as such it is expressive of my will. In humbling myself, I freely submit myself to another in a relation to whom I am given to myself. Humbling myself is something distinctive from humility in and through which I serve another, because in humbling myself, I posit myself as in relation to another, in and through the process of serving another. This can be seen in the case of perceiving someone as superior to me and perhaps more poignantly, with respect to someone perceived as "inferior" to me in some regard.

For example, as a car mechanic, I can devote myself to the repair of cars, or I can aid the head mechanic in his task. This could be simply a matter of service—independently of whether or not I am getting paid for this service. Further, no matter how I may have considered myself in relation to others or to this task, I undertake it, say, without complaint, though I may have had my own ideas of how to do things; or I could undertake my duties without any consideration of the merits of the head mechanic, but do this only with the awareness that he is in charge. In this spirit, I carry out my task as servicing cars. Such an example can be seen as humbling myself in relation to the "master" because the very positions of the relation demand "lowering" myself in relation to him. It is also possible that I humble myself in relation to another because I perceive that the other is in a position of power; from here I can recognize myself as inferior in relation to someone who is superior, and I could do it out of self-preservation (I want to keep my job).

Accordingly, the situation is not unlike the one we find with Odysseus. He feigns to be no one (*outis*) in order to trick the Cyclops and thereby gain control of the situation, defeating the Cyclops in the end. This illustrates, in part, the potential intrinsic to the process of humbling myself, even though factually, it does not have to occur. Intentionally or not, humbling myself enables me to lower myself in order to rise above the other; without the explicit intention of doing so, I could still be attracted to myself by having lowered myself, taking pride in the fact that I have made myself lower, subservient, and in this way, thinking more of myself.

We might consider other examples in which the relation of "humbling myself" is intensified, for instance, when as a car mechanic

I still serve the head mechanic in the same spirit, but I think my ideas, methods, or techniques are superior. This is likewise the case when I, as the head mechanic, inversely work for the new hire—in the spirit of serving—for example, by assisting the new mechanic in his own way. We can find many elaborations of this dynamic, for instance, in the form of professors and students, the Zen master serving the novice monk, or, in the Christian tradition, of Jesus washing the feet of his disciples.

If I do humble myself in these ways, however, I do not do so in a condescending or patronizing manner. I may do this as a courtesy, in an effort to encourage dialogue rather than shut it down, or in order to make another feel comfortable. In terms of bodily comportment, humbling myself can be expressed as bowing down lower than another; or by letting another go first, as when entering a building. *If* it is a matter of humbling myself, then it is more than merely following custom, manners, or mores. I mean by this that humbling myself is irreducible to following rules of behavior or codes of conduct, because whereas the latter might be compulsory, here I am "freely" engaged in the process of humbling myself before another—even if objectively humbling myself and just doing things by social rote might look the same.

I cite these examples of being humbled and humbling myself because they are essentially distinct from humility; and though they may seem to be quite similar, they show by contrast how distinctive the movement of humility is from them. In humility, the humble person does not compare his position with another; the humble person does not position herself in relation to another. She thinks neither highly nor lowly of herself, because I am not the issue. If Jesus washes the feet of his disciples, and *if* this *were* to be an example of *humility* (and not humbling himself), then this would be the case because he loves his disciples, or perhaps because he wants to teach them something by example. But in this case, he does not humble himself. Both being humbled and humbling myself presuppose a comparative relation in which I am somehow an issue. In humility, there is "only" the other that solicits the action or the service in love.

Likewise, when one receives in humility, what is received is not taken as one's "just deserts," but rather as a gift; only post facto is it "humbling"; only after the fact do I feel myself as "undeserving"—which for humility, would find no end. In fact, humility admits of no intention, no fulfillment, no disappointment. Accordingly, Scheler writes that in humility one accepts all things with thanks, from the most subtle pleasure to the grandest bliss; we do this without ever imagining that we deserve even the smallest part.[41] The humble person does not give thought to the proper order of things, but accepts what comes with gratitude and without the thought of merit. Accordingly, Jankélévitch writes that the humble person does not have rights, but only duties.[42]

In humility, I find no end—it goes to infinity—because the very tenor of the movement is governed by ever deeper openness, where the goal is not myself. But in humbling myself, we could come up against a stopping point because it is related to my will. I find it telling that the process of humbling myself is susceptible to a patronizing attitude, whereas humility is not. There is a danger where humbling myself is concerned insofar as this process of humbling myself could slip into being manipulative (for example, I lower myself in order to gain control). Moreover, because it is possible to sense my superiority in humbling myself (and therefore put myself above another by placing myself below another—and also having a positive valence accompany this experience), humbling myself reveals the possibility of superiority in relation to which the earlier being humbled had a negative valence. Thus, being humbled and humbling myself are distinctive experiences from humility.

We can make a final comparison between being humbled and humbling myself by noting that "spatially" speaking, being humbled is characterized by a being-restrained, whereas humbling myself has a self-constraining character.[43] The latter "leaves room" for another; it holds me back, as is the case with modesty, as we will see. In both cases—being humbled and humbling myself—these restraining and constraining movements contribute to what we have called their negative valence. By contrast, humility is not given as a restriction or constraint, since it is immediately and directly an experience of being disposed toward . . . , where the service toward the other is given as expansive. Let us now compare these two experiences, which in their own ways bring the self into relief at least in terms of a comparative relation, with modesty, which also bears on me in a peculiar way.

Modesty. In distinction to being humbled or humbling myself, modesty requires neither lowering nor raising myself. It is also a style of comportment that operates or attempts to operate without pretension, illusion, or self-deception. Not only does modesty presuppose an exposure of myself, but it is simultaneously a refraining from the exposure of myself, a process of not being "showy," where precisely a refraining from myself is brought into relief. In this regard, modesty is more aligned with pride than with shame, since the self-salience in a positive respect emerges and is covered up. Unlike humility (in which I am not at all an issue, since humility is *how I am* as being immediately other-orientated in loving, caring, trusting, etc., only receiving or recovering myself as Myself in this way), in modesty I am still an issue because I am oriented *toward the non-salience of the self.*[44] Thus, modesty emerges in the context of exposing myself or being exposed in a brazen way, and resisting this kind of exposure; modesty holds back from asserting myself in this way.

Further, modesty is impersonal in the sense that it is not oriented toward anyone in particular or toward the personal core of the individual. The reserved character of modesty as a holding myself back makes a gesture both toward a hiding or veiling of insufficiencies, or delicately showing talents, and in this way gestures toward anonymity. Its movement is more a self-retraction than putting myself in my rightful place. But if the latter were the case, then it would always be subordinated to the movement of non-prominence, and hence the former gesture. Even though there is this gesture toward impersonality and anonymity, there is nonetheless a givenness of myself. In modesty, writes Jankélévitch, it is not a matter of the others; or as we would say, it is not a question of a comparison in being humbled or humbling myself before another. But, he asserts, it is all the same still a matter of me, myself.[45] The individual is not a big deal, but what he is, *is something*, however minimally. This is why I am "reserved" in what the French call *pudeur*. In *pudeur*, as well, there is a givenness, a consciousness of self; it is what is "preserved," especially in terms of the body. Thus, there is still something of myself in modesty, but the "self" that is given in modesty is without positive or negative valence; it just is, in whatever manner it is. In this respect, I take myself as neither great nor small, since the experience is not comparative in this way. I am not ostentatious, but innocently only as I appear to be.[46]

In the very movement of openness and service which yields humility, I do not close down my openness, but I am drawn to open myself further. If I get in the way of this movement, it is not due to the movement of humility, but to pride. Whereas in humility the movement is absolute and infinite, in modesty, the movement is relative and finite. It is relative and finite because modesty is qualified by the situation and subject to the self-exposure. I do not harbor any pretensions about myself, but neither is there any question of self-forgetfulness, either as putative goal or unintended consequence. Moderation or the appearance of equilibrium might be a consequence of modesty, but if moderation or equilibrium were the intended outcome, we would only be describing something like propriety. This is because modesty is still a practice related to myself, as a recognition and a suppression of the self-salience.

Humiliation, Affliction, and Humility

We saw previously how shame is lived in a distinctive manner as a diremptive experience, and how shame as self-revelation (which can provoke a positive self-critique) can also issue in (but is irreducible to) a debilitating shame. In fact, the latter presupposes the former such that this kind of self-revelation and self-critique become distorted precisely through a disordered heart, and such that I am given to myself through distortions of value, either on the part of others or myself. We see this in the cases of emotional or physical abuse and cultural forms of domination (like racism) that support and elicit deformative and alienating economic, political, corporeal value ideals such as we get in advertising and in certain forms of commoditization.[47]

The discussion of humiliation actually belongs here, as we will see, namely, in the context of shame and debilitating shame. But because humiliation is often treated alongside the experience of humility (perhaps because of an etymological relatedness), often—misleadingly I think— in terms of a genetic relation of humiliation to humility, I treat the experience of humiliation under the general rubric of humility. I also treat the phenomenon of affliction here. I do this because from the outside, affliction and humiliation appear to be the same; experientially, however, they are quite distinct. Furthermore, it is affliction, not humiliation, that can lead to humility.

Humiliation and debilitating shame. By humiliation I understand a destructive force that is abusive, such as being exposed to mockery, being subject to ridicule, or being reduced to powerlessness before the power of another. It includes being stripped down before others, physically and emotionally—before others who remain in power, where this power is a power over the humiliated one. It targets the basic sense and integrity of the person for all to see. This gives us a clue to the interpersonal status of humiliation. Humiliation is at heart interpersonal; it cannot occur within a *solus ipse,* but it is not expressive of positive interpersonal relations.

The interpersonal nexus that we would find in experiences like love or trust are disoriented. If I am humiliated, I am humiliated by another and before another; I am presupposed as person, yet actively de-personified. This is what makes the process so powerful. I can only be subject to humiliation because there is (at least) an implicit sense of my personal integrity to be humiliated. It is a de-personalization on the basis of an interpersonal nexus.

In this regard, humiliation can also be understood as a diremptive experience, namely, I am given to myself in a way that is in tension with a more basic orientation, or in this case, personal self-presence. There is a diremption in humiliation because I am being reduced to this object, which I as person am not, though I am *made to appear* (= violence) in this light.

Humiliation sustains this active tension actively. I cannot humiliate a person who does not have a sense of him- or herself as a person. However, as opposed to embarrassment or shame, there is nothing "corrective" that can come out of humiliation. Shame, for example, keeps the personal sense of the individual intact—I am thrown back on myself as being revealed to myself as who I "am" in the dynamic sense of becoming. Humiliation, on the other hand, targets me as destroying the personal integrity in question; it is not open to positive critique or to a reorientation of who I am, but only holds me as dis-oriented from who I am before others and as subject to others. Whereas it is courage that might be evoked as a resistance to humiliation, it is rather arrogance that might arise as a resistance to shame.

We can see the difference between shame and humiliation in the following example. I can scold a child in public, saying: "you should be ashamed of yourself" from the perspective of a homeworld. But this is much different from humiliating a child—opening him or her to the derision of others and in a manner that does not allow the child to recover from it. This could include bringing out the child's faults in front of friends or strangers, with no other purpose than bringing attention to the faults and so ridicule the child; for example, it could entail drawing attention to someone who stammers simply to draw attention to it such that the other person just goes deeper and deeper into stammering. When I am humiliated I am made to feel less than who I am, and only that.

Whereas invoking shameful behavior in a scold could still take place in a loving attitude that wants to draw the child back to his or her "true" self, humiliation only wants to disparage, ridicule, and to reduce the other person to an object in order to exert control, but hold the experience at the disorientation, as it were, without futural recovery. Its internal sense is interpersonal since it is realized as violence directed toward a person. But it is not a positive return to my "true" self—which could in a different context lead to repentance, as we have seen above; its internal sense is not humility, as the recovery or reception of myself as Myself. Rather, the sense of humiliation is for this other person to become that de-personified object that I or others could master (e.g., out of anger or hate), where the humiliated person remains a witness to this depersonalization. In this respect, its *meaning* is not the positive interpersonal relation.

Thus, shame, guilt, embarrassment, and humiliation are all diremptive experiences. But whereas shame can point toward the future in the sense of a recovery or a return to Myself (and thus "presence" in the broad sense), humiliation sustains the point of "disorientation" or "diremption" and holds it there, withholding the dimension of recovery or return to the presence of personhood. The devastating quality of humiliation is due in part to closing down the future, holding the individual in the obstinate and abstract "now," making it all the more difficult to recover. Further, while I can be embarrassed before others because of something I do, in humiliation, it is others (real or imagined) who make me appear in this way before others. Finally, humiliation is distinct from insult in the way that embarrassment is distinguished from shame. Insult is an incidental rupture against a basic self or personal experience. Humiliation bears on the core of the personal orientation.

Let's compare this characterization of humiliation with debilitating shame.[48] Debilitating shame appropriates a "false" self-image such that the individual internalizes it, producing or appropriating the same disordered heart. Unlike shame, which is rooted in a genuine self-love, debilitating shame works from self-love, but as we saw above, is transformed into self-hate. Humiliation is an active operation toward another who is acted upon as an object—but where the individual *has not yet* internalized what we would want to call this disordered sense of self. Hence, we can say that debilitating shame can result from an internalized humiliation (though this is not the only source), and why the experience of humiliation belongs properly alongside the thematic of debilitating shame, and not humility.

Paradoxically, in order to humiliate another, in order to execute or sustain a de-personification of him, I have to posit him as "person." And in order for humiliation to work, I have to keep it in process or in an active tension. I have to recognize his personhood in order to destroy it before his eyes, which is to say, before others' eyes—without completely reducing him to the status of an object while attempting to reduce him to the status of an object—so that he can actively witness his own depersonalization against the background of a perceived personhood. Similarly, as the one humiliated, I have to maintain my own personal sense or dignity, while I am being made to appear differently, and I must remain held there at this disequilibrium without the futural movement of return.

However, for humiliation to arise, it is also essential that the personhood of the other cannot be acknowledged explicitly or be made the theme of the actions—such that everyone involved become explicitly cognizant of the personhood of the victim of humiliation.[49] If this were the case, it might be seen as a kind of game, but in any case, it could not result in humiliation. Alternately, this process might "merely" result in torture without humiliation, for example, "mere" physical or psychological abuse (e.g., only to get information, to do to another what she did to me) without the diremptive experience of a denigrated integrity before others, thwarting a futural recovery. Thus, there has to be a co-givenness of personhood, but a personhood that is both being denied by the one humiliating and experienced as such by the one humiliated. For example, if someone tries to humiliate me by shaving my head and exposing me to public ridicule, this will only work if I, too, see a positivity in a full head of hair and a simultaneous denigration in a shaved head (of course the situation can become more poignant if I am strapped down, stripped down, robbed of personal agency, etc.); here we would share *a* homeworld in which the humiliation would arise. (In this way, but only in this way, am I "complicit" in humiliation.) But if it is *only* a matter of the shaved head, and if in fact, a shaved head is actually part of my usual self-comportment, say, as a monk, I will not be humiliated by this singular activity.

Thus, the sense of integrity (the person–person relation) on both sides of humiliating and humiliated must be presupposed in order for humiliation to arise, but it must remain in the background of and resist an active depersonalization. There is thus a double gesture of both ascribing and denying the dignity of the other in humiliation where a diremption is posited, but held there without the possibility of the individual's return to his or her personal integrity.

Humiliation and affliction. Let us draw a further distinction between humiliation and affliction. To do this, it will be helpful to disambiguate affliction and suffering. Following distinctions that can be found in phenomenologists such as Scheler, as well as experientially based writings of mystics—from medieval to contemporary—we can say that suffering is lived as having mundane origins and is something I or another can effect or can in principle remedy. This is the case whether the suffering is physical, psychic, emotional, or spiritual, and whether it occurs at the hand of others, at my own hands, or anonymously by the world in general.

By contrast, affliction is experienced as not having mundane origins, and is not effected by the "I." This is because affliction is not only lived as beyond my own power, or as beyond any "worldly" measures to initiate it or alleviate it, but ultimately because affliction as an inter-Personal movement has a redemptive quality. The fact that I am not self-sufficient in affliction and that the "I" is undone is an initial clue that affliction has a "religious" sense, or put differently, that it occurs on the religious dimension of coexistence. Hence, Simone Weil will distinguish between the "I" that is "destroyed" in a mundane manner, which is what we have called humiliation, and the "I" that is "destroyed" from within an inter-Personal relation, which only within this very movement is viewed as redemptive.[50] The "I" does not do this, but I only yield to it when I co-realize myself as an obstacle to loving.[51]

For Simone Weil, like for Saint John of the Cross, affliction can be given as the experienced absence of God, or as the abandonment by God, as a ground that should be there, but is not. In a similar manner, Mother Teresa reports an experience of being "thrown away by God," forsaken, of a darkness being so dark, of being utterly alone, of the terrible pain of loss, of "God not wanting me," of "God not being God," of "God not really existing."[52]

What is the difference between what we described above as despair in chapter 5 and the phenomenon of affliction? In the moment of the experience, viewed statically, perhaps there is no difference. But viewed generatively, affliction is lived in a more encompassing manner, within the context of faith, say, as a purification of pride, as a radical calling of myself into question. Saint John of the Cross writes: "Yet until a soul is placed by God in the passive purgation of that dark night . . . it cannot purify itself completely of these imperfections or others."[53]

Thus, affliction is lived with or as the full awareness of the Beloved removing Presence, rejecting, distancing, or repulsing, as no-loving, as a complete deprivation of "My" (in the sense of Myself's) greatest personal Good. This is why it is experienced as the worst kind of horror.[54] In affliction, all this is direct, immediate, explicit. On the other hand, despair does not seem to have this immediate, specific, awareness, or as we could also say, despair lacks or at least does not necessarily entail this direct *personal,* or more accurately, *interpersonal* tenor or qualification. Despair, for example, might be experienced as the absence of *any* ground as such, however vague.

Affliction is experienced in terms of a presence that should be there, but is not. Hence, Jonah cries out (to whom?), Jesus cries out (to whom?). This "crying out" points to Immanent or Transcendent presence, something that is more than this experience of abandon; it is a crying out to a presence that is not present (and should be). It is therefore important to note that we cannot simultaneously experience affliction *and* experience affliction as the process of redemption (infinitizing, re-presence of God). It is only after the fact, that is, from the perspective of redemption (for Jonah, the allusion to the Second Temple; for Jesus, the Resurrection) that one could experience affliction as having had a redemptive quality (i.e., disabusing me of myself, negating the "I," being devoted in service).[55] From this latter perspective we could say that there was a presence in the no presence, and it was redemptive. But the latter is not and cannot be given within the experience of affliction itself, as it is taking place. We have been examining affliction by consulting figures who were on the other side of this experience (Saint John of the Cross, Saint Teresa of Avila, and others), and for whom affliction may constitute the removal of obstacles, limits, like any self-attachment.

These experiences have a different tenor depending upon how they are lived, and are not differentiated by virtue of their objective circumstances. For example, it is not the event itself that qualifies it for me as suffering, despair, or affliction. Social degradation, poverty, separation from a loved one, torture, could be lived as either suffering, humiliation, and/or affliction. But in affliction, writes Weil, God is made to appear absent for a time, more absent than a dead man, more absent than light in the utter darkness of a cell. "A kind of horror submerges the whole soul. During this absence there is nothing to love."[56] This suggests an essential difference between humiliation and affliction, namely, "I" can try to resist humiliation, but there is no point to trying to resist affliction in the same way. For example, I can assert in humiliation (at least to myself) that "I have my pride, you know." But "I" am powerless to resist affliction.

From the outside, of course, extreme suffering, humiliation, and affliction can appear indistinguishable. They both essentially occur against my will. Is it others with a political agenda who make me a pariah; is it economic conditions that make me a social outcast; is it God who makes me stand alone or removes my dignity? Within a merely secular experience, humiliation would be limited to something like exerting power over another, on the one hand, and experiencing abuse and destruction of integrity, on the other.

The extent to which something is lived as affliction is the extent to which this complex of experience is lived—at least after the fact—as a tearing down of myself and of the attachment to myself and to things, but does not impair the integrity of the person. Affliction is that which is experienced as occurring within an inter-Personal nexus, eventually so as to allow me to approach others, the world, God in humility, and to live more fully in their presence. In the language we have used above, "I am reduced." After the "reduction" to Myself, I am no longer attached to things or the self, but *Adonai echad*, to God alone, only God. This is why it would be lived not as humiliation, but that as affliction, since what took place is "converted," qualifying me, Myself, as humble. Yet, of course, this is an experiential difference, and nothing one can anticipate in advance or adjudicate from the outside. Such a not being able to adjudicate from the outside, however, belongs to the peculiarities of the experience itself.

If affliction can be characterized as the experience of separation from or the abandonment by God, the Divine, or an Absolute—the greatest horror at the loss of the Beloved—then perhaps we see signs of this as an *Urerlebnis,* a primordial experience, expressed for example in the "creation myths." In the Abrahamic tradition, humanity is (Adam and Eve are) removed from Paradise. Being evicted from Paradise—the immediate presence of God, in which there was no suffering, no affliction—is expressive of such a radical distance from the presence of God. If this narrative is trying to say something about who and how we are as human persons in relation to holiness, then perhaps affliction is not an occasional or a rare occurrence, but expressive of the human condition.

Nevertheless, there seems to be a difference. The book of Bereshit, or Genesis, focuses on something a bit different, namely, that we have removed or distanced ourselves in some way from the Holy (hence the possibility of shame)—though it is true that God is said to banish "humanity" from Paradise. Still, the experience of affliction as we have come to see it tends to be experienced as something that I undergo, but that is initiated on the side of the Holy—but not as punishment. Indeed, there is no "reason" for affliction; it is incomprehensible (and portrayed rather as "dryness," "dark night of the soul," "senseless abandon," "God not being God," etc.).[57] Further, affliction is a radically personal or interpersonal experience. Finally, it is experienced on the other side of the affliction as bringing me closer into the presence of the Beloved (loss of self, there is only God, etc.). Given the strictly interpersonal nature of this experience, and the uniqueness of the individual involved, I would be wary of universalizing affliction as a general concept that applies to all humanity. This would exhibit the same difficulties—in a different direction—as that of "original sin."

Within the context of affliction and abandonment, we can consider a variety of "absolutes." For example, the universe, the military, a loved one (parent), a social system (or collective person) like capitalism or communism could hold the place of the absolute in our lives, whether or not we are consciously aware that they function as absolute. Indeed, we could even feel abandoned by them. But would we experience "affliction"?

To analyze this, we have to consider two things. First, the process of being guided by an absolute having an infinite character is a "religious" movement. This is the process of accepting something with absolute weight, having the unconditionality of the supremely valuable behind which everything else is valued; it is an absolute relation to an infinitely absolute (whether we recognize it as such or call it "God," "acquisition," "fame," "commitment," the "state," etc.). This movement in and of itself has a "religious" tenor, without it being intended as such. Second, there can be a misplacing of the absolute, a "reversal" that takes the form of what we would call idolatry, specifically, religious idolatry.[58] In this case, something relative and finite is accepted or posited in the place of the absolute, or rather is *lived as* absolute. That such a reversal could take place at all, that some*thing* could take on the practical weight of the absolute (even without us being aware of it as such), is already testimony to a religious sphere of experiencing. Since I already made this point elsewhere, I would like to develop its implications where affliction is concerned.

Affliction is an inter-Personal experience. And only to the extent that an absolute is experienced as personal, or as a center of loving, could there be an experience of affliction. This is to say two things. First, the context in which affliction arises cannot be "secular" because the otherwise secular would have a religious meaning, even if we did not actively impute to it a religious significance. Second, affliction tears down the attitude that gives absolute weight to some relative good, an infinite weight to some finite value. This goes even to the finite absoluteness of myself in pride. Thus affliction, properly speaking, belongs to the religious sphere of experiencing as "vertical," and inter-Personal.

Temporality of Humility

We have found that not every futural opening of an experience is an expectation or founded in one. Hoping, for instance, has a different temporal meaning from an expectation. I do not expect or wait for something when I hope; rather, hoping is characterized as a sustainable awaiting-enduringly. The futural temporality of trusting is a "proffering," not an anticipation, and so on. What is the case with humility?

Let's examine the structure of the living-present in order to make this determination. The matter of the living-present can certainly be a topic of its own, but let us present its most basic features to our ends.[59] When something, an object or anything with an object-like structure, is given in a perceiving or in a thinking, it is given "now." But this presentational givenness is also immediately and directly "retained" and lingers with varying affective resonance like a comet's tail on the present. As a retention of the presentational now, there is no possibility of the retention being "disappointed" because it is in fact not an intentional gesture toward anything. This presentational "now–retention" couplet institutes a style of unfolding, advances *how* something to come is to be received, *how* the unfolding is forecast, *how* its givenness will be concordant with what took place. This "how of givenness," which foreshadows what is to come in a concordant manner (in a manner that is harmonious with that which has come before), is called the "protention"; it is a pre-reflective futural mode of givenness. This is how the mode of futural givenness takes shape within the living-present. All of this takes place without us giving any thought to it, like when we step down the stairs while holding an intense conversation with a friend.

As we saw in the example of hope, there can also be a more active futural (concordant) mode of givenness that unfolds with this concordant style given by the present–past relation, and this we call an expectation or anticipation. Thus, we can actively turn our attention toward what is to be expected: one step following another, the outcome of a game, the return on an investment, the behavior of a colleague, or the actions of a friend. Even here, the present and retention constitute a style of unfolding—an unfolding that can be ruptured and disappointed, of course; but they can only undergo rupture or disappointment because that same concordant style is given as projected. Even if they are not exactly an "imposition" of the way things are going to arrive, they are at least an interjection of how things are to pass according to a regular style.

My point here is that in either case, as passive protention or active expectation, these modes of future temporal givenness are eclipsed in humility. We have a first clue that humility is different from the protentional or anticipatory movement of perceptual presentation insofar as there is no expectation functional in humility, or rather, the intentionality of expectation is elided. I have already alluded to this above by saying that in humility, I have no "just deserts" in the sense that I do not expect a return on my efforts; there is no motivation of merit, big or small; there is no regard of justice or injustice to me, due or done; there is no expectation of a fulfillment through what I intend.

Instead, if there is humility, there is an experience of "unwarranted exuberances" (Annie Dillard), of unmerited events, of uncalled-for gifts. One could argue that something lived as "unexpected" is still dependent upon the expected, now as eclipsed. But even here, I would argue, this "unexpected" is not of the mettle of a disappointed perception: precisely nothing is foreshadowed because there is nothing in humility on the basis of which something could be expected. The structure of expectation is put out of play. Thus, even if it is not a common or typical experience, it could happen that I epistemically "expect" that someone may thank me for something I did (knowing his character), but in fact, I never expect anything at all for what I did, not even any kind of acknowledgment, and in this sense, "expecting thanks" does not even cross my mind. A protention or an expectation can be disappointed, but there is nothing to disappoint in humility. We can ascertain, therefore, that humility is lived without teleological purpose in the sense that it is lived without attachment to a result or to what is to come. This is also why the vocabulary of calculation and causation is not fitting for humility.

Accordingly, I do not "try" to efface myself in humility (in which case the structure of expectation would have to be functional, vitiating humility). In humility, no present is expected that is going to fulfill my intention where I am concerned, even though I continue to experience time in this way as objects are given presentationally. Further, humbling myself may lead to humility, but it does not have to do this, since the cultivation of my efforts is not sufficient to provoke an experience like humility, which is the reception of Myself as I am in relation to another.

The inquiry into the futural modes of givenness viv-à-vis humility is related to the question of the motivation for humility, since in presentational givenness, it is the present–retention relation that motivates the protention according to a regular style. We can put this matter in the form of two sorts of questions. First, do I motivate humility or is there an "internal" motivation for humility, where the present–past couplet provokes the humility? To this we would respond, no; we cannot produce humility in the sense of it being related to my power of disposition, which would ultimately be an exercise of pride. Or we can ask: is humility motivated? To this we can respond, yes, in the sense that it arises in the presence of these "unwarranted exuberances," matters accepted as gifts, and even as having received Myself in the presence of others or another. Here we need to distinguish, for example, the practice of disposing myself to things or others in openness, which can yield a loving or a trusting, and which are by nature spontaneous—and humility, which is how I am in such loving and trusting. Further, I can repeat a hoping or hopefulness, but no matter how many times this is repeated, no matter how deeply I am a hopeful person, the hoping is not an expectation. The temporal mode of givenness of hoping is an enduringly-awaiting. The same holds, mutatis mutandis, for humility.

All of this is not to say that humility has no futural or past temporality, but that (like hoping, trusting, repentance, and others) it does not have the structure of an expectation or a retention or a remembering, that is, a temporality like the perception, use, or enjoyment of an object. If we were to identify the presentational structure of givenness with "intentionality," then experiences like these moral emotional ones would have to remain, according to our analyses, "non-intentional" in the phenomenological sense. But I prefer to recognize a broader account of "intentionality" such that it is not exhausted by the "noesis:noema" correlation.[60] For like the other emotional experiences that we have encountered, humility is essentially relational, exhibits a structure of givenness, and is related in some way to "otherness." It is just that its "relational" characteristic is not in the form of an imposition of meaning, but in this case, for instance, as reception or acceptance.

What kind of temporality, then, does humility exhibit? What are the modes of temporal givenness where humility is concerned? In what manner do we characterize these "hows" of temporal givenness in humility? First, humility (or being humble) is qualified as an openness toward and a reception or acceptance of what is given. Its mode of temporality relative to this openness, acceptance, and reception is a presence-at. This mode of presence is a *way in which I am (given)* as being given over to or oriented toward others (things, persons), for example, in loving or in trusting. This kind of presence-at is reflected in a being thankful for. Presence-at and its being thankful for, however, does not motivate anything new to come, it does not anticipate more to be thankful for, so in this sense, it is not taken up in an expectation.

Second, humility is not only related to the way in which something is accepted or received, but it is also a *way in which I receive myself* in and through being other-oriented, and the way in which I receive Myself as having been given to myself prior to being able to choose myself. Thus, I receive "Myself" in humility, which is to say, I receive myself as given to Myself, as not self-grounding. Accordingly, there is a temporal dimension of the past that is not correlative to what I "remember" since being not self-grounding is "before" I could remember or what I could forget. It is what we could call a "generative" past, a prior past before a remembered past, a presence of Myself that is not just retended, but a density that prepares me for who and how I am now. Humility qualifies me as having openly received Myself such that in receiving Myself, a futural unfolding is released (one dimension of which is vocational awareness). If we speak of the receiving Myself in this way, then we can speak of a mode of givenness qualified as an "ante-memorial reception."

Presence-at, as noted, does not motivate anything new to come, it does not anticipate more to be thankful for, and is not lived as an expectation. Nevertheless, there is a futural sense to humility, but this is related to a reception of what is given and an acceptance of whatever is to come, without it being an anticipation of what is to come. As a welcoming of what comes, "infinitely" we might say, the sense of this futural dimension is a disposition toward . . . without the imposition of a telos or a result, and without anticipating an end. To say that I do not deserve something or that I do not merit it is *not* based on a depreciation of myself (in which case the focus would still be on myself), but is grounded in the overflowing or superabundance of what is received or accepted. Futurally, it is a kind of "accepting-ahead" without anticipated end. Accepting-ahead is not a mere passive experience. It bears a density of experience and is expressed "actively" as a devotion toward someone or something. Even though humility is not oriented temporally like an expectation, it does have a temporal meaning, namely, accepting-ahead as devotion.

To sum up briefly, then, humility has a rich temporality peculiar to it and is irreducible to a presentation, retention, and expectation. I qualify these temporal modes of givenness as presence-at which is expressed as a being thankful for, as ante-memorial reception, and as accepting-ahead, reflected in devotion.

Conclusion

Allow me to conclude this chapter on humility by providing a brief summary, and then by relating humility back to the problematic that was raised in the chapter on pride.

Like trust, loving and humility are characterized as moral emotions of otherness. In distinction to trust, loving and humility are understood as having a broader relation to otherness in the sense that they are open and receptive to many kinds of otherness, not just personal otherness. To describe humility, I related it to the experience of loving as a creative act oriented toward another in the fullness of who he, she or what it is in the direction of becoming-being. Loving, in its movement, generates its own normativity intrinsic to the interpersonal relation as emergent from the person. Humility is who I "am" and how I am given to myself in such an orientation. It is a unique kind of self-givenness that is unlike the self-givenness of pride, shame, or guilt.

Humility was also described as foundational for the experience of pride, even if pride has become an historical a priori whereby humility can provide a response to pride. Humility was described as a way of accepting and receiving without the proviso of just deserts. It is distinctive from being humbled and humbling myself insofar as I am not placed or do not place myself in comparison with another; nor is there an attempt in humility to suppress myself, as in the case of modesty. Despite the fact that humiliation seems to be tied to humility, humiliation really belongs to the problematic of shame, and in particular, to the dynamic of debilitating shame. Distinguishing between humiliation and affliction, we say that the latter appears within a religious or inter-Personal context, and that it is this experience, affliction and not humiliation, that could have a genetic relation to humility.

Finally, I described the temporality of humility. Certainly, given the whole person, we live through manifold layers and dimensions of temporality, but just honing in on the experience of temporality in humility, we see unique modes of temporal givenness as presence-at, ante-memorial reception, and accepting-ahead—all of which may go on at the same time as a presentation, retention, and protention—or with the temporal modes of other emotional experiences—but are essentially distinct from them.

Let me now draw out an important feature of this analysis as it concerns the problematic of the self in relation to pride. At the beginning of this work in the chapter on pride, I considered whether or not pride was an essential feature of who we are as human persons. We can recast the issue by asking: Are we given over to pride simply by virtue of the fact that we as persons are radically unique or absolute? Are we "thrown" into pride by taking ourselves up as an ability-to-be—by the fact that we *can* be something, that we *can* make something of ourselves, that we *can* transform a concrete situation and endow it with new meaning, in short, by this very process of transcendence? Are we cast as prideful by being "absolutely Here" in relation to the relativity of objects, by being that spatial zero-point of orientation which for the most part allows us to navigate and master a world? Are we innately prideful because we are subjectively the source of time?

I suggested that such a determination, or rather pre-determination, of pride was not the case. These are indeed fundamental experiences of who we are that can be lived as prideful; but to live them in the way of pride is a creative act. "Being," "Life," "God" does not throw us as "prideful" by abandoning us to transcendence, by withdrawing from givenness, by making us fated to be preoccupied with ourselves as intentional beings. These basic experiences are given; they have inherent value; our uniqueness, our ability-to-do, and so on, have intrinsic worth. As given, we can only take them up; we have no say in this.

But by themselves they are not pride, not the cause of pride, or even the motivation for pride. Indeed, as we have seen, it is pride that simultaneously resists other dimensions of experience that are also given in those fundamental or base experiences. The extent to which pride is subjectively arbitrary is the extent to which it *limits* the very constitution of myself, the world, and thus is self-limiting. These fundamental experiences *can just as well be lived lures for humility.* And it is humility that receives them as ways of being Myself, as interpersonal, as gift.

In the first instance, humility lives the uniqueness of myself as Myself, which is given as not self-grounding, as relational and inter-Personal. At root, it concerns the problematic of vocations. In addition and related to the former, humility receives others as co-constitutive of myself, as well as co-contributing to the meaning of the world. This is why the ability-to-be, who I am, is carried out as participating in the transformation and reparation of the world. Here, humility is realized as devotion both to the "Source" (God, Godhead, the Holy, deities) and as the devotion to others who co-participate in this process of world transformation.

Aesthetically, in the sense we have used the expression above, humility affirms the intercorporeal constitution of sense, not by denying the lived-body as a zero-point of orientation or depreciating the "I can," but by receiving the lived-body ground as not self-grounding; as grounded in the Earth-ground, and by taking up the I can as co-participation, the lived-body ground is co-responsible for *spatial* and *kinesthetic* sense in its self-moving. Aesthetically, humility takes the base experiences as lures for devotion to the Earth-ground as home. It is not, as Heidegger might have it, a "care" for the Earth, which is ultimately rooted in "Dasein." Rather, humility in this register is realized as eco (home)-devotion, which originates from the Earth as ground, and my being grounded in it. Such an eco-devotion is undertaken as intercorporeal devotion, or what Merleau-Ponty might call devotion to intertwining "flesh."

In humility, the ultimate source of meaning in the aesthetic register of temporality is generative temporality in which I am given to myself as self-temporalizing. In this case, I am *given to myself* as self-giving by generative historicity, where Generativity is experienced as the source of this self-giving. Further, temporality is not limited to self-temporalization, but is lived as generatively communal time. This aspect of generative temporal humility is realized as devotion to the reparation of the world to removing limits, and in the broadest sense, liberation or redemption.

Conclusion

Moral Emotions, the Person, and the Social Imaginary

These phenomenological investigations into the moral emotions have provided us with accounts of the meanings and structural characteristics of privileged personal as interpersonal experiences. These investigations have also given us a more expansive notion of the person than we gain through only a perceptual, judicative, or discursive framework; they do so by yielding insights into who we are as persons in emotions that give us to ourselves as we are in relation to others, in emotions that open and close the sphere of personal and interpersonal possibilities, and in emotions that have distinctive temporal and spatial bearing—among other leading characteristics that are too numerous to recount here.

Throughout the individual chapters on the emotions, we have seen the ways in which these moral emotions exhibit distinctive structural characteristics, how they are irreducible to perceptual and judicative acts, how they are not founded in them, and finally, how the moral emotions have their own evidential integrity. In this conclusion, I emphasize the salient features of these emotions (1). The description of these key features, which make up who we are as human persons, allows me to point suggestively to ways in which the moral emotions can and should be integrated into contemporary social and political discourse, the problematic of our contemporary social imaginaries, and how they might play a role in shaping civic life and power relations rather than being sidelined in such discussions (2).

The Distinctive and Fundamental Features of the Moral Emotions for the Meaning of Person

Pride is a creative emergence within the sphere of persons, freely enacted with an interpersonal basis; in effect, it becomes the presupposition for the individualizing and self-oriented tendencies that we witness in many areas of our lives with others. Rather than a straightforward attitude toward the world as taking its sense for granted, pride is a unique, morally significant subjective attitude that—viewed as a whole—is arbitrarily self-limiting. The creative elaboration of certain basic experiences (the ability-to-be, the ability-to-do, etc.) are lived as the refusal of and resistance to others and the others' contributions both to world-meaning and to myself. However, the self-givenness in pride as a subjective attitude is self-dissembling and self-limiting because it presupposes—while it shuts down—the very interpersonal and inter-Personal dimensions intrinsic to self-discovery. It arises as a *historical* a priori in interpersonal existence, presupposing genuine self-love, but focuses on the salience of the subjective, individual self. In so doing, pride informs different expressions of individualism by eschewing the contribution of others and the world to the emergence of meaning.

Shame is one way in which we are revealed to ourselves outside of the limits instituted in pride. As a diremptive experience, that is, an experience in which a situation is given in tension or in conflict with a more basic orientation, shame is a spontaneous, creative way in which that diremption is lived with others, with distinctive implications for myself. To say that shame is creative or spontaneous does not belie the fact that we are thrown back on ourselves, "against our will," as it were, such that shame is able to call pride into question. Rather, by creative, we mean that such a diremption could have been "taken up" spontaneously, say, as embarrassment, as guilt, as humiliation, or not at all. Thus, even though shame in some sense befalls me, it is still an emotional act, and, in this sense, spontaneous, creative, "personal."

Shame is a self-givenness as self-revelation, expressive both of a departure from and alignment with whom we most genuinely are—provided that this is not a debilitating shame. It is a self-givenness as self-revelation that occurs in and through others and with others, such that I am not only exposed before another in shame, but I receive Myself from another. This suggests, further, not only that I am dependent upon others for my self-revelation, not only that I am intimately connected with others for my own bearing, but that we as a community are revealed to ourselves. Being both behind ourselves and ahead of ourselves, shame is given on the basis of self-loving, and makes us susceptible, communally, to shamelessness. Shame, as a diremptive experience, as a lived-through tension, then, is one way in which we can be brought back to ourselves, a way that can motivate *self-critique*. Such a critique is not fundamentally a judgment or assessment, which may come later. The ways of self-critique and how we become on the basis of who we are most deeply are revealed in and through the experience and as guided by our deeper possibilities that are revealed in shame.

Guilt is another creative way in which a diremptive experience emerges in personal experience. It also arises in relation to others as an accomplishment that is mine, but here the relation with others redounds upon Myself as a transgression, issuing in another form of critique. Its futural significance is announced in the possibility of reconciliation with others against whom we have transgressed, and in a possible restoration of ourselves that was revealed through guilt. The intervention of guilt in the otherwise unexamined flow of events calls the prideful self into question, in part, by placing me in the accusative. This occurs on a level of experience that is "prior" to my being able to assume a position of control in assessing myself or judging myself.

While guilt points to a dimension of interpersonal freedom as expressive of the way in which I live my accomplishment in relation to others, it—like shame—is not an act of volition since it, like shame, arises against my will. Further, although guilt emerges in my relation with another, it signals my responsibility to others for a transgression given as a violation of a demand, morally and religiously: morally, in the sense of a transgression of a demand issuing directly from a social other; religiously, as a violation of Myself, and as reversing the movement of holiness, and coevally through the injury to others.

Shame and guilt acquire their deeper significance not simply as independent experiences unto themselves, but elicit the overall movement of repentance. In their own ways, they both provoke a possible self-critique (individually and communally); both appeal to a possible revolution of the heart and liberation from fixed meanings. If shame yields repentance, it is because it bears directly on the becoming of the person interpersonally; if guilt yields repentance, it is because the accomplishment of a deed is not the actual object of the repentance, but only its spur; for it is the personal self as interpersonal that is reexperienced through guilt in repentance.

Viewed in relation to pride, repentance begins the process of replacing ourselves in relation; it possibilizes a future through its movement of reprise and the revolution of the heart. This possibilizing dimension gives repentance a fundamental feature as liberation. Neither a forgetting nor a remembering, nor a revision of the events, repentance operates on a different level; it entails a distinctive existential dispositing and disclaiming peculiar to the interpersonal, moral sphere. Liberating us from fixed meanings of ourselves and of the past deed as one who could accomplish such a deed, as these are revealed to us though shame and guilt, repentance liberates us from limits, which are interpersonal limits. These interpersonal limits are self-limits, both in the sense that they are imposed in a subjectively arbitrary manner, and because they

CONCLUSION

limit interpersonal relations to the preeminence of myself. Although pride is expressive of freedom, as restricted to my will, it is binding and not liberating. Although the freedom of repentance initiates a movement that retrieves my bonds with others, it is liberating.

Repentance, however, is not restricted to the immanence of my intentions, for liberation as reprise and revolution of the heart in the full sense is completed in the transcendence of world transformation. Repentance is a repentant praxis, and this begins with divesting ourselves of what we have gained through the offenses undertaken in the spirit of non-attachment to things, and non-attachment to self. Such a process recovers who we are with and for others, and in some sense requires forgiveness and mercy even though these are not "conditions" of repentance. Finally, what takes place in repentance can be taken up in other ways that we have examined, namely, in hope, trust, loving, and humility.

In addition to repentance, hope and despair were also described under the rubric of the emotions of possibility. Hope and despair are personally engaged possibilities, but more than that, they both have a bearing in relation to a ground of hope. Through hope, a new, different, or even the same future is given as possible, even if it is not expected, and even if it seems impossible. The important and distinctive dimension of hope where such a possibility is concerned is that hope is never frivolous or arbitrary—unlike, say, wishing or imagining. Rather, by being personally engaged in the hoped-for event, what is hoped-for is given *as sustainable*. What is otherwise experienced as impossible is commuted, lived now as sustainable in the act of hope as liberation, and this is why hope is so integral to a politics of liberation. Although hope may coincide with an expectation or can run counter to it, it has its own temporal structure as an awaiting-enduringly. Indeed, as an awaiting-enduringly, hoping, while significant for a politics of liberation, might nevertheless delay taking action. Still, this ground of hope is given in such a way, opening an awaiting-enduringly, that I can be hopeful or have a hopeful disposition.

Thus, in the very hope-act, an other, more precisely, a ground of hope is given without it being the object of an intention or as a fulfillment of an intention, and this ground sustains my very hoping and the hoped-for event, and is sustained through a relation of dependence upon another as already given. In contrast to an impossibility that is commuted to sustainability, despair is lived as the impossibility of a ground that is present as absent. We saw further that not only despair, but the movement of pride cannot exist along with hope as engaged and as sustainable. Because of the ways in which they possibilize, are engaged, and because of their relations of dependence on a ground, or respectively a non-ground, hope and despair are radically distinct from optimism and pessimism, assertion and denial of reality, a laissez-faire attitude and panic.

Like other moral emotions that have been described here, trust exhibits a relation to otherness. But trust is distinctive insofar as it is positively and explicitly oriented toward others, and specifically, others as persons. In fact, trust is only significant as interpersonal. Furthermore, trust is only effective as trust when it presupposes free persons. We saw, for example, that one could not trust if coercion were involved, either by the one trusting, or by the one trusted. But the freedom that takes shape in trust is fundamentally interpersonal because it is one that is realized as being bound to another.

Not being motivated by the security of the past, we expose ourselves to more than can be given in being bound to another in trust; for trust is not reducible to reliability and purely pragmatic relations with others. Instead, trust is oriented toward the other person as mystery, as "transcendence," and thus toward an open future, co-constituting interpersonal social space in a fundamental way. The essential binding character of trust is normative in a unique moral sense, and in its own way directs our modes of comportment with others and our systems of knowledge. This binding character, however, also means that we are essentially vulnerable and susceptible to betrayal. Yet we cannot at the same time trust and rule out the possibility of vulnerability and betrayal.

Being vulnerable as being bound to another in trusting does implicitly go against pride, since in trusting, I have already released control of the situation, as it were, having already realized my freedom as being bound to another, as proffering. Vulnerability and the possibility of betrayal are evident in the trust of a complete stranger, but are implicit in any trusting, even of someone familiar. The opposite movements of distrust and mistrust, however, tend to fragment and to isolate. They are unable to constitute sociality as interpersonal space. This is why a society that attempts to found social cohesion on mistrust or distrust will in the best of circumstances remain in conflict with itself; in the end, however, it will destroy itself internally by having to remove freedom (which is a presupposition of trust) in order to manage sociality, rather than preserve freedom.

Proffering ourselves—the unique temporal mode of trust—in the presence of this transcendent, free other, with whom we are bound to their and our destinies, even if for that moment or in that mode, trusting as a moral emotion of otherness is not the same as assessing risk or ruling out gullibility. I do not originally "decide" to trust, since it is not an expression of autonomy. Proffering ourselves, however, can be an invitation to trust and an imposition of trustworthiness, and in this respect be generative of trust.

While trusting is oriented toward a personal other, a movement that realizes freedom as being bound to the other, loving is an opening to any other whatsoever, from the inorganic to the holy. Loving opens itself to the integrity and flourishing of the other as it *is* in the dynamic sense of becoming, while being open toward the fullest realization of what it is with respect to its own sphere of being and givenness. In loving, even an "object" is never just an object, since loving is a process through which what gives itself is de-limited, and in this respect partakes in the process of redemption, of liberation as infinitization or removing limits. With respect to the expansiveness of loving and the orientation to flourishing in loving, which constitutes a loving community, loving is broader than trusting. Humility is connected to the movement of loving, but as how I am self-given in the acceptance of what is given and in the reception of myself as Myself.

In relation to pride as historically instituted through personal actions, humility can be understood as a recovery of the interpersonal Myself. This happens in humility, in part, not as imposing my will or expecting something in return for what I do, but as the acceptance of what is given without just deserts. Humility therefore does not share the structure of intention and fulfillment that is evident in the noeis/noema correlation. Further, the acceptance without just deserts in humility takes place as not having others at my power of disposition or asserting myself as the sole or main conveyor of meaning, but instead as participating with others in meaning-giving, and as the reception of myself as Myself. Here, Myself is given relationally as not self-grounding, though not in a way that would give me in comparison with others. Even though it is characterized as acceptance and reception, the "density" of humility has a futural resonance. Humility is expressed in this case as devotion, namely, as a devotion toward the things themselves, toward others, and toward Myself, that is, as vocational experience.

The project of *Moral Emotions,* and a phenomenology of the emotions more generally, is not an attempt to give a so-called universal account of the emotions as if it would be an ahistorical, abstract statement valid neutrally across all cultures and irrespective of all traditions. These moral emotions, which have emerged historically and creatively through personal as interpersonal acts, hold essentially for a set of "personal" traditions, for example, the Abrahamic tradition, Western modernity, and so on. Indeed, it is also my contention that some emotions may not make sense within a different spiritual tradition, like Zen Buddhism. Given the core of experience rooted in *sunyata* or emptiness, the Zen Buddhist, for example, will not and "should" not (in every sense of the term) experience guilt. The basic framework for this was clarified in *Home and Beyond*, and in *Phenomenology and Mysticism*, so I will not go into further detail here.

But this does not mean that such an account of the moral emotions given here is merely arbitrary or relative, either. Such a descriptive enterprise does attempt to clarify the *essential structures* of these experiences which emerge or have emerged, generatively, as concrete a prioris. This suggests that given the experience, an emotion will have such and such a structure, no matter when, where, or who experiences it. Thus, if I hope, in whatever circumstance I hope, from the most "mundane" to the most "profound" content of that experience, it will be lived as an engaged and sustainable possibility, it will be lived as an awaiting-enduringly, and so on. This is not to prescribe when and where and for what I should hope. Instead, it is a matter of observing certain essential features of the act. For example, to go to one extreme, a total deprivation of trust would leave one completely suspicious and isolated even if (one might maintain) we need to be this suspicious on a particular occasion. This is not a predetermination like "you should always trust," nor is it an exercise in justifying to another or to myself why I trust this person; rather, descriptively it says that trust opens up an interpersonal dimension of being with others, and it is one of the founding experiences for interpersonal and intercultural relations such that without it, we tend toward isolation to the point of a pathological solipsism.

Further, one can ascertain in some cases certain internal connections between the emotions. For example, there are intrinsic relations between pride, shame, guilt, repentance, humility, and so on. Shame, for instance, is such that it can furnish a reply to pride, and further that without any kind of disorientation lived as a diremptive experience, there would be no shame. But these movements and interrelations are intrinsic to the experiences themselves, and are not something imposed on the outside or linked coincidentally, as if we were constructing an idea of the person or theorizing what it means to be a virtuous human being.

Finally, while such a phenomenological description is not a matter of imposing norms of experience on the emotions, for example, determining when one should hope, how one should feel guilty, and so on, some of the emotions we have considered do have an internal, self-critical normative bearing. But again, this has to be considered in the context within which the emotion emerges. Within the Abrahamic tradition, for instance, which is a personal as interpersonal tradition, pride shows itself as internally problematic. That is, pride refuses the interpersonal nexus that it presupposes, and in the process, pride is self-dissimulating because it obfuscates the interpersonal contribution of meaning, subjectively restricting it to myself, concealing the interpersonal dimension of the self as Myself. This suggests a critique of pride with normative weight, a critique, however, that is disclosed through countervailing experiences *within* experience itself, like in shame, guilt, repentance, and humility, and is imposed neither according to an abstract norm or because of a commitment to a rational principle. As we saw above, loving, in its creative spontaneity, bears its own improvisational intrinsic normativity, instituting its own normative demands vis-à-vis the beloved in this concrete interpersonal nexus.[1]

Social Imaginary, Freedom, and Modernity

The moral emotions have far-reaching consequences not only for how we view our place in the world, but for world-transformation. Because we have conflicting views of freedom, for example, (1) from pride—as individual, subjective self-will—and (2) from the internal normative critiques of pride given in other moral emotions such as trust—freedom as interpersonal—the moral emotions have important implications, consequences, and significance for our modern social imaginaries as well as for its postmodern variants.

I understand by "social imaginary" that configuration of convictions and practices, institutional procedures, customs and techniques of living, as well as ideas and pre-reflective experiences that articulate interactions in the social sphere. In effect, the social imaginary orders and expresses how we interact with one another.[2] The political philosopher Claude Lefort, for example, describes a pre-ideological or pre-critical social imaginary, on the one hand, and the era of ideology, on the other, which is a novel mode of the social imaginary and which ushers in new forms of Western modernity (or modernities).[3]

In the pre-modern social imaginary, in which power regulates social life and its hierarchies in specific ways, the social sphere was governed by a power or powers *outside* of the social sphere. A sphere of "transcendence" directed the interactions within the social without necessarily being a part of the social interaction, giving some persons different worth and integrity than others. For example, God and God's representative on earth, the king—with the king's two bodies,[4] the clergy, and others—articulated a social hierarchy (e.g., *oratores, bellatores,* and *laboratores*), but this was accomplished essentially from outside of that social sphere in which these divisions and power relations are played out.[5]

With the advent of an innovative social imaginary, what Lefort calls the "era of ideology," a new framework for the confluence of power and the social, of the political and civil space emerges. Transcendence is now integrated into immanence such that it is the sphere of immanence which accounts for the movement of transcendence. The social imaginary in which the monarch ruled and devised the people is overcome, and this overcoming can be symbolized in the effects of the guillotine and the image of the "body politic." Modernity is, in part, this project of giving an account of transcendence by a turn vis-à-vis transcendence in and through the *critical* (reflective or pre-reflective) turn to immanence. One can see this philosophically from Kant to Husserl to Derrida, and in a way that postmodernity is itself a further working out of modernity.

This is also why Charles Taylor can rightly designate this movement as radical *secularity*. Secularity is not the fact that "God" cannot be present in the internal lives of individual believers in this social imaginary, what we call the era of ideology: "God" can be present in our political identity as in "my" individual life; in fact, we do see this in the West in the Protestant Reformation all the way down to the myriad forms of evangelism. The decisive point, however, is that sacredness does not govern the action carried out within the social sphere. Rather than social action taking place from "higher times," it occurs literally in a secular manner, in profane time, mono-dimensionally: foundings are common actions in profane time.[6] In the secularism of this kind, Scheler and Taylor would agree, impersonal benevolence of a practical kind as a teleological striving or duty replaces the movement of infinite loving.[7]

Politically one can see this in the French and American revolutions, in bourgeois ideology, capitalism, fascist and communist variants of totalitarian ideology, and popular movements peculiar to postmodern ideology. Put in different terms, according to Lefort, the era of ideology is the promissory note of unifying power and civic life, the political and the social, by claiming to nullify the stratifications and divisions that were imposed from the outside on the social sphere. But at each turn, we witness new divisions and hierarchies that were not supposed to have emerged. For instance, in a bourgeois ideology, which, for example, challenged the power relations and divisions among the king and his subjects, there insidiously emerged new divisions. In the attempt to unify the social from within the social, investing the "citizens" with power and equality, different rifts surfaced between those who express themselves according to the universal idea, essence, norm, rationality as subject and hence as "free" and having access to power—and those who do not have access to the rule, the norm, rationality and thus appear as uncivilized, non-subject, abnormal, irrational, non-autonomous. In the process of this articulation, this ideology obfuscates the very historical emergence of this social order as an institution because it has already aligned itself with the universal, and thus, its economic order and values appear as eternal and non-emergent.

A totalitarian ideology, in both its fascist and communist variants, however, sought to eradicate these presuppositions and divisions by unifying the social and the political, identifying power and the people by claiming a seamless accord between the state and civil society, denying divisions among special sectors (economic, educational, legal, personal, etc.). In this way, it purported to master its own harmonious and integral organization, providing a univocal, integrated discourse of and meaning to history. Possessing a predetermined teleology of sense, it could identify and solve "crises." The social is indeed unified, but at the cost of reallocating divisions, now by virtue of a different sphere called, appropriately, the "anti-social" (the nonconformists, the "waste," the "vermin," in short, those who putatively threaten the integrity of the social). Here the purity of the social is at once maintained through the impurity of the antisocial.

Within the reputed social whole, however, other divisions surreptitiously sprang up, namely, those between the leaders and followers; some are closer to the center of power as absolute power, nearer to the essential meaning and judgment of history; some are purer, higher, better than others; some are at or nearer the origin and more "original" while others are farther, and mere supplements to "the Truth"; yet these others who are lower or subservient can still share in power and lord it over others (e.g., as informants).

The dismantling of this ideology has led to more contemporary efforts to overcome the once clandestine and now obvious divisions, an effort that I have called elsewhere the homogeneity of power, and Lefort has called an invisible ideology.[8] This new social imaginary in the era of ideology has sought to accomplish what the totalitarian ideology promised but was unable to deliver, namely, the people as one ("power to the people"), the unity of power and civic life. It attempts to accomplish this integration by ridding society of divisive in-groups and out-groups, eradicating hierarchies of all kinds, refraining from passing value-judgments or making discriminations, ultimately self-surrendering the exercise of power in all forms, because after all, it is thought, power is divisive, corrupting, malevolent, and authoritarian.

Thus, people sit in circles so as to be equidistant from the center or the place of power; there is no "head of the class"; there are no leaders or followers, but facilitators and associates; there are no value-judgments, assertions, or discriminations, but "I statements" of one's feelings; there are no insiders and outsiders, but rather "affinity groups"; there are no strangers or foreigners, but internationals; there is no Truth, but truths. Knowledge is only permitted as the homogeneity of knowledges or epistemes, and since knowledge is power, power is self-sacrificed in the name of social cohesion, where "power" is eschewed and permitted only in the guise of the homogeneity of power. In fact, all differences are permitted—but so long as no difference can make a difference, historically, because it is contended that then we would putatively place ourselves back into a totalitarian framework. Whereas previously, through the technological innovations of modernity through Galileo—according to Husserl—"to be" means to be mathematizable or quantifiable, now reality has a different sense; "to be" means to be interchangeable. There are no absolutes, no essences, no foundation, since these are oppressive and harken back to static power relations of domination and the treacheries of fascisms and communisms.

To be sure, this movement that characterizes the homogeneity of power and that is characteristic of postmodernism does have a liberating moment, because it holds back an oppressive hierarchy and gives the disenfranchised an opportunity to participate in social and political affairs, yielding the voice to others who had been traditionally or formerly excluded; it has the intention of being non-dogmatic by not ruling out other perspectives in advance, but by allowing them to come out into the open.

The problem is that there is only a pretension of participation in or contribution to meaning-making, because if sense or meaning (*sens*) emerges, it cannot have a direction (*sens*) that will make a difference in the bearing of history or social transformation, because this would imply that it has a priority of over others; the fear is that it will introduce new divisions, and that direction or orientation will revert to predetermination. Thus, in the homogeneity of power, we can only "play" at making a difference, and validate them only as they are important to me and how I feel—thus excluding in its own way the transformative role of the moral emotions. I no longer engage in creative activity (writing, dancing, composing, etc.) to participate in transforming the world in some way, but only to express my inner feelings.

This form of postmodernism, however, is really just a fulfillment of the selfsame movement of modernity and most recently totalitarianism, because they all share the same presuppositions. The presuppositions are these: power *is* identical with exercising control over others; hierarchy *is* domination; freedom *is* the autonomy of the subjective will; rationality *is* the province of meaning and truth; emotions are only individual, non-significant, and non-evidentiary feelings.

Yet the homogeneity of power (and postmodernism) is more than

CONCLUSION

this; it is the power of homogeneity. It is so effective because it hides itself *as* power, which is how the homogeneity of power is really the power of homogeneity, and why it makes sense for Lefort to call it "invisible" ideology. The real efficacy of the homogeneity of power is the fact that it eclipses itself as such by advancing a set of power relations in which, miraculously, there is no eclipse. It, too, hides its own historicity (in the name of non-essentialism), its role of power in societal relations, and its emergence as a form of power in them as controlling social relations from outside of social relations. It controls a situation universally *in and through* everyone giving up control and power individually. It is a logic of self-effacement that becomes powerful through an apparent loss of power, since everyone participates through self-sacrifice in advance.

That it is the power of homogeneity is evident, for example, when anyone steps out of line in this model of power relations: he or she is either immediately reprimanded, or the assessments of the situation *must be* converted into "I statements" ("I guess I feel that . . ."). There are no in-groups and out-groups, but there is also no living social interaction because everyone is fragmented from one another in an equality of "simple location" (Whitehead) of his or her own individual, autonomous "I statements" who "cannot." And, of course, *no one* is in a position of power; *no one* is expounding the Truth, *no one* has a claim on history, so we cannot pinpoint the source of power (as we could previously, say, in a totalitarian ideology). The homogeneity of power dominates as the power of homogeneity, clandestinely—and can only function this way—because it is supported by those who it dominates having self-avowedly already surrendered power and the process of making history. The homogeneity of power relies on our willingness to see power only in totalitarian terms so that it can continue to hide itself as universal and as power that regulates the social; it enters history unhistorically as a social imaginary, but keeps power from the social, affirming only powerlessness and implicitly sanctioning the status quo. I do not have the occasion here to go into more detail in tracing the contours of the era of ideology, its promises and its disappointments; this would take us beyond the scope of this work. But I do want to use this occasion to make the following observations where the moral emotions and social imaginaries are concerned.

The postmodern is not a place of refuge from the modern. If we find ourselves at an impasse today with the postmodern, facing the same problems concerning the articulations of power and civil society, but in different form, it is not only due to the fact that the postmodern recasts in a more insidious manner the same problems and meanings of power and society as the modern in its reconfiguration of immanence and transcendence. Rather, the impasse is also due in part to the way in which modernity established itself *by* dismissing the spiritual and evidentiary role of the emotions, especially what we call the moral emotions as interpersonal, that is, by acknowledging or including them in a discourse only by excluding them from social and political coexistence and as incapable of making any significant contribution. In a sense, the emotions were not "irrational" because they lacked reason, but because they did not conform to the "innovations" of modern rationality.

Accordingly, not only was a distinctive concept of freedom instituted within the era of ideology, one in which freedom was closely knit to the ingenuity of modern individualism and the individual's autonomy, to the idea of reason, and to the possibility of critique. At the same time, the emotions, especially the moral emotions, were cast aside as irrational, "internal," as privately ethical concerns, to be dealt with psychologically; they were in practice considered to be devoid of spiritual sense, incapable of yielding their own kind of evidence as interpersonally revelatory, and of having any liberating or critical potential.

If we, along with the Frankfurt school and later critical theorists, have found dissatisfaction with "Enlightenment rationality"; if postmodernity is really a peculiar ratification of modernity, and if it has run its course such that now we are wont to speak—uncritically and infelicitously—of a post-postmodernity—it is *nevertheless impossible to go back to a pre-critical social imaginary,* even if we wished to do so, and even if the wish were accompanied by the awareness that modernity like postmodernity (and the social arrangements of power they express) are historical. The attempt to resurrect a Transcendence to govern an immanence, for instance, could only amount to abandoning ourselves to a naive theocracy or to what we witness today as *fundamentalism* and fundamentalist violence.[9]

Certainly, there have been attempts to deal with the permutations of Enlightenment rationality and our era of ideology by turning to aesthetics (Adorno), to a refined sense of political judgment (Lyotard), and even to a communicative rationality (Habermas). While these attempts are not oriented toward trying to escape modernity, while they do not long for a pre-critical social imaginary, there is still a problem that these and other figures have in common. They ignore what modernity has ignored, namely the *role of the moral emotions* and the possibilities opened by them. Through the moral emotions, it is possible *to retrieve what was excluded in modernity* without trying to go back abstractly to an earlier, pre-critical social imaginary, and yet to go forward beyond our current modern predicament and postmodern impasse by appropriating these resources. Experiences like loving, humility, trust, repentance, even shame, guilt, and pride reveal the person as *interpersonal;* we dis-

CONCLUSION

cover in our self-revelations that we are inherently relational and not self-grounding, the "self" given most deeply relationally as Myself. As opposed to secularity, holiness is revealed (in moral emotions like loving, humility, etc., in experiences of not being self-grounding) not as dominating or controlling over another, but "vertically" as serving another or in love, trust, humility, mutual respect, and only in this sense from what Taylor calls "higher times."

The moral emotions were evident in modernity, but ignored and even denigrated in favor of other values that came to the fore, like subjectivity, rationality, and autonomy. Here the value of the distinctiveness of the individual took on the shape of a reversal such that now the individual is asserted as self-grounding. But the moral emotions belong to us as persons just as much as do reason and judgment, or even aesthetics and communication; indeed, they are at the heart of what it means to be "person." If we insist on the moral emotions being able to provide a new opening, we do so without sacrificing the idea of freedom, critique, normativity, or power, but instead propose reevaluating their scope according to what is revealed in these emotions. But I want to be clear: the moral emotions only provide a "new" opening in the sense that it is relatively new for modernity and postmodernity, or new for us now. Taking up the moral emotions in the way suggested here amounts to recovering what has been excluded and reversing the reversal. If we are wont to speak of crisis today, then it is not really a crisis of "Reason" or the crisis of the sciences, no matter how broadly understood—to allude to Husserl's theme. Nor is it a matter of a second beginning, as Heidegger might have it. If there is a "crisis," it is not in Reason, but in the fact that the emotions have been excluded from the meaning of person, and made the subset of Reason, or sensibility, which amounts to the same thing. Reversing the reversal as recovering what was excluded, we would say that it is the interpersonal movement that we find in the emotional sphere (like we find in loving or trusting) that founds the epistemic movement of knowing objects.[10] It is not a matter of finding a new beginning, because the emotions have been there all along in modernity—no matter how far we trace it back. Or to express it differently, it is not only a matter of seeing the ways in which the emotions—having their own kinds of evidence—offer distinctive modes of existence as coexistence; it is also a matter of understanding how the emotions have already been functional where persons are concerned, but excluded in favor of other preferences. This kind of crisis shows up in our social imaginaries.

In this case, we do not let freedom be colonized by the idea of subjective autonomy, and we disambiguate it from its identification with my individual will; it is not a matter of critique being something egoically initiated by rational prowess or reducing transcendence to immanence; it is not a matter of power being equated with the mastery over another such that it refuses otherness; it is not a matter of hierarchy being tantamount to lording over or belittling another. If we can speak of "progress" in the human person, it is not because we overcome a crisis in the teleology of reason, or because we have unveiled a secret plan to world history, or because we now conform to a standard imposed on us; rather it is because we not only can live up to and generate "norms" as revealed, for example, in the depth of loving, trusting, or humility, or in the discrepancies disclosed through shame, guilt, and in liberating possibilities emergent in repentance and hope—but also because we can reveal each time anew, creatively, the interpersonal and inter-Personal nexus. The normative demands issue from the beloved in the loving or trusting, and possibility of critique emerges in felt violation of those interpersonal relations through experiences like shame and guilt. These are at least experiential openings, founding ones, if not exclusive ones.

For the moral emotions to take on such a role for us, they, *the moral emotions, for example, shame, guilt, hope, repentance, loving, trusting, humility, and even pride need to be reintegrated explicitly into our social and political discourses and practices;* they recommend themselves to be invested or reinvested with their social and political significances, along with their ethical, economic, ecological, and religious ones. It is the moral emotions that give us a unique chance of working through and with modernity into the future, creatively, working with what we have gained in this social imaginary, but with new, previously dismissed senses of ourselves as persons. If "critical theory" wants to be more than a theory about theory, but about transformation and liberation, then it is to the moral emotions that it can turn for such a possibility of critique.

Understood in light of the moral emotions, then, the reductions that take place in modernity, like the equation of freedom to the autonomy of the self-grounding subjective will, would be interpreted precisely as expressions of *pride*. Pride, not Enlightenment rationality, would provide the leading clue for critique. Pride, as we saw, cannot be reduced to the basic experiences (absolute uniqueness, the ability-to-be, absolute Hereness, the ability-to-do or the I can, self-temporalization); for pride is a creative appropriation of them as self-limiting and self-dissimulating in manifold ways. Likewise, freedom cannot be equated with subjective, rational autonomy, or with humanistic immanence. Rather, sovereignty expressive of pride is one way in which these basic experiences have been *historically* appropriated, but not the only way, let alone functioning as the most significant clues to power, freedom, hierarchy, or critique. To realize this is to realize its historical contingency,

CONCLUSION

as well as the individualism and economic structures grounded in it, and that there are other emotions which take up or recover the person *as* interpersonal, as co-contributors of meaning, and as not self-grounding, as being bound to one another, and so on.

For example, we see different, interpersonal senses of freedom stemming from the moral emotions. We have discovered, for instance, the meaning of freedom expressed as being bound to others, as a liberation from a fixed past, as a liberation for the possibility of change and as a commutation of the impossible; we have seen it realized in the reconstitution of being with others and reconciliation, in disposing ourselves to others as being vulnerable, as receiving ourselves from others. This is something different from the freedom of "deliberation" that tends to be current today. We have seen different models of critique that are not immanent, dialectical, or rational, but that are instigated by another, for example, in shame or in guilt, and that have revolutionary potential, as Marx himself saw. Shame, as we have seen, gives us a lived example of the contextual, historical, social critique of the present in light of a co-given past and future because of the normativity inherent in the experienced tension or diremption lived *as* shame.

We have seen other types of power that are not a matter of physical force or of forcing my will on another, but for example in loving as an invitational "force," or in trusting that is imposing and is generative of trust. We have seen a "binding" character of experience that is not of necessity or to a norm, but expressed as freedom in trusting and loving, and to persons. We have also seen the possibility of interpersonal hierarchies in experiences in which I am given as not self-grounding; we have encountered "vertical" emotions of otherness like in loving, trusting, humility, and devotion—none of which are a matter of dominating, controlling, or belittling another; in fact, through them I am revealed as vulnerable before another. It is through these emotions and experiences that we are able to conduct a critique of power and social relations that are destructive or hateful, for example, debilitating shame and humiliation.

All of this is not to say that the emotions are political in the sense of reducing their meaning to this sphere of personal existence—any more than it would be to say that economic relations define interpersonal relations. It is certainly not to undermine the important role that reason, rational discourse, and critical judgments play in our collective lives and in the formation of more democratic institutions. However, it is to acknowledge and to underscore that there are other sources of critique, normativity, freedom, and power, and that they have a different tenor as emergent and expressive of the person. It is to bring to the fore a fundamental dimension of personal coexistence that has been left out of account, namely, the moral emotions, and to emphasize that they have *political, social, economic, and ecological significance,* not just "internal" private, psychological, or so-called ethical ones. Finally, it is to admit that they possess a religious significance that is irreducible to fundamentalism, religious fanaticism, or theocracy, a significance that is evoked, for example, in the sacredness that arises in the emotional act of loving or humility. In this way, social action does take place from "higher times" in loving, in humility, in trusting, and has already taken place, even in modernity.

Fundamentalism, religious fanaticism, and the like are what Bergson would term forms of "static" religion that would found a "closed" morality.[11] Yet, trusting, loving, humility, hoping, repentance, shame, guilt, and pride play as much a role in collective life as communicative rationality, rhetoric, and bio-politics, and I argue in fact really play a more fundamental role where persons are concerned because they are both founding for and expressive of interpersonal relations. They not only reveal different forms of power and critique, but provide essential, vital insights into interpersonal relations. They do not replace power and civil society, but I would dare say that they provide radically unique ways of living into and understanding our social and political institutions from the direction of holiness. These are not merely "post-secular," but in a newly qualified sense, religious and moral.

It is interesting in this regard that the moral emotions have occasionally surfaced in discourses on power and civic life in the last century, for example, in Bloch's and Lash's work on hope,[12] and more recently, in Agamben's earlier evocation and later dedication of a chapter to shame in his *Remnants of Auschwitz*. It is also interesting that at the turn of the twenty-first century, the Parliament in Turkey passed a "repentance law" that could grant immunity from prosecution, and that South Africa introduced a "Truth and Reconciliation Commission." These were not traditional political categories. The humiliation of the Germans with the Treaty of Versailles, which imposed reparations that were not grounded in repentance, has social and political significance. Perhaps the attention today to the humiliation of accused political terrorists and prisoners in Guantanamo Bay is a heart-pang in this direction. Elemental shame— the shame of being human in the face of atrocities—writes Hannah Arendt, is what is left of our sense of international solidarity, and it has not yet found an adequate political expression.[13] Even in these difficult situations, bringing the moral emotions (like issues of shame, guilt, trust, humility, loving, devotion, etc.) to the fore in such discussions as categories for evaluation and practice would put us on a different footing and open different horizons for us as persons within our contemporary social imaginary.

It is not a matter of imposing laws on how to act, primarily because this would vitiate the creative dimension of the personal and interpersonal interaction. These relations are not and cannot be realized according to fixed norms, since they are optimalizing, creative of norms, and liberating in an interpersonal register. Instead, it is a matter of the way in which we begin to be and to think with one another. The very experience of trust, for example, shows that the possibilities of action are not dependent upon the past, even if they occur in a historical context and emerge from historical presuppositions. Trust is initiated freely in the direct presence of and with another; it is a creative emergence that ultimately need not be scripted from the past. The moral emotions are not normative as realized according to a predetermined structure, but are historically creative of interpersonal structures, something both desirable and necessary as we attend our impasse of postmodernism.

Notes

Introduction

1. Max Scheler, "Ordo Amoris," in *Schriften aus dem Nachlaß*, vol. 1, in *Gesammelte Werke*, vol. 10, ed. Maria Scheler (Bern: Francke, 1957), 364–66. English translation, David R. Lachterman, "Ordo Amoris," in *Selected Philosophical Essays* (Evanston, Ill.: Northwestern University Press, 1973), 119–23.

2. From the standpoint of rational evidence, the emotions tend to be regarded as unfounded matters of instinct, and as devoid of internal evidence and meaning, dependent upon our psychophysical organization, leaving out human spirit, because it has been equated with the rational. If they are to be made meaningful, they must become the province of judgment; if they are not rational, they are to find a home in the soul or become the object of psychoanalysis; if they are to be real, they are to be naturalized or to be quantified. If rationality is coupled with profit and capital, then emotions that might call the latter into question (like shame or guilt) would have to be deemed highly "irrational." See Max Scheler, *Formalismus in der Ethik und die Materiale Wertethik*, in *Gesammelte Werke*, vol. 2, ed. Maria Scheler (Bern: Francke, 1966), esp. 259–64, 82–84.

3. Scheler, "Ordo Amoris," 364–66; "Ordo Amoris" (English translation), 119–23. See also Max Scheler, "Erkenntkis und Arbeit," in *Die Wissenformen und die Gesellschaft, in Gesammelte Werke*, vol. 8, ed. Maria Scheler (Bern: Francke, 1960, 2nd ed., 1960), 191–382.

4. See Jesse Prinz, *The Emotional Construction of Morals* (Oxford: Oxford University Press, 2009).

5. Friedrich Nietzsche, *Zur Genealogie der Moral*, in *Sämtliche Werke*, vol. 5, ed. Giorgio Colli and Mazzino Montinari (Berlin: De Gruyter, 1980). And see Søren Kierkegaard, *Works of Love*, ed. and trans. Howard V. Hong and Edna H. Hong (Princeton, N.J.: Princeton University Press, 1995).

6. Martin Heidegger, *Sein und Zeit* (Tübingen: Niemeyer, 1979). And see Jean-Paul Sartre, *Esquisse d'une théorie des emotions* (Paris: Hermann, 1948); Gabriel Marcel, *Homo Viator: Introduction to a Metaphysic of Hope*, trans. Emma Craufurd (New York: Harper Torchbooks, 1962); S. Strasser, *Das Gemüt* (Freiburg: Verlag Herder, 1956).

7. Vladimir Jankélévitch, *Philosophie morale*, ed., Françoise Schwab (Paris: Flammarion, 1998); Bernhard Waldenfels, *Phänomenologie der Aufmerksamkeit* (Frankfurt am Main: Suhrkamp, 2004), and much more recently, Bernhard Waldenfels, *Hyper-phänomene: Modi hyperbolischer Erfahrung* (Frankfurt am Main:

Suhrkamp, 2012); Francisco Varela and Natalie Depraz, "At the Source of Time Valence and the Constitutional Dynamics of Affect," *Journal of Consciousness Studies, Emotion, Experience* 12, no. 8 (2005): 61–81; Evan Thompson, *Mind in Life: Biology, Phenomenology, and the Sciences of Mind* (Cambridge, Mass.: Harvard University Press, 2007); Dan Zahavi, *Subjectivity and Selfhood: Investigating the First-Person Perspective* (Cambridge, Mass.: MIT Press, 2005); Adrian Johnston and Catherine Malabou, *Self and Emotional Life: Philosophy, Psychoanalysis, and Neuroscience* (New York: Columbia University Press, 2013). See, too, Maxine Sheets-Johnstone, "Emotions and Movement: A Beginning Empirical-Phenomenological Analysis of Their Relationship," *Journal of Consciousness Studies*, 6, no. 11–12 (2000): 259–77; Robert Solomon, *True to Our Feelings: What Our Emotions Are Really Telling Us* (Oxford: Oxford University Press, 2007). Also contributing along these lines, see Glen Mazis, *Emotions and Embodiment* (New York: Peter Lang, 1994).

8. Anthony J. Steinbock, "Introduction" to *Phenomenology and Mysticism: The Verticality of Religious Experience* (Bloomington: Indiana University Press, 2007).

9. See, too, John Drummond, "'Cognitive Impenetrability' and the Complex Intentionality of the Emotions," *Journal of Consciousness Studies* 11, no. 10–11 (2004): 109–26; and John Drummond, "Moral Phenomenology and Moral Intentionality," *Phenomenology and the Cognitive Sciences* 7 (2008): 35–49.

10. Edmund Husserl, *Logische Untersuchungen: Band II: Untersuchungen zur Phänomenologie und Theorie der Erkenntnis,* part 1 (Tübingen: Niemeyer, 1968), 493–94: "Wir dürfen nämlich sagen: Jedes intentionale Erlebnis ist entweder ein objektivierender Akt oder hat einen solchen Akt zur 'Grundlage,' d.h. er hat in diesem letzten Falle einen objektivierenden Akt notwendig als Bestandstück in sich, dessen Gesamtmaterie zugleich, und zwar individuell identisch *seine* Gesamtmaterie ist." See Robert Sokowloski, *The Formation of Husserl's Concept of Constitution* (The Hague: Martinus Nijhoff, 1964); Donn Welton, *The Origins of Meaning: A Critical Study of the Thresholds of Husserlian Phenomenology* (The Hague: Martinus Nijhoff, 1983).

11. Edmund Husserl, *Ideen zu einer reinen Phänomenologie und phänomenologischen Philosophie: Erstes Buch: Allgemeine Einführung in die reine Phänomenologie,* ed. W. Biemel, *Husserliana* vol. 3 (The Hague: Martinus Nijhoff, 1950). Hereafter referred to as Hua 3. See especially part 3, chapter 3.

12. Husserl, Hua 3, §§94–95.

13. Husserl, Hua 3, §95, §117. English translation by F. Kersten, *Ideas Pertaining to a Pure Phenomenology and to a Phenomenological Philosophy,* First Book (The Hague: Martinus Nijhoff, 1983).

14. Husserl, Hua 3, §93.

15. Husserl, Hua 3, §95: "Dabei sind die Schichtungen, allgemein gesprochen, so, dass oberste Schichten des Gesamtphänomens 'fortfallen' können, ohne dass das Übrige aufhörte, ein konkrete vollständiges intentionales Erlebnis zu sein...."

16. Husserl, Hua 3, §95.

17. Ibid., §116.

18. Ibid., §95.

19. Husserl, *Logische Untersuchungen,* II/1, part 3, §14

NOTES TO PAGES 10-13

20. Husserl, Hua 3, §94. See also Edmund Husserl, *Analyses Concerning Passive and Active Synthesis: Lectures on Transcendental Logic*, trans., Anthony J. Steinbock (Dordrecht: Kluwer, 2001), division 1 on "Modalization" of part 2.

21. See Eugen Fink, "Operative Begriffe in Husserls Phänomenologie" (1957) in *Nähe unde Distanz: Phänomenologische Vortäge und Aufsätze* (Alber: 1976), 180–204.

22. See Maurice Merleau-Ponty, *Phénoménologie de la perception* (Paris: Gallimard, 1945), 451. English translation by Donald Landes, *Phenomenology of Perception* (Routledge, 2012).

23. Husserl, Hua 3, §116.

24. Zahavi, *Subjectivity and Selfhood*.

25. Dan Zahavi, "Self and Other: The Limits of Narrative Understanding," in *Narrative and Understanding Persons*, ed. D. D. Hutto, Royal Institute of Philosophy Supplement 60 (Cambridge: Cambridge University Press, 2007), 179–201. See also J. Bruner, *Making Stories: Law, Literature, Life* (Cambridge, Mass.: Harvard University Press); and K. Young and J. L. Saver, "The Neurology of Narrative," *Substance*, 30, no. 1–2 (2001): 72–84.

26. This is explored in my *Vocations and Exemplars: The Verticality of Moral Experience*, in preparation.

27. See S. Strasser, *Das Gemüt* (Freiburg: Verlag Herder, 1956).

28. I do not consider here the way in which emotions, for example, in rasa "are" the performance in bodily experience, and how the experience of emotions induces religious response. See Susan L. Schwartz, *Rasa: Performing the Divine in India* (New York: Columbia University Press, 2004). See also Maxine Sheets-Johnstone, *The Roots of Morality* (University Park: Penn State University Press, 2008). Nor is it my task to enter the debate concerning whether or not facial expressions universally reveal what others consider "emotions." See Paul Ekman, *Emotions Revealed: Recognizing Faces and Feelings to Improve Communication and Emotional Life*, 2nd ed. (New York: Henry Holt, 2007). See also Charles Darwin, *The Expression of the Emotions in Man and Animals* (1872; Whitefish, Mont.: Kessinger, 2010). And see R. E. Jack, O. G. B. Garrod, H. Yu, R. Caldara, and P. G. Schyns, "Facial Expressions of Emotion Are Not Culturally Universal" in *Proceedings of the National Academy of Sciences of the United States of America*, vol. 109/19 (2012), 7241–44.

29. Prinz, *The Emotional Construction of Morals*.

30. See Mark Timmons, *Morality without Foundations: A Defense of Ethical Contextualism* (Oxford: Oxford University Press, 1999). And see Mark Timmons, *Moral Theory* (New York: Rowman & Littlefield, 2002); and *Metaethics after Moore*, ed. Terry Horgan and Mark Timmons (Oxford: Clarendon, 2006).

31. Thus, I use "moral" in a different sense than does Solomon, who prefers the expression "ethical," although he does not seem to distinguish "moral" (or his "ethical") as essentially interpersonal emotions from other kinds of emotions, feelings, or affects. But to the extent that he wants to explore the "wisdom of the heart" (alluding to Pascal), these projects go in the same general direction, even if the details of the analyses and consequences differ. See Solomon, *True to Our Feelings*, especially his "Introduction."

32. Steinbock, *Phenomenology and Mysticism*, esp. "Introduction" and "Epilogue."

33. The expression "inter-Personal" is the expression I use to designate the relation between finite absolute human persons and infinite absolute Person, or the Holy. As such, it is to be distinguished, but not separate from an interpersonal relation that obtains between finite human persons. See my *Phenomenology and Mysticism*.

34. See especially Carol Gilligan, *In a Different Voice: Psychological Theory and Women's Development* (Cambridge, Mass.: Harvard University Press, 1982); and *An Ethic of Care: Feminist and Interdisciplinary Perspectives*, ed. Mary Jeanne Larrabee (New York: Routledge, 1993).

35. Henri Bergson, *Les deux sources de la morale et de la religion* (1932; Paris: Presses Universitaires de France, 1984). English translation by R. Ashley Audra and Cloudesley Brereton, *The Two Sources of Morality and Religion* (Notre Dame: University of Notre Dame Press, 1977).

36. See Steinbock, *Phenomenology and Mysticism*, "Introduction."

37. Although there are spatial implications of the moral emotions, such as being expansive or contracting, the moral emotions are not directly spatial in the way that they are temporal.

38. See Scheler, *Formalismus*. See *Emotion Experience: Journal of Consciousness Studies*, eds. Giovanna Colombetti and Evan Thompson; vol. 12, no. 8–10 (2005). See also Sylvan S. Tomkins, *Affect Imagery Consciousness: The Positive Affects* (New York: Springer, 1962); Sylvan S. Tomkins *Affect Imagery Consciousness: The Negative Affects* (vol. 2) (New York: Springer, 1963); Daniel C. Batson, Laura L. Shaw, and Kathryn C. Oleson, "Differentiating Affect, Mood, and Emotion: Toward Functionally Based Conceptual Distinctions," *Emotion: Review of Personality and Social Psychology*, no. 13, ed. Margaret S. Clark (Thousand Oaks, CA: Sage Publications, 1992), 294–326; and E. A. Blechman, *Moods, Affect, and Emotions* (Hillsdale, N.J.: Lawrence Erlbaum Associates, 1990). See also Martha C. Nussbaum, *The Therapy of Desire* (Princeton, N.J.: Princeton University Press, 1994). Finally, what Freud refers to in his "The Unconscious" as *Affektbildungen, Affekte, Gefühle*, and *Empfindungen*, would not correspond to what I describe as "moral emotions."

39. Ludwig Wittgenstein, "Philosophy of Psychology—A Fragment," in *Philosophical Investigations*, 4th ed. (Malden, Mass.: Wiley-Blackwell, 2009), i. I.

40. This was the point of investigating the structures of a unique religious sphere of experiencing and evidence in *Phenomenology and Mysticism*.

41. Compare, for example, Jean-Paul Sartre, *Esquisse d'une théorie des emotions* (Paris: Le Livre de Poche, 2000).

42. For early comparisons of the two methods, see John Wild, "Is There a World of Ordinary Language?" *Philosophical Review* (October 1958): 460–76; Maurice Natanson, "Phenomenology and the Natural Attitude," in *Literature, Philosophy and the Social Sciences* (The Hague: Martinus Nijhoff, 1962), 34–43; Eugene TeHennepe, "The Life-World and the World of Ordinary Language," in *An Invitation to Phenomenology: Studies in the Philosophy of Experience*, ed. James M. Edie (Chicago: Quadrangle Books, 1965), 133–46.

43. Edmund Husserl, *Logische Untersuchungen, Vol. II: Elemente einer phänomenologischen Aufklärung der Erkenntnis, Part II* (Tübingen: Niemeyer, 1968).

44. Max Scheler, *Wesen und Formen der Sympathie*, in *Gesammelte Werke*, vol. 7, ed. Manfred Frings (Bern: Francke, 1973), 71. See A. R. Luther, *Persons in Love: A Study of Max Scheler's "Wesen und Formen der Sympathie"* (The Hague: Martinus Nijhoff, 1972), 71.

45. For a more detailed explication of "leading clue," see Anthony J. Steinbock, *Home and Beyond: Generative Phenomenology after Husserl* (Evanston, Ill.: Northwestern University Press, 1995).

46. Since there is not a neutral intersubjectivity, forcing phenomenology to make abstract universal claims, and since this is encompassed by generativity, phenomenology is also led to investigate orders of experience that give themselves concordantly, optimally, typically, and in familiar ways such that any such analysis into essential structures has to take into account their *generative* configurations, more specifically, in terms of the irreducible structure of homeworlds and alienworlds. One can still speak of essential structures, but those structures may be in generation, as peculiar to some generatively dense homeworlds and not—from the perspective of the "home"—some alienworlds. See Steinbock, *Home and Beyond*. See also Anthony J. Steinbock, "Facticity and Insight as Problems of the Lifeworld: On Individuation," *Continental Philosophy Review* 37, no. 2 (2004): 241–61.

47. Phenomenology can detect the rule of the social imaginary over the social and the political within the social and political, and in principle can examine those relations of power, economic, and institutional practices that have effaced their own historical founding, and have come to be taken as "natural" or as if they have always already been there.

48. J. L. Austin, "A Plea for Excuses," in *Philosophical Papers*, ed. J. O. Urmson and G. J. Warnock (New York: Oxford University Press, 1970), 175–204.

49. J. L. Austin, *How to Do Things with Words*, ed. J. O. Urmson and Marina Sbisa (Cambridge, Mass.: Harvard University Press, 1975).

50. Austin, "A Plea for Excuses," 181.

51. Ibid., 182.

52. Ludwig Wittgenstein, *The Blue and Brown Books: Preliminary Studies for the "Philosophical Investigations"* (Malden, Mass.: Blackwell, 1969), "Blue Book," p. 4.

53. Wittgenstein, *Philosophical Investigations*, 43.

54. Ibid., 19, 23, 241.

55. Austin, "A Plea for Excuses," 186.

56. Ibid., 182. This is also how Husserl describes phenomenology's attitude in relation to the "natural attitude," namely, removing the blinkers (*Scheuklappen*).

57. TeHennepe, "The Life-World and the World of Ordinary Language," 145. See also Oswald Hanfling, *Philosophy and Ordinary Language: Bent and Genius of Our Tongue* (New York: Routledge, 2000).

58. See Bertrand Russell, *The Analysis of Matter* (Nottingham, Eng.: Spokesman Books, 2007), 155.

59. TeHennepe, "The Life-World and the World of Ordinary Language," 136. See also Stuart Hampshire, *Thought and Action* (Notre Dame, Ind.: Univer-

sity of Notre Dame Press, 1981). And see *Ordinary Language Criticism: Literary Thinking after Cavell after Wittgenstein,* ed. Denneth Dauber and Walter Jost (Evanston, Ill.: Northwestern University Press, 2003).

60. Austin, "A Plea for Excuses," 182–85.

61. Ibid., 182.

62. See Steinbock, *Home and Beyond.*

63. The lifeworld is both perceptual and linguistic; it is not non-linguistic. It is just that linguistic meanings can also be presupposed as they "circulate" back into what we take for granted. Both the broader natural and the more specific naturalistic (scientific, exact sciences) are naive. See Steinbock, *Home and Beyond,* section 2.

64. Austin, "A Plea for Excuses," 181.

65. For example, Saint Teresa of Avila writes: "For a long time, even though God favored me, I didn't know what words to use to explain His favors: and this was no small trial." Or we can examine what are called "ecstatic expressions" of Sufi mystics, which in many instances had no direct concept prior to the experience or attempt at linguistic formulation. This is perhaps one reason why they had to wait to create their own audience, if they were not killed as heretics first. See Steinbock, *Phenomenology and Mysticism,* esp. chapters 2–4.

66. Herbert Marcuse, *One-Dimensional Man: Studies in the Ideology of Advanced Industrial Society* (Boston: Beacon, 1964), 181.

67. Wittgenstein, *Blue and Brown Books,* "Brown Book," 127.

68. Marcuse, *One-Dimensional Man,* 195.

Part 1

1. See Gabriele Taylor, *Pride, Shame and Guilt: Emotions of Self-Assessment* (Oxford: Oxford University Press, 1985), 1–16.

2. Fabrice Teroni and Julien A. Deonna, "Differentiating Shame from Guilt," *Consciousness and Cognition* 17 (2008): 725–40.

3. June Price Tangney and Kurt W. Fischer, eds., *Self-Conscious Emotions: The Psychology of Shame, Guilt, Embarrassment, and Pride* (New York: Guilford, 1995).

4. See Carolyn Zahn-Waxler and Joann Robinson, "Empathy and Guilt: Early Origins of Feelings of Responsibility," in Tangney and Fischer, *Self-Conscious Emotions,* 143–73, who include guilt and empathy as "moral emotions."

5. For example, see I. J. Roseman, "Cognitive Determinants of Emotions: A Structural Theory," in P. Shaver, ed., *Review of Personality and Social Psychology,* vol. 5: 11–36; Drummond, "'Cognitive Impenetrability'"; C. Hookway, "Emotions and Epistemic Evaluations," in *The Cognitive Basis of Science,* ed. P. Carruthers et al. (Cambridge: Cambridge University Press, 2002); K. N. Ochsner and J. J. Gross, "The Cognitive Control of Emotion," *Trends in Cognitive Science* 9, no. 5 (2005): 242–49.

6. See P. Shaver, J. Schwartz, D. Kirson, and C. O'Connor, "Emotion Knowledge: Further Exploration of a Prototype Approach," *Journal of Personality and Social Psychology,* vol. 52 (1987): 1061–86.

Chapter 1

1. Donald L. Nathanson, "A Timetable for Shame," in *The Many Faces of Shame*, ed. Donald L. Nathanson (New York: Guilford, 1987), 34.

2. This situation would not be ameliorated by conceiving interpersonal relations as adding another already abstractive "I." This would only be to adjunct solitude upon solitude, and presuppose at root that the self is self-sufficient in a collocation of complete self-sufficient selves.

3. As does Kirill in Tarkovsky's *Andrei Rublev*.

4. See Simone de Beauvoir, *Le deuxième sexe* (1949; Paris: Éditions Champion, 2004); and Simone de Beauvoir, *Pour une morale de l'ambiguïté* (Paris: Gallimard, 1947). I am especially grateful to Sara Heinämaa for her comments and references to de Beauvoir in this regard.

5. It is interesting to note that for Freud, the narcissist has no capacity for transference, and therefore is inaccessible to psychoanalytic efforts. Sigmund Freud, *Vorlesungen zur Einführung in die Psychoanalyse*, in *Gesammelte Werke*, vol. 11 (Frankfurt am Main: Fischer Verlag, 1969), 465.

Further, according to the Fourth Edition of the *Diagnostic and Statistical Manual of Mental Disorders* (DSM-IV), narcissism is still classified as a "personality disorder." According to *The Mental Health Diagnostic Desk Reference*, a guide to the DSM-IV, narcissism is classified in Cluster B of personality disorders, and to be diagnosed as such, it should be met by at least five of nine characteristics. Among them is being interpersonally exploitive as taking advantage of others to get needs met, and a grandiose sense of self-importance. (See Carlton E. Munson, *The Mental Health Diagnostic Desk Reference: Visual Gudies and More for Learning to Use the Diagnostic and Statistical Manual (DSM-IV-TR)*, 2nd ed. [New York: Haworth, 2001], 257–59.) Cases are documented as examples of such disorders in the *DSM-IV-TR Casebook* (e.g., "My Fan Club," and "False Rumors"). (See *DSM-IV-TR Casebook: A Learning Companion to the Diagnostic and Statistical Manual of Mental Disorders, Fourth Edition*, ed. Robert L. Spitzer et al. [Washington, D.C.: American Psychiatric Publishing, 2002), esp. 84–85, 23–42.) For me, these are instead spiritual or personal elaborations of what I characterize below in terms of personal uniqueness or the ability-to-be, yielding pride, and not most fundamentally a psychological disorder, even if they can be evaluated psychologically.

It is difficult to take many of these diagnostic metrics seriously, especially when, beginning with the publication of the Fifth Edition (DSM-5, May 2013), what is essentially a temper tantrum will now be classified as "Disruptive Mood Dysregulation Disorder." In this vein, it is curious that narcissism will no longer be classified as a personality disorder, but will be recognized as a subset of "antagonism personality domain." Despite the arbitrariness of this classification on many levels, it may have the advantage of recognizing narcissism as an interpersonal refusal at the very basis of any self-aggrandizement. I would like to thank Joona Taipale for conversations on this matter, and to acknowledge his unpublished manuscript, "Disturbances of Empathy in Narcissistic Disorders."

6. I could be proud of my pride, but then this being proud of would occur

on a different level of experience, and would be irreducible to the movement of pride (see below, this chapter).

7. For this reason, the "will-to-power" cannot in any meaningful sense be a matter of pride. Within this context, it is rather sheer expressive meaning-giving. See Friedrich Nietzsche, *Jenseits von Gut und Böse*, in *Sämtliche Werke*, vol. 5, ed. Giorgio Colli and Mazzino Montinari (Berlin: De Gruyter, 1980). English translation by Walter Kaufman, *Beyond Good and Evil* (New York: Vintage Books, 1989). And see Friedrich Nietzsche, *The Will to Power*, trans. Walter Kaufman and R. J. Hollingdale, ed. Walter Kaufman (New York: Vintage Books, 1968).

8. See Taylor, *Pride, Shame and Guilt*, 44.

9. On self-esteem in a critique of Rawls, see John Deigh, "Shame and Self-Esteem: A Critique," in *Ethics* 93 (January 1983): 225–45.

10. For example, see Max Scheler, *Vom Umsturz der Werte*, ed. Maria Scheler, 4th ed. (Bern: Francke Verlag, 1955), 20.

11. Again, to resist the presence of others is to experience the presence of others in some way, in and through the very occlusion: their inclusion in my experience is constituted through this exclusion in the assertion of myself as the only or highest source.

12. René Descartes, *The Philosophical Works of Descartes*, vol. 1, trans. Elizabeth S. Haldane and G. R. T. Ross (Cambridge: Cambridge University Press, 1981), 402–4 ("The Passions of the Soul," Arts. CLIV-CLVIII).

13. See Thomas Hobbes, *Leviathan*, ed. C. B. Macpherson (New York: Penguin Books, 1985), part 1, chapter 8, p. 140.

14. J. J. Rousseau, *Émile ou de l'éducation* (Paris: Garnier Frère, 1904), 43; Jean-Jacques Rousseau, *Emile, or On Education*, trans. Allan Bloom (Basic Books, 1979), 67. And Rousseau writes : "Voyez, mon fils, à quelle absurdité mènent l'orgueil et l'intolérance, quand chacun veut abonder dans son sens, et croire avoir raison exclusivement au reste du genre humain." *Émile*, 365.

15. Dante Alighieri, *The Divine Comedy*, trans. C. H. Sisson (Oxford: Oxford University Press, 1993), esp. cantos I–XI.

16. See Steinbock, *Phenomenology and Mysticism*, chapters 6–7.

17. Hence, Luther calls person an intrinsic coherence of dynamic orientation. See Luther, *Persons in Love*.

18. See Steinbock, *Phenomenology and Mysticism*, chapter 7.

19. Again, this is the topic of a work in preparation as *Vocations and Exemplars*.

20. And can be seen in a psychoanalytic register as narcissism. See above note 5.

21. See Husserl, *Analyses Concerning Passive and Active Synthesis*.

22. See Edmund Husserl, *Ideen zu einer reinen Phänomenologie und phänomenologische Philosophie, Zweites Buch, Husserliana* 4, ed. Marly Biemel (The Hague: Martinus Nijhoff, 1952); hereafter, Hua 4. And see Merleau-Ponty, *Phénoménologie de la perception*.

23. See Husserl, Hua 4.

24. On the matter of sexual difference and the experience of the body within a phenomenological framework, see Sara Heinämaa, *Toward a Phenomenol-*

ogy of Sexual Difference: Husserl, Merleau-Ponty, Beauvoir (New York: Rowman and Littlefield, 2003). See also Elizabeth Grosz, *Volatile Bodies: Toward a Corporeal Feminism* (Bloomington: Indiana University Press, 1994). And see Iris Marion Young, *On Female Body Experience: "Throwing Like a Girl" and Other Essays* (Oxford: Oxford University Press, 2005).

It can be argued that transcendental features of embodiment differ according to gender difference, and for example, meaning constitution varies according to different bodily experiences. In this case, there would be generative structural differences in meaning constitution that could be discerned in phenomenology by a generative phenomenology.

Nevertheless, I hold that there are formal, transcendental features, even aesthetic, bodily ones that are not determined by sexual or gender difference. For example, that a perception always has a retention which immediately lingers on the present; that the couplet present-retention as temporal modes of givenness forecast or "protend" something to come along the pattern of givenness sketched out by this present-retention (even if the experience does not continue to unfold along this way); that something which comes into relief in a context, and comes into relief affectively in the perceptual sphere—these are fundamental regular lawful structures for any human psychophysical being (and perhaps for all psychophysical beings) in order for there to be a unity of sense. This does not say *what* is perceived or protended; it does not determine *how long* something is retained or anticipated; it does not speak to *which* aspects come into affective relief. These aspects of meaning-constitution could and can vary according to sexual difference and cultural contexts. This is not to say, however—to agree with Heinämaa—that temporality and gender are a minor empirical problem.

I am not in a position to specify how pregnancy might affect the experience of the lived-body as a zero-point of orientation, or how as a fetus and the experience of my lived-body was grounded in my mother's body as ground-body, as grounded in the Earth as Earth-ground. If these are the guiding experiences (experiences of being co-grounding, not self-grounding, or of "intertwining" as Merleau-Ponty might say), however, then I would suspect that they would not tend toward what I am calling here "aesthetic pride."

25. See Husserl, *Analyses Concerning Passive and Active Synthesis;* See also Merleau-Ponty, *Phénoménologie de la perception,* esp., the final chapter on freedom, "La liberté."

26. Michel Henry, *L'essence de la manifestation,* 2nd ed. (Paris: Presses Universitaires de France, 1990); Dan Zahavi, *Self-Awareness and Alterity: A Phenomenological Investigation* (Evanston, Ill.: Northwestern University Press, 1999).

27. See Dan Zahavi, "Michel Henry and the Phenomenology of the Invisible," *Continental Philosophy Review,* Special Issue, ed. Anthony J. Steinbock, vol. 32, no. 3 (1999): 223–40. And see Zahavi, *Self-Awareness and Alterity.*

28. See Anthony J. Steinbock, "Limit-Phenomena and the Liminality of Experience," *Alter: Revue de Phénoménologie,* vol. 6 (1998): 275–96.

29. Husserl, *Analyses,* 68. See Anthony J. Steinbock, "From Phenomenological Immortality to Phenomenological Natality," in *Rethinking Facticity,* ed. Eric Nelson and Francois Raffoul (Albany: SUNY Press, 2008), 25–40.

30. Husserl, *Analyses*, 466–67. Husserl writes: "Just as the cessation is conceivable only insofar as it is in process, though the cessation of the process itself is inconceivable, so too is the beginning only conceivable in process, though not conceivable as the beginning of the process" (*Analyses*, 468).

31. Husserl, *Analyses*, 468–69.

32. Ibid., 467, 470.

33. Ibid., 467, 469, 471.

34. I can always find myself in time after the fact, as it were, as past. But this is because self-temporalization is itself the primordial source for the "first transcendent," namely, the transcendent self, which in the immanence of original time is primordially instituted, and then through rememberings comes to self-givenness. But in the functions (perception, retention, protention), and acts (remembering, expectation, etc.) themselves, I am given precisely as the source of time and as unable to be posited completely like an object.

35. Husserl, *Analyses*, 471.

36. Edmund Husserl, *Die Krisis der europäischen Wissenschaften und die transzendentale Phänomenologie: Einleitung in die phänomenologische Philosophie*, ed. Walter Biemel, *Husserliana* 6 (The Hague: Martinus Nijhoff, 1954), §36. See Steinbock, *Home and Beyond*, esp. chapter 6.

37. See Steinbock, *Phenomenology and Mysticism*, esp. "Introduction."

38. Usually, "attitude" refers to the dancer's pose in which one arm is raised and one leg, with knee bent, is raised, front or back. See, too, F. J. J. Buytendijk, *Attitudes et mouvements: Étude fonctionnelle du movement humain*, trans. Louis van Haecht (Paris: Desclée de Brouwer, 1957), esp. 125–61.

39. See Zahavi, *Self-Awareness and Alterity*.

40. In this way, the epistemic natural attitude does not take into consideration all the evidence available, and is thus phenomenologically naive or "mundane." For example, we could note on the level of passive associative synthesis, as we find in Husserl, that objects or aspects of objects or unities of sense that have an object-like structure exercise an affective allure on the perceiver in order to be constituted as such, and in this way contribute to the constitution of their own sense. We could also note how one is given to oneself intercorporeally, such as we might find in erotic perception, or more generally in terms of what Merleau-Ponty has called the reversibility of the flesh. See, for example, Anthony J. Steinbock, "Perception érotique, histoire et honte" ["Erotic Perception, History, and Shame"], French translation by Pierre-Jean Renaudie, in *Alter: Revue de Phénoménologie* (2011), 175–94.

41. Saint Augustine, *The City of God*, trans. Marcus Dods (New York: Modern Library, 2000); Dante, *Purgatorio*, canto IV.

42. Bernard of Clairvaux articulates twelve steps of pride that correlate with Saint Benedict's twelve steps of humility described in his *Rule*. These steps of pride are the following: (1) curiosity and wandering eyes, (2) levity of mind leading to envy others or seeing them as inferior, (3) giddiness and being saddened by the goodness of others, (4) boasting and bragging that one is better than others, (5) singularity, or wanting to be seen as better rather than wanting really to be better, (6) self-conceit or thinking one is holier than others,

NOTES TO PAGES 48–52

and wanting the good opinion of others, (7) presumption, or putting oneself before others, (8) self-justification or excusing one's sins, (9) hypocritical confession, (10) revolt or contempt for superiors and others, (11) freedom in sinning, (12) habit of sinning. See Bernard of Clairvaux, *The Steps of Humility and Pride*, trans. Jean Leclercq and Henri Rochais (Trappist, Ky.: Cistercian Publications, 1973), 57–78.

43. Rousseau, *Émile*, 281–82; *Emile*, 245.
44. Rousseau, *Émile*, 225; *Emile*, 201.
45. Taylor, *Pride, Shame, and Guilt*, 44–45.
46. Dobh Baer of Lubavitch, *Tract on Ecstasy*, trans. Louis Jacobs (London: Vallentine, Mitchell, 1963), 161–63.
47. Santa Teresa de Jesus, *Obras Completas*, ed. Efren de La Madre de Dios and Otger Steggink (Madrid: Biblioteca de Autores Cristianos, 1997), 136–37; hereafter, *Obras*. My citations of the English follow *The Collected Works of St. Teresa of Avila*, trans. Kieran Kavanaugh and Otilio Rodriguez, vol. 1 (Washington, D.C.: ICS Publications, 1976), chapter 25, pp. 9–13; hereafter, *Collected Works*, vol. 1.
48. Georges Bernanos, *The Diary of a Country Priest*, trans. Pamela Morris (New York: Carroll and Graf, 1965), 249. See San Juan de la Cruz, *Obras Completas*, ed. Licinio Ruano de la Iglesia (Madrid: Biblioteca de Autores Cristianos, 1982), 323. Saint John of the Cross, *The Collected Works of Saint John of the Cross*, rev. ed., trans. Kieran Kavanaugh and Otilio Rodriguez (Washington, D.C.: ICS Publications, 1991), 364: "Sometimes they minimize their faults, and at other times they become discouraged by them, since they felt they were already saints, and they become impatient and angry with themselves, which is yet another fault."
49. David Hume, *A Treatise on Human Nature*, ed. L. A. Selby-Bigge (Clarendon, 1967), book 2, part 1 (sec. VI, p. 291).
50. See Max Scheler, "Das Ressentiment im Aufbau der Moralen," in *Vom Umsturz der Werte*, in *Gesammelte Werke*. vol. 3, ed. Maria Scheler (Bern: Francke, 1955), 33–147. See Friedrich Nietzsche, *Zur Genealogie der Moral*, in *Sämtliche Werke*, vol. 5, ed. Giorgio Colli and Mazzino Montinari (Berlin: De Gruyter, 1980), esp. 268–69, 270–74, 281–83.
51. Ruzbihan Baqli, *Unveiling of Secrets: Diary of a Sufi Master*, trans. Carl W. Ernst (Chapel Hill, N.C.: Parvardigar, 1997).
52. Henry, *L'essence*, 389–90/312–13. See Anthony J. Steinbock, "The Problem of Forgetfulness in Michel Henry," in *Continental Philosophy Review: The Philosophy of Michel Henry*, ed. Anthony J. Steinbock, vol. 32, no. 3 (1999): 271–302.
53. Etymologically, *fierté* is related to the Latin *ferus*, and accordingly means "wild," "intrepid," "courageous," and in this sense relates to being superior to others, extending to arrogance. *L'orgueil*, which is more closely related to how I understand "pride" here, is more the insistence of the personal value to the detriment of consideration due to others. Voltaire wrote in his entry on *fierté* that within the soul *fierté* is grandeur, but in exteriority, in society, it is *l'orgueil* (Voltaire, *Encyclopédie, ou Dictionnaire raisonné des sciences, des arts et des métiers*, vol. 6 [1756], 719).
54. Jean-Paul Sartre, *L'être et le neant: Essai d'ontologie phénoménologique* (Paris: Gallimard, 1943), 337; see also 309, 314; English translation by Hazel E.

Barnes, *Being and Nothingness: A Phenomenological Essay on Ontology* (New York: Washington Square, 1956), 386; see also 352, 358.

55. In the genesis of the individual, empirical research has shown that so-called self-related evaluative experiences like pride, shame, and guilt can be observed in children between the ages of 24 and 36 months—something supported by psychoanalytic literature. Of course, this is assuming that there is a correlation between what we are describing and what they are observing (for example, they seem to be taking "being proud of" for "pride" in the way that we have clarified it). See Michael Lewis, *Shame: The Exposed Self* (New York: Free Press, 1995).

More interestingly, Lewis also cites Geppert and Kuster, who found that while children around thirty months exhibited expressions of shame and guilt, pride was not observed until some months later. See Lewis, *Shame*, 250. See also S. S. Tomkins, *Affect, Imagery, and Consciousness, Vol. 1, Positive Affects* (New York: Springer, 1962); and S. S. Tomkins, *Imagery, and Consciousness, Vol. 2, Negative Affects* (New York: Springer, 1963). And see U. Geppert and U. Kuster, "The Emergence of 'Wanting to Do It Oneself': A Precursor of Achievement Motivation," *International Journal of Behavioral Development* 6 (1983): 355–70.

56. See the section below on "self-love."

57. And later characterized by Heidegger co-grounding in the relation of difference determined by a *belonging* together of beings and Being. Martin Heidegger, *Identität und Differenz* (Tübingen: Neske, 1982). English translation by Joan Stambaugh, *Identity and Difference* (New York: Harper and Row, 1969).

58. See Martin Heidegger, *Zur Sache des Denkens* (Tübingen, Niemeyer, 1976). Martin Heidegger, *On Time and Being*, trans. Joan Stambaugh (New York: Harper and Row, 1972).

59. Steinbock, *Phenomenology and Mysticism*, chapter 6.

60. See Steinbock, "Erotic Perception, History, and Shame."

61. Edmund Husserl, "Grundlegende Untersuchungen zum phänomenologischen Ursprung der Räumlichkeit der Natur," (1934) in *Philosophical Essays in Memory of Edmund Husserl*, ed. M. Garber (Cambridge, Mass.: Harvard University Press, 1940), 317.

62. Husserl, "Ursprung," 308.

63. See Edmund Husserl, *Zur Phänomenologie der Intersubjektivität: Texte aus dem Nachlaß, Dritter Teil: 1929–1935, Husserliana* 15, ed. Iso Kern (The Hague: Martinus Nijhoff, 1973), *Beilage* 10, text no. 14. See also Steinbock, "Limit-Phenomena and the Liminality of Experience."

64. See below, chapter 7.

65. Expressions I take from Jana Trajtelová and Art Luther, respectively. See below, chapter 7.

66. Alphonso Lingis, *The Imperative* (Bloomington: Indiana University Press, 1998).

67. See, for example, W. H. Walsh, "Pride, Shame and Responsibility," in *Philosophical Quarterly* 20, no. 78 (1970): 1–13.

68. See Steinbock, *Home and Beyond*, section 4.

69. Or it could move in the direction of a genuine asceticism, as Scheler

notes. Scheler, *Ressentiment*, 128–31. See also Margaret R. Miles, *Fullness of Life: Historical Foundations for a New Asceticism* (Philadelphia: Westminster, 1981).

70. Georges Canguilhem, *Le normal et le pathologique* (Paris: Presses Universitaires de France, 1966).

71. Or we could admire ourselves. Self-admiration may not issue in pride, however, but may issue in "vanity." Vanity, however, is not reducible to pride, because the former is a concern with how I appear to another, even if that "other" is myself. It does not go to the depths of the constitutive source of meaning as does pride, though vanity can have its roots in pride.

72. See also Gabriele Taylor, who also correctly identifies both characteristics of being proud of, namely, the recognition of value and the "relation of belonging." Taylor, *Pride, Shame and Guilt*, esp. 32, 38, 41. The difficulty I find in her analysis, however, concerns an implicit conflation at times with pride and being proud of.

73. See Scheler, *Vom Umsturz der Werte*, 18–19.

74. Michael Lewis, *Shame: The Exposed Self* (New York: Free Press, 1995), 78–79.

75. See Michael F. Mascolo and Kurt W. Fischer, "Developmental Transformations in Appraisals for Pride, Shame, and Guilt," in Tangney and Fischer, *Self-Conscious Emotions*, 64–113.

76. The situation can be modified of course if "gay pride" comes to mean "anti-heterosexual" or "white pride" means anti-black, anti-Jewish, anti-Catholic, and so on.

77. See Taylor, *Pride, Shame, and Guilt*, 47.

78. At a particularly poignant episode, Charlotte's so-called renewed "attention" to her daughter (at age fourteen) over one summer becomes an even more insidious form of pride.

79. See Carl W. Ernst, *Rūzbihān Baqlī: Mysticism and the Rhetoric of Sainthood in Persian Sufism* (Richmond Surrey, Eng.: Curzon, 1996), 44–45. And see Carl W. Ernst, *Words of Ecstasy in Sufism* (New York: SUNY Press, 1985).

80. Ernst, *Ruzbihan Baqlī*, 146.

81. Of course, insofar as we are dealing with an immediate present, it is somewhat misleading to speak of a temporal "orientation" because strictly speaking, there is no intentional directedness in a radical immediacy. But because we can speak of a temporal orientation in other emotional experiences treated in this work, I use the expression for the sake of continuity.

Chapter 2

1. G. W. F. Hegel, *Phänomenologie des Geistes* (Hamburg: Felix Meiner, 1952), esp. 145–50. Further, by deflecting vital death, anxiety enables death to be raised to a spiritual significance. As a possibility, death, as expressive of the power of "negativity," becomes the determining characteristic of a self-conscious being. Moreover, the burgeoning self-consciousness that has taken up the principle of negativity as it is found in life in general has made it its *own* principle

of negativity. In so doing, the negativity peculiar to life in general has become a *conscious* principle of negativity as something possible for self-consciousness. Finally, anxiety showed to the particular form of life in general the necessity of maintaining specific determinations and the essential role they have in the process of negativity.

2. See G. W. F. Hegel, *Enzyklopädie der philosophischen Wissenschaften im Grundrisse (1830), Erster Teil, Werke* 8 (Frankfurt am Main: Suhrkamp, 1970), 89–90.

3. Max Scheler, "Über Scham und Schamgefühl," in *Schriften aus dem Nachlass, Band 1: Zur Ethik und Erkenntneslehre* (Bern: Francke, 1957), 68. Rotenstreich also draws a comparison between Hegel and Scheler in his chapter on shame in Nathan Rotenstreich, *On the Human Subject: Studies in the Phenomenology of Ethics and Politics* (Springfield, Ill.: Charles C. Thomas, 1966), esp. 110ff.

4. Scheler, "Über Scham," 69. See also 145.

5. Ibid., 90.

6. Taylor, *Pride, Shame and Guilt*, 81. Accordingly, shame is not most fundamentally, as Taylor writes, "the emotion of self-protection." Nor does such self-protection imply the prevention of doing something in the future.

7. Scheler, "Über Scham," 82, 101, 141, 142.

8. Giorgio Agamben, *Means without End: Notes on Politics*, trans. Vincenzo Binetti and Cesare Casarino (Minneapolis: University of Minnesota Press, 2000), esp. 3–12, 37–45; and Giorgio Agamben, *Homo Sacer: Sovereign Power and Bare Life*, trans. Daniel Heller-Roazen (Stanford, Calif.: Stanford University Press, 1998), esp. 1–12, 15.

9. See Agamben, *Homo sacer*, 166ff. Agamben, *Means without End*, 37–45; *Homo Sacer*, 168; *Means without End*, 44: "To an order without localization (that is, the state of exception during which the law is suspended) corresponds now a localization without order (that is, the camp as permanent space of exception)."

The camp is the space of this coincidence in non-coincidence of bare life and politics, touching all modern life such that there is "no so-called democratic state today that is not compromised and up to its neck in such a massive production of human misery" (Agamben, *Means without End*, 133).

10. Agamben, *Homo Sacer*, 71–86, 114.

11. Ibid., 8.

12. Agamben writes that one of the paradoxes of the state of exception is that here it is impossible to distinguish the transgression of the law from the execution of the law. Thus, he writes, a person who goes for a walk during the curfew is not transgressing the law any more than the soldier who kills him is executing it (*Homo Sacer*, 57).

13. Karl Marx, "From Letter to Arnold Ruge" (1843), in *The Letters of Karl Marx*, trans. Saul K. Padover (Englewood Cliffs, N.J.: Prentice-Hall, 1979).

14. Agamben, *Means without End*, 132: "And it is a shame of this type, as it has been rightly pointed out, that we feel today when faced by too great a vulgarity of thought, when watching certain TV shows, when confronted with the faces of their hosts and with the self-assured smiles of those 'experts' who jovially lend their qualifications to the political game of the media."

NOTES TO PAGES 71–75

15. Giorgio Agamben, *Remnants of Auschwitz: The Witness and the Archive*, trans. Daniel Heller-Roazen (New York: Zone Books, 2002), 87–135.

16. It is no wonder, then, that Agamben finds Levinas's early account of shame to be exemplary.

17. Agamben, *Homo Sacer*, 8: "Politics therefore appears as the truly fundamental structure of Western metaphysics insofar as it occupies the threshold on which the relation between the living being and the *logos* is realized. In the "politicization" of bare life—the metaphysical task *par excellence*—the humanity of living man is decided."

18. Agamben, *Remnants of Auschwitz*, 106; see 107. "We can therefore propose a first, provisional definition of shame. It is nothing less than the fundamental sentiment of being a *subject*, in the two apparently opposed senses of this phrase: to be subjected and to be sovereign."

19. Agamben, *Remnants of Auschwitz*, for example, 121–23.

20. Ibid., 128–29.

21. Ibid., 133.

22. For example, see Jean-Luc Donnet, *L'humour et la honte* (Paris: Presses Universitaires de France, 2009), who treats this experience in relation to Conrad's *Lord Jim*. On the assessment of psychoanalytic literature on shame, see Lewis, *Shame: The Exposed Self*.

23. Taylor is correct in maintaining that it makes more sense to speak of different cases of shame, but not of different "kinds" of shame in the sense that the latter would have different structures. It is articulating their shared structure that is part of the phenomenological project. See Taylor, *Pride, Shame, and Guilt*, 54, 76.

See Guenter Harry Seidler, *In Others' Eyes: An Analysis of Shame*, trans. Andrew Jenkins (Madison, Conn.: International University Press, 2000), who gives a thorough account of shame from psychoanalytic perspectives with a basic phenomenological orientation in relation to subject-object relations.

24. For example, see Frankl's exposition of vocational meaning in Viktor E. Frankl, *Man's Search for Meaning*, trans. Ilse Lasch (Boston: Beacon, 2006), 104–5.

25. See Steinbock, *Home and Beyond*, esp. section 3.

26. See Taylor, *Pride, Shame, and Guilt*, 69–75. See also Deigh, "Shame and Self-Esteem," 225–26.

27. Lewis, *Shame: The Exposed Self*, 81–83. Nor, as Solomon maintains, is embarrassment different from shame and guilt by being an "innocent" emotion. See Solomon, *True to Our Feelings*, 93.

28. If an event in shame were not given with the sense of a constitutive abnormality—against the background of the experienced and even taken for granted "normal" internal coherence of the person—there would not be an experience of shame in the first place.

29. The Tree of Life is the Tree of the knowledge of Good and Evil. Adam and Eve do not yet know good and evil, so they cannot be expected to know right from wrong in the sense of being obedient. (Conversation, Joseph Steinbock.)

After they eat the fruit, God asks Adam and Eve what happened. Rather than taking responsibility, Adam blames Eve; Eve blames the serpent.

After the "Fall," Adam and Eve are said to appear before each other *as naked*, as exposed before each other, and this sense of exposure before another is ostensibly the motivation for their experience of shame. They subsequently fashioned loincloths to cover their "nakedness," their genitals or what in German are sometimes referred to as *"Schamteile"*—literally "shame parts," or what we would call "private parts." The term *Schamteile*, however, suggests that these are private parts that should have remained private, but as exposed to another are shame-inducing.

The most familiar interpretation of this parable, then, is that the experience of shame is motivated by my intimate *exposure before others*, and the experience of a *diremption* between how I am for myself, and how I appear before others. At the heart of this more fundamentally, according to Max Scheler, is the very diremption or tension between life (*Drang*) and spirit (*Geist*).

30. While I do observe certain similarities with shame between the "West" and the "East," I do not consider shame in this work from the perspective of the "East," even though one can glean certain common structures (as we will see below with regard to the issue of proleptic shame) and even though the East is commonly associated with shame. Certainly, we can find abundant examples that strike us as experiences of shame, from Dōgen's *Shōbōgenzō* (see Dōgen's *Shōbōgenzō: The Treasure House of the Eye of the True Teaching*, trans. Hubert Nearman [Mount Shasta, Calif.: Shasta Abbey, 2007]: for example, in the "Genjō Kōan," or in "Uji," in "Sansuikyō," in "Gyōji," or in "Bukkyō") to Taira Shigesuke in the *Bushido*. But I am hesitant to reduce the experience of shame in Dōgen, for example, to shame in the Abrahamic tradition without being sensitive to potential fundamental differences between the insight into generativity, on the one hand, and emptiness, on the other. See Steinbock, *Home and Beyond*, section 4. Also, by virtue of the analyses here, I reject the commonplace and prevalent distinction often made between a "shame culture" (the East) and a "guilt culture" (the West). See Ruth Benedict, *The Chrysanthemum and the Sword: Patterns of Japanese Culture* (Boston: Houghton Mifflin, 1946). It is interesting, however, as Dan Zahavi notes, that there are said to be 113 shame-related expressions in Chinese. See Dan Zahavi, "Self, Consciousness, and Shame," in *The Oxford Handbook of Contemporary Phenomenology*, ed. Dan Zahavi (Oxford: Oxford University Press, 2012), 304–23. But a comparative analysis that would take this into account requires a different study.

31. We could, however, interpret this not being in control here as what Williams could mean by his statement. See also Bernard Williams, *Shame and Necessity* (Berkeley: University of California Press, 1993), 220.

32. Even if I am objectively wrong about a circumstance in which I am involved in shame, and am revealed to myself as how I am in shame, there is still an inherent truth about the self-revelation; it is still meaningful to me as a revelation of Myself to Myself. In a self-reflection, however, I can delude myself. In self-awareness there is a mineness of experience which is not subject to delusion, but there is also a higher-level self-awareness in which I can be "wrong." A self-

revelation could impede upon a self-awareness (say, as a corrective) and reorient a self-awareness. (I am aware of myself as a great cyclist, but am revealed to myself in shame as a poor one; now I have a different self-awareness.)

33. See Steinbock, *Phenomenology and Mysticism*, chapter 8. That this dimension of shame is "primary" in relation to other kinds of shame, or that it is "primary" in relation to an experience like guilt does not mean that it comes first temporally, but that it is more fundamental to the person in and through its self-revelatory dimension.

34. See Scheler, "Über Scham," 148–49. Hart in his discussion of shame also holds that shame always presupposes original self-love. See James G. Hart, *Who One Is: Book 2: Existenz and Transcendental Phenomenology* (Boston: Springer, 2009), 338–51.

35. Scheler, "Über Scham," 142.

36. See ibid., 82, 100–1 142, 149.

37. Agamben, *Means without End*, 132.

38. Scheler, "Über Scham,"115.

39. *Euripides' Hippolytus*, trans. Michael R. Halleran (Newburyport, Mass.: Focus, 2001), v. 244–49.

40. As Dōgen writes in the *Shōbōgenzō:* "Without shame for past or present, and with a befuddled mind, they make a mishmash of what the Buddha said."

41. See Aristotle, *Rhetoric*, book 2, chapter 6, in *The Basic Works of Aristotle*, ed. and trans. Richard McKeon (New York: Random House, 1941).

42. Phil Hutchinson, *Shame and Philosophy* (New York: Palgrave Macmillan, 2008), 146–47.

43. Leon Wurmser, *The Mask of Shame* (Baltimore: Johns Hopkins University Press, 1981), 41–44. Taylor also goes in this direction when she writes of judging oneself adversely or of shame as a "sophisticated type of self-consciousness"; see *Pride, Shame, and Guilt*, 61, 67, 68.

44. I am not "stiff-necked" in shame, but appear before the other as supplicant, flushed. On blushing in shame, see John T. MacCurdy, "The Biological Significance of Blushing and Shame," *British Journal of Psychology* 21 (1930): 174–82.

45. In distinction to Michael Lewis, "Shame and Stigma," in *Shame: Interpersonal Behavior, Psychopathology, and Culture*, ed., Paul Gilbert and Bernice Andrews (New York: Oxford University Press, 1998), 126–27.

46. I find it interesting that James Hart rather spontaneously uses the expression "revelation" or being revealed to ourselves in the context of shame. See Hart, *Who One Is: Book 2*, esp. 338–51.

47. Auto-affection according to Agamben is only an analogy of shame, but not the definition of shame. See Agamben, *Remnants of Auschwitz*, 110.

48. See Scheler, "Ordo Amoris." The notion of the disordered heart (Scheler) corresponds in a different way to Johnston's and Malabou's contention that feelings can be other than what they are (mis)taken to be by the person having them. This, they contend, is one of the fundamental lessons of psychoanalysis. See Johnston and Malabou, *Self and Emotional Life*, 86.

49. This is probably what Helen Block Lewis is trying to suggest when she writes that shame is an "affective-cognitive state of low self-esteem," but in doing

so reduces shame to this function. See Helen Block Lewis, *The Role of Shame in Symptoms Formation* (Hillside, N.J.: Lawrence Erlbaum, 1987), 39. See also Jane Middelton-Moz, *Shame and Guilt: Masters of Disguise* (Deerfield Beach, Fla.: Health Communications, 1990).

50. See Lewis, *Shame: The Exposed Self,* esp. chapters 8 and 9.

51. James Gilligan, *Violence: Reflections on a National Epidemic* (New York: Vintage, 1997); see 48–65. See also Hart, *Who One Is: Book 2,* 347–51.

52. Conversation with Claudia Welz.

53. W. E. B Du Bois, *The Oxford W. E. B. Du Bois Reader,* ed. Eric J. Sundquist (New York: Oxford University Press, 1996), 72–76.

54. Aristotle, *Rhetoric,* book 2, chapter 6.

55. René Descartes, "The Passions of the Soul," in *The Philosophical Works of Descartes,* article CCV: "Shame, on the contrary, is a species of sadness, also founded on self-love, which proceeds from the apprehension or the fear which we possess of being blamed; besides that it is a species of modesty or humility and mistrust of self. For when we esteem ourselves so highly that we cannot imagine ourselves to be disdained by any, we cannot easily be ashamed."

56. Benedict de Spinoza, *Ethics,* in *On the Improvement of the Understanding, Ethics, Correspondence,* trans. R. H. M. Elwes (New York: Dover, 1955). See part 3, prop. 2, def. 3, prop. 9, prop. 30, prop. 39.

57. Immanuel Kant, *Immanuel Kant's "Anthropologie in pragmatischer Hinsicht"* (Lepizig: Immanuel Müller, 1833), §76. English translation, *Anthropology from a Pragmatic Point of View,* ed., and trans. Robert B. Louden (New York: Cambridge University Press, 2006), §76.

58. See also Lisa Guenther, "Shame and the Temporality of Social Life," in *Continental Philosophy Review* 44, no. 1 (2011): 23–39.

59. See Sartre, *L'être et néant,* 310–11; *Being and Nothingness,* 354.

60. Sartre, *L'être et néant,* 308; *Being and Nothingness,* 351. Shame, writes Sartre, is "the feeling of being finally what I am but elsewhere, over there for the Other." *L'être et néant,* 314; *Being and Nothingness,* 358. "And the one who I am—and who on principle escapes me—I am he *in the midst of the world* in so far as he escapes me." *L'être et néant,* 310; *Being and Nothingness,* 353. This is distinct from slavery, or the feeling of the alienation of all my possibilities, as well as from fear, or the feeling of being in danger before the Other's freedom. *L'être et néant,* 314; *Being and Nothingness,* 358.

61. Sartre, *L'être et néant* 306, 319; *Being and Nothingness,* 349, 364.

62. Sartre, *L'être et néant,* 319, *Being and Nothingness,* 364.

63. Sartre, *L'être et néant,* 307; *Being and Nothingness,* 350.

64. Sartre, *L'être et néant,* 310. *Being and Nothingness,* 352: "Shame—like pride—is the apprehension of myself as a nature although that very nature escapes me and is unknowable as such. Strictly speaking, it is not that I perceive myself losing my freedom in order to become a *thing,* but my nature is—over there, outside my lived freedom—as a given attribute of this being which I am for the Other." See Sartre, *L'être et néant,* 307; *Being and Nothingness,* 350.

65. When I experience shame, I experience the other's *expectation* (of me), whether this is objectively accurate or not. Phenomenologically, we are not ad-

ducing whether the other person actually expects something of us, but rather, in order for shame to be a matter of experience, I have to have experienced the expectation of the other or others. We don't experience their remembering, for example. But we do experience what another expects of us. Again, this is not to say that I experience his experiencing, but in the case of shame, I experience an expectation on his part (whether or not I am objectively correct about this).

66. This is not so say that such an interpersonal nexus will motivate shame. It may never happen. Or again, such an "I-You encounter" might provoke only embarrassment precisely because of an accepting, open attitude on the part of another. I might be before an esteemed music teacher, play a wrong note, and feel embarrassed. It is interesting, in fact, that quite often when one plays a wrong note, the musician or student will spontaneously apologize. This might be from two motivations: first, it does not do justice to the music, second, it might "offend" the listener.

67. Although Levinas does write in *Totality and Infinity* of the Other being ashamed of its nakedness, which is to say, the nudity of the face as being revealed and absolved from disclosure. The account in *Totality and Infinity* differs from the account of shame given in *De l'evasion*, which confines shame to an intra-subjective experience. Levinas describes shame as the experience of discovering myself as being chained to myself; it is expressive of being radically intimate with the whole of being, and yet incapable of escaping this presence; it is the experience of being consigned to what is always assumed, but as unable to assume it. This structure of subjectivity itself, which is exposed in shame, is something Levinas will call later "ontological solitude." See Agamben, *Remnants of Auschwitz*, 104–5; Emanuel Levinas, *De l'evasion* (Paris: Fata Morgana), esp., sections 5 and 6. Emmanuel Levinas, *Le temps et l'autre* (Paris: Fata Morgana, 1979), esp. 17–44.

68. Emmanuel Levinas, *Totalité et infini* (The Hague: Martinus Nijhoff, 1961), 55–56, 58. English translation by Alphonso Lingis, *Totality and Infinity* (Pittsburgh: Duquesne University Press, 1969), 83–84, 86.

69. Levinas, *Totalité*, 56; *Totality*, 84:

70. See Levinas, *Totalité*, 55–61; *Totality*, 83–89. "The freedom that can be ashamed of itself founds truth. . . ." Thus, revelation (the givenness of the Other) is founding for the disclosure of objects (or for another as an object).

71. The Other is *revealed* (as face, as the trace of God), not disclosed (as a thing meaningful in the context of things); it intrudes vertically, as it were, in the horizontal world of disclosure from "On High." In the face of the Other, I can discover my self-occupation—my freedom—as "murderous in its very exercise" because its initial impulse is to disclose the "Other" as a thing and appropriate it in terms of my self-occupation. But where the Other is given, revealed, as interlocutor (in what Levinas calls "Discourse" and "Desire"), as over whom I *can*-not have power, whom I cannot murder—I experience *shame*.

72. Levinas, *Totalité*, 230; *Totality*, 252.

73. Levinas, *Totalité*, 56; *Totality*, 84.

74. See Lewis, *Shame: The Exposed Self*. See also Taylor, *Pride, Shame and Guilt*.

75. Seidler, *In Others' Eyes*, 260.

76. While he does not put it precisely in these terms, I believe Zahavi would

agree with this analysis insofar as he claims that intrapersonal shame is founded in interpersonal shame. His point is that being thrown back on myself (intrapersonal) is not a sufficient characterization of shame. See Zahavi, "Self, Consciousness, Shame," 319–20. For me, the self-revelatory character of shame is interpersonal.

77. But this anonymity is secondary. As Deigh suggests, children experience shame without having discrete and stable aims and ideals against which the child would measure him- or herself. See Deigh, "Shame and Self-Esteem," 234. And see Fabrice Teroni and Julien A. Deonna, "Is Shame a Social Emotion?," in *Self-Evaluation: Affective and Social Grounds of Intentionality*, eds., Anita Konzelmann Ziv, Keith Lehrer & Hans Bernard Schmid (Dordrecht: Springer 2011), esp., sect. 6.

78. For example, at least in the West, a man might feel shame at crying openly. It is not the crying, but insofar as crying would be perceived as a sign of weakness or softness, and further, this is not valued as something masculine (the "icon" of rough and tough machismo, "the Marlboro Man," would hardly be seen crying). On the other extreme, if the Marlboro Man wanted to be perceived as sensitive, or if sensitivity or empathy, say, were valued for the Marlboro Man, crying would not be experienced as shameful. Odysseus, too, is ashamed to be seen crying.

79. This is a problematic treated in my *Vocations and Exemplars: The Verticality of Moral Experience*, in preparation.

80. See also, for example, Taylor's discussion in *Pride, Shame, and Guilt*, 58.

81. As in Robert Bresson's film of that name.

82. We can take the example of presenting a paper before others. (I thank Christina Gould for presenting this example.) See also Teroni and Deonna, "Is Shame a Social Emotion?," who make use of a similar example. In this scenario, one brackets the question of an "outside" other where the evident source of the diremption would be something like self and other. In fact, we could imagine an example in which I did not even care about others, or about what they thought. To make this example more extreme, all I might care about is myself and how I appear to myself, say, as in a usual expression of pride.

I still experience shame, but now the present others are bracketed, so to speak, and do not play a role in the experience of shame. They are not disappointed in my work; in fact, they are not even neutral. They are pleased with it; it even exceeded their demands, say. This is also interesting because with this example, shame is not a matter of fulfilling or not fulfilling demands. (I meet their demands, fulfill their expectations, I even exceed them.) It is true that, in distinction to shame, guilt might arise because I "owe" them more than they expect, beyond what they demand or can demand. Despite the others' appraisal, still, I am ashamed. I might be ashamed because even though they do not know it, I let them down; I have led them astray with my poor effort, and the fact that they are happy only makes it worse, because now I also feel guilty and responsible for having led them astray (they think work like this is good). This makes me all the more ashamed. I am ashamed that it came before them in this way, and I am ashamed "of myself," before myself. I might not be living up to God,

I might not be living up to my vocational self (Myself as given to myself); I might not be living up to my expectations of myself, to my teacher, to Socrates, or to the meaning of philosophy.

83. See my *Home and Beyond,* esp. section 4.

84. It is possible in this context to bring shame upon others as another social mode of shame. In this case, it is not I who experience shame because I do not measure up to perceived social expectations or norms. Rather, the shame takes place within the collective person (a community, a family), even if I as an individual never experience that shame. Thus, a team might lose an important match, and bring shame on the hometown or country, even if the team members themselves experience no such shame; or we could take the example of the youth who has a liaison outside of wedlock, bringing shame on a community with traditional "family" values.

85. We can also recognize a shame that is brought on me by another. This kind of shame has the same objective configuration as the one above, but is articulated from the side of the one who experiences shame. A public figure (an athlete, a public servant) has an affair (known or unknown to his or her spouse), but when it is made public, the injured party experiences shame because the affair says something about her or his person, makes her or him "look bad," perhaps that they were somehow inadequate, not as good a lover, a poor spouse. The individual feels shame whether or not the offending party does or not, and even if the "public" thinks that it is the offending party that should be ashamed.

In a different configuration, we could say that another "puts me to shame" because someone does something (the same thing) better than I do, and by comparison, another "makes me" feel shame.

86. See chapter 6, below.

87. Rainer Krause, "Psychodynamik der Emotionsstörungen," in *Enzyklopaedie der Psychologie,* ed. K. R. Scherer, vol. C/IV/3: Emotion (Goettingen: Hogrefe, 1990), 630–705.

88. Primo Levi, *The Reawakening,* trans. Stuart Woolf (New York: Simon and Schuster, 1965), 16.

89. Shamelessness could yield a "retroactive shame" that occurs when I initially do something with no consciousness of wrongdoing; in fact, it may even be counted by others as honorable. Only subsequently is the action denounced as, for example, dishonorable, and now possibly giving rise to shame. Obvious examples in this direction include participants in a war effort, whose efforts are revealed in a new light after the war. The point here is that the same action was at one time experienced as honorable, and at a later time retroactively constituted as shameful for myself and/or for others.

I think that Phil Hutchinson is off the mark when, relying on the example of Diogenes, he remarks that shamelessness is actually a product of *training* such that what he calls (misleadingly) "concepts" becomes fundamentally altered. See Phil Hutchinson, *Shame and Philosophy* (New York: Palgrave Macmillan, 2008), 106–8.

90. See also Spinoza, *Ethics,* prop. 58.

91. Lewis, *Shame: The Exposed Self:* "Denial and forgetting require a refo-

cusing, removing attention from the events that caused the shame or from the shaming experience itself" (139–40). See also 168–73 in relation to the etiology of MPD (multiple personality disorders).

92. It is possible that as I age, I become ashamed that I can no longer do what I used to do; I cannot compete as well in a sport, I am out of shape, and so on; I do not want to appear before others to avoid my shame, even though, strictly speaking, there is nothing I can do about it; still, if I experience shame, there is something of my participation in my aging, say, for which I am ashamed. It is not that another can forgive me, for there is nothing to forgive. But another can participate in altering the context. For example, I may no longer compete with young people, but with others "my age"; others might not hold me to the same standards that I hold myself (rightly or wrongly), and perceiving this, I no longer feel shame. The point is that what has modified is the *basic context* in which the shame emerged. It is not the liberation of the meaning of the past (as in repentance or forgiveness), but a modification of the present context.

93. See the example treated by Zahavi in "Self, Consciousness, and Shame."

94. Nietzsche, *Jenseits von Gut und Böse*, section 40. In the first instance, the overman wants to obscure the perception of himself by others—all the way down to the close circle of intimates—of any generous deeds. For these others might attribute some quality of goodness to him, rather than just letting the generosity be dynamically generous. The mystics, Nietzsche writes, had to have felt something of this very compulsion to conceal their actions or confuse those who want to imitate blindly. If there is going to be a diremption, then make it radical. Thus, the overman will issue contradictory messages, for the opposite of what appears holy might be the proper mask of a god in order to avoid shame.

In the second instance, Nietzsche tackles the most pernicious of witnesses, the self. Here, others are not the issue, but the self as other; my own memory is "another" which not only can misinterpret or expose myself to profound misunderstanding; through my memory, I can reify myself; witnessing my own good deeds I could become prideful, which is to say, fixate on "myself" as something (of import). The inventive overman, then, will conceal himself even from his own memory.

What is interesting in Nietzsche's example is that shame is not just a problem of exposure before others, but the exposure to the most intimate recesses of the self, where one's own memory is the culprit. It concerns the memory as a witness to my action. It is not that memory misremembers, but that it *retends a self,* as Husserl might say; it holds onto and potentially recalls a self; as such, it can give me a false, that is, static sense of self. For Nietzsche, shame is a spiritual matter that is not limited to my *being* with others, as it is with Sartre, but is already found as a problem in relation to the individual him- or herself, where I am another to myself. This testifies to a diremption of self within the self—and not just one between me and my body, or me and others.

95. Taira Shigesuke, *Code of the Samurai: A Modern Translation of the Bushido Shoshinsu,* trans. Thomas Cleary (Rutland, Vt.: Tuttle, 1999), esp. 18–21.

96. See also Williams, *Shame and Necessity,* 79, in relation to Odysseus: "The

NOTES TO PAGES 98-101

Avoidance of shame in these cases serves as a motive: you anticipate how you will feel if someone sees you."

97. On the role of shame in a democratic politics, see Christina Tarnopolsky, "Prudes, Perverts, and Tyrants: Plato and the Contemporary Politics of Shame," *Political Theory* 32, no. 4 (2004): 468–94.

Chapter 3

1. See especially St. Augustine, Bishop of Hippo, *The Works of St. Augustine: Answer to the Pelagians,* ed. John E. Rotelle, trans. Roland J. Teske (Hyde Park, N.Y.: New City, 1997), 40, 110, 167, 229–42, 457.

2. See Immanuel Kant, *Die Religion innerhalb der Grenzen der bloßen Vernunft,* ed. Karl Vorländer (Hamburg: Meiner Verlag, 1990), esp. 37–40, 77.

3. And early on at least acquires the meaning of "crime." See Hegel, *Phänomenologie des Geistes,* esp. 334–60.

4. Sigmund Freud, "Das Ich und das Es," in *Gesammelte Werke,* vol. 13, 4th ed. (Frankfurt am Main: Fischer Verlag, 1963), 235–89; and "Das ökonomishe Problem des Masochismus," in *Gesammelte Werke,* vol. 13, 369–89. See also "Einige Charaktertypen aus der psychoanalytischen Arbeit," in *Gesammelte Werke,* vol. 10, 3rd ed. (Frankfurt am Main: Fischer Verlag, 1963), 363–91; "Zeitgemässes über Krieg und Tod," in *Gesammelte Werke,* vol. 10, 323–55. See also Gerhart Piers and Milton B. Singer, *Shame and Guilt* (Springfield, Ill.: Charles C. Thomas, 1953).

5. M. L. Hoffman, "Development of Prosocial Motivation: Empathy and Guilt," in *The Development of Prosocial Behavior,* ed. N. Eisenberg (New York: Academic, 1982), 281–13. See also J. Kagan, *The Second Year: The Emergence of Self-Awareness* (Cambridge, Mass.: Harvard University Press, 1981).

6. R. Lazarus, *Emotion and Adaptation* (New York: Oxford University Press, 1991).

7. J. Tangney "Situational Determinants of Shame and Guilt in Young Adulthood," *Personality and Social Psychology Bulletin* 18: 199–206; H. B. Lewis "Guilt in Obsession and Paranoia," in *Emotions in Personality and Psychopathology,* ed. C. E. Izard (New York: Plenum, 1979), 399–414; E. J. Wertheim and J. C. Schwarz, "Depression, Guilt, and Self-Management of Pleasant and Unpleasant Events," *Journal of Personality and Social Psychology* 45: 884–89; Roy F. Baumeister et al., "Interpersonal Aspects of Guilt: Evidence from Narrative Studies," in *Self-Conscious Emotions: The Psychology of Shame, Guilt, Embarrassment, and Pride,* ed. June Price Tangney and Kurt W. Fischer (New York: Guilford, 1995), 255–73.

8. See Harald G. Wallbott and Klaus R. Scherer, "Cultural Determinants in Experiencing Shame and Guilt, in Tangney and Fischer, *Self-Conscious Emotions,* 465–87; Kazuo Miyake and Kosuke Yamazaki, "Self-Conscious Emotions, Child Rearing, and Child Psychopathology in Japanese Culture," in Tangney and Fischer, *Self-Conscious Emotions,* 488–504; Mille R. Creighton, "Revisiting Shame and Guilt Cultures: A Forty-Year Pilgrimage," in *Ethos* 18, no. 3 (1990): 279–307.

9. Karl Jaspers, *Die Schuldfrage: Ein Beitrag zur deutschen Frage* (1947; Mu-

nich: Piper Verlag, 1965). English translation, *The Question of German Guilt*, trans. E. B. Ashton (New York: Fordham University Press, 2000).

10. Jaspers, *Schuldfrage*, 10–11; *The Question of German Guilt*, 25–26. See also Sami Philström, who also understands guilt in this metaphysical sense that he calls "transcendental." See Sami Philström, *Transcendental Guilt: Reflections on Ethical Finitude* (New York: Lexington Books, 2011).

11. Translation slightly modified.

12. Jaspers, *Schuldfrage*, 15; *The Question of German Guilt*, 30. See also Merold Westphal, *God, Guilt, and Death: An Existential Phenomenology of Religion* (Bloomington: Indiana University Press, 1987).

13. The status of guilt as a moral emotion vs. a legal concept is ambiguous in Taylor—who wants to contrast shame and guilt by suggesting that guilt *is* (and not merely can be) a legal concept. See Taylor, *Pride, Shame, and Guilt*, 85, 89.

14. Although I regard guilt as an emotion, for reasons specified above, for guilt interpreted as a foundational affect, see Johnston and Malabou, *Self and Emotional Life*, 75–101.

15. Eugène Minkowski, *Lived Time: Phenomenological and Psychopathological Studies*, trans. Nancy Metzel (Evanston, Ill.: Northwestern University Press, 1970), 59.

16. Note also that such an experience of complicity is ultimately an intersubjective phenomenon.

17. See especially Fyodor Dostoevsky, *The Brothers Karamoazov*, trans. Richard Pevear and Larissa Volokhonsky (New York: Vintage Books, 1991); and Fyodor Dostoevsky, *Crime and Punishment*, trans. Richard Pevear and Larissa Volokhonsky (New York: Vintage Books, 1993).

18. Though guilt is mine, we cannot assert, as does Ricoeur, that guilt is an individual phenomenon in relation to sin which is collective, such that there is a phenomenology of guilt and an ontology of sin. Guilt is an individual and a collective experience, and sin is also susceptible to individual experience and phenomenological description. Paul Ricoeur, *The Symbolism of Evil*, trans. Emerson Buchanan (Boston: Beacon, 1967), 107. See also Paul Ricoeur, *Finitude et culpabilité* (Paris: Éditions Montaigne, 1960).

19. Jaspers, *Schuldfrage*, 49–50; *The Question of German Guilt*, 65–66.

20. Jaspers, *Schuldfrage*, 49; *The Question of German Guilt*, 65.

21. Jaspers, *Schuldfrage*, 49; *The Question of German Guilt*, 66; translation slightly modified.

22. See the accounts reported by Minkowski, *Lived Time*, 285.

23. See Husserl, *Analyses Concerning Passive and Active Synthesis*, 129, 458, 467. Although a retention is susceptible to a "retroactive crossing-out" in the case of a revision of the objective sense (see part 2, §7).

24. This is what Husserl calls in the *Analyses* the "unconscious"; see especially 201, 214, 221.

25. In terms of genetic development, cognitive research has shown that a sense of personal responsibility can emerge as early as the second year of life. See Carolyn Zahn-Waxler and Joann Robinson, "Empathy and Guilt: Early Origins of Feelings of Responsibility," in Tangney and Fischer, *Self-Conscious Emo-*

tions, 143–73. This is earlier than Darwin's observation of guilt at two years and seven months of age. See Darwin, *The Expression of the Emotions in Man and Animals,* 262–63.

For us this means, however, that guilt is an emotion that arises as a possibility within the global becoming of person. It need not arise at all or at a specific time, but—if it is indeed the same experience under consideration—it has been observed with consistency during the second year of life.

26. K. M. McGraw, "Guilt Following Transgression: An Attribution of Responsibility Approach," *Journal of Personality and Social Psychology,* vol. 53 (1987): 247–56.

27. Bernhard Waldenfels, *Antwortregister* (Suhrkamp: Frankfurt am Main, 1994), see esp. 320–98.

28. See, for example, the analysis by Roy F. Baumeister, Arlene M. Stillwell, and Todd F. Heatherton, "Interpersonal Aspects of Guilt: Evidence from Narrative Studies," in Tangney and Fischer, *Self-Conscious Emotions,* 255–73.

29. See Husserl, *Analyses Concerning Passive and Active Synthesis,* 61. And see 41: "And it calls out to us, as it were, in these referential implications: 'There is still more to see here, turn me so you can see all my sides, let your gaze run through me, draw closer to me, open me up, divide me up; keep on looking me over again and again, turning me to see all sides. You will get to know me like this, all that I am, all my surface qualities, all my inner sensible qualities,' etc."

30. Alfred North Whitehead, *Process and Reality* (New York: Free Press, 1978); Alfred North Whitehead, *Science and the Modern World* (New York: Free Press, 1953); Alfred North Whitehead, *Adventures of Ideas* (New York: Free Press, 1961); Anthony J. Steinbock, "Whitehead's 'Theory' of Propositions," *Process Studies* 18, no. 1 (Spring 1989): 19–29.

31. Lingis, *The Imperative.*

32. But ultimately, the demand, where guilt is concerned, issues from another (who sets the norm or standard), even if it seems to come from "myself."

33. Guilt is a response to a perceived demand, even if another person does not express it as such or never even thought of it; I can always (rightly or wrongly) impute it to another. We can think of Lance Armstrong feeling guilty about coming in third at the Olympics, apologizing to his team when they did not expect him to win it anyway, and moreover when one of his teammates won it.

34. See Levinas, *Totalité et infini;* Levinas, *Totality and Infinity.*

35. Taylor, *Pride, Shame, and Guilt,* 87, 90, 98. See John Rawls, *A Theory of Justice* (Cambridge, Mass.: Harvard University Press, 2005), 474.

36. Instead, we would have to consider atonement as the appropriate response for transgression of a moral demand. This is why one at most is responsive and can be responsible.

37. Martin Buber, *Schuld und Schuldgefühle* (Heidelberg: Verlag Lambert Schneider, 1958), 67. English translation by Paul Roazen, *Martin Buber on Psychology and Psychotherapy,* ed. Judith Buber Agassi (New York: Syracuse University Press, 1999), 137.

38. Ricoeur, *The Symbolism of Evil,* 107. See also Vladimir Jankélévitch, *Philosophie morale,* ed. Françoise Schwab (Paris: Flammarion, 1998), esp. 321–39.

39. For example, in the Catholic tradition, one can *experience* a difference in the weight of a venial sin or a mortal sin.

40. Ricoeur, *The Symbolism of Evil*, 106–7.

41. Taylor, *Pride, Shame, and Guilt*, 97.

42. See Max Scheler, *Vom Ewigen im Menschen*, in *Gesammelte Werke*, vol. 5., 4th ed., ed. Maria Scheler (Bern: Francke, 1954), 40.

43. See Rudolf Otto, *The Idea of the Holy*, trans. John W. Harvey (New York: Oxford University Press, 1958), 10–23. And see Westphal's treatment of existential guilt and its relation to the Sacred as *mysterium tremendum* in *God, Guilt, and Death*, esp. 69–89. However, I do not view guilt fundamentally in this way vis-à-vis the possibility of punishment.

44. Martin Heidegger, *Sein und Zeit* (Tübingen: Niemeyer, 1979), 289–90.

45. Ibid., 284.

46. Ibid., 287, 294.

47. See, for example, Karen Caplovitz Barrett, "A Functionalist Approach to Shame and Guilt," in Tangney and Fischer, *Self-Conscious Emotions*, 25–63.

48. Heidegger, *Sein und Zeit*, 283–84.

49. Ibid., 285: Heidegger writes, "But freedom *is* only in the choice of one possibility, which is to say, in bearing the weight of not having chosen, and also not being able to choose the other possibilities."

50. For a more detailed explication, see Steinbock, *Phenomenology and Mysticism*, chapter 6.

51. Heidegger, *Sein und Zeit*, 187–88. And not, as it is mistakenly interpreted, given as an individual alone (*allein*) in relation to other individuals. Thus, the individualizing down to itself in anxiety allows Dasein to be with others who are also "there" authentically, as there in a co-being-there.

52. Ibid., 286.

53. Ibid., 293.

54. Ibid., 287.

55. Ibid., 296–97, 288.

56. Claude Romano, *Au coeur de la raison, la phénoménologie* (Paris: Gallimard, 2010).

57. Ibid., 699.

58. Ibid., 700–701.

59. Ibid., 701–2.

60. Ibid., 709. He writes: "Here we have a new kind of possibility, an 'existential' possibility, in Heidegger's terminology. Something is 'possible' in the existential sense if it is compatible with the sort of 'being' (of entity, of *Dasein*) I aspire to be—if it is in keeping with the way I understand myself, with the way I see or envision my own existence. In other words, something is possible, in the existential sense of the term, if it is in conformity with a life project, or a project of existence." Translation by Michael Smith.

61. Ibid., 701–3.

62. Ibid., 712: "Existence is such that one must project oneself into it and make it possible in this or that way in order for it to be the *existence* that it is." Translation by Michael Smith.

63. See Paulo Freire, *Pedagogy of the Oppressed,* trans. Myra Bergman Ramos (New York: Continuum, 2001).

64. I do not explicate this inter-personal dimension of vocation here, but do determine this sense of vocation in *Vocations and Exemplars*.

65. On the passive character of emergence in Heidegger's thought, see Arthur R. Luther, "Original Emergence in Heidegger and Nishida," in *Philosophy Today* 26, no. 4/4 (1982): 345–56.

66. Frankl, *Man's Search for Meaning,* 79–80.

67. Buber, *Schuld und Schuldgefühle,* 35–42; *Martin Buber on Psychology and Psychotherapy,* 123–26. Buber understands conscience as the capacity to distinguish between past and future actions which should be approved and those which should be disapproved.

68. Buber, *Schuld und Schuldgefühle,* 40–42; *Martin Buber on Psychology and Psychotherapy,* 125–26.

69. Buber, *Schuld und Schuldgefühle,* 44; *Martin Buber on Psychology and Psychotherapy,* 127: "What he is now obliged to do cannot be accomplished in any other place than in the abyss of I-with-me, and it is just this abyss that must be illuminated. . . . As for the illumination of essence, it is in its most real moments not even a monologue, much less a real conversation between an ego and a superego: all speech is exhausted; what takes place here is the mute shudder of self-being."

70. Buber, *Schuld und Schuldgefühle,* 63–64; *Martin Buber on Psychology and Psychotherapy,* 135–36.

71. Scheler, *Formalismus,* 482; Scheler, *Formalism,* 490.

72. See Teroni and Deonna, "Differentiating Shame from Guilt," 725–40.

73. Ibid., 726–28. Taylor, too, sees that shame tends to bear on the shape of who I am and guilt on what I have done. Teroni and Deonna, for their part, hold that the first and the fourth criteria do not have any constitutive truth, but exhibit only typicality effects. However, in support of the second and third, they contend that the relation between shame and guilt is not conflictual, but instead issues in a unified view of them. See also Teroni and Deonna, "Differentiating Shame from Guilt," 736.

74. Compare Benedict, *The Chrysanthemum and the Sword,* and Creighton, "Revisiting Shame and Guilt Cultures: A Forty-Year Pilgrimage," *Ethos,* 18, 279–307.

75. See Scheler, *Vom Ewigen im Menschen,* 40, 42.

76. Ibid., 40, 42.

77. Buber, *Schuld und Schuldgefühle,* 67; *Martin Buber on Psychology and Psychotherapy,* 137.

78. Scheler, *Vom Ewigen im Menschen,* 55.

Chapter 4

A previous version of the chapter on repentance has appeared as "Repentance as a Response to Violence in the Dynamic of Forgiveness" in Michael Staudigl, ed., *Phenomenologies of Violence* (Leiden-Boston: Brill, 2013), 181–205.

1. Simon Wiesenthal, *The Sunflower: On the Possibilities and Limits of Forgiveness*, trans. H. A. Pichler (New York: Schocken Books, 1998).
2. See Scheler, *Formalismus*, 522–23.
3. "*Vayomer Adonai, salachti kid'varecha*," "And God said, I have forgiven you, as I have promised" (Numbers 14:19–20).
4. Scheler, *Vom Ewigen*, 50.
5. Spinoza, *Ethics*, see 4, prop. 54: "Repentance is not a virtue, or does not arise from reason; but he who repents of an action is doubly wretched or infirm. . . . For, if all men who are a prey to emotion were all equally proud, they would shrink from nothing, and would fear nothing. . . . Indeed those who are a prey to these emotions [humility, repentance, and reverence] may be led much more easily than others to live under the guidance of reason."
See also *Repentance: A Comparative Perspective*, ed. Amitai Etzoni with David E. Carney (Rowman and Littlefield, 1997).
6. Husserl, *Analyses Concerning Passive and Active Synthesis;* Merleau-Ponty, *Phénoménologie de la perception;* Minkowski, *Lived Time.*
7. See Husserl, *Analyses Concerning Passive and Active Synthesis,* esp. div. 3, and appendix 8.
8. We distinguish this sense of the past in time from, for example, the Levinasian past as the "Immemorial," the "Father," or the "Origin" which constitutes us (as "being Jewish") in terms of election and vocation. Emmanuel Levinas, *Confluences*, 1947, année 7, nos. 15–17, 253–64. English translation, Mary Beth Mader, "Being Jewish," *Continental Philosophy Review* 40, no. 3 (2007): 205–10.
9. Natalie Depraz, in a different context, refers to the temporality of *metanoia* as a reflexive conversion, as a "preparatory time," which is also the time of verbal confession:

"Ainsi, le temps préparatoire correspond bien à ce mouvement de conversion réflexive dont parle Husserl, par lequel je me déprends des objets externes et fais retour sur mes actes, les examine pour eux-mêmes; le temps proprement dit de la confession verbale au prêtre se donne comme un geste de suspension de mon système de défense, où l'on se perd soi-même de vue: il renvoie très clairement à une *épochè* . . . ; le temps immédiatement subséquent donne naissance à un laisser-être ou à un lâcher-prise qui met en mouvement l'ouverture de l'ego et le processus d'une possible libération de soi-même." Natalie Depraz, *Le corps glorieux: Phénoménologie pratique de la Philocalie des Pères du désert et des Pères de l'Eglise* (Louvain: Éditions Peeters, 2008).

10. See Steinbock, *Phenomenology and Mysticism,* esp., chapters 2–4.
11. Kant, *Die Religion*, 51–52. English translation, *Religion within the Limits of Reason Alone* (New York: Harper Torchbooks, 1960).
12. See Jankélévitch, *Philosophie morale,* esp. 117–27.
13. Descartes seems to misidentify repentance, thinking we could anticipate it, given a lack of resolution or feeble use of free will. See *The Philosophical Works of Descartes,* "The Passions of the Soul," Third Part, art. clix.
14. Dostoevsky, *Crime and Punishment.*
15. *Martin Buber, Tales of the Hasidim,* trans. Olga Marx (New York: Schocken Books, 1991), 315; text slightly modified.

NOTES TO PAGES 148-154

16. Shakespeare, *Hamlet*, act 3, scene 3, ll. 36-72.

17. Karl Marx, *Grundrisse der Kritik der politischen Ökonomie*, in *Karl Marx, Friedrich Engels Werke*, vol. 42: *Ökonomische Manuskripte 1857/1858* (Berlin: Dietz Verlag, 1983), 59. English translation by Marin Nicolaus, *Grundrisse* (London: Penguin Books, 1973), 123.

18. Isaiah 58:2-7:

. . .

"Why, when we fasted, did You not see?
When we starved our bodies, did You pay no heed?"
Because on your fast day
You see to your business
And oppress all your laborers!
Because you fast in strife and contention,
And you strike with a wicked fist!
Your fasting today is not such
As to make your voice heard on high.
Is such the fast I desire,
A day for men to starve their bodies?
Is it bowing the head like a bulrush
And lying in sackcloth and ashes?
Do you call that a fast,
A day when the Lord is favorable?
No, this is the fast I desire:
To unlock fetters of wickedness,
And untie the cords of the yoke
To let the oppressed go free;
To break off every yoke.
It is to share your bread with the hungry,
And to take the wretched poor into your home;
When you see the naked, to clothe him,
And not to ignore your own kin.

19. Scheler, *Vom Ewigen*, 41.

20. We can think here of the example from Gandhi. He instructs the man who killed another boy's father to take care of that man's son, serving in some way the one who has been injured. The extent to which the man cared about the dying Gandhi or listened to him is the extent to which we could speak of a repentant heart, at the very least, even though he may not have been explicitly or completely repentant. It is here that acts of atonement could themselves spur a guilt about the past offense or open one up to a more profound repentance, where repentance could at last "begin."

21. Scheler, *Vom Ewigen*, 38, 42.

22. Notice also that while apology is a linguistic act, repentance is "pre-linguistic" or "a-linguistic." Repentance does not require a verbal statement to be lived through in the way, say, a promise does.

23. Scheler writes that one experiences repentance in relation to a "law" that is given as holy, and in such a way that we could not have prescribed to

ourselves. For this reason, repentance gets it full meaning and is fully articulate within a *religious* context and within religious experiencing. See Scheler, *Vom Ewigen*.

24. See Steinbock, *Phenomenology and Mysticism*, chapter 7.

25. This is a topic I am preparing in another work, *Earth as Ground: The Verticality of Ecological Experience*.

26. See for example, Michael Barber, *Equality and Diversity: Phenomenological Investigations of Prejudice and Discrimination* (Amherst, N.Y.: Humanity Books, 2001).

27. "The repentant sinner should strive to do good with the same faculties with which he sinned. . . . With whatever part of the body he sinned, he should now engage in good deeds. If his feet had run to sin, let them now run to the performance of the good. If his mouth had spoken falsehood, let it now be opened in wisdom. Violent hands should now open in charity. . . . The trouble-maker should now become a peace-maker." Rabbi Johan Gerondi, *The Gates of Repentance*, trans. Yaakov Feldman (Northvale, N.J.: Jason Aronson, 1999).

28. While forgiveness is interpersonally relevant, I do not take up forgiveness thematically in this work, primarily because it does not give itself as a moral *emotion* (as do, say, loving, hating, humility).

Chapter 5

Parts of this chapter have appeared previously in abridged versions: "Time, Otherness, and Possibility in the Experience of Hope" in *Issues in Interpretation Theory*, ed. Pol Vandevelde (Milwaukee, Wisc.: Marquette University Press, 2006): 271–89; and "A Phenomenology of Despair," *International Journal of Philosophical Studies* 15, no. 3 (2007): 435–51.

1. See Albert Camus, *Le mythe de Sisyphe* (Paris: Gallimard, 1942). English translation, *Myth of Sisyphus* (New York: Vintage International, 1991). In my "Introduction" to *Vocations and Exemplars*, I explicate Camus with respect to secular and ethical humanism vis-à-vis moral experience.

2. Søren Kierkegaard, *Works of Love*, ed. and trans. Howard V. Hong and Edna H. Hong (Princeton, N.J.: Princeton University Press, 1995); Søren Kierkegaard, *The Sickness unto Death: A Christian Psychological Exposition for Upbuilding and Awakening*, ed. and trans. Howard V. Hong and Edna H. Hong (Princeton, N.J.: Princeton University Press, 1980).

3. Ernst Bloch, *Daz Prinzip Hoffnung*, 3 vols. (Frankfurt am Main: Suhrkamp, 1959).

4. Gabriel Marcel, *Homo Viator: Introduction to a Metaphysic of Hope*, trans. Emma Craufurd (New York: Harper Torchbooks, 1962). And see Gabriel Marcel, "Desire and Hope," trans. Nathaniel Lawrence, in *Readings in Existential Phenomenology*, ed. Nathaniel Lawrence and Daniel O'Connor (Englewood Cliffs, N.J.: Prentice Hall, 1967), 277–85.

5. Paul Ricoeur, *Figuring the Sacred: Religion, Narrative, and Imagination*, ed. Mark I. Wallace, trans. David Pellauer (Minneapolis: Fortress, 1995). See

also Rebecca K. Huskey, *Paul Ricoeur on Hope: Expecting the Good* (New York: Peter Lang, 2009).

6. Martin Heidegger, *Phänomenologie des religiösen Lebens*, Gesamtausgabe 60 (Frankfurt am Main : Klostermann, 1995); Martin Heidegger, *The Phenomenology of the Religious Life*, trans. Matthias Fritsch and Jennifer Anna Gosetti-Ferencei (Bloomington: Indiana University Press, 2004).

7. Jürgen Moltmann, *Theologie der Hoffnung: Untersuchungen zur Begründung und zu den Konsequenzen einer christlichen Eschatologie* (Munich: Christian Kaiser, 1965).

8. See the early phenomenological treatment of hope (1937) by Heinrich Middendorf, *Phänomenologie der Hoffnung* (Würzburg: Königshausen & Neumann, 1985). See also the contemporary phenomenological work on this topic by Klaus Held, "Idee einer Phänomenologie der Hoffnung," in *Interdisziplinäre Perspektiven der Phänomenologie* (Dordrecht: Springer, 2006), 126–41.

9. In contrast to Schmacher/Pieper's contention. See Bernard Schumacher, *Josef Pieper and the Contemporary Debate on Hope*, trans. D. C. Schindler (New York: Fordham University Press, 2003), esp. 66–96. There are, however, similar distinctions made with respect to expectation and hope.

10. On this distinction between passive and active, see Husserl, *Analyses Concerning Passive and Active Synthesis*.

11. Accordingly, I agree with Klaus Held's appraisal concerning the uniqueness of hoping in relation both to expectation and as we will see, optimism. See Held, "Idee einer Phänomenologie der Hoffnung."

12. There are of course other modalizations: doubt, negation, reaffirmation, and so on.

13. Moltmann, *Theologie der Hoffnung*, esp. chapter 2; English translation, James W. Leitch, *Theology of Hope: On the Ground and the Implications of a Christian Eschatology* (Minneapolis: Fortress, 1993), esp. chapter 2. See also Jürgen Moltman, *The Future of Hope: Theology as Eschatology*, ed. Frederick Herzog (New York: Herder and Herder, 1970).

14. I think that this is what Held is trying to evoke when he writes of the "Gefühl des Urvertrauens in den Fortbestand der Welt." See Held, "Idee einer Phänomenologie der Hoffnung."

15. Otto, *The Idea of the Holy*, 10–23.

16. See Steinbock, *Phenomenology and Mysticism*.

17. There is thus not only an inter-Personal dependence, but an interpersonal one as well in the experience of hope.

18. I do not mean this in Levinas's sense of a movement initiated from the Other. Desire here would correspond roughly to what he means by "need."

19. See also Marcel, "Desire and Hope," 278–79.

20. I am given to myself as sustainable by this ground. On the one hand, being sustainable in the matter of who I become means that I am not determined in advance. If it were given as determined, neither hope nor fatalism could emerge as possible experiences (a point I will come back to below—since hopelessness presupposes hope). On the other hand, being sustain*able* in the matter of who I can become means developing "my way" is sustainable on the

basis of hope. If my emergence were arbitrary (say, in the case of vitalism), there would be no sustainability for "my way," no experience of a "vocation," and no "ground" for the hope of the sustainability of my way, and no basis for experience of hope to emerge.

21. Nicholas Lash, *A Matter of Hope: A Theologian's Reflections on the Thought of Karl Marx* (Notre Dame, Ind.: University of Notre Dame Press, 1984), 266–68.

22. See Max Horkheimer and Theodor W. Adorno, *Dialectic of Enlightenment,* trans. John Cumming (New York: Continuum, 1982).

23. See Steinbock, *Phenomenology and Mysticism,* chapter 8.

24. St. Teresa, *Obras,* 106–7; *Collected Works,* vol. 1, chapter 19.11.

25. See Steinbock, *Phenomenology and Mysticism,* "Introduction," and chapter 5.

26. Lash, *A Matter of Hope,* 269–70.

27. I take this expression from Michael Smith, who offered this distinction.

28. See Marcel, who similarly understands the temporality of hope as an "active waiting." Marcel, "Desire and Hope," 280–81.

29. Hesiod, *Works and Days and Theogony,* trans. Stanley Lombardo (Indianapolis: Hackett, 1993).

30. Aristotle, *Nicomachean Ethics,* III, *Physics,* VII, in *The Basic Works of Aristotle.* However, Aristotle is cited by Diogenes Laertius as regarding hope to be nothing but a waking dream. See Diogenes Laertius, *Lives of Eminent Philosophers,* trans. R. D. Hicks, volume 1, (Cambridge, Mass.: Loeb Classical Library, 1925), book 5, chapter 1.

31. St. Augustine, *Enchiridion: On Faith, Hope, and Love,* trans. J. B. Shaw (Washington, D.C.: Regnery, 1996), VIII.

32. St. Thomas Aquinas, *Summa Theologiae,* vol. 33, trans. W. J. Hill (New York: McGraw-Hill, 1966), 2a2ae, Q. 17, art. 1, 5.

33. Spinoza, *Ethics,* part 3, prop. 18, note 2.

34. John Locke, *An Essay Concerning Human Understanding,* ed. Alexander Campbell Fraser (New York: Dover, 1959), book 2, chapter 20.

35. In Dante's "Paradise," for example, there is no hope (no longer hope) because hope is fulfilled. (To hope for anything beyond what is given in paradise would be a sign of pride and mitigate the attitude of humility and acceptance peculiar to paradise.)

36. Camus, *Le mythe de Sisyphe,* 126; *The Myth of Sisyphus,* 91.

37. Kierkegaard, *The Sickness unto Death.*

38. This expressive, purposive activity, as witnessed in the unhampered persistence of the boy through the creation of the gigantic bell, signaled or "rang" to him the significance of creation in spite of all else. It struck him on the level of his despair and called him to himself and out of despair.

Part 3

1. Annette C. Baier, "What Do Women Want in a Moral Theory?" *Noûs* 19, no. 1 (1985): 53–63.

2. See my gesture in this direction, "Perception érotique, histoire et honte" ["Erotic Perception, History, and Shame"], French translation by Pierre-Jean Renaudie, *Alter: Revue de Phénoménologie* (2011), 175–94.

3. See, for example, the work of Sara Heinämaa, for whom generosity acknowledges the other's contribution of meaning: "Generosity and Wonder: Two Future-Oriented Emotions," unpublished manuscript.

Chapter 6

An earlier, abridged version of the chapter on trust appeared as "Temporality, Transcendence, and Being Bound to Others in Trust" in *Trust, Sociality, Selfhood* (Tübingen: Mohr Siebeck, 2010), ed. Arne Grøn and Claudia Welz: 83–102.

1. See, for example, J. David Lewis and A. Weigert, "Trust as a Social Reality," *Social Forces* 63 (1985): 967–85; Niklas Luhmann, *Trust and Power* (Chichester: Wiley, 1979); R. Peters, V. Covello, and D. McCallum, "The Determinants of Trust and Credibility in Environmental Risk Communication: An Empirical Study," *Risk Analysis* 17 (1997): 43–54; O. Renn and D. Levine, "Credibility and Trust in Risk Communication: An Empirical Study," in *Communicating Risks to the Public: International Perspectives,* ed. R. Kasperson and P. Stallen (Boston: Kluwer, 1991), 175–218; J. Scholz, "Adaptive Political Attitudes: Duty, Trust, and Fear as Monitors of Tax Policy" (with Mark Lubell), *American Journal of Political Science,* 42 (1998): 903–20; A. Markovits and K. Deutsch, *Fear of Science—Trust in Science: Conditions for Change in the Climate of Opinion* (Cambridge, Mass.: Oelgeschlager, Gunn & Hain, 1980). See also Amy Mullin, "Trust, Social Norms, and Motherhood," *Journal of Social Philosophy* 36, no. 3 (2005): 316–30.

2. Reliability is a normatively significant mode of experience in this respect. See Steinbock, *Home and Beyond,* section 3.

3. Giving oneself over to the will of God is expressed in the Islamic tradition in the trial with Ishmael (*Qur'an,* 37:100–107).

4. The social dimension to trust is an implicit starting point in, for example, Lewis and Weigert, "Trust as a Social Reality," 967–985; Mullin, "Trust, Social Norms, and Motherhood," and Luhmann, *Trust and Power.*

5. Strictly speaking, even if a person were factually alone, the individual could never be conceived as separate or isolated (even though one can have experiences of exclusion or ostracism from a group; in fact, even isolation presupposes an intention toward others). See Scheler, *Formalismus,* 511.

6. I do not consider in the context of this work other aspects of trust, like trusting the stray dog.

7. Again, in a generative phenomenology we can understand the temptation to associate familiarity and the familiar as a mode of normality (in German *Vertrautheit*) with trust (*Vertrauen*), but there is an essential independence of trust in relation to familiarity, as we will see.

8. See John G. Holmes and John K. Rempel, "Trust in Close Relationships," *Review of Personality and Social Psychology,* vol. 10 (1989): 187–220; see esp. 188.

9. See Rochat, who basically, and misleadingly, I think, defines trust in

terms of reliability. Philippe Rochat, "Trust in Early Development," in *Trust, Sociality, Selfhood,* ed. Arne Grøn and Claudia Welz (Tübingen: Mohr Siebeck, 2010), 31–43.

10. Alphonso Lingis, *The First Person Singular* (Evanston, Ill.: Northwestern University Press, 2007). See also Alphonso Lingis, *Trust* (Minneapolis: University of Minnesota Press, 2004). On the immediacy of trust, see Arne Grøn, "Trust, Sociality, Selfhood," in Grøn and Welz, *Trust, Sociality, Selfhood,* 13–30.

11. See, for example, Isaacs et al., "Faith, Trust and Gullibility," *International Journal of Psychoanalysis,* vol. 44 (1963): 461–69.

12. Kelly Oliver also points out that the German term *Pflicht,* which is often translated as "duty" (Kant) also means more literally "pledge" or "plight," and is accordingly related to the Middle High German *Pflëgen,* or care. Thus, in this context, trust as giving myself over to another can be at the root of a "pledge," and for Kant, the basis of duty. See Kelly Oliver, "The Plight of Ethics," in *The Fiftieth Anniversary Special Issue with the Society for Phenomenology and Existential Philosophy: Journal of Speculative Philosophy* 26, no. 2 (2012), esp. 119–20.

13. I thank Christian Lotz for bringing this observation to my attention.

14. See my *Home and Beyond,* esp. section 4.

15. See, for example, Markovits and Deutsch, *Fear of Science.* And see T. Porter, *Trust in Numbers: The Pursuit of Objectivity in Science and Public Life* (Princeton, N.J.: Princeton University Press, 1995). See also R. Crease, "The Paradox of Trust in Science," *Physics World,* March 2004, 18.

16. But see the issue of transitive trust below

17. For Hobbes, because there is a relative isomorphism of desires and aversions, a relative natural equality of power, an unbounded liberty to preserve one's life and to possess, a presupposition of scarcity, and a natural diffidence, trust is not a founding emotion for human beings. It is only when the desires and aversions are regulated by science (rooted in speech or logos) that we can organize the *same telos* and *same means* to organize "The" desire for all (peace and aversion to war) and "The" means for all (articles of peace and the covenant), in short, that as a *social* form we are able to circumvent the problem of trust and authorize a Sovereign by means of a contract with one another. See Thomas Hobbes, *Leviathan* (Mineola, N.Y.: Dover, 2006).

18. See also Claudia Welz, "Trust as Basic Openness and Self-Transcendence," in Grøn and Welz, *Trust, Sociality, Selfhood,* 45–64.

19. See Morton Deutsch, *The Resolution of Conflict: Constructive and Destructive Processes* (New Haven, Conn.: Yale University Press, 1973), esp. 149ff.

20. Russell Hardin, "Trustworthiness," *Ethics* 107, no. 1 (1996): 26–42.

21. Hence, skepticism unfolds on a different level of experience than does mistrust.

22. Accordingly, I disagree with Hamrick's contention that "trust must be conjugated with suspicion." William S. Hamrick, *Kindness and the Good Society: Connections of the Heart* (New York: SUNY Press, 2002), esp. 240.

23. We can think here of the related phenomenon of forgiveness: "If you do this again, I will not be your friend . . . I will leave you, etc." This is essentially contradictory and vitiates the experience of forgiveness.

NOTES TO PAGES 209-224

24. On trust and distrust, see Trudy Govier, *Dilemmas of Trust* (Montreal: McGill-Queen's University Press, 1998). This work takes up trust on an "interpersonal" level. For her reflections on trust are a broader social and political context; see Trudy Govier, *Social Trust and Human Communities* (Montreal: McGill-Queen's University Press, 1997).

25. See Steinbock, *Home and Beyond*, section 3.

26. Annette Baier, "Trust and Anti-Trust," *Ethics* 96, no. 2 (1986): 231-60.

27. See also Isaacs et al. "Faith, Trust and Gullibility," esp. 462.

28. Isaacs et al. contends, "Faith, Trust and Gullibility," 465.

29. Richard Holton, "Deciding to Trust, Coming to Believe," *Australasian Journal of Philosophy* 72, no. 1 (March 1994): 63-76.

30. See Bernd Lahno, "On the Emotional Character of Trust," *Ethical Theory and Moral Practice*, vol. 4 (2001): 171-89.

31. See Steinbock, *Phenomenology and Mysticism*.

32. I thank Marilyn Frye and Helen Fielding for prompting these reflections on the imposing nature of trust.

33. See Olli Lagerspetz, *Trust: The Tacit Demand* (Dordrecht: Kluwer Academic, 1998), esp. 150ff. I disagree, however, that "to recognize trust is to respect the demand that is made"; rather, it consists in becoming trustworthy.

34. Baier, "Trust and Anti-Trust"; Carolyn McLeod, "Our Attitude Towards the Motivation of Those We Trust" *Southern Journal of Philosophy*, vol. 38 (2000): 465-80.

35. See Husserl, *Analyses Concerning Passive and Active Synthesis*, esp. part 2, div. 3.

36. See McLeod, "Our Attitude," esp. 475-77. Jones, too, shares many of these presuppositions. Despite the fact that she correctly places trust in the emotional sphere and recognizes in it a "significant cognitive component," she nevertheless asserts that trust is an attitude of optimism that the goodwill of another will extend to our interaction with another. See Karen Jones, "Trust as an Affective Attitude" *Ethics* 107, no. 1 (1996): 4-25.

37. Lawrence C. Becker, "Trust as Noncognitive Security about Motives," *Ethics* 107, no. 1 (1996): 43-61.

38. See McLeod, "Our Attitude," and Jones, "Trust as an Affective Attitude."

39. In this, I disagree with Mullin's contention in "Trust, Social Norms, and Motherhood." See especially 322ff.

40. See Hardin, "Trustworthiness," 26ff.

41. See Isaacs et al., "Faith, Trust and Gullibility," 464.

Chapter 7

The epigraph for this chapter is from Annie Dillard, *Pilgrim at Tinker Creek* (New York: Harper Collins, 1999), 139.

1. See Steinbock, *Phenomenology and Mysticism*, "Introduction" and chapter 5.

2. Scheler, *Wesen und Formen der Sympathie*, 146-47, 156; Scheler, *Formalismus*, 524-25; *Formalism*, 536-37.

3. Scheler, *Wesen und Formen der Sympathie*, 151–52. For Scheler, values are given in and peculiar to the emotional sphere of experience. As such, they can be given in a "value-ception" and felt in some way (depending upon the order of givenness) without being an object of judgment or reflection. Value is the way something is given in the relational experience encompassed by "feeling" and more specifically in the concrete unity of the human person (the interpenetration of the vital and the spiritual), the emotions.

4. This is the topic of another work on the "Verticality of Manifestation."

5. Scheler, *Wesen und Formen der Sympathie*, 159, 161–62. See the attempt to carry out a phenomenology of loving and hatred with respect to Husserl's work by Peter Hadreas, *A Phenomenology of Love and Hate* (Burlington, Vt.: Ashgate, 2007).

6. I take the expression of "nonviolent insistence" from Jana Trajtelová, an expression that is also relevant for vocational experience.

7. I also employ the expression "as from another," from Art Luther, an expression that I find evocative for the experience of vocations.

8. See, for example, Scheler, *Formalismus*, 483, 489–90; *Formalism*, 491, 498.

9. Scheler, "Ordo Amoris," 358–59; English translation, "Ordo Amoris," 113.

10. Scheler, *Wesen und Formen der Sympathie*, 156, 159, 160; see too 131, 136.

11. Ibid., 157, 160–61. See Luther, *Persons in Love*, 108, 111–22.

12. Thus we understand Scheler: "This highest form of the love of God is not to have love 'for' God, the All-merciful—that is, of a thing, but the *co-execution* of His love for the world (amare mundaum in Deo), and for Himself (amare Deum in Deo); that is, it is what the scholastics, the mystics, and before them, Saint Augustine called 'amare in Deo.'" Scheler, *Wesen und Formen der Sympathie*, 166.

13. Scheler, *Wesen und Formen der Sympathie*, 157.

14. Ibid., 145–46.

15. Also Frankl, *Man's Search for Meaning*, 111.

16. Scheler writes: "The root of this X, the motivating moment for the execution of the acts which lead to some form of participation, can only be the *taking-part* transcending itself and its being. We call this, in the most formal sense, '*love*.' Knowledge exists and only exists where the being-thus as strict identity is *both extra mente*, namely *in re, and also* and simultaneously *in mente* as 'ens intentionale' or 'object.'" And further: "Consciousness or knowledge of knowledge (con-scientia) already presupposes the having of ecstatic knowledge and can come to givenness through a reflexive act that directs itself originally to the knowledge-giving act. Without a tendency in the being that knows of moving from and out of itself to participate in a different being, no "knowledge" whatsoever is possible. I can see no other name for this tendency than 'love,' 'devotion.'" And see: "All activities such as thinking, observing, and cognizing are only operations that lead to a 'knowledge,' but are not themselves knowledge.

"If this 'knowledge' is knowledge in the most general sense of the word, then it is clear that because knowledge is an ontological relation, its *goal*, that 'for which' knowledge is and thus sought, cannot further be knowledge, but rather must in every case be a *becoming*, a *becoming other*." Max Scheler, "Erkenntnis und Arbeit," in *Gesammelte Werke*, vol. 8, ed. Maria Scheler (Bern: Franke Verlag, 1960), 204; English translation by Zachary Davis, *Cognition and Work* (forthcoming, Evanston, Ill.: Northwestern University Press).

17. Scheler, *Wesen und Formen der Sympathie*, 161.

18. Ibid., 161–62.

19. Ibid., 162–64.

20. See Jana Trajtelová, *Vzdialenost' a blízkost' mystiky: Fenomenologická štúdia fundamentálnych pohybov v tradičnej mystike západu* (Trnava a Towarzystwo Słowaków w Polsce: Studa Minorum, 2011) [*Distance and Proximity of Mysticism: Phenomenological Study of Fundamental Movements in Traditional Western Mysticism*].

21. See Steinbock, *Phenomenology and Mysticism*, chapter 8.

22. Ibid., chapter 8.

23. Frankl, *Man's Search for Meaning*, 38.

24. See, for example, Scheler, "Ordo Amoris," 353–54. English translation, 106–7.

25. See Max Scheler, "Zur Rehabilitierung der Tugend," in *Vom Umsturz der Werte: Abhandlungen und Aufsätze*, ed. Maria Scheler (Bern: Francke Verlag, 1955), 15–17.

26. See "Introduction," above.

27. Descartes, "The Passions of the Soul," part 2, art. 54.

28. I use humility and being humble interchangeably, primarily for the ease of expression. I distinguish below humility/being humble from being humbled and humbling myself.

29. St. Teresa of Avila, *Obras*, 76; *Collected Works*, vol. 1, 12.5.

30. St. Teresa of Avila, *Obras*, 88–90; *Collected Works*, vol. 1, 15.3–9; *Obras*, 92; *Collected Works*, vol. 1, 15.14.

31. Dillard, *Pilgrim at Tinker Creek*, 262–63.

32. Vladimir Jankélévitch, *Les vertus et l'amour*, vol. 1 (Paris: Flammarion, 1986), 388.

33. Ibid., 389

34. St. Benedict describes twelve "steps" of humility in his *Rule*, intended, here, for monastics in a religious order. In ascending order they are, in brief, the following: (1) obeying God's Commandments (which is to say, not doing one's own will), (2) not trying to please oneself in loving one's will, (3) submitting in obedience to a superior, (4) putting up patiently and quietly with everything inflicted on the individual, (5) confessing evil thoughts and acts, (6) accepting, as a worthless workman, contentedly all that is crude and harsh, (7) not only confessing one's inferiority, but believing it, (8) doing only what the common rule or the example of elders demands, (9) practicing silence, speaking only when asked a question, (10) refraining from laughter and frivolity, (11) speaking gently, without jests, simply, seriously, softly, (12) showing humility in one's heart and appearance and actions. Saint Benedict, *The Rule of St. Benedict*, trans. Anthony C. Meisel and M. L. del Mastro (New York: Doubleday, 1975), 56–61.

35. Steinbock, *Phenomenology and Mysticism*, chapter 8.

36. See Taylor, *Pride, Shame, and Guilt*, as well as the contributions in Tangney and Fischer, *Self-Conscious Emotions*.

37. Jankélévitch, *Les vertus et l'amour,* 363: "Car sa presence est en fait indiscernable de son absence. . . . "

38. For the notion of verticality, see Steinbock, *Phenomenology and Mysticism,* "Introduction."

39. See *Coltrane on Coltrane: The John Coltrane Interviews,* ed. Chris DeVito (Chicago: Chicago Review, 2010).

40. We do not want to confuse the valence of the particular emotion experienced with the assessment of the emotions within a philosophical anthropology—even though in my view a philosophical anthropology is necessary for such an assessment—for example, in weighing how or when shame is good, necessary, and so on.

41. Scheler, *Vom Umsturz der Werte,* 18.

42. Jankélévitch, *Les vertus et l'amour,* 398.

43. Chris Paone, conversation.

44. See also Dōgen's *Kesa Kudoku,* or *On the Spiritual Merits of the Kesa.* Here we read: "The World-honored One, in advising the monk Jnanaprabha ('He Whose Wise Discernment Is Radiant'), spoke thus:

The Dharma robe, based on its material, color, and dimensions, acquires ten superb benefits.

First, because it blankets your body well, it keeps feelings of shame or embarrassment at bay and shields you with a sense of modesty, so that you may train with the good Dharma and put It into practice." Dōgen, *Shōbōgenzō,* 961.

45. Jankélévitch, *Les vertus et l'amour,* 333: "Ce n'est que moi, mais c'est tout de même moi."

46. It seems Jankélévitch conflates what we would call being humbled with modesty when he attributes the recognition of being of little or no account to modesty; see *Les vertus et l'amour,* 337–38.

47. The difficulty with debilitating shame therefore is not shame, but the disordered value orientation at the root of this debilitating form.

48. See Karmen MacKendrick, "Humiliated Subjects," in *Pornotopia: Image, Apocalypse, Desire,* ed. Louis Armand, Jane Lewty, and Andrew Mitchell (Prague, Czech Republic: Univerzita Karlova v Praze, 2008), 145–63.

49. I would like to thank Reginald Slavkovský for this observation.

50. See Simone Weil, *Le pesanteur et la grâce* (Paris: Librairie Plon, 1988), 35; English translation *Gravity and Grace,* trans. Emma Crawford and Mario von der Ruhr (New York: Routledge, 2002), 26. See also Simone Weil, *Attente de Dieu* (Paris: La Colombe, 1963), 84–85; English translation *Waiting for God,* trans. Emma Craufurd (New York: Perennial Classics, 2001), 70–71.

51. I am grateful to Jana Trajtelová for noting this distinction.

52. Based on a report from Barbara Bradley Hagerty, NPR, "Mother Teresa Beatified," October, 14, 2003. See also Mother Teresa, *A Simple Path,* ed. Lucinda Vardey (New York: Ballantine Books, 1995), 65.

53. San Juan de la Cruz, *Obras Comletas,* 326; Saint John of the Cross, *The Collected Works of Saint John of the Cross,* 366.

54. See Trajtelová, *Vzdialenost' a blízkost' mystiky,* 154–60.

NOTES TO PAGES 251-269

55. There are redemptive moments in Dostoevsky; or the work of Dostoevsky is a narrative of redemption, but we do not find this dimension, say, in Camus's *Myth of Sisyphus*. This is probably one of the reasons why Camus did not think Dostoevsky was radical enough in carrying out the existentialist insight—which leads to the absurd. Likewise, there is no "re-presencing" in Kafka, no "death," only transformations, mysterious disappearances, and so on. Affliction is lived as affliction when a return is made impossible on our part, and accomplished only on the part of God or the infinite Absolute. This is how such an experience can evoke humility.

56. Weil, *Attente*, 84; *Waiting*, 70.
57. See Trajtelová, *Vzdialenosť a blízkosť mystiky*, 188–94.
58. See Steinbock, *Phenomenology and Mysticism*, chapter 8.
59. See Klaus Held, *Lebendige Gegenwart: Die Frage nach der Seinsweise des transzendentalen Ich bei Edmund Husserl, entwickelt am Leitfaden der Zeitproblematik* (The Hague: Nijhoff, 1966). And see Edmund Husserl, *On the Phenomenology of the Consciousness of Internal Time* (1893–1917), trans. John Brough (Dordrecht: Springer, 2008). See also Husserl, *Analyses Concerning Passive and Active Synthesis*.
60. See Steinbock, *Phenomenology and Mysticism;* and see Levinas, *Totalité*, xvii; *Totality*, 29; see also xvi; 27–28.

Conclusion

1. Running throughout the experience of these moral emotions is the experience of vocations and that of Myself, in the dynamic, inter-Personal sense. It is the project of a related work mentioned above, *Vocations and Exemplars: The Verticality of Moral Experience*, and connected to this, another work planned that focuses on the verticality of "manifestation" as a mode of givenness, entitled *Icons and Idols*. The work that deals with the ecological implications of these experiences is provisionally entitled *Earth as Ground: The Verticality of Ecological Experience* (in preparation).
2. Similarly, Charles Taylor understands the social imaginary as the way in which we collectively imagine, pre-theoretically and reflectively, too, our social life in the contemporary Western world. See Charles Taylor, *Modern Social Imaginaries* (Durham, N.C.: Duke University Press, 2007), esp. 23, 50.
3. Claude Lefort, *Les formes de l'histoire* (Paris: Gallimard, 1978); Claude Lefort, *Éléments d'une critique de la bureaucratie* (Paris: Gallimard, 1979); Claude Lefort, *L'invention démocratique* (Paris: Fayard, 1981). See also Reinhart Koselleck, *Kritik und Krise: Eine Studie zur Pathogenese der bürgerlichen Welt* (Frankfurt am Main: Suhrkamp, 1973).
4. Ernst H. Kantorowicz, *The King's Two Bodies: A Study in Medieval Political Theology* (Princeton, N.J.: Princeton University Press, 1957).
5. Taylor, *Modern Social Imaginaries*, 11.
6. Ibid., esp. 95–99, 186, 194.
7. Ibid., 117; Scheler, *Wesen und Formen der Sympathie*, 145–46.

8. Lefort, *Les formes de l'histoire*, 318ff.; Anthony J. Steinbock, "Totalitarianism, Homogeneity of Power, Depth: Towards a Socio-Political Ontology," *Tijdschrift voor Filosofie* 51, no. 4 (December 1989): 621–48.

9. See Martin E. Marty and R. Scott Appleby, eds., *Fundamentalism Observed* (Chicago: University of Chicago Press, 1994); also, Martin E. Marty and R. Scott Appleby, eds., *Fundamentalisms Comprehended* (Chicago: University of Chicago Press, 2004). See Michel Foucault, *Power/Knowledge: Selected Interviews and Other Writings, 1972–1977,* ed. Colin Gordon (New York: Pantheon, 1980).

10. See above, note 16 to chapter 7.

11. Bergson, *Les deux sources de la morale et de la religion.*

12. Bloch, *Daz Prinzip Hoffnung;* Lash, *A Matter of Hope.*

13. Hannah Arendt, "Organized Guilt and Universal Responsibility," in *Collective Responsibility: Five Decades of Debate in Theoretical and Applied Ethics,* ed. Larry May and Stacey Hoffman (New York: Rowman and Littlefield, 1991), 281–82.

Bibliography

Agamben, Giorgio. *Homo Sacer: Sovereign Power and Bare Life.* Trans. Daniel Heller-Roazen. Stanford, Calif.: Stanford University Press, 1998.
———. *Means without End: Notes on Politics.* Trans. Vincenzo Binetti and Ceasre Casarino. Minneapolis: University of Minnesota Press, 2000.
———. *Remnants of Auschwitz: The Witness and the Archive.* Trans. Daniel Heller-Roazen. New York: Zone Books, 2002.
Alighieri, Dante. *The Divine Comedy.* Trans. C. H. Sisson. Oxford: Oxford University Press, 1993.
Aquinas, Saint Thomas. *Summa Theologiae,* vol. 33. Trans. W. J. Hill. New York: McGraw-Hill, 1966.
Arendt, Hannah, "Organized Guilt and Universal Responsibility." In *Collective Responsibility: Five Decades of Debate in Theoretical and Applied Ethics,* ed. Larry May and Stacey Hoffman, 273–83. New York: Rowman and Littlefield, 1991.
Aristotle. *The Basic Works of Aristotle.* Ed. and trans. Richard McKeon. New York: Random House, 1941.
Augustine, Saint. *The City of God.* Trans. Marcus Dods. New York: Modern Library, 2000.
———. *The Confessions.* Trans. Maria Boulding. Hyde Park, N.Y.: New City, 1997.
———. *Enchiridion: On Faith, Hope, and Love.* Trans. J. B. Shaw. Washington, D.C.: Regnery, 1996.
———. *The Works of Saint Augustine: Answer to the Pelagians.* Trans. Roland J. Teske, ed. John E. Rotelle. Hyde Park, N.Y.: New City, 1997.
Austin, J. L. *How to Do Things with Words,* ed. J. O. Urmson and Marina Sbisa. Cambridge, Mass.: Harvard University Press, 1975.
———. "A Plea for Excuses." In *Philosophical Papers,* ed. J. O. Urmson and G. J. Warnock, 175–204. New York: Oxford University Press, 1970.
Backström, Joel. *The Fear of Openness: An Essay on Friendship and the Roots of Morality.* Turku, Finland: Åbo Akademi University Press, 2007.
Baier, Annette C. "Trust and Anti-Trust." *Ethics* 96, no. 2 (1986): 231–60.
———. "What Do Women Want in a Moral Theory?" *Noûs* 19, no. 1 (1985): 53–63.
Baqli, Ruzbihan. *Unveiling of Secrets: Diary of a Sufi Master.* Trans. Carl W. Ernst. Chapel Hill. North Carolina: Parvardigar, 1997.
Barber, Michael. *Equality and Diversity: Phenomenological Investigations of Prejudice and Discrimination.* Amherst, N.Y.: Humanity Books, 2001.

BIBLIOGRAPHY

Barrett, Karen Caplovitz. "A Functionalist Approach to Shame and Guilt." In *Self-Conscious Emotions: The Psychology of Shame, Guilt, Embarrassment, and Pride*, ed. June Price Tangney and Kurt W. Fischer, 25–63. New York: Guilford, 1995.

Batson, Daniel C., Laura L. Shaw, and Kathryn C. Oleson. "Differentiating Affect, Mood, and Emotion: Toward Functionally Based Conceptual Distinctions." In *Emotion: Review of Personality and Social Psychology* no. 13: 294–326. Ed. Margaret S. Clark. Thousand Oaks, Calif.: Sage, 1992.

Baumeister, Roy F., et al. "Interpersonal Aspects of Guilt: Evidence from Narrative Studies." In *Self-Conscious Emotions: The Psychology of Shame, Guilt, Embarrassment, and Pride*, ed. June Price Tangney and Kurt W. Fischer, 255–73. New York: Guilford, 1995.

Beauvoir, Simone de. *Le deuxième sexe*. Paris: Éditions Champion, 2004.

———. *Pour une morale de l'ambiguïté*. Paris: Gallimard, 1947.

Becker, Lawrence C. "Trust as Noncognitive Security about Motives." *Ethics* 107, no. 1 (1996): 43–61.

Benedict, Ruth. *The Chrysanthemum and the Sword: Patterns of Japanese Culture*. Boston: Houghton Mifflin, 1946.

Benedict, Saint. *The Rule of St. Benedict*. Trans. Anthony C. Meisel and M. L. del Mastro. New York: Doubleday, 1975.

Bergson, Henri. *Les deux sources de la morale et de la religion*. Paris: Presses Universitaires de France, 1984.

———. *The Two Sources of Morality and Religion*. Trans. R. Ashley Audra and Cloudesley Brereton. Notre Dame, Ind.: University of Notre Dame Press, 1977.

Bernanos, Georges. *The Diary of a Country Priest*. Trans. Pamela Morris. New York: Carroll and Graf, 1965.

Blechman, E. A. *Moods, Affect, and Emotions*. Hillsdale, N.J.: Lawrence Erlbaum Associates, 1990.

Bloch, Ernst. *Daz Prinzip Hoffnung*. 3 vols. Frankfurt am Main: Suhrkamp, 1959.

Bruner, J. *Making Stories: Law, Literature, Life*. Cambridge, Mass.: Harvard University Press, 2002.

Buber, Martin. *Martin Buber on Psychology and Psychotherapy*. Ed. Judith Buber Agassi, trans. Paul Roazen. New York: Syracuse University Press, 1999.

———. *Schuld und Schuldgefühle*. Heidelberg: Verlag Lambert Schneider, 1958.

———. *Tales of the Hasidim*. Trans. Olga Marx. New York: Schocken Books, 1991.

Buytendijk, F. J. J. *Attitudes et mouvements: Étude fonctionnelle du movement humain*. Trans. Louis van Haecht. Paris: Desclée de Brouwer, 1957.

Camus, Albert. *Le mythe de Sisyphe*. Paris: Gallimard, 1942.

———. *The Myth of Sisyphus*. Trans. Justin O'Brien. New York: Vintage Books, 1983.

Canguilhem, Georges. *Le normal et le pathologique*. Paris: Presses Universitaires de France, 1966.

Clairvaux, Bernard of. *The Steps of Humility and Pride*. Trans. Jean Leclercq and Henri Rochais. Trappist, Ky.: Cistercian, 1973.

Colombetti, Giovanna, and Evan Thompson, eds. *Emotion Experience: Journal of Consciousness Studies* 12, no. 8–10 (2005).

BIBLIOGRAPHY

Coltrane on Coltrane: The John Coltrane Interviews. Ed. Chris DeVito. Chicago: Chicago Review, 2010.
Crease, Robert. "The Paradox of Trust in Science." *Physics World,* March 2004.
Creighton, Mille R. "Revisiting Shame and Guilt Cultures: A Forty-Year Pilgrimage." *Ethos* 18, no. 3 (1990): 279–307.
Darwin, Charles. *The Expression of the Emotions in Man and Animals.* Whitefish, Mont.: Kessinger, 2010.
Dauber, Denneth, and Walter Jost, eds. *Ordinary Language Criticism: Literary Thinking after Cavell after Wittgenstein.* Evanston, Ill.: Northwestern University Press, 2003.
Deigh, John. "Shame and Self-Esteem: A Critique." *Ethics* 93, no. 2 (January 1983): 225–45.
Depraz, Natalie. *Le corps glorieux: Phénoménologie pratique de la Philocalie des Pères du désert et des Pères de l'Eglise.* Louvain: Éditions Peeters, 2008.
Descartes, René. *The Philosophical Works of Descartes.* Vol. 1. Trans. Elizabeth S. Haldane and G. R. T. Ross. Cambridge: Cambridge University Press, 1981.
Deutsch, Morton. *The Resolution of Conflict: Constructive and Destructive Processes.* New Haven, Conn.: Yale University Press, 1973.
Dillard, Annie. *Pilgrim at Tinker Creek.* New York: Harper Collins, 1999.
Dobh Baer of Lubavitch. *Tract on Ecstasy.* Trans. Louis Jacobs. London, Vallentine, Mitchell, 1963.
Dōgen. *Shōbōgenzō: The Treasure House of the Eye of the True Teaching.* (*A Trainee's Translation of Great Master Dōgen's Spiritual Masterpiece*). Trans. Hubert Nearman. Mount Shasta, Calif.: Shasta Abbey, 2007.
Donnet, Jean-Luc. *L'humour et la honte.* Paris: Presses Universitaires de France, 2009.
Dostoevsky, Fyodor. *The Brothers Karamoazov.* Trans. Richard Pevear and Larissa Volokhonsky. New York: Vintage Books, 1991.
———. *Crime and Punishment.* Trans. Richard Pevear and Larissa Volokhonsky. New York: Vintage Books, 1993.
Drummond, J. "'Cognitive Impenetrability' and the Complex Intentionality of the Emotions." *Journal of Consciousness Studies* 11, no. 10–11 (2004): 109–26.
———. "Moral Phenomenology and Moral Intentionality," *Phenomenology and the Cognitive Sciences* 7 (2008): 35–49.
DSM-IV-TR Casebook: A Learning Companion to the Diagnostic and Statistical Manual of Mental Disorders. 4th ed. Ed. Robert L. Spitzer et al. Washington, D.C.: American Psychiatric Publishing, 2002.
Du Bois, W. E. B. *The Oxford W.E.B. Du Bois Reader.* Ed. Eric J. Sundquist. New York: Oxford University Press, 1996.
Ekman, Paul. *Emotions Revealed: Recognizing Faces and Feelings to Improve Communication and Emotional Life.* 2nd ed. New York: Henry Holt, 2007.
Ernst, Carl W. *Ruzbihan Baqlī: Mysticism and the Rhetoric of Sainthood in Persian Sufism.* Richmond Surrey, Eng.: Curzon, 1996.
———. *Words of Ecstasy in Sufism.* New York: SUNY Press, 1985.
Etzoni, Amitai, with David E. Carney, eds. *Repentance: A Comparative Perspective.* Rowman and Littlefield, 1997.

Euripides. *Euripides' Hippolytus.* Trans. Michael R. Halleran. Newburyport, Mass.: Focus, 2001.
Fink, Eugen. "Operative Begriffe in Husserls Phänomenologie." In *Nähe unde Distanz: Phänomenologische Vortäge und Aufsätze,* 180–204. Alber, 1976.
Foucault, Michel. *Power/Knowledge: Selected Interviews and Other Writings, 1972–1977.* Ed. Colin Gordon. New York: Pantheon, 1980.
Frankl, Viktor E. *Man's Search for Meaning.* Trans. Ilse Lasch. Boston: Beacon, 2006.
Freire, Paulo. *Pedagogy of the Oppressed.* Trans. Myra Bergman Ramos. New York: Continuum, 2001.
Freud, Sigmund. "Das Ich und das Es." In *Gesammelte Werke,* vol. 13:. 235–89. 4th ed. Frankfurt am Main: Fischer Verlag, 1963.
———. "Das ökonomishe Problem des Masochismus." In *Gesammelte Werke,* vol. 13: 369–89. 4th ed. Frankfurt am Main: Fischer Verlag, 1963.
———. "Einige Charaktertypen aus der psychoanalytischen Arbeit." In *Gesammelte Werke.* vol. 10: 363–91. 3rd ed. Frankfurt am Main: Fischer Verlag, 1963.
———. *Vorlesungen zur Einführung in die Psychoanalyse.* In *Gesammelte Werke,* vol. 11. Frankfurt am Main: Fischer Verlag, 1969.
———. "Zeitgemässes über Krieg und Tod." In *Gesammelte Werke,* vol. 10: 323–55. 3rd ed. Frankfurt am Main: Fischer Verlag, 1963.
Gerondi, Rabbi Johan. *The Gates of Repentance.* Trans. Yaakov Feldman. Northvale, N.J.: Jason Aronson, 1999.
Gilligan, Carol. *In a Different Voice: Psychological Theory and Women's Development.* Cambridge, Mass.: Harvard University Press, 1982.
Gilligan, James. *Violence: Reflections on a National Epidemic.* New York: Vintage, 1997.
Govier, Trudy. *Dilemmas of Trust.* Montreal: McGill-Queen's University Press, 1998.
———. *Social Trust and Human Communities.* Montreal: McGill-Queen's University Press, 1997.
Grosz, Elizabeth. *Volatile Bodies: Toward a Corporeal Feminism.* Bloomington: Indiana University Press, 1994.
Guenther, Lisa. "Shame and the Temporality of Social Life." *Continental Philosophy Review* 44, no. 1 (2011): 23–39.
Hadreas, Peter. *A Phenomenology of Love and Hate.* Burlington, Vt.: Ashgate, 2007.
Hampshire, Stuart. *Thought and Action.* Notre Dame, Ind.: University of Notre Dame Press, 1981.
Hamrick, William S. *Kindness and the Good Society: Connections of the Heart.* New York: SUNY Press, 2002.
Hardin, Russell. "Trustworthiness." *Ethics* 107, no. 1 (1996): 26–42.
Hart, James G. *Who One Is: Book 1: Meontology of the "I": A Transcendental Phenomenology.* Boston: Springer, 2009.
———. *Who One Is: Book 2: Existenz and Transcendental Phenomenology.* Boston: Springer, 2009.
Hegel, G. W. F. *Enzyklopädie der philosophischen Wissenschaften im Grundrisse (1830), Erster Teil. Werke* 8. Frankfurt am Main: Suhrkamp, 1970.
———. *Phänomenologie des Geistes.* Hamburg: Felix Meiner, 1952.

BIBLIOGRAPHY

Heidegger, Martin. *Identität und Differenz.* Tübingen: Neske, 1982.
———. *Identity and Difference.* Trans. Joan Stambaugh. New York: Harper and Row, 1969.
———. *On Time and Being.* Trans. Joan Stambaugh. New York: Harper and Row, 1972.
———. *Phänomenologie des religiösen Lebens,* Gesamtausgabe 60. Frankfurt am Main: Klostermann, 1995.
———. *The Phenomenology of the Religious Life.* Trans. Matthias Fritsch and Jennifer Anna Gosetti-Ferencei. Bloomington: Indiana University Press, 2004.
———. *Sein und Zeit.* Tübingen: Niemeyer, 1979.
———. *Zur Sache des Denkens.* Tübingen, Niemeyer, 1976.
Heinämaa, Sara. *Toward a Phenomenology of Sexual Difference: Husserl, Merleau-Ponty, Beauvoir.* New York: Rowman and Littlefield, 2003.
Held, Klaus. "Idee einer Phänomenologie der Hoffnung." In *Interdisziplinäre Perspektiven der Phänomenologie,* 126–41. Dordrecht: Springer, 2006.
———. *Lebendige Gegenwart: Die Frage nach der Seinsweise des transzendentalen Ich bei Edmund Husserl, entwickelt am Leitfaden der Zeitproblematik.* The Hague: Nijhoff, 1966.
Henry, Michel. *L'essence de la manifestation.* 2nd ed. Paris: Presses Universitaires de France, 1990.
Herzog, Frederick, ed. *The Future of Hope: Theology as Eschatology.* New York: Herder and Herder, 1970.
Hesiod. *Works and Days and Theogony.* Trans. Stanley Lombardo. Indianapolis, Ind.: Hackett, 1993.
Hobbes, Thomas. *Leviathan.* Ed. C. B. Macpherson. New York: Penguin Books, 1985.
Hoffman, M. L. "Development of Prosocial Motivation: Empathy and Guilt." In *The Development of Prosocial Behavior,* ed. N. Eisenberg, 281–313. New York: Academic, 1982.
Holmes, John G., and John K. Rempel. "Trust in Close Relationships." *Review of Personality and Social Psychology,* vol. 10 (1989): 187–220.
Holton, Richard. "Deciding to Trust, Coming to Believe." *Australasian Journal of Philosophy* 72, no. 1 (March 1994): 63–76.
Hookway, C. "Emotions and Epistemic Evaluations." In *The Cognitive Basis of Science,* ed. P. Carruthers et al. Cambridge: Cambridge University Press, 2002.
Horgan, Terry, and Mark Timmons, eds. *Metaethics after Moore.* Oxford: Clarendon, 2006.
Horkheimer, Max, and Theodor W. Adorno. *Dialectic of Enlightenment.* Trans. John Cumming. New York: Continuum, 1982.
Hume, David. *A Treatise on Human Nature.* Ed. L. A. Selby-Bigge. Clarendon, 1967.
Huskey, Rebecca K. *Paul Ricoeur on Hope: Expecting the Good.* New York: Peter Lang, 2009.
Husserl, Edmund. *Analyses Concerning Passive and Active Synthesis: Lectures on Transcendental Logic.* Trans. Anthony J. Steinbock. Boston: Kluwer Academic, 2001.

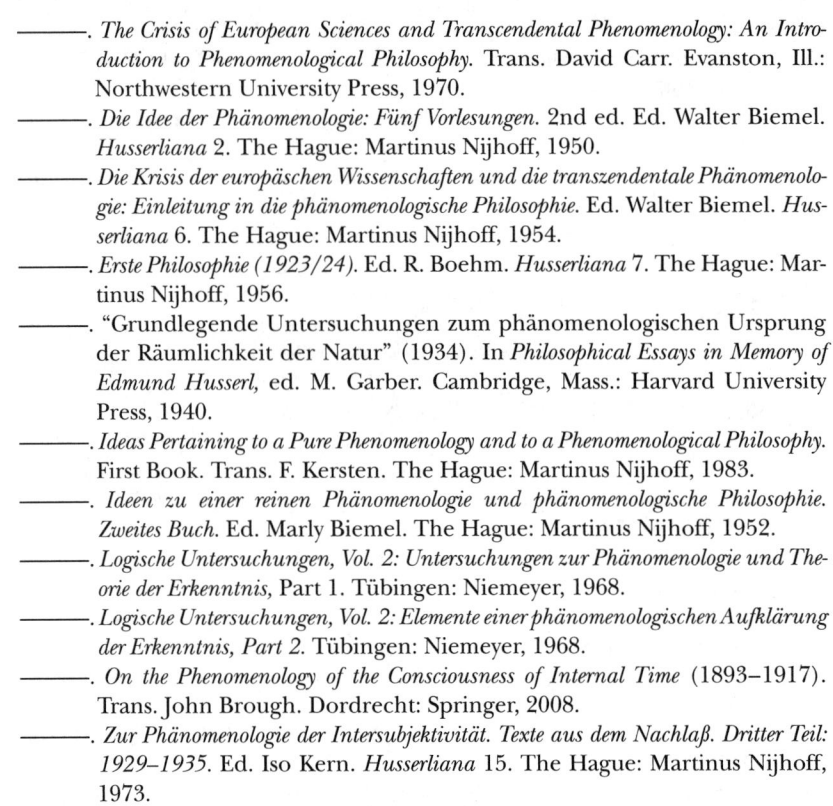

———. *The Crisis of European Sciences and Transcendental Phenomenology: An Introduction to Phenomenological Philosophy.* Trans. David Carr. Evanston, Ill.: Northwestern University Press, 1970.

———. *Die Idee der Phänomenologie: Fünf Vorlesungen.* 2nd ed. Ed. Walter Biemel. Husserliana 2. The Hague: Martinus Nijhoff, 1950.

———. *Die Krisis der europäschen Wissenschaften und die transzendentale Phänomenologie: Einleitung in die phänomenologische Philosophie.* Ed. Walter Biemel. Husserliana 6. The Hague: Martinus Nijhoff, 1954.

———. *Erste Philosophie (1923/24).* Ed. R. Boehm. Husserliana 7. The Hague: Martinus Nijhoff, 1956.

———. "Grundlegende Untersuchungen zum phänomenologischen Ursprung der Räumlichkeit der Natur" (1934). In *Philosophical Essays in Memory of Edmund Husserl,* ed. M. Garber. Cambridge, Mass.: Harvard University Press, 1940.

———. *Ideas Pertaining to a Pure Phenomenology and to a Phenomenological Philosophy.* First Book. Trans. F. Kersten. The Hague: Martinus Nijhoff, 1983.

———. *Ideen zu einer reinen Phänomenologie und phänomenologische Philosophie. Zweites Buch.* Ed. Marly Biemel. The Hague: Martinus Nijhoff, 1952.

———. *Logische Untersuchungen, Vol. 2: Untersuchungen zur Phänomenologie und Theorie der Erkenntnis,* Part 1. Tübingen: Niemeyer, 1968.

———. *Logische Untersuchungen, Vol. 2: Elemente einer phänomenologischen Aufklärung der Erkenntnis, Part 2.* Tübingen: Niemeyer, 1968.

———. *On the Phenomenology of the Consciousness of Internal Time* (1893–1917). Trans. John Brough. Dordrecht: Springer, 2008.

———. *Zur Phänomenologie der Intersubjektivität. Texte aus dem Nachlaß. Dritter Teil: 1929–1935.* Ed. Iso Kern. Husserliana 15. The Hague: Martinus Nijhoff, 1973.

Hutchinson, Phil. *Shame and Philosophy.* New York: Palgrave Macmillan, 2008.

Isaacs, K. S., James M. Alexander, and Ernest A. Haggard. "Faith, Trust and Gullibility." *International Journal of Psychoanalysis,* vol. 44 (1963): 461–69.

Jack, R. E., O. G. B. Garrod, H. Yu, R. Caldara, and P. G. Schyns. "Facial Expressions of Emotion Are Not Culturally Universal." In *Proceedings of the National Academy of Sciences of the United States of America,* vol. 109/19 (2012): 7241–44.

Jankélévitch, Vladimir. *Philosophie morale,* ed. Françoise Schwab. Paris: Flammarion, 1998.

Jaspers, Karl. *Die Schuldfrage: Ein Beitrag zur deutschen Frage.* Munich: Piper Verlag, 1965.

———. *The Question of German Guilt.* Trans. E. B. Ashton. New York: Fordham University Press, 2000.

Juan de la Cruz, San. *Obras Completas.* Ed. Licinio Ruano de la Iglesia. Madrid: Biblioteca de Autores Cristianos, 1982.

John of the Cross, Saint. *The Collected Works of Saint John of the Cross.* Rev. ed. Trans. Kieran Kavanaugh and Otilio Rodriguez. Washington, D.C.: ICS Publications, 1991.

BIBLIOGRAPHY

Johnston, Adrian, and Catherine Malabou. *Self and Emotional Life: Philosophy, Psychoanalysis, and Neuroscience.* New York: Columbia University Press, 2013.
Kagan, J. *The Second Year: The Emergence of Self-Awareness.* Cambridge, Mass.: Harvard University Press, 1981.
Kant, Immanuel. *Anthropology from a Pragmatic Point of View.* Ed. and trans. Robert B. Louden. New York: Cambridge University Press, 2006.
———. *Die Religion innerhalb der Grenzen der bloßen Vernunft.* Ed. Karl Vorländer. Hamburg: Meiner Verlag, 1990.
———. *Immanuel Kant's Anthropologie in pragmatischer Hinsicht.* Leipzig: Immanuel Müller, 1833.
———. *Kritik der reinen Vernunft.* Ed. Raymund Schmidt. Hamburg: Meiner, 1956.
———. *Religion within the Limits of Reason Alone.* New York: Harper Torchbooks, 1960.
Kantorowicz, Ernst H. *The King's Two Bodies: A Study in Medieval Political Theology.* Princeton, N.J.: Princeton University Press, 1957.
Kierkegaard, Søren. *The Sickness unto Death: A Christian Psychological Exposition for Upbuilding and Awakening,* Ed. and trans. Howard V. Hong and Edna H. Hong. Princeton, N.J.: Princeton University Press, 1980.
———. *Works of Love.* Ed. and trans. Howard V. Hong and Edna H. Hong Princeton, N.J.: Princeton University Press, 1995.
Koselleck, Reinhart. *Kritik und Krise: Eine Studie zur Pathogenese der bürgerlichen Welt.* Frankfurt am Main: Suhrkamp, 1973.
Krause, Rainer. "Psychodynamik der Emotionsstörungen." In *Enzyklopaedie der Psychologie,* ed. K. R. Scherer. Vol 3: *Psychologie der Emotionen,* 630–705. Goettingen: Hogrefe, 1990.
Laertius, Diogenes. *Lives of Eminent Philosophers.* Trans. R. D. Hicks. Volume I. Cambridge, Mass.: Loeb Classical Library, 1925.
Lagerspetz, Olli. *Trust: The Tacit Demand.* Dordrecht: Kluwer Academic, 1998.
Lahno, Bernd. "On the Emotional Character of Trust." *Ethical Theory and Moral Practice,* vol. 4 (2001): 171–89.
Larrabee, Mary Jeanne, ed. *An Ethic of Care: Feminist and Interdisciplinary Perspectives.* New York: Routledge, 1993.
Lash, Nicholas. *A Matter of Hope: A Theologian's Reflections on the Thought of Karl Marx.* Notre Dame, Ind.: University of Notre Dame Press, 1984.
Lazarus, R. *Emotion and Adaptation.* New York: Oxford University Press, 1991.
Lefort, Claude. *Éléments d'une critique de la bureaucratie.* Paris: Gallimard, 1979.
———. *Les formes de l'histoire.* Paris: Gallimard, 1978.
———. *L'invention démocratique.* Paris: Fayard, 1981.
Leitch, James W. *Theology of Hope: On the Ground and the Implications of a Christian Eschatology.* Minneapolis, Minn.: Fortress, 1993.
Lewis, Helen Block. "Guilt in Obsession and Paranoia." In *Emotions in Personality and Psychopathology,* ed. C. E. Izard, 399–414. New York: Plenum, 1979.
———. *The Role of Shame in Symptoms Formation.* Hillside, N.J.: Lawrence Erlbaum, 1987.

BIBLIOGRAPHY

Lewis, J. David, and A. Weigert. "Trust as a Social Reality." *Social Forces*, vol. 63 (1985): 967–85.
Lewis, Michael. "Shame and Stigma." In *Shame: Interpersonal Behavior, Psychopathology, and Culture*, ed. Paul Gilbert and Bernice Andrews, 126–40. New York: Oxford University Press, 1998.
———. *Shame: The Exposed Self.* New York: Free Press, 1995.
Levi, Primo. *The Reawakening.* Trans. Stuart Woolf. New York: Simon and Schuster, 1965.
Levinas, Emmanuel. "Being Jewish." Trans. Mary Beth Mader. *Continental Philosophy Review* 40, no. 3 (2007): 205–10.
———. *De l'evasion.* Paris: Fata Morgana, 1982.
———. *Le temps et l'autre.* Paris: Fata Morgana, 1979.
———. *Totalité et infini.* The Hague: Martinus Nijhoff, 1961.
———. *Totality and Infinity.* Trans. Alphonso Lingis. Pittsburgh: Duquesne University Press, 1969.
Lingis, Alphonso. *The First Person Singular.* Evanston, Ill.: Northwestern University Press, 2007.
———. *The Imperative.* Bloomington: Indiana University Press, 1998.
———. *Trust.* Minneapolis: University of Minnesota Press, 2004
Locke, John. *An Essay Concerning Human Understanding.* Ed. Alexander Campbell Fraser. New York: Dover, 1959.
Luhmann, Niklas. *Trust and Power.* Chichester, Eng.: Wiley, 1979.
Luther, A. R. "Original Emergence in Heidegger and Nishida." *Philosophy Today* 26, no. 4/4 (1982): 345–56.
———. *Persons in Love: A Study of Max Scheler's "Wesen und Formen der Sympathie."* The Hague: Martinus Nijhoff, 1972.
MacCurdy, John T. "The Biological Significance of Blushing and Shame." *British Journal of Psychology* 21 (1930): 174–82.
Marcel, Gabriel. "Desire and Hope." Trans. Nathaniel Lawrence, in *Readings in Existential Phenomenology,* ed. Nathaniel Lawrence and Daniel O'Connor, 77–285. Englewood Cliffs, N.J.: Prentice Hall, 1967.
———. *Homo Viator: Introduction to a Metaphysic of Hope.* Trans. Emma Craufurd. New York: Harper Torchbooks, 1962.
Marcuse, Herbert. *One-Dimensional Man: Studies in the Ideology of Advanced Industrial Society.* Boston: Beacon, 1964.
Markovits, A., and K. Deutsch. *Fear of Science—Trust in Science: Conditions for Change in the Climate of Opinion.* Cambridge, Mass.: Oelgeschlager, Gunn & Hain, 1980.
Marty, Martin E., and R. Scott Appleby, eds. *Fundamentalism Observed.* Chicago: University of Chicago Press, 1994.
———. *Fundamentalisms Comprehended.* Chicago: University of Chicago Press, 2004.
Marx, Karl. "From Letter to Arnold Ruge, 1843." In *The Letters of Karl Marx,* trans. Saul K. Padover. Englewood Cliffs, N.J.: Prentice-Hall, 1979.
———. *Grundrisse.* Trans. Marin Nicolaus. London: Penguin Books, 1973.

BIBLIOGRAPHY

———. *Grundrisse der Kritik der politischen Ökonomie.* In *Karl Marx, Friedrich Engels Werke,* vol. 42: *Ökonomische Manuskripte 1857/1858.* Berlin: Dietz Verlag, 1983.
Mascolo, Michael F., and Kurt W. Fischer. "Developmental Transformations in Appraisals for Pride, Shame, and Guilt." In *Self-Conscious Emotions: The Psychology of Shame, Guilt, Embarrassment, and Pride,* ed. June Price Tangney and Kurt W. Fischer. New York: Guilford, 1995.
Mazis, Glen. *Emotions and Embodiment.* New York: Peter Lang, 1994.
McGraw, K. M. "Guilt Following Transgression: An Attribution of Responsibility Approach." *Journal of Personality and Social Psychology,* vol. 53 (1987): 247–56.
McLeod, Carolyn. "Our Attitude Towards the Motivation of Those We Trust." *Southern Journal of Philosophy,* vol. 38 (2000): 465–80.
Merleau-Ponty, Maurice. *Phénoménologie de la perception.* Paris: Gallimard, 1945.
———. *Phenomenology of Perception.* Trans. Donald Landes. Routledge, 2012.
Middelton-Moz, Jane. *Shame and Guilt: Masters of Disguise.* Deerfield Beach, Fla.: Health Communications, 1990.
Middendorf, Heinrich. *Phänomenologie der Hoffnung.* Würzburg: Königshausen & Neumann, 1985.
Miles, Margaret R. *Fullness of Life: Historical Foundations for a New Asceticism.* Philadelphia: Westminster, 1981.
Minkowski, Eugène. *Lived Time: Phenomenological and Psychopathological Studies* Trans. Nancy Metzel. Evanston, Ill.: Northwestern University Press, 1970.
Miyake, Kazuo, and Kosuke Yamazaki. "Self-Conscious Emotions, Child Rearing, and Child Psychopathology in Japanese Culture." In *Self-Conscious Emotions: The Psychology of Shame, Guilt, Embarrassment, and Pride,* ed. June Price Tangney and Kurt W. Fischer, 488–504. New York: Guilford, 1995.
Moltmann, Jürgen. *Theologie der Hoffnung: Untersuchungen zur Begründung und zu den Konsequenzen einer christlichen Eschatologie.* Munich: Christian Kaiser, 1965.
Mullin, Amy. "Trust, Social Norms, and Motherhood." *Journal of Social Philosophy* 36, no. 3 (2005): 316–30.
Munson, Carlton E. *The Mental Health Diagnostic Desk Reference: Visual Guides and More for Learning to Use the Diagnostic and Statistical Manual (DSM-IV-TR).* 2nd ed. New York: Haworth, 2001.
Natanson, Maurice. "Phenomenology and the Natural Attitude." In *Literature, Philosophy and the Social Sciences,* 34–43. The Hague: Martinus Nijhoff, 1962.
Nathanson, Donald L. "A Timetable for Shame." In *The Many Faces of Shame,* ed. Donald L. Nathanson. New York: Guilford, 1987.
Nietzsche, Friedrich. *Beyond Good and Evil.* Trans. Walter Kaufman. New York: Vintage Books, 1989.
———. *Jenseits von Gut und Böse. Sämtliche Werke,* vol. 5. Ed. Giorgio Colli and Mazzino Montinari. Berlin: De Gruyter, 1980.
———. *The Will to Power.* Trans. Walter Kaufman and R. J. Hollingdale, ed. Walter Kaufman. New York: Vintage Books, 1968.

BIBLIOGRAPHY

———. *Zur Genealogie der Moral. Sämtliche Werke*, vol. 5. Ed. Giorgio Colli and Mazzino Montinari. Berlin: De Gruyter, 1980.
Nussbaum, Martha C. *The Therapy of Desire*. Princeton, N.J.: Princeton University Press, 1994.
Otto, Rudolf. *The Idea of the Holy*. Trans. John W. Harvey. New York: Oxford University Press, 1958.
Peters, R., V. Covello, and D. McCallum. "The Determinants of Trust and Credibility in Environmental Risk Communication: An Empirical Study." *Risk Analysis*, vol. 17 (1997): 43–54.
Philström, Sami. *Transcendental Guilt: Reflections on Ethical Finitude*. New York: Lexington Books, 2011.
Piers, Gerhart, and Milton B. Singer, *Shame and Guilt*. Springfield, Ill: Charles C. Thomas, 1953.
Porter, T. *Trust in Numbers: The Pursuit of Objectivity in Science and Public Life*. Princeton, N.J.: Princeton University Press, 1995.
Prinz, Jesse. *The Emotional Construction of Morals*. Oxford: Oxford University Press, 2009.
Rawls, John. *A Theory of Justice*. Cambridge, Mass.: Harvard University Press, 2005.
Renn, O., and D. Levine. "Credibility and Trust in Risk Communication: An Empirical Study." In *Communicating Risks to the Public: International Perspectives*, ed. R. Kasperson and P. Stallen, 175–218. Boston: Kluwer, 1991.
Ricoeur, Paul. *Figuring the Sacred: Religion, Narrative, and Imagination*. Ed. Mark I. Wallace, trans. David Pellauer. Minneapolis, Minn.: Fortress, 1995.
———. *Finitude et culpabilité*. Paris: Éditions Montaigne, 1960.
———. *The Symbolism of Evil*. Trans. Emerson Buchanan. Boston: Beacon, 1967.
Rochat, Philippe. "Trust in Early Development." In *Trust, Sociality, Selfhood*, ed. Arne Grøn and Claudia Welz, 31–43. Tübingen: Mohr Siebeck, 2010.
Romano, Claude. *Au coeur de la raison, la phénoménologie*. Paris: Gallimard, 2010.
Roseman, I. J. "Cognitive Determinants of Emotions: A Structural Theory." In *Review of Personality and Social Psychology*, ed. P. Shaver, vol. 5:11–36.
Rotenstreich, Nathan. *On the Human Subject: Studies in the Phenomenology of Ethics and Politics*. Springfield, Ill.: Charles C. Thomas, 1966.
Rousseau, Jean-Jacques. *Emile, or On Education*. Trans. Allan Bloom. Basic Books, 1979.
———. *Émile, ou de l'éducation*. Paris: Garnier Frère, 1904.
Russell, Bertrand. *The Analysis of Matter*. Nottingham, Eng.: Spokesman Books, 2007.
Sartre, Jean-Paul. *Being and Nothingness: A Phenomenological Essay on Ontology*. Trans. Hazel E. Barnes. New York: Washington Square, 1956.
———. *Esquisse d'une théorie des emotions*. Paris: Hermann, 1948.
———. *L'être et le neant: Essai d'ontologie phénoménologique*. Paris: Gallimard, 1943.
Scheler, Max. *Cognition and Work: A Study Concerning the Value and Limits of the Pragmatic Motifs in the Cognition of the World*. Trans. Zachary Davis. Evanston, Ill.: Northwestern University Press (forthcoming).
———. "Das Ressentiment im Aufbau der Moralen." In *Vom Umsturz der Werte, Gesammelte Werke*, vol. 3: 33–147. Ed. Maria Scheler. Bern: Francke, 1955.

BIBLIOGRAPHY

———. "Die Demut." In *Vom Umsturz der Werte, Gesammelte Werke,* vol. 3, pp. 17–26. Ed., Maria Scheler. Bern: Francke, 1955.

———. "Die Stellung des Menschung im Kosmos." *Gesammelte Werke,* vol. 9. Ed. Manfred S. Frings. Munich: Francke Verlag, 1976.

———. "Erkenntknis und Arbeit." In *Die Wissenformen und die Gesellschaft. Gesammelte Werke,* vol. 8: 191–382. 2nd ed. Ed. Maria Scheler. Bern: Francke, 1960.

———. *Formalism in Ethics and Non-Formal Ethics of Value.* Trans. Manfred S. Frings and Roger L. Funk. Evanston, Ill.: Northwestern University Press, 1973.

———. *Formalismus in der Ethik und die Materiale Wertethik. Gesammelte Werke,* vol. 2. Ed. Maria Scheler. Bern: Francke, 1966.

———. "Ordo Amoris." In *Selected Philosophical Essays,* 98–135. Evanston, Ill.: Northwestern University Press, 1973.

———. "Ordo Amoris." In *Schriften aus dem Nachlaß,* vol 1. *Gesammelte Werke,* vol. 10: 345–76. Ed. Maria Scheler. Bern: Francke, 1957.

———. "Über Scham und Schamgefühl." *Schriften aus dem Nachlass,* vol. 1: *Zur Ethik und Erkenntneslehre,* 67–154. Bern: Francke, 1957.

———. *Vom Ewigen im Menschen. Gesammelte Werke,* vol. 5. 4th ed. Ed. Maria Scheler. Bern: Francke, 1954.

———. *Wesen und Formen der Sympathie. Gesammelte Werke,* vol. 7. Ed. Manfred Frings. Bern: Francke, 1973.

Scholz, J. and Mark Lubell. "Adaptive Political Attitudes: Duty, Trust, and Fear as Monitors of Tax Policy." *American Journal of Political Science,* vol. 42 (1998): 903–20.

Schumacher, Bernard. *Josef Pieper and the Contemporary Debate on Hope.* Trans. D. C. Schindler. New York: Fordham University Press, 2003.

Schwartz, Susan L. *Rasa: Performing the Divine in India.* New York: Columbia University Press, 2004.

Seidler, Guenter Harry. *In Others' Eyes: An Analysis of Shame.* Trans. Andrew Jenkins. Madison, Conn.: International University Press, 2000.

Shaver, P., J. Schwartz, D. Kirson, and C. O'Connor. "Emotion Knowledge: Further Exploration of a Prototype Approach." *Journal of Personality and Social Psychology,* vol. 52 (1987): 1061–86.

Sheets-Johnstone, Maxine, "Emotions and Movement: A Beginning Empirical Phenomenological Analysis of Their Relationship." *Journal of Consciousness Studies* 6, no. 11–12 (2000): 259–77.

———. *The Roots of Morality.* University Park, Pa.: Penn State University Press, 2008.

Shigesuke, Taira. *Code of the Samurai: A Modern Translation of the Bushido Shoshinsu.* Trans. Thomas Cleary. Rutland, Vt.: Tuttle Publishing, 1999.

Sokowloski, Robert. *The Formation of Husserl's Concept of Constitution.* The Hague: Martinus Nijhoff, 1964.

Solomon, Robert. *True to Our Feelings: What Our Emotions Are Really Telling Us.* Oxford: Oxford University Press, 2007.

Spinoza, Benedict de. *On the Improvement of the Understanding, Ethics, Correspondence.* Trans. R. H. M. Elwes. New York: Dover, 1955.

Steinbock, Anthony J. "Facticity and Insight as Problems of the Lifeworld: On Individuation." *Continental Philosophy Review* 37, no. 2 (2004): 241–61.
———. "From Phenomenological Immortality to Phenomenological Natality." In *Rethinking Facticity*, ed. Eric Nelson and Francois Raffoul, 25–40. Albany, N.Y.: SUNY Press, 2008: 25–40.
———. *Home and Beyond: Generative Phenomenology after Husserl*. Evanston, Ill.: Northwestern University Press, 1995.
———. "Limit-Phenomena and the Liminality of Experience." *Alter: Revue de Phenomenologie*, vol. 6 (1998): 275–96.
———. "Perception érotique, histoire et honte." *Alter: Revue de Phénoménologie*. Trans. Pierre-Jean Renaudie (forthcoming).
———. *Phenomenology and Mysticism: The Verticality of Religious Experience*. Bloomington: Indiana University Press, 2007.
———. "The Problem of Forgetfulness in Michel Henry." In *Continental Philosophy Review: The Philosophy of Michel Henry*. Ed. Anthony J. Steinbock. Vol. 32, No. 3, 1999:271–302.
———. "Totalitarianism, Homogeneity of Power, Depth: Towards a Socio-Political Ontology." *Tijdschrift voor Filosofie* 51, no. 4 (December 1989): 621–48.
———. "Whitehead's 'Theory' of Propositions." *Process Studies* 18, no. 1 (Spring 1989): 19–29.
Strasser, S. *Das Gemüt*. Freiburg: Verlag Herder, 1956.
Taipale, Joona, "Disturbances of Empathy in Narcissistic Disorders," unpublished manuscript.
Tangney, J. "Situational Determinants of Shame and Guilt in Young Adulthood." *Personality and Social Psychology Bulletin*, vol. 18, pp. 199–206.
Tangney, June Price, and Kurt W. Fischer, eds. *Self-Conscious Emotions: The Psychology of Shame, Guilt, Embarrassment, and Pride*. New York: Guilford, 1995.
Tarnopolsky, Christina. "Prudes, Perverts, and Tyrants: Plato and the Contemporary Politics of Shame." *Political Theory* 32, no. 4 (2004): 468–94.
Taylor, Charles. *Modern Social Imaginaries*. Durham, N.C.: Duke University Press, 2007.
Taylor, Gabriele. *Pride, Shame and Guilt: Emotions of Self-Assessment*. Oxford: Oxford University Press, 1985.
TeHennepe, Eugene. "The Life-World and the World of Ordinary Language." In *An Invitation to Phenomenology: Studies in the Philosophy of Expeience*, ed. James M. Edie, 133–46. Chicago: Quadrangle Books, 1965.
Teresa, Mother. *A Simple Path*. Ed. Lucinda Vardey. New York: Ballantine Books, 1995.
Teresa of Avila, Saint. *The Collected Works of St. Teresa of Avila*. Trans. Kieran Kavanaugh and Otilio Rodriguez. Washington D.C.: ICS Publications, vol. 1, 1976.
Teresa de Jesus, Santa. *Obras Completas*. Ed. Efren de La Madre de Dios and Otger Steggink. Madrid: Biblioteca de Autores Cristianos, 1997.
Teroni, Fabrice, and Julien A. Deonna. "Differentiating Shame from Guilt." *Consciousness and Cognition*, vol. 17 (2008): 725–40.

BIBLIOGRAPHY

———. "Is Shame a Social Emotion?" In *Self-Evaluation: Affective and Social Grounds of Intentionality,* ed. Anita Konzelmann Ziv, Keith Lehrer, and Hans Bernard Schmid. Dordrecht: Springer, 2011: 193–214.
Thompson, Evan. *Mind in Life: Biology, Phenomenology, and the Sciences of Mind.* Cambridge, Mass.: Harvard University Press, 2007.
Timmons, Mark. *Moral Theory.* New York: Rowman and Littlefield, 2002.
———. *Morality without Foundations: A Defense of Ethical Contextualism.* Oxford: Oxford University Press, 1999.
Tomkins, Sylvan S. *Affect Imagery Consciousness: The Positive Affects.* Vol. 1. New York: Springer, 1962.
———. *Affect Imagery Consciousness: The Negative Affects.* Vol. 2. New York: Springer, 1963.
Trajtelová, Jana. *Vzdialenosť a blízkosť mystiky: Fenomenologická štúdia fundamentálnych pohybov v tradičnej mystike západu.* Trnava a Towarzystwo Słowaków w Polsce: Studa Minorum, 2011.
Varela, Francisco, and Natalie Depraz. "At the Source of Time Valence and the Constitutional Dynamics of Affect." *Journal of Consciousness Studies, Emotion, Experience* 12, no. 8 (2005): 61–81.
Voltaire. *Encyclopédie, ou Dictionnaire raisonné des sciences, des arts et des métie.* Vol. 6, 1756.
Waldenfels, Bernhard. *Antwortregister.* Suhrkamp: Frankfurt am Main, 1994.
———. *Hyper-phänomene: Modi hyperbolischer Erfahrung.* Frankfurt am Main: Suhrkamp, 2012.
Wallbott, Harald G., and Klaus R. Scherer. "Cultural Determinants in Experiencing Shame and Guilt." In *Self-Conscious Emotions: The Psychology of Shame, Guilt, Embarrassment, and Pride,* ed. June Price Tangney and Kurt W. Fischer, 465–87. New York: Guilford, 1995.
Walsh, W. H. "Pride, Shame and Responsibility." *Philosophical Quarterly* 20, no. 78 (1970): 1–13.
Weil, Simone. *Attente de Dieu.* Paris: La Colombe, 1963.
———. *Gravity and Grace.* Trans. Emma Crawford and Mario von der Ruhr. New York: Routledge, 2002.
———. *Le pesanteur et la grâce.* Paris: Librairie Plon, 1988.
Welton, Donn. *The Origins of Meaning: A Critical Study of the Thresholds of Husserlian Phenomenology.* The Hague: Martinus Nijhoff, 1983.
Wertheim, E. J., and J. C. Schwarz. "Depression, Guilt, and Self-Management of Pleasant and Unpleasant Events." *Journal of Personality and Social Psychology* 45: 884–89.
Westphal, Merold. *God, Guilt, and Death: An Existential Phenomenology of Religion.* Bloomington: Indiana University Press, 1987.
Whitehead, Alfred North. *Adventures of Ideas.* New York: Free Press, 1961.
———. *Process and Reality.* New York: Free Press, 1978.
———. *Science and the Modern World.* New York: Free Press, 1953.
Wiesenthal, Simon. *The Sunflower: On the Possibilities and Limits of Forgiveness.* Trans. H. A. Pichler. New York: Schocken Books, 1998.

Wild, John. "Is There a World of Ordinary Language?" *Philosophical Review,* October 1958, 460–76.
Williams, Bernard. *Shame and Necessity.* Berkeley: University of California Press, 1993.
Wittgenstein, Ludwig. *The Blue and Brown Books: Preliminary Studies for the "Philosophical Investigations."* Malden, Mass.: Blackwell, 1969.
———. *Philosophical Investigations,* "Philosophy of Psychology—A Fragment." 4th ed. Malden, Mass.: Wiley-Blackwell, 2009.
Wurmser, Leon. *The Mask of Shame.* Baltimore: Johns Hopkins University Press, 1981.
Young, Iris Marion. *On Female Body Experience: "Throwing Like a Girl" and Other Essays.* Oxford: Oxford University Press, 2005.
Young, K., and J. L. Saver, "The Neurology of Narrative." *Substance* 30, no. 1–2 (2001): 72–84.
Zahavi, Dan. "Michel Henry and the Phenomenology of the Invisible." *Continental Philosophy Review,* special issue, ed. Anthony J. Steinbock, vol. 32, no. 3 (1999): 223–40.
———. "Self and Other: The Limits of Narrative Understanding." In *Narrative and Understanding Persons,* ed. D. D. Hutto, 179–201. Royal Institute of Philosophy Supplement 60. Cambridge: Cambridge University Press, 2007.
Self-Awareness and Alterity: A Phenomenological Investigation. Evanston, Ill.: Northwestern University Press, 1999.
———. "Self, Consciousness, and Shame." In *The Oxford Handbook of Contemporary Phenomenology,* ed. Dan Zahavi, 304–23. Oxford: Oxford University Press, 2012.
———. *Subjectivity and Selfhood: Investigating the First-Person Perspective.* Cambridge, Mass.: MIT Press, 2005.
Zahn-Waxler, Carolyn, and Joann Robinson. "Empathy and Guilt: Early Origins of Feelings of Responsibility." In *Self-Conscious Emotions: The Psychology of Shame, Guilt, Embarrassment, and Pride,* ed. June Price Tangney and Kurt W. Fischer, 143–73. New York: Guilford, 1995.

Index

ability-to-be, 38–39, 43, 121–22, 200, 259, 285n5
ability-to-do, 40, 43, 200, 259
Abraham, 75, 201
Abrahamic tradition: and affliction, 252–53; and covenant, 218; and freedom, 201; and hope, 178; and idolatry, 60; and Person, 54, 169, 212; and repentance, 152; and shame, 75, 83, 90
absurdity (the absurd), 160, 189–90, 193
accomplishment, 93–94, 103–4, 110, 130
accusation, 109, 115, 119
act: definition, 140
Adorno, Theodor, 170, 273
aesthetic absolute presence, 39–40, 55. *See also* Earth
affect: and emotion, 16–17, 98, 153; auto-affection, 76–77, 80
affliction, 250–55, 258, 317n55; as inter-Personal, 250, 252, 254. *See also* humiliation; humility
Agamben, Giorgio, 33, 277; on pride, 70; on shame, 70–71, 77, 97–98, 295n47
alienworld, 87, 156, 206. *See also* homeworld
anxiety: in Heidegger, 122–23; in Hegel, 68
Aquinas, Saint Thomas: on hope, 178
Arendt, Hannah, 277
Aristotle: on hope, 178; on shame, 79, 83
arrogance, 34, 61, 248
atonement, 150, 307n20
attitude, 44: belief, 207; natural, 19–20, 44–45, 46; and pride, 46, 52
Augustine, Saint: on guilt, 101; on hope, 178; on pride, 48
Austen, Jane, 34, 49
Austin, J. L., 21–24
auto-affection, 76–77, 80

Baer, Rabbi Dov, 49, 212
Baier, Annette, 195, 209, 215
Baqlī, Rūzbihān, 50–51, 212. *See also* Sufism
basic experiences (in relation to pride), 36–37, 43–44, 50, 259, 262, 275; aesthetic, 39–43; personal, 37–39. *See also* pride
Becker, Lawrence, 216
belief: as founded in trust, 215
Benedict, Ruth, 294n30
Benedict, Saint, 288n42, 315n34
Bergman, Ingmar: *Autumn Sonata*, 62–63; *Shame*, 78
Bergson, Henri, 14, 277
Bernanos, Georges, 50
Bernard of Clairvaux, 288n42
Bloch, Ernst, 277
bracketing. *See under* phenomenological method
Bresson, Robert, 184
Buber, Marin: on conscience, 305n67; on guilt, 115, 128–30; on repentance, 132

Camus, Albert, 160, 189, 193, 317n55
charity, 149
cognition: and emotion, 5, 9, 11, 28, 101, 216
Coltrane, John, 241
commitment, 217–19
concordance, 65, 73–74, 147, 254–55
critical theory, 4, 135, 178, 273, 275
critique, 19, 47, 268, 273–75; self-critique, 51, 76, 78, 82, 99, 117, 132, 240, 262–63, 267

Dante Alighieri, 35, 48
Darwin, Charles, 303n25
Dasein, 54, 120–21

333

INDEX

Deigh, John, 286n9, 298n77
de-limitation, 13, 154, 226, 229, 231, 239
demand: aesthetic, 112–13; epistemic, 111–12; moral, 110, 113–15
denial, 173–75. *See also* hope
Deonna, Julien, 27, 131, 305n73
Depraz, Natalie, 6, 306n9
Descartes, René: on humility, 234; on pride, 34–35; on repentance, 306n13; on shame, 83
deserving, 34, 236, 244, 255–57. *See also* just deserts
despair, 136, 160, 189–94, 264–65; and affliction, 251-52; and hopelessness, 136, 190–92; and pessimism, 191; temporality of, 192. *See also* hope
desperation, 179–80
Deutsch, Morton, 207
devotion, 236–37, 257, 260
Dillard, Annie, 236, 255
diremptive experience: defined, 72–73. *See* embarrassment; guilt; humiliation; shame
disappointment, 79, 161, 179, 183–84
disordered heart, 80–81, 247, 295n48
distrust. *See under* trust
Dōgen, 95, 294n30, 295n40, 316n44
Donnet, Jean-Luc, 293n22
Dostoevsky, Fyodor: on guilt, 104, 105, 109; and redemption, 317n55
Du Bois, W. E. B.: on shame, 81

Earth: Earth-alienation, 55–56; as ground, 55, 113, 260, 287n25
Ekman, Paul, 281n28
embarrassment, 73–74, 87, 117, 297n66; as a diremptive experience, 73
embodiment, 286n24
emotion, 11–12, 28, 233, 261, 267, 279n2; and affects, 16–17, 98, 153; and distinct givenness, 15, 19–21, 103; emotional sphere, 5–7, 10, 16, 38, 223, 274, 313n36, 314n3; and modernity, 3–4, 268, 271–78; as moral, 11–14, 35, 159, 196, 229, 238, 281n31; of otherness, 195–96, 258; of possibility, 135–36, 158–59, 264; of self-givenness, 27, 28–29, 238–39, 241
epoché. *See* phenomenological method, bracketing

Ernst, Carl, 64
ethics of care, 13, 195
Euripides, 78
evidence, 5–6, 15, 273, 279n2; and external perception, 41; and mystical experience, 64; of the past, 65; and presentation, 170, 224

familiarity, 26, 198, 206, 209
Fielding, Helen, 313n32
Fink, Eugen, 10
Fischer, Kurt, 27, 62
forgetfulness: and natural attitude, 20, 44; of self, 151–52, 235–36, 239
forgiveness, 137, 157, 308n28
foundation, 7–10, 232–33
Frankl, Viktor, 126–27, 230
freedom, 276; ability-to-be, 38; ability-to-do, 40; as being bound to another, 159, 195, 201, 222; as creative, 38, 72–73, 76, 104, 127, 130, 140; as interpersonal, 14; and pride, 51–52, 54, 66. *See also* liberation
Freire, Paulo, 125
Freud, Sigmund, 131, 285n5
Frye, Marilyn, 313n32

Gandhi, 307n20
Generativity, 60, 156; temporality, 56–57, 260
Genesis (book of), 75, 90, 252–53, 293n29
Geppert, U., 290n55
Gerondi, Rabbi Johan, 308n27
gift, 244, 255–56
Gilligan, James, 81
givenness: how of, 18–20, 24, 45, 254; presentational, 6, 256; self-givenness, 27–28, 40–41, 99, 240
Gould, Christina, 298n82
guilt: and demand, 114–15; as a diremptive experience, 117–18, 131, 263; in Heidegger, 119–23; as interpersonal, 107–9, 113–15, 118–19, 128, 130–31; as metaphysical, 102, 104–5, 116, 128; mineness, 103–5; as religious, 128, 130–31; and self-critique, 100, 107, 115, 117–19, 130, 263; and shame, 94, 131–32; temporality of, 105–8, 118; valence, 107, 119; and vocation, 125, 127–28

INDEX

Habermas, Jürgen, 273
Hadreas, Peter, 314n5
Hamlet, 148–50, 152, 157
Hamrick, William, 312n22
Hardin, Russell, 208
Hart, James: on shame, 81, 295n34, 295n46
hate, 226; self-hate, 50, 81, 234, 240, 249. *See also* love
heart: as disordered, 80–81, 247, 295n48; order of the, 12, 116; revolution of the, 136, 142, 147
Hegel, G. W. F.: on guilt, 101; master/slave, 242–43; on self-givenness 41; on shame, 68
Heidegger, Martin, 6, 54, 124, 127–28; on guilt, 120–23; on moods, 14; on self-givenness, 41; on sense-giving, 45
Heinämaa, Sara, 285n4, 286n24
Held, Klaus, 309n8, 309n11, 309n14
Henry, Michel, 41, 51
Hesiod, 177–78
historicity, 56–57
Hobbes, Thomas: and covenant, 312n17; on pride, 35
Holmes, John, 204
Holton, Richard, 211
Homer, 243
homeworld, 57, 60, 87–88, 90, 156, 206. *See also* alienworld
homogeneity of power, 270, 271–72
hope, 136, 160, 169, 175, 182–83, 264; absence of, 189; awaiting-enduring, 175–77; commutation of the impossible, 173, 177, 184, 186, 264, 276; and desire, 169, 177, 188–89; and desperation, 180–81; as engaged, 166; and expectation, 162–64; ground of, 168–69, 170; hopefulness, 171, 183; as inoperative, 178–79; as liberating, 136, 164–65, 177, 186, 192, 193, 264; and longing, 166–67, 188; and possibility, 164–65, 171–73, 184–85, 188, 264, 267; as sustainable, 136, 167, 171–73, 264, 309n20; temporality of, 161–63, 174–77; and waiting for, 175–76; and wishing, 162, 166. *See also* despair
hopelessness, 182, 183–85; and despair, 136, 190–92; and disappointed hope, 183, 188–89; and the ground of hope, 185, 189; specificity of occasion, 136, 184; temporality of, 186–88
Horgan, Terry, 13
Horkheimer, Max, 170
Hume, David: on pride, 50
humiliation, 247–49; and affliction, 250, 252, 258; as a diremptive experience, 247, 248–50; and personhood, 249–50; political, 277
humility, 231, 240, 244–45, 259–60, 266; being humbled, 242–43; in Bernard of Clairvaux, 288n42; and eco-devotion, 260; as founding, 233; humbling myself, 243–45; and humiliation, 248; and Jesus, 251; and just deserts, 236, 244, 255; as liberating, 260; and modesty, 245–46; as moral emotion, 196, 232; and Moses, 237; and pride, 233–35, 241; in Saint Benedict, 315n34; and self-givenness, 239–41; temporality, 256–58, 260
Husserl, Edmund, 6, 7–11, 23, 40, 45, 48, 119, 196, 269, 283n56, 288n30, 306n9; and Earth-ground, 55–56; and modernity, 271, 274; on sense-constitution, 111, 147, 280n10, 280n15, 288n40, 303n29; on time-consciousness, 41–42, 139, 300n94, 302n23
Hutchinson, Phil, 79, 299n89

ideology: bourgeois, 269; era of, 269, 273; invisible, 270, 272; pre-ideological era, 268; totalitarian, 269, 270, 272. *See also* social imaginary
idolatry, 170, 253; and pride, 60, 238; and repentance, 149–50
imagination, 165–66
individuation, 37–38, 122
intentionality: defined, 7–9, 256; epistemic, 10, 96, 111–12; of expectation, 41–42, 255; and hoping, 136, 169–72, 183, 193; and loving, 225–27; and retention, 106, 254; in Sartre, 83–84; in Scheler, 314n16; and subjectivity, 40–41; and trust, 221–22
intercorporeality, 56, 57; and erotic perception, 288n40; sense-constitution, 55, 260
Isaiah, 149

Jankélévitch, Vladimir, 6; on humility, 238, 240, 245; on modesty, 246; on remorse, 143
Jaspers, Karl: on guilt, 101–3, 104–5
John of the Cross, Saint: on affliction, 251; on pride, 289n48
Johnston, Adrian, 6, 295n48
Jones, Karen, 313n36
judgment (judicative acts), 6–7, 10, 207–8. *See also* presentation
just deserts: and humility, 236, 244, 255. *See also* humility

Kafka, Franz: on guilt, 109; and redemption, 317n55
Kant, Immanuel: on change of heart, 142; on guilt, 101; on shame, 83
Kierkegaard, Søren, 6, 160; on despair, 190
kinestheses, 40, 55
Krause, Rainer, 89
Kuster, U., 290n55

Lagerspetz, Olli, 214
Lahno, Bernd, 211
Lash, Nicholas, 169, 174, 277
Lefort, Claude, 268–69, 270
Levi, Primo: on shame, 89
Levinas, Emmanuel, 50, 210; on demand, 114; on metaphysical Desire, 153; and need, 309n18; on temporality, 306n8; on shame, 83, 85–86, 297n67, 297n71
Lewis, Helen Block, 295n49
Lewis, J. David, 311n4
Lewis, Michael: on being proud, 62; on shame, 73, 86, 94, 290n55
liberation, 94, 135, 273; and expectation, 164; in hope, 136, 164–65, 177, 186, 192, 193, 264; in humility, 260; in loving, 230, 266; through phenomenology, 17, 239; in remembering, 139; in repentance, 136, 144, 146–47, 152, 157–59, 263–64
life, 16, 37–38, 68–71, 97
lifeworld, 23, 26, 45, 206, 284n63
Lingis, Alphonso: on imperatives, 58, 113; on trust, 204
lived-body, 39–40, 54–56, 260, 287n24
Locke, John: on hope, 178

Lotz, Christian, 312n13
love, 25, 57–58, 127, 196, 212–13, 219–20, 223–24; and humility, 231; as liberating, 230, 266; as movement, 224–26, 228; and objects, 229–30; and person, 57, 224, 227–28; self-love, 58–59, 77, 82, 98, 231, 249, 262; temporality of, 230
Lublin, Rabbi of, 144
Luhmann, Niklas, 311n4
lure, 36–37. *See also* pride
Luther, A. R., 286n7, 305n65, 314n7
Lyotard, Jean-François, 273

MacCurdy, John T., 295n44
Malabou, Catherine, 6, 295n48
Marcel, Gabriel, 6, 160, 178, 310n8
Marcuse, Herbert, 26
Marx, Karl, 48, 58, 135, 138, 151; on charity, 149; on hope, 174; on shame, 67, 70, 77, 276; value disordering, 80–81
Mascolo, Michael, 62
Mazis, Glen, 280n7
McLeod, Carolyn, 215–16
meaning: and language, 26; and phenomenology, 18–19, 20–21, 45; and pride, 33, 39–43; and sense, 9–10
Merleau-Ponty, Maurice, 139, 196, 260, 287n24, 288n40; on reflection, 119; on self-givenness, 41, 242
Minkowski, Eugène, 103, 139
mistrust. *See under* trust
modernity, 3, 4–5, 178, 269, 271–73
modesty, 245–46. *See also* humility
Moltman, Jürgen, 164
moral emotion. *See under* emotion
moral reduction, 48–51, 75, 235, 252
moral sphere, 12–14, 44, 46–47, 113, 147, 194, 206–7, 210, 216, 239, 263
motivation, 139, 145, 163, 172, 205, 215–16, 256–57
Mullin, Amy, 313n39
Myself, 12, 48, 53, 86, 93, 119, 127–28, 218, 276; as inter-Personal, 13, 51, 58, 126, 218, 231, 259; as interpersonal, 51, 53, 59, 128, 136, 196; as not self-grounding, 12, 28, 48, 51, 77, 99, 119, 127, 130, 136, 154, 158, 183, 218, 236, 239, 241, 257–60, 266, 274; as optimal,

INDEX

87, 93, 147; and self-love, 58–60, 77, 82, 231, 240. *See also* vocational self
mysticism, 26, 50–51, 63–64, 158, 201

narcissism: and pride, 34, 285n5
natural attitude, 19–20, 44–45, 46. *See also* phenomenological method
Nietzsche, Friedrich, 6, 34, 160, 235; on ressentiment, 50; on shame, 95, 300n94; will-to-power, 286n7
normality, 105, 147. *See also* concordance; optimality
normativity: as interpersonal, 13, 267–68; and love, 58, 113–14, 229, 258; and shame, 99; and trust, 206, 222
not self-grounding. *See under* Myself

objectivating acts: and non-objectivating acts, 8–9, 11, 221, 232. *See also* presentation
Oliver, Kelly, 312n12
optimality, 87, 92–93, 147, 206, 278
optimism, 164–65, 181–82. *See also* hope
ordinary language philosophy, 17, 1–23
Otto, Rudolf, 119, 169

panic, 181, 182, 265
patience, 175–77. *See also* hope
perception: and founding, 9–10; and objects, 41, 111–12, 179, 225–26, 287n24; and trusting, 205, 221
person, 11–12, 17, 37, 147, 261, 267, 273–74, 275–77; basic experiences of, 36–39; collective, 60, 70, 86, 87–88, 102, 156; and emotions, 14–15, 16, 28, 159; as free/creative, 14, 31, 36, 38–39, 40, 54, 66, 67, 72–73, 76, 82, 99, 104, 118, 126, 127, 130, 132, 135–36, 140, 158–59, 194, 202, 224, 231, 236, 262; interpersonal, 12, 14, 17, 32, 37, 59, 118, 131, 157, 196, 201, 309n17; interpersonal nexus, 14, 15, 33, 46, 54, 116, 119, 275; as not specifically human, 16, 28; sphere of, 12, 66, 76, 147; uniqueness, 12, 37–38, 77, 126–27, 137. *See also* Myself
Person (absolute infinite), 14, 54, 76, 102, 120, 130, 138, 141, 154, 169, 212; inter-Personal, 13, 14, 58, 75, 120, 126, 128, 218, 250, 282n33, 309n17, 317n1;

inter-Personal nexus, 126, 127, 218, 252, 275
pessimism, 181–82. *See also* hope
phenomenological method, 17–18, 20–21, 25, 44–45; bracketing, 18–20, 48, 51, 239, 298n82; constitutive analysis, 18, 45; generative phenomenology, 23, 283n46; lifeworld, 23, 26, 45, 206, 284n63; reduction, 18, 239; static, 19
Philström, Sami, 302n10
Plato: on shame, 95
possibility: emotions of, 135–36, 158, 160, 177, 194, 264; engaged, 166; in Heidegger, 121–25, 304n60; in hope, 164–65, 171–73, 177, 179, 184–85, 188, 264, 267; hyper-factual, 166; impossibility, 173, 177, 184–89, 193, 264; and love, 225–28; and person, 75, 204, 219, 225, 227, 262, 273, 275; pure open, 165–66; in repentance, 138, 146, 155, 159, 263; as sustainable, 171–72, 264; and vocation, 128–28
postmodernity, 3, 21, 195, 269, 271–73
power, 270–71. *See also* homogeneity of power
presentation, 6–7, 15, 170–71, 237, 254, 256
pride, 31, 49, 52, 259, 261–62, 275; aesthetic lure, 39–44; deserving, 34; and freedom, 51–52, 54, 66; and guilt, 115; and humility, 233–35; as interpersonal, 32–34, 36, 46, 51, 66, 202; personal lure for, 37–39; resistance or refusal, 33–35, 46, 53–54; and revelation, 48; and self-confidence, 64–65; as self-dissembling, 32–33, 48, 52–55, 57, 234–35, 262; and self-grounding, 34–35, 46–47, 50, 52–54, 56, 59–60, 66, 90, 234, 275; as self-limiting, 52, 57, 133, 262; as sovereignty, 33, 54, 70, 275; temporality of, 56–57, 64–65, 291n81; valence, 36, 50. *See also* love, self-love
proud of, 61–63
psychoanalysis, 49, 54, 279n2, 290n55, 293n22, 293n23, 295n48; and narcissism, 34, 285n5; and shame, 72
psychology: and emotions, 5, 16, 27–28, 37; and narcissism, 285n5; and shame, 72

INDEX

reconciliation, 115, 129, 132, 155, 158–59, 263
reduction, 18, 239; as epistemic, 51; moral, 48–51, 75, 235. *See also* phenomenological method
regret, 142–43
reliability, 198–200, 215–16. *See also* trust
religious, 77, 119, 128, 169, 212, 253–54
remembering, 42, 106–8, 139, 257, 288n34, 300n94
remorse, 143
Rempel, John, 204
repentance, 132–33, 135–36, 138, 141, 152, 263–64; before another, 153, 154–55; dis-position, 145–46, 152; and freedom, 147, 158; and guilt, 119; immanence and transcendence, 149–51; as liberating, 94, 136, 144, 146–47, 152, 157–59, 263–64; as re-action, 139–40; as religious, 152, 154, 158–59; reprise, 140–41; revolution of the heart, 136, 142, 147; valence of, 144–45
responsivity, 110, 126, 128
revelation, 170–71, 224, 226: of the Other, 297n71; self-revelation, 75, 80, 98–99, 212. *See also* verticality
Ricoeur, Paul: on guilt and sin, 302n18
Robinson, Joann, 284n4, 302n25
Rochat, Philippe, 311n9
Romano, Claude, 124–25
Rotenstreich, Nathan, 292n3
Rousseau, Jean-Jacques: on pride, 35, 48, 49
Russell, Bertrand, 22–23

samurai, 82, 95
Sartre, Jean-Paul, 6, 160; on pride, 52; on shame, 83–84
Saussure, Ferdinand de, 71
Scheler, Max, 5, 6, 18, 54, 116, 210, 269, 279n2, 311n5; on the disordered heart, 80; good-in-itself-for-me, 77, 129, 226; on guilt, 130, 132; on humility, 244; on love, 225–26, 228, 314n12, 314n16; normativity, 113–14; on repentance, 138, 150, 153, 307n23; on shame, 68–69, 72, 77, 95, 294n29; on suffering, 250; on value, 290n69, 314n3
Schwartz, Susan L., 281n28

secular, 46, 234, 269, 277
Seidler, Guenter, 86, 293n23
self: definition, 12
self-awareness, 294n32
self-esteem, 34, 62, 80. *See also* pride
self-forgetfulness, 151–52, 235–36, 239
self-genesis, 42–43
self-givenness, 27–28, 40–41, 99, 240; and self-assessment, 27
self-grounding, 13, 43, 54–55, 57, 90, 155, 168, 231, 274; in pride, 34–35, 46–47, 50, 52–54, 56, 59–60, 66, 90, 234, 275. *See* Myself, not self-grounding
self-hatred, 50, 81, 234
self-judgment, 238; and self-critique, 28, 262–63; and shame, 79
self-love. *See under* love
self-revelation, 80, 98–99, 117, 210–12, 274; and loving, 225; and pride, 31–32, 48, 52, 66; and shame, 52, 67, 71, 72–73, 75–77, 82, 86, 89, 94, 263, 298n76, 294n32. *See also* diremptive experience
self-revision: and repentance, 144, 146–47, 159
self-temporalization, 41–43, 56; as immortality, 41–42
shame: and Abrahamic tradition, 75, 83, 90; absence of, 89; as collective, 87–88, 89; debilitating shame, 80–82, 249; as a diremptive experience, 52, 67, 73–74, 85, 99, 131, 262; and embarrassment, 73; as exposure before another, 75, 86; and guilt, 131–32; as interpersonal, 84–88, 298n82, 299nn84–85; and self-critique, 72, 76, 78, 80–82, 86, 99, 246–47, 248, 262; and self-revelation, 75–76, 80, 94, 98; shamelessness, 89–91, 299n89; temporality of, 91–95; valence of, 78–79
Shakespeare, William, 148–50, 152, 157
Sheets-Johnstone, Maxine, 6, 281n28
Shigeskue, 95–96
shyness, 96
singularity, 37; singularizing acts, 28, 201
Slavkovský, Reginald, 316n49
social imaginary, 261, 268, 283n47; and modernity, 4, 269–75; and moral emotions, 3–4, 16, 196, 197, 277. *See also* ideology
solidarity, 102, 128, 157, 218, 277

INDEX

Solomon, Robert, 6, 281n31, 293n27
sovereignty: in Agamben, 69–70; and pride, 33, 54, 70, 275
Spinoza, Benedict de: on hope, 178; on repentance, 138; on shame, 83, 90
Steinbock, Joseph, 293n29
Strasser, S., 6
suffering: versus affliction, 250
Sufism: and boasting, 63–64; and language, 284n65; self-annihilation, 50–51
synthesis: active and passive, 6, 10, 139, 288n40

Taipale, Joona, 285n5
Talmud Yoma, 148
Tangney, June, 27
Tarkovsky, Andrei: *Andrei Rublev*, 191, 241, 285n3; *Nostalghia*, 90
Tarnopolsky, Christina, 301n97
Taylor, Charles, 269, 274, 317n2
Taylor, Gabriele, 27, 49, 69, 73, 114, 117, 291n72, 292n6, 293n23, 295n43, 302n13, 305n73
TeHennepe, Eugene, 22–23
temporality: expectation, 162–64, 175; living-present, 254; of emotions, 15, 282n37; protention, 106, 111–12, 162; remembering, 42, 106–7, 108, 139, 257, 288n34, 300n94; retention, 106–7; self-temporalization, 41–43, 56; time-constitution, 42
temporal meaning and temporal orientation, 15; in guilt, 105, 108, as distinct, 118, 130–31; in hope, 161, 175; in humility, 254, 257; in love, as distinct, 230; in pride, 64–65; in repentance, as distinct, 146–47; in shame, 93–94, 131; in trust, 205, 213
Teresa of Avila, Saint, 230, 235–36; on hope, 170; and language, 284n65; and prayer, 212; on pride, 49
Teresa, Mother, 115, 251
Teroni, Fabrice, 27, 131, 305n73
Thomas Aquinas, Saint: on hope, 178
Thompson, Evan, 6
Timmons, Mark, 13

Trajtelová, Jana, 314n6, 315n20
trust, 195, 197, 265–66; anti-trust, 209–10; as being bound, 206–8, 211, 218–29; and betrayal, 210–12; and commitment, 218–19; deciding to trust, 211; distrust, 195, 206, 209–11, 222; and freedom, 200–201, 202, 213, 219, 221–22; and gullibility, 208; as imposition, 214–15; as interpersonal, 201–2; mistrust, 195, 206, 209–11, 222; as modally specified, 220–21; as proffering, 205–6; and reliability, 199, 203; temporality of, 204–5; as transitive, 213
t'shuvah, 146, 149
tzedakah, 51, 86, 149

uniqueness. See *under* person

valence, 24, 36–37, 316n40
vanity, 34. See also pride
Varela, Francisco, 6
verticality, 13, 218, 240, 254, 274
virtue, 231–32
vocational self, 38, 58, 86, 93, 124–26, 128, 154, 231. See also Myself
Voltaire: on pride, 289n53
vulnerability, 207–8, 210, 211–12. See also trust

Waldenfels, Bernhard, 6; on responsivity, 110
Weigert, A., 311n4
Weil, Simone, 250–51, 252
Welz, Claudia, 296n52
Westphal, Merold, 304n43
Whitehead, Alfred North, 272; on epistemic lure, 111–12
Wiesenthal, Simon, 137, 138, 155
Wild, John, 282n42
Williams, Bernard, 76
Wittgenstein, Ludwig, 16, 22–23, 26
Wurmser, Leon, 79

Zahavi, Dan, 6; on the self, 12; on shame, 294n30, 297n76
Zahn-Waxler, Carolyn, 284n4, 302n25

About the Author

Anthony J. Steinbock is a professor of philosophy and the director of the Phenomenology Research Center at Southern Illinois University. He is the editor in chief of *Continental Philosophy Review;* his previous books include *Phenomenology and Mysticism: The Verticality of Religious Experience* (2007) and *Home and Beyond: Generative Phenomenology after Husserl* (Northwestern, 1995).